Inuit Art

An Anthology

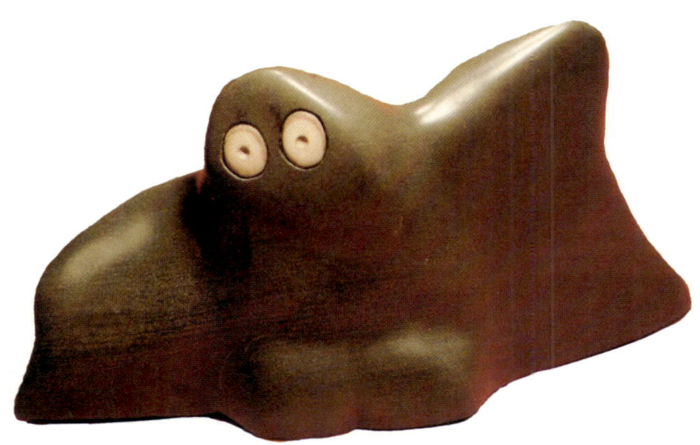

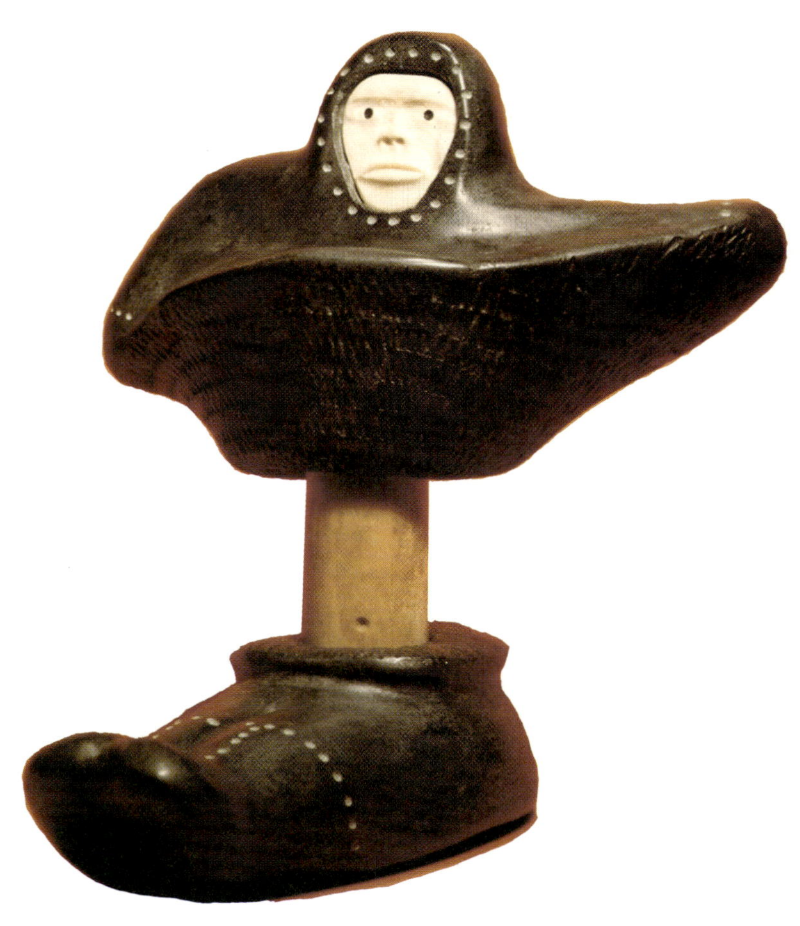

Inuit Art

Introduction by ALMA HOUSTON

WINNIPEG, MANITOBA

© 1988 by Watson & Dwyer Publishing

All rights reserved

ISBN 0-929486-21-5 pa.
ISBN 0-920486-22-3 bd.

Watson & Dwyer Publishing Ltd.
232 Academy Road
Winnipeg, Manitoba R3M 0E7

Canadian Cataloguing in Publication Data

Main entry under title:

Inuit art : an anthology

Includes articles originally appearing in The Beaver.
ISBN 0-920486-21-5 pa. ISBN 0-920486-22-3 bd.

1. Inuit—Canada—Art*. 2. Artists, Inuit—Canada—Art*.

E99.E7I58 1987 704'.0397 C87-098136-6

The publication of this book has been supported by grants from the Canada Council and the Manitoba Arts Council.

Cover: *Sea Goddess* by Osuitok Ipeelee of Cape Dorset

Title Page: *Owl* by Mattiusi Iyaituk of Ivugivik
Soapstone and caribou antler
11.5 x 24.3 x 7.7 cm
Private collection, San Francisco

Title Page: (over) *Man Getting Dressed in the Morning*
by Mattiusi Iyaituk
Soapstone, caribou antler and ivory
23.1 x 23.1 x 25.6 cm
Collection: Images of the North, San Francisco

Printed in Canada by
D. W. Friesen & Sons Ltd.
Altona, Manitoba

Acknowledgements

Most of the articles that comprise this anthology were originally published in *The Beaver* magazine between 1972 and 1984. The editor during those years, Helen Burgess, commissioned the manuscripts after discussions with Alma Houston; the aim was to present a variety of subjects related to Inuit art, by informed and fluent writers.

Not all authors approached responded with contributions; nor were all aspects of the subject covered. Much of the story remains to be told.

The editor and publisher acknowledge with gratitude, permission granted by the Hudson's Bay Company to compile and publish this selection of material from *The Beaver.*

The kind co-operation of the authors in granting permission to present their articles in this anthology is also acknowledged.

We are indebted too, to Jean Blodgett and Marybelle Myers for the opportunity to include their personal interviews with Osuitok Ipeelee of Cape Dorset and Nutaraaluk and Mattiusi Iyaituk of Ivugivik. The comments of these thoughtful artists who spoke openly about their art and their hopes for the future, is a valued addition to the book.

We also acknowledge the permission of the Inuit artists to reproduce their works of art, by arrangements made on their behalf with the Eskimo Arts Council.

Biographical Notes

Betty Bell:

For thirteen years, Mrs Alistair Bell was buyer of Inuit Art for the Gallery Shop in the Vancouver Art Gallery.

Jean Blodgett:

Jean Blodgett, former Curator of Inuit Art at the Winnipeg Art Gallery, is now Adjunct Curator of Inuit Art at the Art Gallery of Ontario, Toronto and Adjunct Professor at Carleton University, Ottawa. She has mounted a number of prestigious exhibitions of Inuit art: 'The Coming and Going of the Shaman', 'Grasp Tight the Old Ways' and most recently, the Jessie Oonark Retrospective for the Winnipeg Art Gallery.

Sheila Butler:

In 1969 Sheila and Jack Butler went to Baker Lake, N.W.T, to extend the federal government's sculpture program and to establish printmaking. During the three years that they lived and worked with the Baker Lake artists, they collaborated with the women to develop wall hangings and decorated clothing.

The Butlers returned to Winnipeg in 1972 to pursue their own highly successful careers as artists. Jack Butler continued to commute to Baker Lake as an advisor until 1976; Sheila last visited Baker Lake in 1975.

Mary Craig:

Mary Craig has been directly involved with the marketing and promotion of Inuit art for twenty-five years. During her years with the Fine Arts Section of Canadian Arctic Producers she handled sales of the first collections of prints from Cape Dorset.

In 1976, Mary Craig joined La Fédération des Coopératives, Montreal, representing Inuit co-operatives in Arctic Quebec. She is director of Fine Arts at La Fédération.

Alma Houston:

Alma Houston lived among the Cape Dorset artists from 1952 to 1965. In the following years, as Head, Fine Arts Division of Canadian Arctic Producers, she was a catalyst in presenting the art of the Inuit to the world in a prestigious and reputable way. She now owns and manages the Houston North Gallery in Lunenberg, Nova Scotia.

Charlotte Lindgren:

Charlotte Lindgren, a fibre artist, was consultant for the Pangnirtung weaving shop for three years. Her husband, architect Edward Lindgren, worked on projects for native communities at the University of Manitoba.

Robert McGhee:

Robert McGhee is an archaeologist with the Archaeological Survey directed by the National Museums of Canada.

Marybelle Myers:

Marybelle Myers, former manager of arts and crafts development for La Fédération des Coopératives, Montreal, is now editor of the *Inuit Art Quarterly*.

Terry Ryan:

Terry Ryan has been Manager of the West Baffin Eskimo Co-operative at Cape Dorset since 1962.

Contents

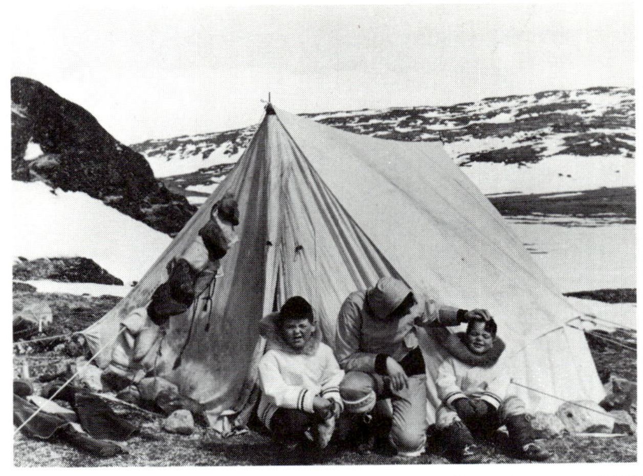

Alma Houston with sons John and Sam, near Cape Dorset. c. 1957.

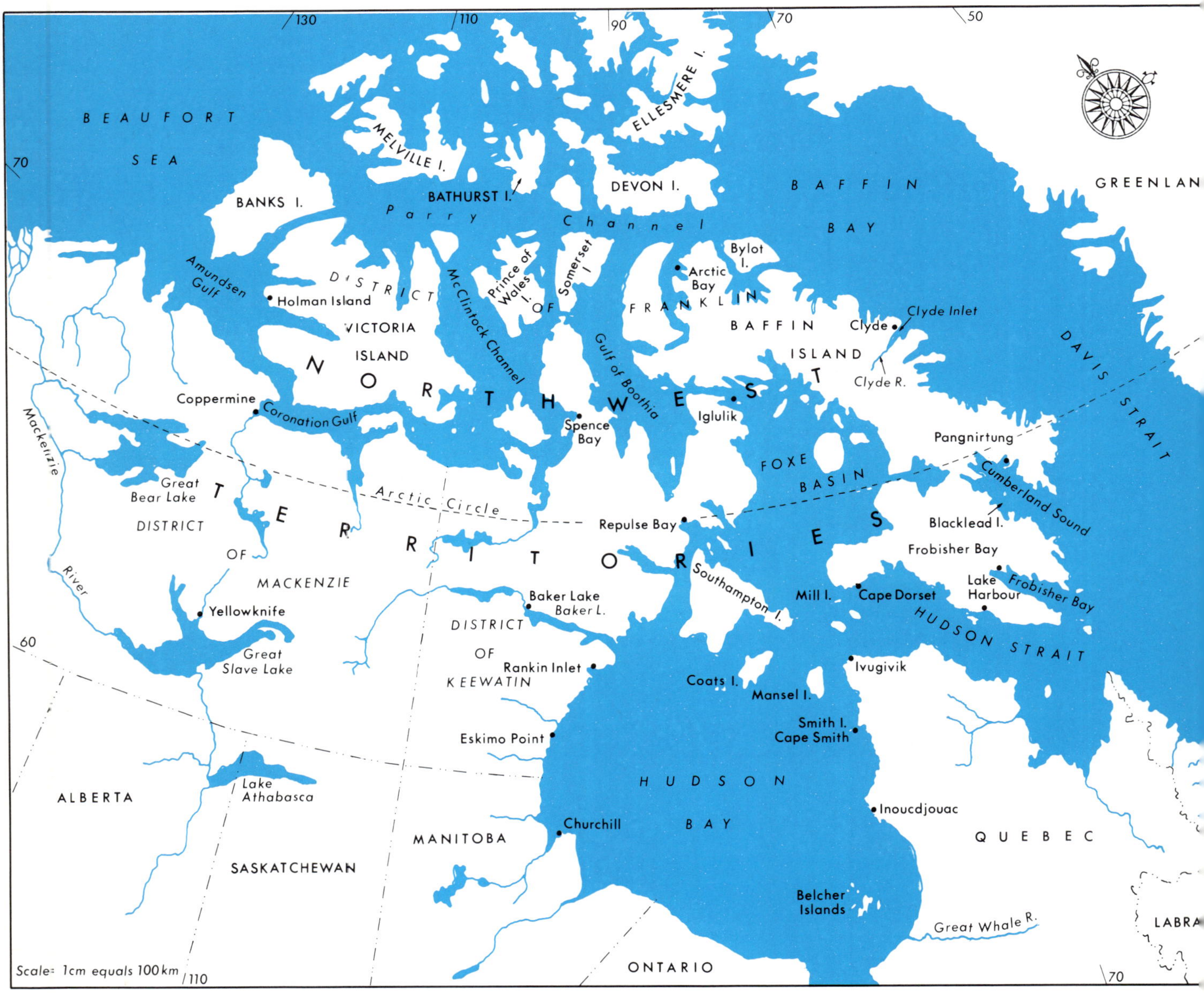

Introduction

RE-READING THE ARTICLES in this book, from Robert McGhee's lucid 'The Prehistory and Prehistoric Art of the Canadian Inuit', to Jean Blodgett's interview with Osuitok, brought back memories of those eventful years when Inuit art was introduced to the South and won overwhelming acclaim. Each article set me off on thoughts of my own; I have been examining the past all over again.

The past nearly forty years of Canadian Inuit art is a record of remarkable achievement in the face of staggering odds. The barriers of distance, language, culture and economics, have forced the artists to put their faith and their work into the hands of agents from down south.

Southern artists who can work directly with galleries, and who meet their public from time to time, would find it strange and awkward to deal through such indirect means. The Inuit artists cannot even monitor their 'spokesmen' who write in English, French, German, Japanese; all inaccessible to them. And Inuit artists have usually been represented simplistically; who would have suspected how rich their language, how enlightened their thoughts could be? When in the mid-1960s, the Carruthers Commission into Government in the Northwest Territories held their hearings in Clyde River, the commissioners were astounded at the eloquence of this particular small band of Inuit. Their interpreter in that place was the arctic scholar, Robert Williamson, whose excellent command of Inuktitut reflected his mastery of English, and his facility in a number of other languages. As well, he had at his command those insights which come only from living among the people.

Another perception, often expressed, is that Inuit art cannot survive, which is to say that Inuit artists are a vanishing species. This opinion is always with us. Original peoples are supposed to vanish. I find that personal contact with Inuit artists tends to dispel any fears I might have for their survival. Individually, the Inuit appear to be at least as whole and as connected to their culture as the other artists I meet. In fact, Marshall McLuhan would probably have given them survival odds over both dealers and southern artists, because of their tribal consciousness. To that, I would add their humour, their kindness, their utter lack of pretentiousness, and above all, their closeness to nature.

As Jean Blodgett reminds us in her article 'The Historic Period in Canadian Inuit Art', contemporary Inuit art dates from the year that James Houston arrived in the Arctic in 1948. We have learned the story through reading, oral history, or, for the silver-haired group including me, by having been there. We were involved, enthusiastic, and excited. We were proud to be the first owners of the usually very small, vital, and innocent carvings from Port Harrison, Povungnituk, and Cape Smith.

Line-ups for the first Inuit carvings, offered for sale at the Canadian Handicrafts Guild in Montreal, stretched along Peel Street, and around the corner on Burnside, and preceded by a decade the famous all-night vigils for Cape Dorset prints. Inuit art caught the attention of some of Montreal's most interesting art patrons, as well as the Canadian press.

The National Gallery of Canada held its first exhibition of Inuit art in 1951. During the coronation of HRH Elizabeth II, the eyes of the world were on London, and Canadian Inuit art came into its own, in an exhibition at Gimpel Fils Gallery in that city. Owner Charles Gimpel, who handled the works of Henry Moore and Barbara Hepworth, believed that Inuit sculpture was the best art coming out of Canada. Through his efforts, works by the Arctic's great sculptors: Qaqaq, Osuitok, Johnny Inukpuk, and Tiktak, were exhibited and sold internationally. Charles Gimpel was not impressed by the Canadian dealers in Inuit art of that time. He told me that he felt that no-one in Canada really understood the true value of Inuit sculpture. I wonder what he would think of the Inuit art scene in Canada, circa 1988?

The first experimental Inuit stonecut and stencil prints, described by Mary Craig in her article on the Cape Dorset prints, were offered for sale in the Hudson's Bay store in Winnipeg in the pre-Christmas season, 1958. In the summer of the following year, the first documented collection emerged rather quietly, at Stratford, Ontario. Who could have known that the experiment at Cape Dorset would so capture the imagination of the Inuit? Printmaking took hold and spread across the Arctic, to become part of the Inuit tradition.

One of our best friends and supporters during that early period of the 1950s was the Honourable Vincent Massey, who bought Inuit sculpture and original prints to be given as gifts of state. He was the first Governor General to visit the Eastern Arctic, and later commissioned the Great Mace of the Northwest Territories.

Highlights of the 1960s include the formation of the Canadian Eskimo Arts Committee, and the beginning of printmaking at Povungnituk, both in 1961. Baker Lake sculpture appeared on the scene at Winnipeg in 1964. Two other milestones, in 1965, were the incorporation of the first Inuit marketing organization, Canadian Arctic Producers, in Ottawa, and the first issue of prints from Holman Island, introduced in New Brunswick, at the Beaverbrook Museum. The film *Kenojuak*, by the National Film Board of Canada, was released, translated into several languages and distributed around the world.

The great Canadian exposition that marked Canada's first hundred years as a nation, honoured Inuit, along with other Canadian art. Royalty, heads of state, dignitaries from every country visited Expo '67 and the nation's capital. Many returned home bearing gifts of Inuit art. The fledgling Canadian Arctic Producers arranged several selling exhibitions in North America and Europe, while the Department of External Affairs was showing Inuit prints and drawings abroad. The year 1967 was a hallmark year for Inuit artists. An indication of their growing recognition in Canada was the reproduction of Kenojuak's *The Enchanted Owl*, on a postage stamp. In the inaugural year of the Order of Canada, Kenojuak was among the first visual artists to be honoured.

Still in 1967, *The Beaver* magazine published a special issue on Inuit art; a total of 80,000 copies were distributed. The National Gallery of Canada opened the Centennial Year with an exhibition: 'Cape Dorset, A Decade of Sculpture and Prints'. Inuit art was entering a period of great popularity and critical recognition that would grow steadily for another ten years. Then a recession would seriously damage the network of producers, co-operatives, distributors, retailers, and collectors.

In the meantime, the seventies saw Inuit art exhibited internationally; first the landmark 'Masterworks Exhibition', followed by 'The Inuit Print'. The most exciting event of the 1970s was the emergence of the Baker Lake prints; powerful from the start. After several years of reports from officials of that region that there was 'no interest in printmaking on the part of the Baker Lake Inuit', Jack and Sheila Butler went in there and helped the Inuit artists to make it happen. Then from Pangnirtung came the first superlatively woven tapestries, and in 1973, the first collection of Pangnirtung prints. Their gentle figurative landscapes could not have been more different from the bold spiritual landscapes of Baker Lake. To the west, at Spence Bay, women were experimenting with natural dyes, and designing their own line of Inuit parkas, their 'packing animals', and other highly original creations. Jewellery was being made in precious metals at Cape Dorset and Frobisher Bay, and the diversity of talents of the Cape Dorset people was further demonstrated by their winning of an international prize for animated film at Zagreb, Yugoslavia.

Pitseolak Ashoona, O.C., R.C.A., of Cape Dorset was winning new admirers for her fabulous drawings and prints through the release of *Pitseolak: Pictures Out of My Life*, her autobiographical book with Dorothy Eber, and the National Film Board film.

At Canadian Arctic Producers in Ottawa, we were reserving works of the great artists for special shows, in anticipation of the demand that would follow the exhibition 'Sculpture/Inuit'. The first exhibition of Canadian art ever to be held in the Soviet Union, 'Sculpture/Inuit' drew hundreds of thousands of viewers at the Hermitage in Leningrad, and the Pushkin in Moscow. This major event in Inuit art history was conceived by Doris Shadbolt of the Canadian Eskimo Arts Council, and realized with the assistance of the Departments of Indian and Northern Affairs, and External Affairs. The exhibition began its international tour at the Vancouver Art Gallery, and went on to Paris, Copenhagen, London, Philadelphia and back in Canada, to the Montreal Museum of Fine Arts, and the National Gallery of Canada. I remember feeling that the presence of Inuit artists, at each and every opening, lent a touch of reality to the wonder of it all.

As we expected, the effect of 'Sculpture/Inuit' was to heighten critical recognition, and to greatly increase the demand for major works by individual sculptors. Today, these sculptors are still referred to as 'Masterworks artists'. The demand for Inuit sculpture and prints in general was at its peak by 1975, and the auction houses, in Toronto, Montreal, and New York jumped in. In Toronto, among the several auction houses, as many as five large sales a year were held, and this continued into the early eighties. While these sales attracted a lot of attention, in the long run the effect on Inuit art was not beneficial. The market was flooded, and it took the recession to restore a measure of saneness.

By the time it becomes possible to have any perspective on the '80s, I am hoping we will have seen a reversal of some of the current trends.

In 1986 Canadian Arctic Producers amalgamated with La Fédération des Coopératives du Nouveau Québec and transferred to new corporate headquarters in Winnipeg. Meanwhile, given easy accessibility to the Arctic, private speculators, large and small, have begun to offer more serious competition to the Inuit co-operatives. The goal of orderly marketing, once part of the mandate of the Canadian Eskimo Arts Council, appears to have been forgotten, or has become impossible to control. The artists themselves sense the danger of this change. In his interview with Marybelle Myers, Nutaraaluk of Arctic Quebec expresses concern repeatedly for his future as a carver and for the future of the co-operative as a marketing outlet.

While storm clouds are gathering above the co-ops and their marketing organizations, there are rays of hope in the growing interest of the public galleries. The Winnipeg Art Gallery continues to hold catalogued exhibitions of Inuit art; expanding with the acquisition of the Ian Lindsay collection, and launching the marvellous Jessie Oonark retrospective. The Art Gallery of Ontario showed 'Grasp Tight the Old Ways', the Klamer collection and book. Kenojuak was elevated to Companion of the Order of Canada, with a retrospective at the McMichael Collection. The *Inuit Art Quarterly*, edited by Marybelle Myers, became our new forum, filling the void left by *Arts & Culture of the North.* And the National Gallery of Canada opened its arms at last to Inuit art.

The eighties have not been years of expansiveness, although Inuit art is gradually recovering from the recession. In this new world of information exchange, one might have expected to have greater input from the Inuit artists themselves. Communication continues to be indirect, as if it came out of a tin. Gallery visits from the artists are still rare and special events. Even videotapes of artists would make them more real to those who have kept the art alive these many years: the dealers, the public galleries, and the collectors. As it stands now, we can pass on rather crisp curriculum vitae, more suited to the investment minded than to art lovers, and leaf through books and catalogues for possible photographs.

We who lived through nearly four decades of revelation and acclaim, cannot help but feel nostalgic about those opening nights of a new exhibition or the launching of new art forms. Back in those early years all of Canada knew that the Ministers of Northern Affairs were Inuit art enthusiasts, for they—both Arthur Laing and then Jean Chrétien—collected, and they proudly officiated at openings, standing at the side of the Inuit artists themselves, who had travelled south to attend the event.

But time moves on. Inuit art still pays its way, as it always has. We see more and more 'players', as they call themselves, getting into the business, presumably not for altruistic reasons. Simultaneously, we hear that there isn't enough 'quality' sculpture to go around. With the players threatening to outnumber the artists, the market is fragmented and confusing to artist and collector alike. It is time for decisive action. As a nation, we have enjoyed decades of praise and honour for our enlightened support of Inuit art. It has enriched our lives, and has become part of our identity as Canadians.

For the sake of Inuit artists and generations of Inuit to come, let us hope that before the end of the 1980s decisive steps are taken to ensure that it is the art that is being managed by a proper system, and not the system that is being maintained by the art.

Alma Houston
Lunenburg, Nova Scotia
March, 1988

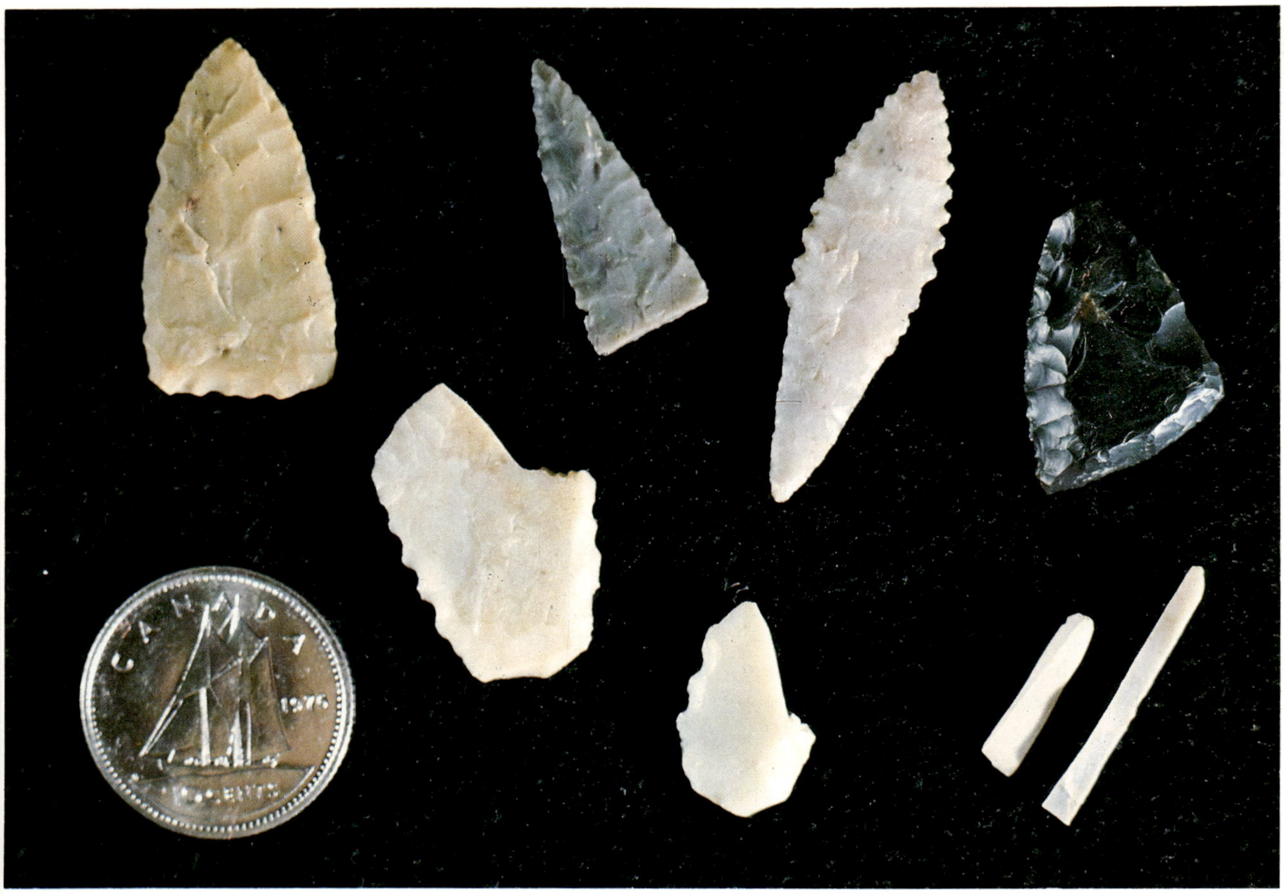

Miniature tools chipped from coloured flint by early Arctic Small Tool tradition hunters; the largest object is only 55 mm long. A Canadian dime is used for scale.

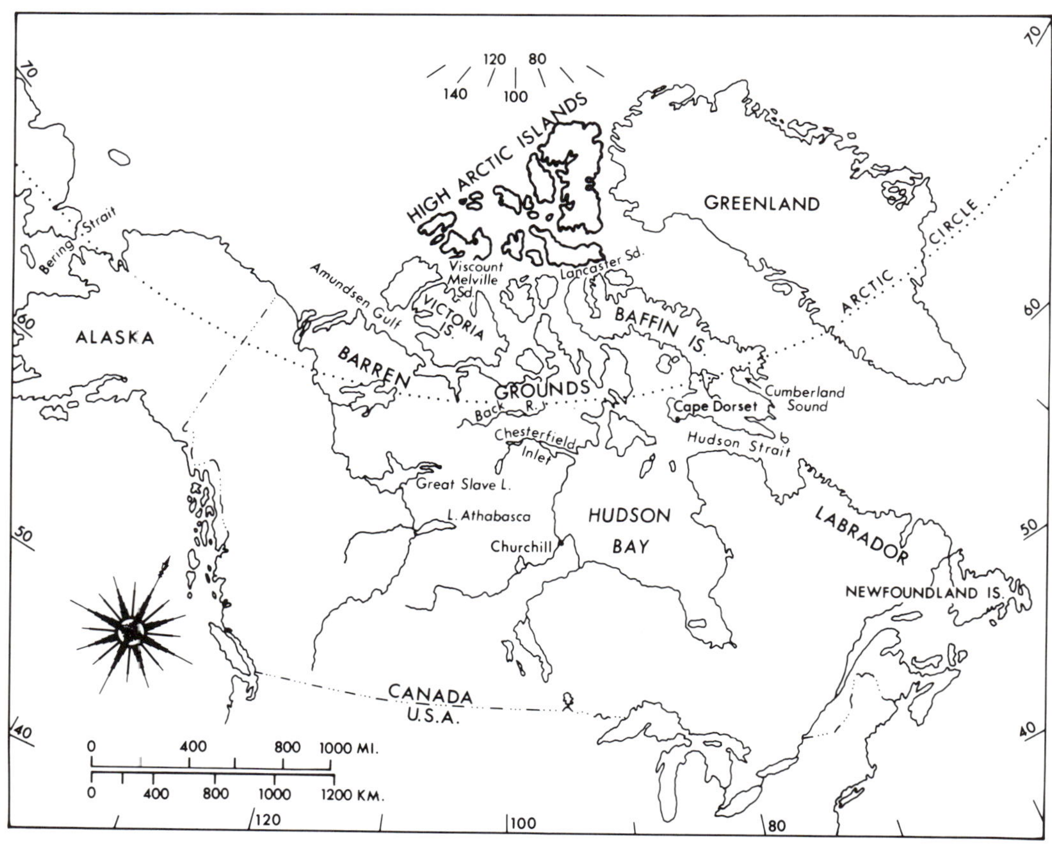

From *The Beaver*, Summer 1981.

The Prehistory and Prehistoric Art of the Canadian Inuit

By Robert McGhee

OVER THE PAST THREE DECADES there has been a growing interest in the art forms being produced by the Inuit of Arctic Canada. In the early days of this phenomenon there were many naive statements made by collectors, and claims made by dealers, that Inuit soapstone carving was the culmination of an artistic tradition which had gradually developed over the centuries, or even over millennia of prehistoric time. Another view, and one which is more fashionable today, treats Inuit art as an entirely new art form, rapidly evolving, changing as it grows, developing its own traditions, and which can be appreciated without reference to its origins or to the past.

Neither of these views is entirely satisfactory. We do not find soapstone carvings, nor the remains of any other modern art forms, on archaeological sites of the later prehistoric period; these developments belong to the mid-twentieth century. Nevertheless, although there is little resemblance between modern art forms and those of the prehistoric past, art has been produced in Arctic Canada for the last 4,000 years. Over this period the art took many forms. There was no simple development over time, either in Inuit culture or in its arts; yet perhaps some of these arts may have expressed concepts similar to those of modern Inuit art. A brief sketch of the history of the Canadian Inuit and of their art may serve as a useful background in appreciating the artistic productions of the Inuit today.

The Arctic seen by the first Inuit was probably very similar in most respects to that of the present day. By about 8,000 years ago the glaciers of the last Ice Age had retreated to the mountains of Labrador and the eastern arctic islands, where they remain today as relics of the Pleistocene. By this time whales and smaller sea mammals had penetrated the bays and channels of the arctic coast, and the tree-line was moving rapidly northward to well beyond its present position. To the north of tree-line the animals of the the tundra were becoming established. Caribou and musk-oxen, and the wolves and foxes which preyed upon and scavenged their herds, must have moved into the Arctic by this time, and waterfowl were probably establishing summer nesting areas. These animals were followed by Indian hunters who, by 8,000 years ago, were travelling northward along the coast of Labrador and in the Barren Grounds to the west of Hudson Bay. Our archaeological evidence suggests, however, that these Indians did not winter on the tundra, but stayed close enough to the tree-line so that they could retreat to the forest which provided fuel and shelter from the arctic winter. For several thousand years the arctic mainland and the arctic archipelago remained uninhabited, not through lack of food resources, but because the human knowledge needed to survive the winter in this bleak land was lacking.

Such knowledge was being developed far to the west, probably in the northeastern regions of Siberia. Here, Neolithic hunters of the northern Asiatic forests may have discovered the rich sea-mammal resources of the Bering Sea coast, and decided that they could winter in the area while subsisting on sea-mammal meat and fat stored from the summer hunt. Their traditional cultures may already have developed tailored skin clothing which allowed them to better insulate themselves from the winter cold and wind; these conditions the Indians survived only through the use of wood fires within the shelter of the forest. Or perhaps the factor which first allowed full-time occupation of the tundra was merely the development of attitudes which placed a higher value on being well fed than on being warm and dry. It is interesting to note that the Chipewyan Indians with whom Samuel Hearne travelled the Barren Grounds during the 1770s treated hunger as a joke but, wretchedly clothed, they were greatly inconvenienced by cold and wet weather. On the other hand, Europeans have always been impressed by the ability of the Inuit to live and work cheerfully in appalling weather conditions; the greatest fear of the traditional Inuit family was not cold, but inadequate supplies of food. Perhaps the development of the

---

All photographs are by the author, unless otherwise indicated.

attitude that body heat should be supplied by food, that energy should be used internally and conserved by insulating clothing rather than externally through the use of wood fires, helped to develop the first permanent habitation of the tundra regions.

If such an attitude had been evolved in the cultures of early Siberian hunters, the arctic tundras and coasts of North America were certainly good areas in which to put it into practice. Although the Arctic may seem barren to the modern urban dweller—and perhaps even more so to the farmer—to a hunter, the Arctic is a relatively productive place to live and work. Although the Arctic supports a small number of animal species relative to temperate and tropical regions, these animals occur in large numbers and dense seasonal congregations which can be very efficiently exploited by a hunting population. The cold temperatures of the region allow meat to be easily stored for a time when resources are scarce, either on a seasonal basis or over a period of years. Once a hunter knows the country, knows where to find the summer fish runs and the autumn caribou-migration routes and the spots where sea mammals congregate during the winter, he is in a better situation than many of his southern compatriots.

The remains of the first camps of such tundra and coastal hunters are found in western Alaska in the centuries just prior to 2000 B.C. By the latter date, similar camps existed across the arctic coast of Canada and in northern Greenland. Today, the sites of these camps are marked by rings of stones or gravel which once held down the edges of their tents, and by stone slabs which formed a hearth and storage areas within the tents. The arrangement of the central hearth and storage areas in a mid-passage arrangement separating working or sleeping areas on either side of the tent, resembles an old Eurasiatic house style which survived among the Lapps of northern Europe until the nineteenth century, and probably reflects the Asiatic ancestry of the first arctic hunters. Around the remains of such camps we find scatters of chipped flint tools: points for arrows or spears, knives, scrapers and burins, which have led archaeologists to call this culture the Arctic Small Tool tradition (an unwieldy name usually shortened to ASTt).

The early ASTt people may have been attracted eastward across Arctic Canada by the presence of animals which had never been hunted, and which were therefore more curious about than wary of human hunters. For whatever reason, these people seem to have established a thin veneer of occupation throughout most of the area within a very few centuries. They adapted their subsistence economy to the resources of local areas, in some regions concentrating on the hunting of musk-oxen, in others on seals, while in some camps we find that most of the refuse bones are those of waterfowl, fox and other small game. Apparently lacking dogsleds, snowhouses, oil lamps and float-harpoons, their economy seems to have been more insecure, and their life more uncomfortable, than that of more recent Inuit.

We do not usually expect to find evidence of artistic activity among people living this meager sort of life, and indeed very few carvings or engravings on bone are known from the ASTt. On the other hand, their chipped flint tools and weapon points are surprisingly well and carefully made, and may approach what we could call an art form. The chipping of flint is one of mankind's oldest crafts; yet very few cultures have developed the skills of the ASTt people in handling this intractable material. It is apparent that ASTt craftsmen were interested in more than functional aspects of stone tools; they selected multicoloured flints, chipped them very evenly and symmetrically, often with decorative edge serration, and their extremely small size suggests that there was a high value on the skill necessary to create such miniature pieces. If we can call this an art form, it would appear to have been one perfectly suited to the lifestyle of the ASTt people: useful, portable, and probably increasing the interest and significance of the everyday hunting and household tasks for which the tools were used.

After about 1500 B.C. the climate of Arctic Canada began to deteriorate from conditions which may have been slightly warmer than those of the present day. Cooler summers may have allowed an increase in the thickness and extent of sea ice, thus restricting the ranges and populations of seals and other sea mammals. Land mammal populations may have been reduced as well, or their migration routes suddenly and unexpectedly changed, especially in areas such as the Barren Grounds where the tree-line retreated south by over 200 kilometres after what appears to have been a disastrous series of fires. About this time ASTt people abandoned some areas, including the north coast of Greenland and the High Arctic Islands north of Lancaster Sound. Others began to move into the interior of the Barren Grounds and became caribou hunters, displacing for several centuries the traditional Indian occupants of the region as far south as Great Slave Lake and Lake Athabasca.

During the first millennium B.C., in the context of increasingly severe climate and ice conditions, the ASTt people of Baffin Island, northern Hudson Bay and Hudson Strait developed more efficient hunting techniques, what appears to have been a more secure and sedentary way of life, new types of tools and new forms of art. Together, these new elements formed what is known archaeologically as the Dorset culture, named for Cape Dorset where the culture was first recognized. During the following centuries the Dorset people spread out from their relatively rich home area, reoccupying the islands of the High Arctic, moving down the Labrador coast to form the primary occupation of the island of Newfoundland for almost a millennium, and occasionally extending

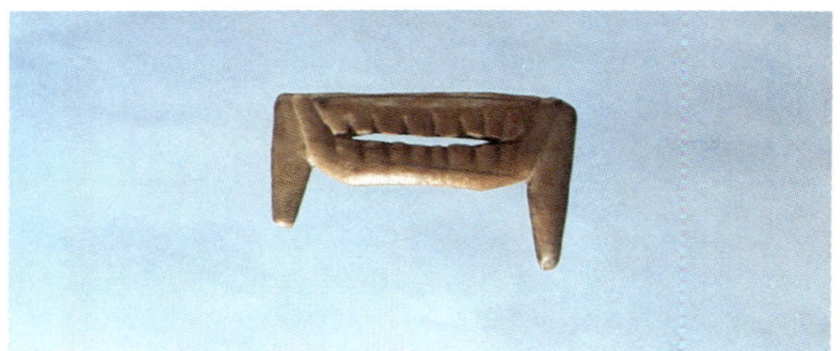

A set of ivory animal teeth, designed to be worn in the mouth of a Dorset shaman.

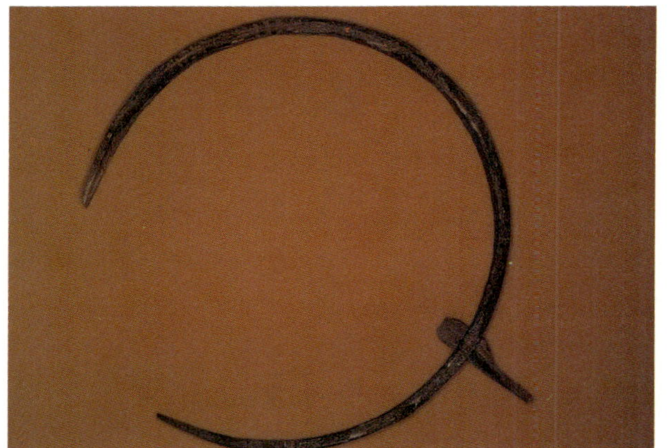

The Dorset shaman used a small drum with wooden rim, such as this specimen from Bylot Island.

their territory westward as far as the eastern shores of Amundsen Gulf. Although some of these areas were occupied only sporadically, the Dorset way of life dominated Arctic Canada for almost 2,000 years.

The Dorset people lived in settlements which appear to have been larger and more permanent than those of their ASTt ancestors. In some areas they built semi-subterranean winter houses with turf walls, while in others they seem to have used domed snowhouses heated with oil lamps carved from soapstone. Both types of structures must have been vast improvements over the tents heated with small fires of driftwood and animal bones which seem to have been the winter dwellings of the early ASTt people. There is some evidence that they now possessed kayaks, and the ones found around their camps indicate that they were efficient hunters of sea mammals as large as walrus and narwhal. In some regions they killed large numbers of caribou, and may have built some of the stone drive-lanes used by later Inuit caribou hunters.

Perhaps it was the increased security provided by this new way of life which allowed or encouraged the development of a new art form: the carving of small figures in ivory or wood. The majority of Dorset carvings represent animals, occasionally humans, and perhaps spirits, both in realistic and highly abstract forms. Most scholars interpret Dorset art objects as intimately connected to shamanistic religious practices similar to those described by anthropologists for many people around the northern world. Items such as life-sized wooden masks, drums and sucking tubes

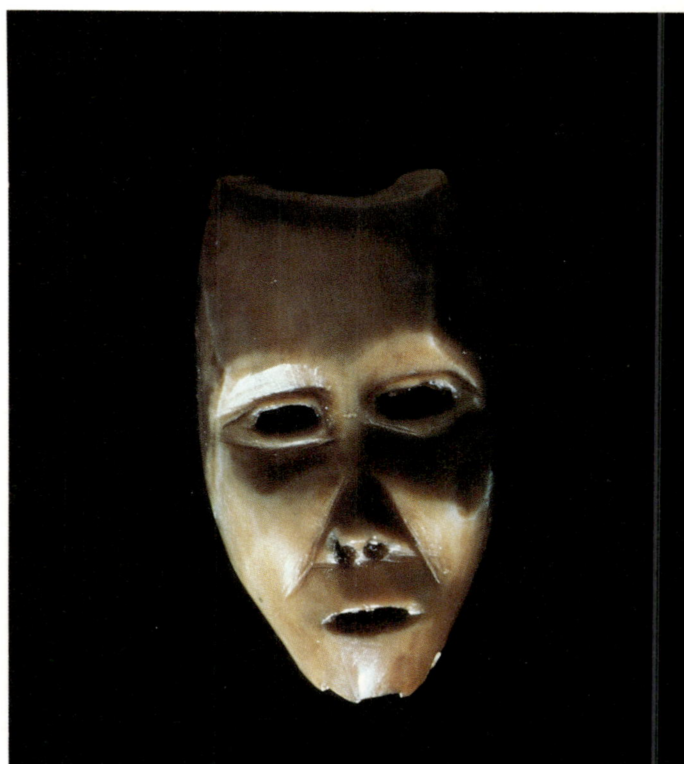

A Dorset masquette in ivory, 35 mm high, from Arctic Quebec.

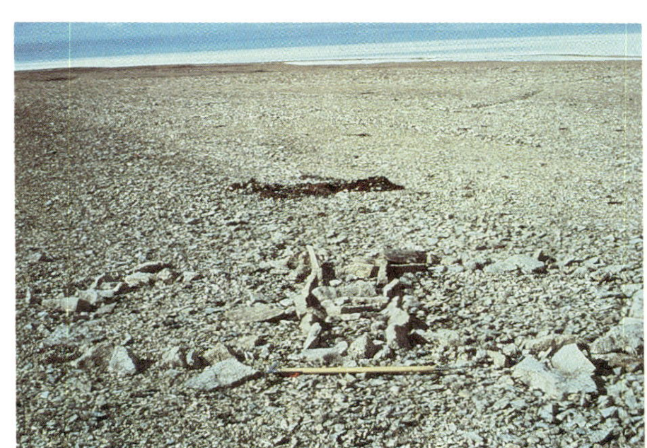

A well-preserved Early Dorset tent, showing the mid-passage arrangement built of vertical slabs of rock.

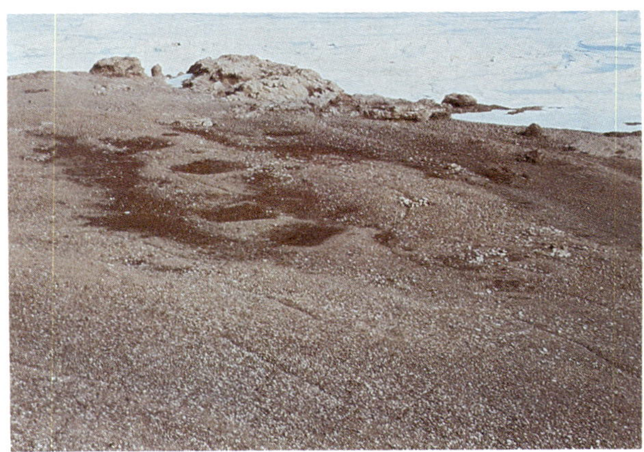

The remains of winter houses are marked by four rectangular patches of vegetation at this Late Dorset site on southern Ellesmere Island.

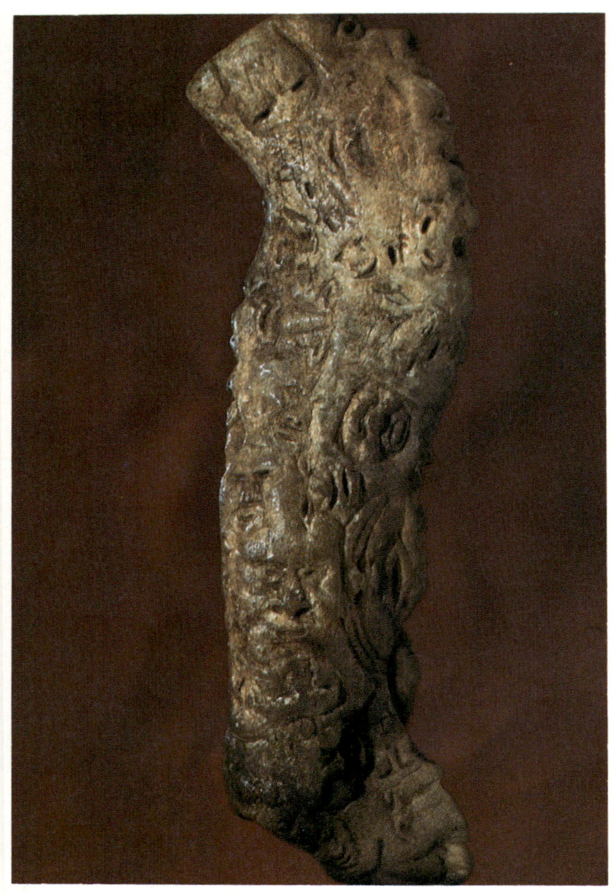

This piece of caribou antler is covered with carvings of approximately sixty faces. A few similar objects have been found at other Late Dorset sites.

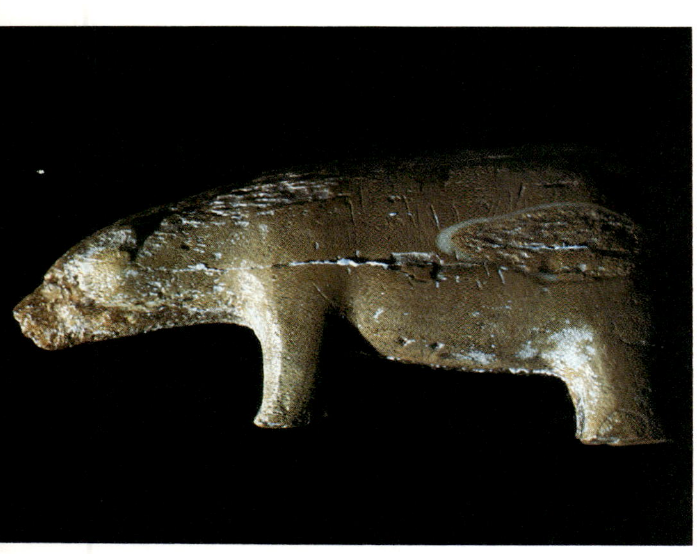

An ivory carving of a bear, found at a Late Dorset site on Bathurst Island.

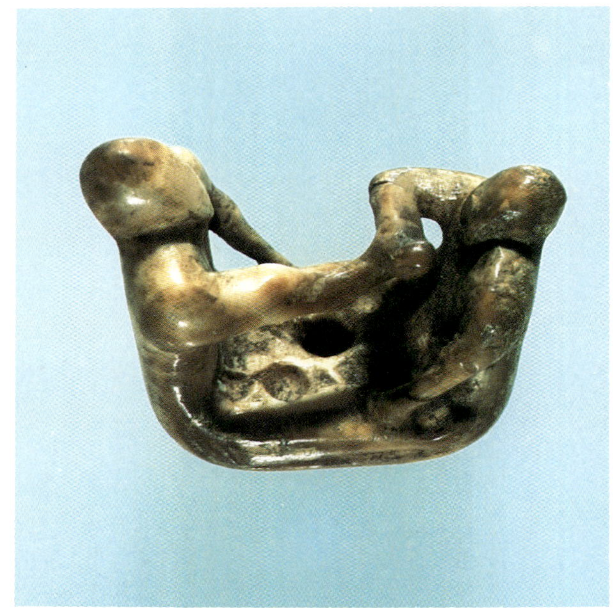

Dorset ivory carving of two men wrestling.

were almost certainly used by the shaman. Miniature harpoon heads may have been magical weapons, and figures of humans and bears with a hole in the chest or throat, sometimes containing a sliver of wood, were probably associated with attempts at sympathetic magic.

Other items are not so clearly associated with shamanism, but may have been objects of magical power. In this category we might place carvings of bears, more or less stylized but consistently engraved with lines representing elements of the animal's skeleton and joints. It has been suggested that these 'X-ray' figures may represent the helping bear spirit of the shaman rather than an actual bear. Other such objects are pieces of caribou antler covered with carvings of up to sixty faces, perhaps representing the people in a local community, the patients whom a shaman had cured, or the spirits upon which the shaman could call. Naturalistic carvings of animals—bears, falcons, caribou, musk-oxen—and occasionally of humans, may not have been associated with magic; yet many of these are perforated so that they could be hung from a string, and may have been worn as personal amulets. The rarest form of Dorset art is found along the Hudson Strait coast of northern Quebec. Here, at a few localities, cliffs of soapstone have been carved with numerous human faces, similar to the clusters of faces on antler tines found elsewhere.

Although carvings occur in all phases of Dorset culture, there appears to have been a major increase in the numbers and variety produced during the closing centuries of the Dorset period, somewhere between 500 and 1000 A.D. This was also the period in which Dorset culture reached its maximum extent, expanding northward to reoccupy the High Arctic as far as northwestern Greenland. At the end of this expansion, however, Dorset culture disappeared from all areas except Arctic Quebec where Dorset people appear to have survived for a few more centuries.

This remarkably sudden disappearance of a population which had occupied Arctic Canada for three millennia can best be explained in terms of a well-documented historical event: the invasion of the area by Alaskans, the ancestors of the modern Canadian Inuit. Inuit legend states that when their ancestors came to Arctic Canada they found it occupied by a race of people called *Tunit* whom the Inuit eventually killed or drove away. The legend supports the archaeological evidence of Dorset disappearance, and perhaps explains what occurred approximately 1,000 years ago. From the *Tunit* the invading Inuit may have learned how to build domed snowhouses, learned the locations of soapstone quarries from which they could carve lamps and cooking pots; and a few other elements of Dorset culture that may have found their way into the culture of the Inuit. It is also possible that some Dorset people were incorporated into the Inuit population, although there is presently no evidence to support this idea.

The ultimate origin of the Alaskan Inuit is still uncertain. They may have developed from ASTt people who remained in western and northern Alaska after their relatives had moved east to Arctic Canada, or they may have originated in an older population which had settled the Pacific coast of Alaska approximately 10,000 years ago during the closing stages of the Bering Land Bridge. In either case, we know that by about 2,500 years ago ancestral Inuit were living in western Alaska, and were gradually developing the efficient open-water hunting techniques which led to the sophisticated Old Bering Sea culture on both sides of Bering Strait in the centuries around 1 A.D. These people had kayaks and larger skin boats, float harpoons which allowed them to easily kill large sea mammals, and their consequent ability to accumulate and store food for the winter allowed them to build large permanent villages. These villages, some of which were inhabited for several centuries, were composed of large semi-subterranean, log-walled houses, covered with turf for insulation, and heated by lamps burning sea-mammal oil.

The ivory carvings and complex engraving style of the Old Bering Sea people have been justly celebrated since the first artifacts were discovered about fifty years ago. The artistic styles, as well as those of the contemporaneous and vaguely related Ipiutak people of northern Alaska, have been compared with, and tenuously linked to, styles emanating from Indian cultures of the Northwest Coast and with those of eastern Asia and northern China. They are decidedly different from, and show no relationship to, the contemporaneous styles of Dorset art in

Ivory weapons of the Old Bering Sea culture. The butterfly-shaped object may have been a harpoon rest from the front of a hunting boat.

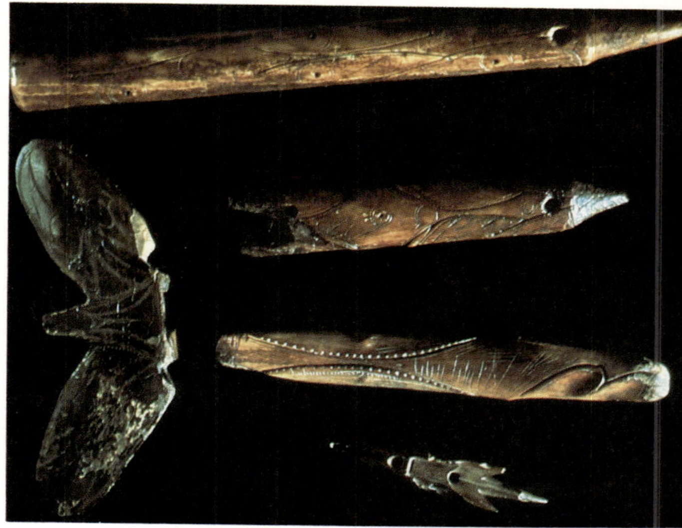

Arctic Canada, being much less clearly linked with shamanistic activities. The fact that the most highly decorated objects are generally weapons for sea-mammal hunting suggests that perhaps the art of the early Alaskan Inuit may, rather, have been associated primarily with hunting magic.

By about 1,000 years ago the Inuit of North Alaska had learned to hunt the large bowhead whales which migrate eastward each spring through narrow leads in the ice close to the North Alaskan coast. At approximately the same time, the climate throughout the northern hemisphere began to warm rapidly. In Europe, zones of agriculture moved northward, and the warming climate has been suggested as a cause for the contemporaneous Norse expansion out of Scandinavia. The relatively calm and ice-free sailing conditions which allowed the Norse to reach Greenland and the eastern coast of North America may also have encouraged a wave of Inuit expansion eastward across the Arctic. When the Inuit and Norse met, probably in northern Greenland at some time during the twelfth century A.D., mankind had first circled the arctic world.

These immigrant whale hunters, the ancestors of the Inuit, are known to archaeologists as the Thule culture, named for the area in northwestern Greenland where their remains were first recognized. Travelling and hunting in open skin-covered boats up to ten metres long, and in winter by dogsled, the Thule people seem to have moved across the entire Arctic within one or two centuries. They established permanent winter villages similar to those of their Alaskan ancestors, but their houses were now built of stone and whale bones rather than driftwood logs, which were not available in most areas of their new country. The villages were smaller than those of Alaska, and most appear to have been occupied for a shorter

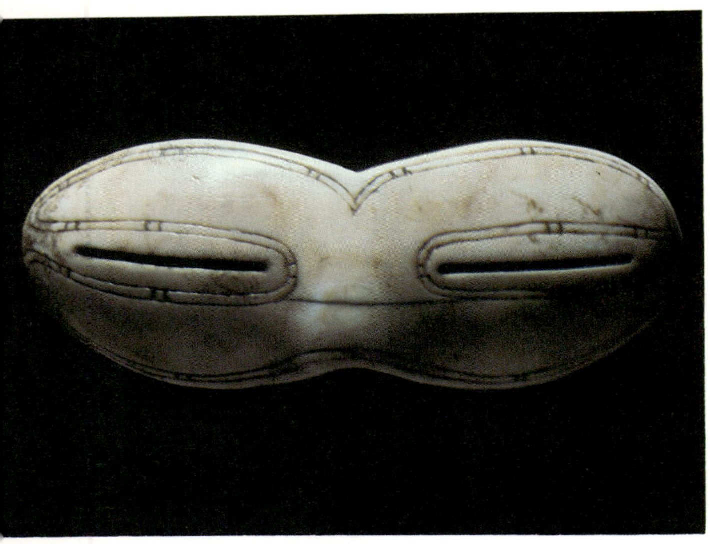

Thule snow goggles, carved from ivory and decorated with incised lines.

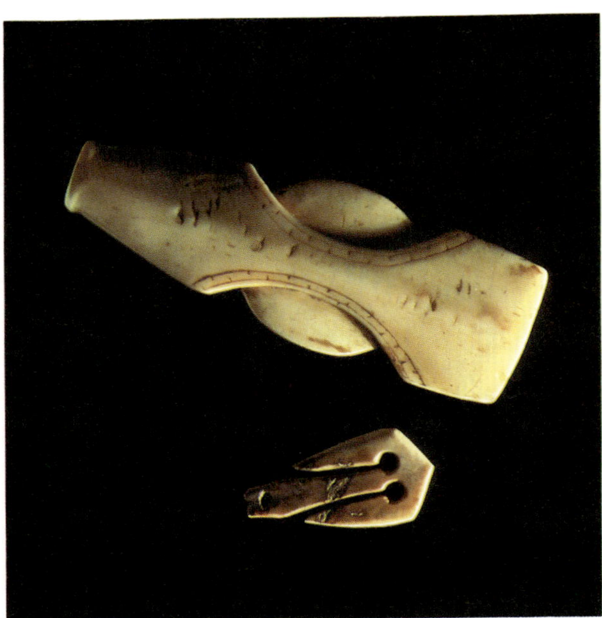

Ivory needle case and thimble holder, from a Thule site on northern Ellesmere Island.

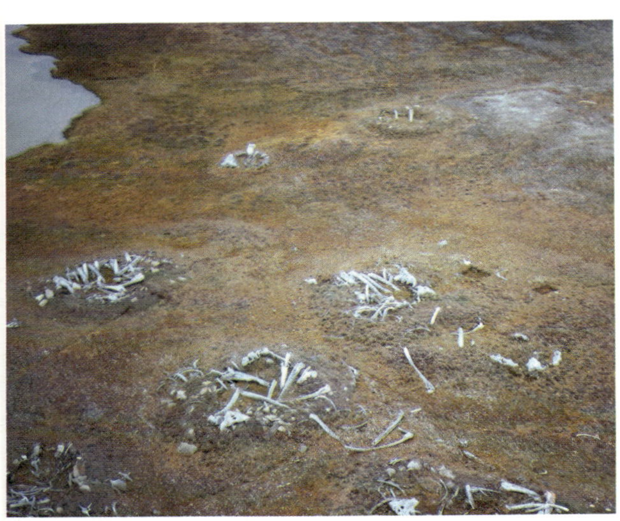

Thule winter village on Bathurst Island. The whale bones are the collapsed roof supports of the winter houses. Below is a Thule winter house with the roof reconstructed after excavation.

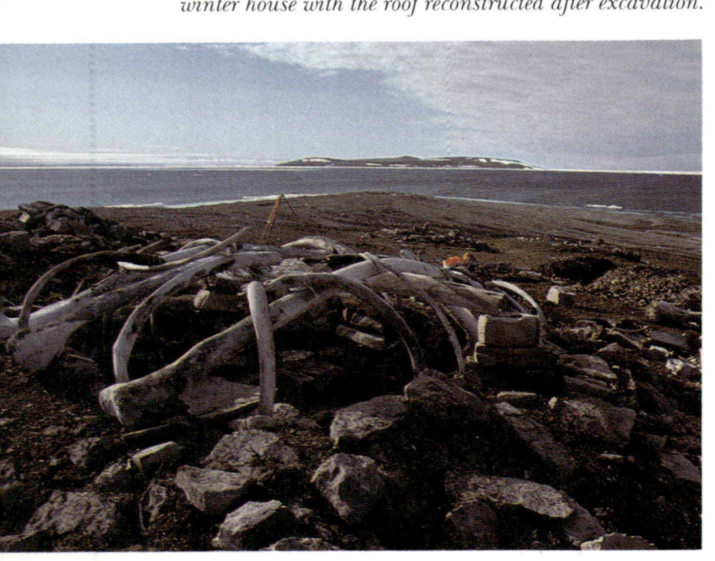

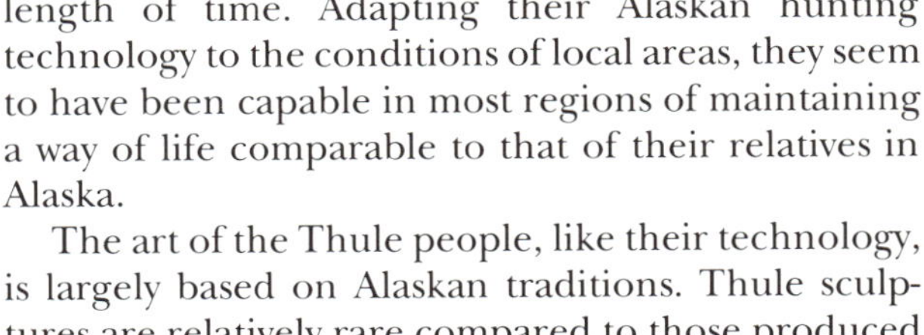

length of time. Adapting their Alaskan hunting technology to the conditions of local areas, they seem to have been capable in most regions of maintaining a way of life comparable to that of their relatives in Alaska.

The art of the Thule people, like their technology, is largely based on Alaskan traditions. Thule sculptures are relatively rare compared to those produced by their Dorset predecessors, and made in a very few standardized forms. Most are simple silhouette figures in wood or ivory, representing women with flat uncarved faces and stumpy arms; some of these may have been children's dolls, and others perhaps amulets or charms. Another standardized form consists of small birds or birds with women's heads, carved with a flat base so that they resemble birds sitting on the water; all are made from ivory or sea-mammal tooth, and in the historic period similar objects were used in a hand-game. The occasional toggle or line-stopper carved in the form of an animal's head, and a few small whale effigies, make up most of the remainder of Thule sculptural art.

The Thule people did, however, add engraved designs to many of their artifacts: single or double marginal lines, sometimes joined with hatch-marks or ticks, 'Y' designs or stick-figure humans, and occasional representations of animals or entire panels showing hunting and camp scenes. The majority of such decoration is found on ivory objects, and mostly on either weapons used in hunting sea mammals, or tools and other objects associated with women, such as needle cases, combs and decorative pendants. I have argued elsewhere that the use of ivory in the manufacture of such objects, and perhaps the related decoration, is associated with the Thule view of the world as dimly reflected in the

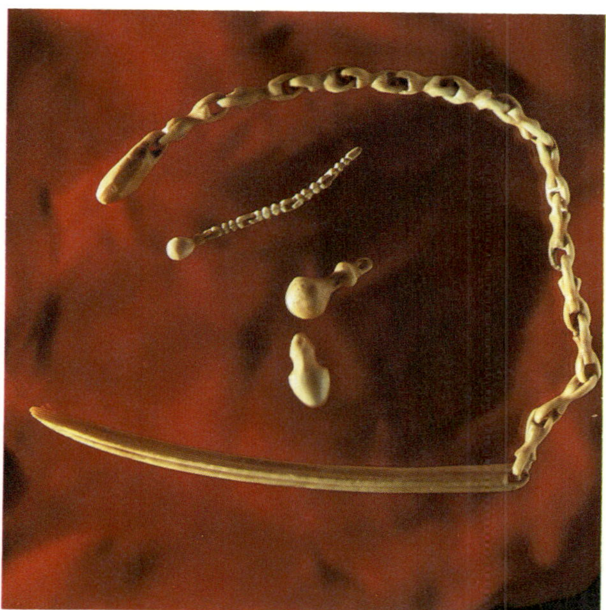

Thule ivory carvings from Bathurst Island: two chains and two pendants.

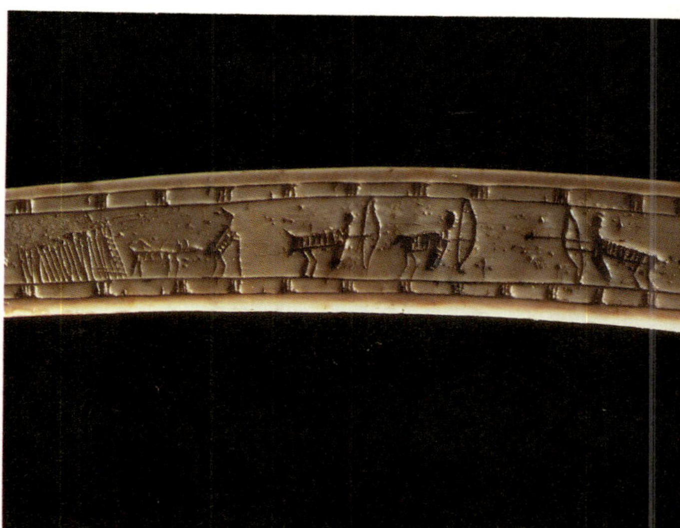

Engraved fighting scene from an ivory bow drill recovered from a Thule grave near Arctic Bay.

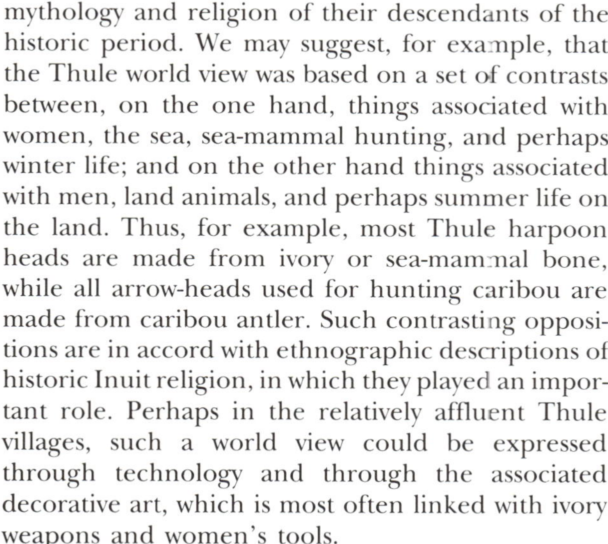

mythology and religion of their descendants of the historic period. We may suggest, for example, that the Thule world view was based on a set of contrasts between, on the one hand, things associated with women, the sea, sea-mammal hunting, and perhaps winter life; and on the other hand things associated with men, land animals, and perhaps summer life on the land. Thus, for example, most Thule harpoon heads are made from ivory or sea-mammal bone, while all arrow-heads used for hunting caribou are made from caribou antler. Such contrasting oppositions are in accord with ethnographic descriptions of historic Inuit religion, in which they played an important role. Perhaps in the relatively affluent Thule villages, such a world view could be expressed through technology and through the associated decorative art, which is most often linked with ivory weapons and women's tools.

What happened to the Thule people? Five centuries ago their winter villages, supplied with food and fuel accumulated during the summer open-water hunting of sea mammals, were scattered across most of Arctic Canada. Yet by the time that European explorers began to penetrate the area in the eighteenth century, much of the region was unoccupied and in the inhabited regions people were following a more nomadic life in small bands, living in tent camps during the summer and in temporary winter villages of snowhouses. Only in Labrador, southwestern Greenland and in some parts of Baffin Island did something like a Thule lifestyle continue.

The most likely explanation for this change involves a climatic deterioration, the onset of the Little Ice Age which, between approximately 1600 and 1850 A.D. affected the entire northern hemisphere. Throughout Europe there were disastrous crop failures, the sea ice in the vicinity of Iceland became much more severe than during the preceding centuries, and similar conditions must have occurred in arctic North America. Shorter ice-free summer seasons and increasing amounts of both fast and drift ice in most regions must have decreased the range of whales and other large sea mammals, and also made hunting more difficult. Faced with this sudden and unexpected change in their environment, various regional groups of Inuit reacted in different ways.

The islands of the High Arctic were abandoned, except for the dwindling population of Polar Eskimos clustered around the open water and bird cliffs of northwestern Greenland. Through most of the Central Arctic, summer sea hunting must have become increasingly difficult, and people began to look to the interior for summer food supplies. Small bands consisting of one or a few families began to wander inland, fishing in the lakes and rivers, intercepting the caribou migrations, and occasionally hunting musk-oxen and other animals. Following such a pattern, they could not accumulate or transport enough food to last through the winter in the permanent winter villages of their ancestors. In most areas, winter life depended primarily on hunting the small ringed seal, which winters beneath the ice and can be caught at leads and breathing holes. In order to hunt these animals efficiently, the Inuit needed temporary villages of snowhouses, which could be abandoned when the local seal population had been hunted out. The technology and knowledge necessary for these new hunting and living patterns had been developed during Thule times, but the onset of colder climatic conditions now rapidly increased their importance.

There may have been a general population

decline as people tried to adjust to the new conditions, although we cannot be certain of this, as our knowledge of Thule population size is very vague. Many elements of Thule technology disappeared; items such as large skin boats and whaling gear were simply no longer useful, and were abandoned and forgotten in most areas. In the Central Arctic, kayaks were adapted for river hunting of caribou and were no longer used for sea hunting. Among the Polar Eskimos the art of kayak construction was lost, and they also seem to have forgotten the use of the bow and the fish spear. At the same time, there was a general and drastic decrease in the amount and quality of plastic and decorative art being produced. It is difficult to understand why this should have occurred. The usual explanation is that, with deteriorating environmental conditions, people were so busy making a living that there was no time left over for artistic activities. This cannot be true, however, since poor weather forces long periods of inactivity in any arctic hunting camp. Although there must still have been plenty of time to carve, perhaps the increasing insecurity of life produced a lack of will, a simple decline in interest in applying the customary decorations to hunting weapons and sewing tools. This lack of interest may have extended to other spheres of life, such as mythology and religion; those of the Canadian Inuit of the historic period were generally much less complex than those of their Alaskan and Greenlandic relatives, perhaps due to an impoverishment which occurred during the Little Ice Age.

Another possible cause for the decline of art in this period lies in contact with European technology which penetrated the entire area during the eighteenth and nineteenth centuries, usually far ahead of the Europeans themselves. In some parts of the world, such as the Northwest Coast of British Columbia, the introduction of metal tools may have led to florescence in artistic activity. Among the Canadian Inuit, however, one has the impression that the new materials are associated with a decline in traditional art and even in traditional technology; as metal carving tools became increasingly available, traditional artifacts made with these tools were not as skilfully done or finely finished as those made in earlier times when metal was scarce. One can only speculate on the influence of an obviously superior technology on a people whose tools and weapons had always been considered to be more efficient and sophisticated than those of any others in the known world. Only when direct contact with Europeans occurred, and a market was established for Inuit carvings and engravings, do we find the rebirth of these art forms.

From the foregoing, it can be seen that there was no simple and direct development of prehistoric Inuit culture or art in Arctic Canada. The Inuit are often naively seen as a people who, over the millennia, have gradually developed a lifestyle finely adapted to their harsh environment, and an artistic tradition reflecting that way of life. Such a view makes it difficult to understand the nature of Inuit life and art. Archaeology shows that the Canadian Inuit are relatively recent immigrants to the area, arriving from Alaska during the past millennium and bringing with them a rich and sophisticated hunting culture. Their artistic traditions were developed in the Bering Sea area, and were perhaps influenced both by the artistic styles of Bronze Age Asia and those of the Indian cultures of northwestern North America. Arriving in Arctic Canada, they met and were perhaps influenced by the Dorset people, whose ancestors had inhabited the area for 3,000 years and developed a unique way of life and fascinating and compelling art styles. As recently as 500 years ago the Canadian Inuit had a productive and relatively secure economy, and a culture perhaps as advanced as that of any other hunting people on earth. Only during the few centuries prior to European contact was this way of life reduced by the hazards of climatic change. The Inuit life described by early European explorers and anthropologists was not the culmination of thousands of years of gradual development, but of a recent and rapid adaptation to a deteriorating environment.

As part of this adaptation, Inuit plastic art practically disappeared for a period of a few centuries. Only in the 1950s did carving once again become a prominent activity. Although occasional carvings have been made for sale to Europeans for the past century, the florescence of the past three decades has been in response to the creation of an organized export market which provided a continuing economic incentive for the production of carvings and other items. On the surface, these new forms of artistic expressions bear little resemblance to those of the prehistoric past. Yet there was a great deal of variability among prehistoric art forms. The complex engraved decoration of the Old Bering Sea culture bears no closer relationship to the magical carvings of the Dorset people than it does to contemporary Inuit carving. In each of these cases, artistic activity appears to have been encouraged for different reasons, and to have used different modes of expression. In this context, modern Inuit art may be seen as an integral part of an Inuit artistic heritage, a heritage marked by diversity and occasional florescence rather than by gradual and uniform development. ♦

Jean Blodgett

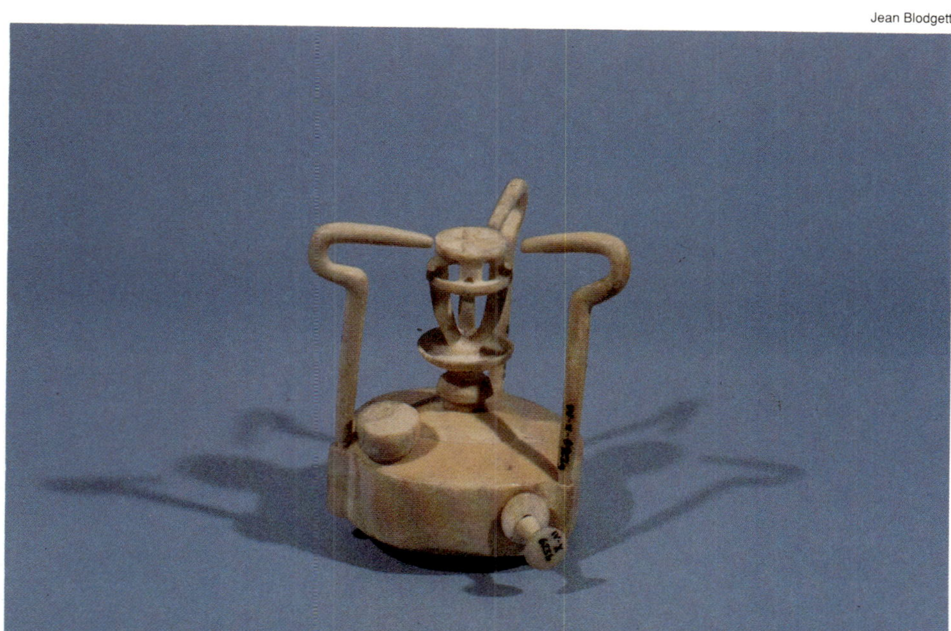

The Historic Period in Canadian Eskimo Art

By Jean Blodgett

THE HISTORY OF CANADIAN INUIT ART is usually divided into three major time periods, the prehistoric, historic, and contemporary; a chronology based on significant events within the sequence of arctic cultures. In Canada, the prehistoric period, which includes the Dorset, Thule and earlier cultures, extends from approximately 2000 B.C. to c. 1700 A.D. The historic period dates from the late 1700s and continues to 1948 when James Houston first visited the Arctic. Mr Houston's trip north and the very successful sale in Montreal of Inuit artworks collected by him on a second trip in 1949 heralded the beginning of a new period in Inuit art. Although previous attempts had been made earlier in the century to market Inuit carvings, it was not until the late 1940s that conditions were ripe for such a development. The years since that time have been characterized by the consistent and ongoing production and exportation of artworks for sale in the South.

The contemporary period, defined as dating from the time of James Houston's first northern ventures and continuing to the present, is particularly well known, and the subject of increasing study and research. The work in this area is, in addition, supported by considerable documentation and analysis of the Dorset and Thule cultures and their art, carried out primarily by archaeologists. Falling between these two major areas is the historic period,

---

Model primus stove in ivory, from the Eastern Canadian Arctic in the 1930s. Height: 8 cm. Canadian Museum of Civilization, Ottawa.

From *The Beaver,* Summer 1979.

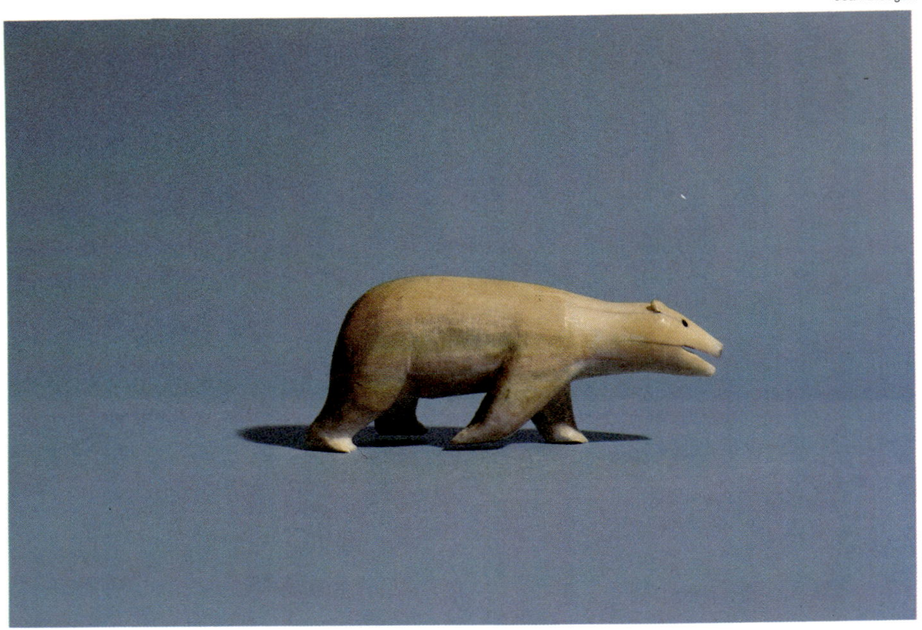

Bear in ivory, 1925, from Cape Dorset. Height: 4.5 cm. Collected by J. Dewey Soper, Canadian Museum of Civilization, Ottawa.

an ill-defined and poorly documented time span which is often only briefly acknowledged within the history of Inuit art.

It would appear that a number of factors have contributed to the historic period's particular position in Inuit history. In contrast to the scientific study of prehistoric archaeology and the accessibility of contemporary research, the historic phase is plagued with misconceptions and lack of visual data, as well as problems of definition, provenance, dating, and documentation. Not only has little been written about the art of this period, but only a few publications reproduce examples of the actual artworks.[1] As a result there is insufficient visual material readily available to provide the basis for thorough analysis and comparison. The lack of published information is not compatible with the volume of artifacts observed and collected during this period by explorers, whalers, ethnologists, anthropologists, missionaries, Hudson's Bay Company and government employees, and tourists, for we find that those working or travelling in the Arctic generally returned home with some memento of their sojourn in the North. Unfortunately much of the material which was acquired by private individuals remains inaccessible or unknown, and even collections in major institutions often came to the museums incompletely documented. With the exception of those collectors who were making a scientific study of the artifacts, the historic collector, in keeping with the attitude of the times, was usually unconcerned with documenting the object or its maker. The situation becomes somewhat better from 1850 on, and the early part of the 20th century is the most thoroughly documented of this period. The majority of works discussed and reproduced here date from the turn of the century or later.

In addition to the lack of precise and scientific collecting procedures and dearth of documentation, the historic period is, in itself, simply difficult to define. Two major events are inextricably tied with the development of the historic phase; the Little Ice Age (1600-1850) and white contact.[2] During the 17th century, an increasingly colder climate resulted in changes in animal populations and distribution. The Thule people responded to these new conditions by making considerable adaptations in their hunting technology and lifestyle. These developments significantly altered their traditional culture, in effect bringing to an end the Thule phase. At the same time, more and more outsiders were making their way to the Arctic. Not only were these foreigners able to record their travels, thus instituting our first written accounts, or history, of the arctic people, but they—like the climatic changes—had a significant effect on the indigenous population.

Explorers had ventured to the northern coasts of Canada since as early as about 1000 A.D., but these trips were sporadic and of short duration. By the mid-19th century, however, the traffic north in some areas had increased to such an extent that the Inuit were in continuous contact with non-Inuit.[3] The presence of these foreigners, particularly the whalers, missionaries and traders, had a tremendous influence on the traditional Inuit culture, for these outsiders came to stay and they brought with them new jobs, new implements, new clothing and food, and a new religion.

Yet the amount and duration of contact with outsiders varied considerably throughout the North;

Ernest Mayer

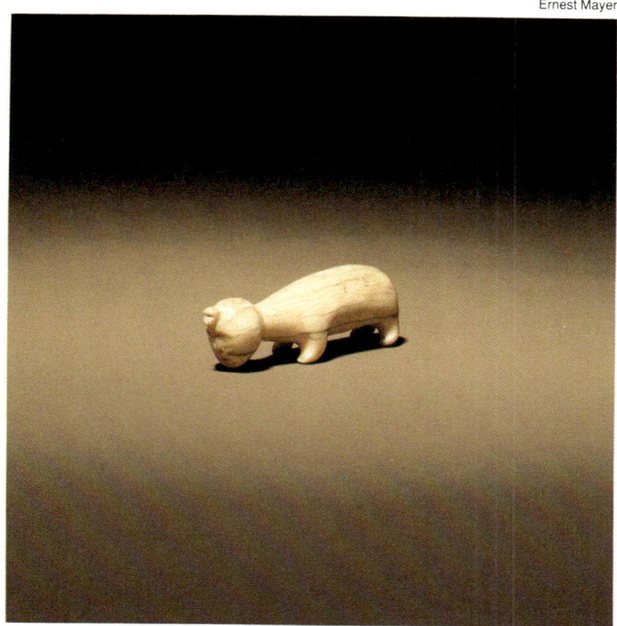

Bear with spirit head, amulet in ivory, pre-1923, from Blacklead Island. Height: 2.1 cm. Royal Ontario Museum, Toronto.

Ernest Mayer

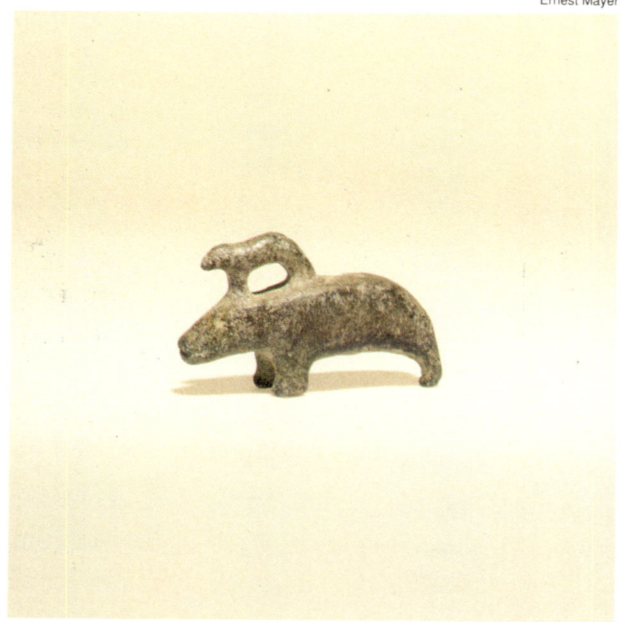

Bears, c. 1915, in grey-brown stone from the west coast of Hudson Bay. Height: 3.4 cm. Canadian Museum of Civilization, Ottawa. Collected by Christian Leden.

Jean Blodgett

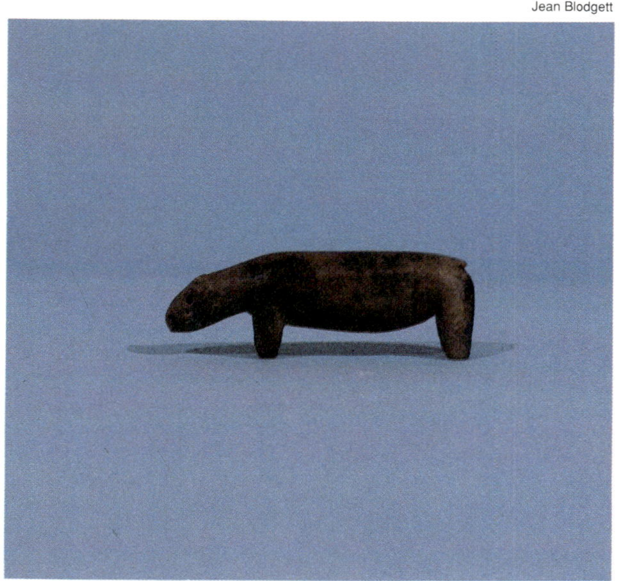

Bear, 1915, in horn, from Chesterfield Inlet. Height: 2.8 cm. Canadian Museum of Civilization, Ottawa. Collected by C. Leden.

for example, in Labrador the Moravians established a permanent mission at Nain in 1771, while the Iglulik Eskimos were generally without steady contact until late in the 19th century. Thus one specific date for the beginning of white contact cannot be established, just as one date cannot be assigned to mark the end of the Thule culture. From 1600 on, the Inuit culture underwent considerable change as a result of both the climatic conditions and increasing association with non-Inuit, but this was a gradual process, and one which occurred in different parts of the Canadian Arctic at different times. The historic period, then, is one arising from cultural changes, and it is essentially a period of transition. The artworks from these years reflect this state of transition and change.

During the historic period, the Inuit people, like their predecessors, continued to make decorated items and carvings (as well as unadorned, functional tools and equipment which are not considered here). These objects, which range from everyday implements to articles of special significance, include toys and games such as dolls and *ayagaks* or personal adornments and equipment such as ivory combs and pipes; and ceremonial and religious items: skin masks, head ornaments, shaman belts, amulets and fetishes.[4] It is important to note that not only were these objects made by the Inuit for their own use, but their crafting shows obvious signs of the attention devoted to non-functional and aesthetic concerns. The artifacts are sensitively decorated and adorned with patterns or representative figures, and complementary or unusual materials are used for finishing details. A number of the objects, particularly the carvings, are associated with the religious practices of the Inuit. For example, the bear, an animal often connected with shamanism as a popular helping spirit, is well represented in several different guises in the historic period.

An examination of these various bears, however, indicates yet another concern related to the carvings made during the historic period. Of the bears illustrated, the one from Cape Dorset is distinctive; it has a new, clean look to it, it has a more animated or illustrative quality, and it has protruding extremities which make it less of a contained unit than the bear from Chesterfield Inlet. In fact, the Cape Dorset bear does not look as if it has been used by the people who made it. This consideration, of the ultimate function of the object, is a major factor in the historic period. In contrast to the art objects made by the Inuit of this period for their own use, we find an even greater number of items which appear to have been made purely for sale or trade to non-Inuit. Although it is not always possible to establish with certainty whether the objects the Inuit made were intended for themselves or not, those things destined for the outsiders are generally characterized by such factors as an unused look, a free-standing and more open sculptural form with protruding extremities thus making the object more suited to display than to being handled or held, orientation to a base, untraditional or even alien function or subject matter, and an illustrative quality. As we have seen, from the early 1800s on, there was a marked increase in the traffic north, and these visitors acquired virtually any and all objects that they could from the Inuit, stimulated by scientific investigation, simple curiosity, or the desire for souvenirs and mementoes. The presence of these outsiders and their modern equipment, as well as their acquisitiveness, influenced the culture they observed, and the Inuit began to produce objects which were of no use to themselves, but which were predestined for sale to the visitors.

Although their function had thus changed, many of the artworks still represented traditional and indigenous subjects. Whether as a result of a request or search for information on the buyer's part, or as a result of his own familiarity with such subjects, the Inuit artist often depicted things and events within his native tradition and experience. In keeping with the concerns of a hunting economy, the carvers depicted the various animals of the North, including musk-oxen, caribou, walrus, seals, whales, narwhals, bears and even fish, dogs, hares and birds.[5] In addition to these single representations, the artists also turned their attention to some fairly complex hunting and animal scenes,[6] usually portraying the action on a large, single piece of ivory, but in some instances using separate parts to compose the scene. The artists also depicted themselves and their fellow men in a striking variety of representative poses and attitudes; in groups, alone, or engaged in domestic tasks.[7] Models were also popular, and we find a number of examples of small-scale igloos, sleds and kayaks,[8] some of which are embellished with very fine and minutely detailed hunting equipment. In fact, there are all kinds of precisely finished miniature models of implements such as harpoons, spears, ulus, knives, scrapers, fishing jiggers and snow-shovels. The attention to detail in these implements and models, as well as the realistic and animate carvings of the people and animals of the North, seem to suggest an illustrative intent on the part of the maker, as though he was trying to show outsiders his native culture and environment.

At the same time during this period, traditional technical skills were also employed in the making of

Tom Prescott

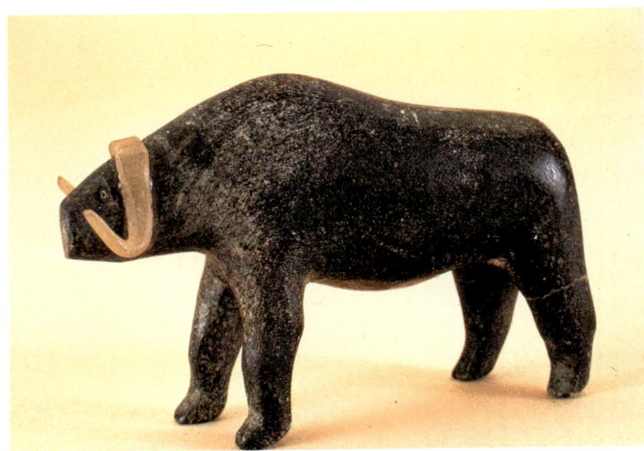

Musk-ox in grey stone and horn. Presented to Dr L. E. Borden, physician on the 'Neptune' wintering at Cape Fullerton on the west coast of Hudson Bay, 1903-04. Height: 6.5 cm. Canadian Museum of Civilization, Ottawa.

Jean Blodgett

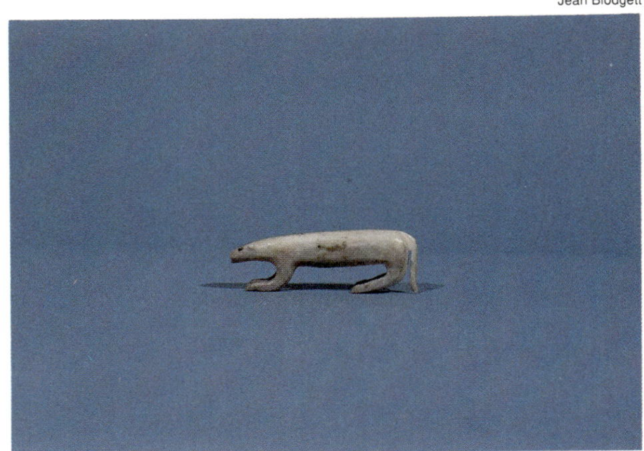

Dog in ivory, c. 1920 from North Baffin Island. Collected by R. J. Kidston. Canadian Museum of Civilization, Ottawa.

Jean Blodgett

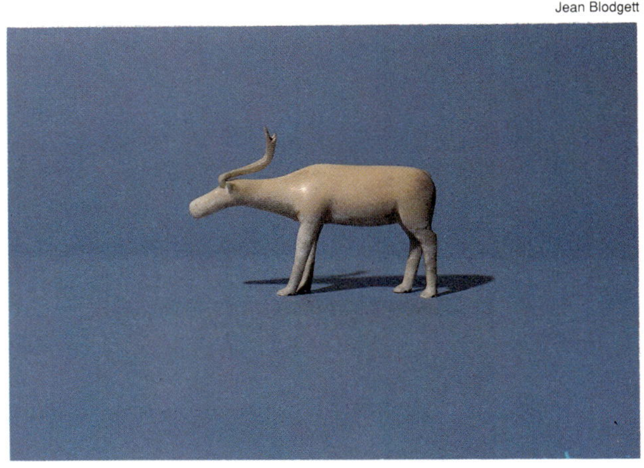

Caribou in ivory, 1925. Collected at Cape Dorset by J. D. Soper during a period of research. Canadian Museum of Civilization.

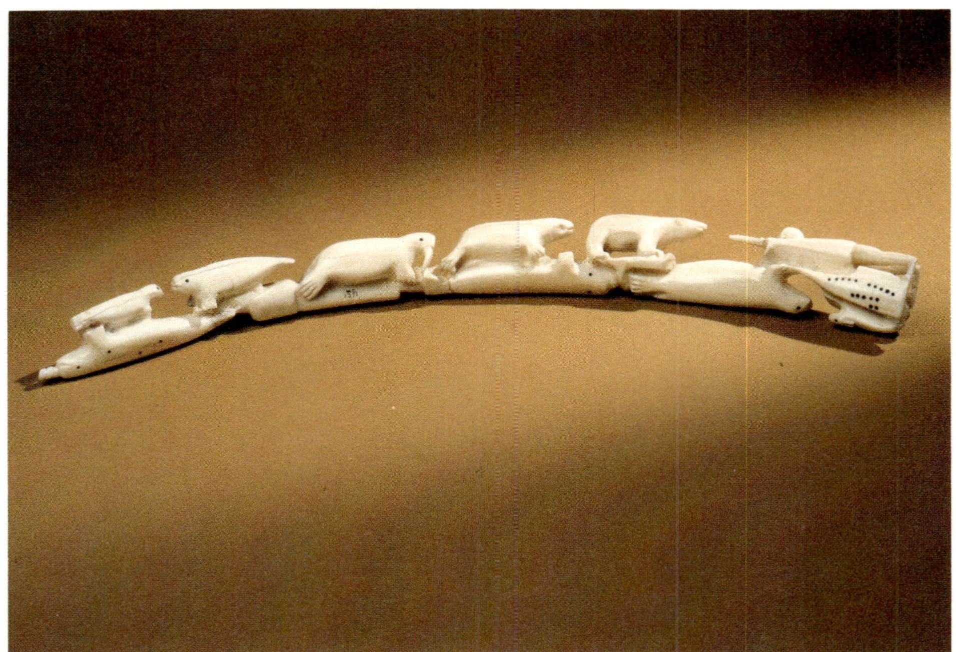

Scene with hunter and animals in ivory. Pre-1914. Collected by Robert Flaherty in the Eastern Canadian Arctic. Length: 41.5 cm. Royal Ontario Museum, Toronto.

Jean Blodgett

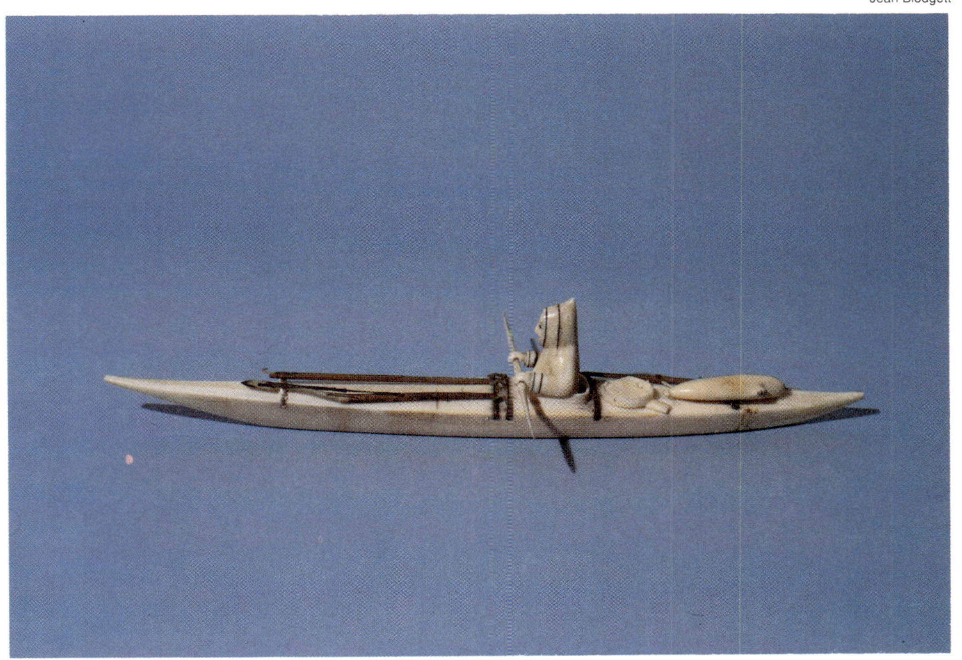

Model kayak in ivory with wood, hide, metal and sinew, 1924. Collected by L. T. Burwash, Cape Dorset. Length: 22.9 cm. Canadian Museum of Civilization, Ottawa.

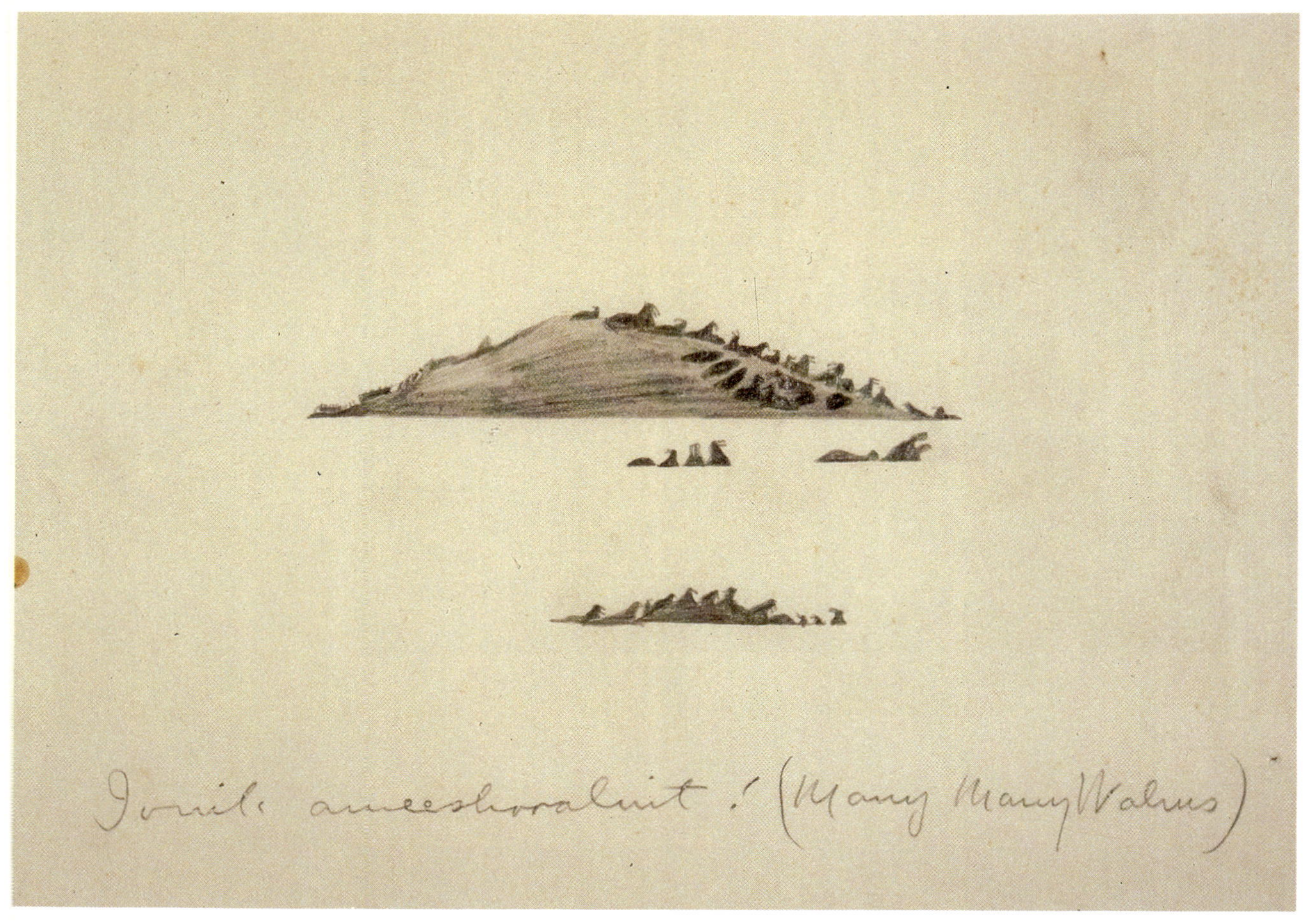

'Many Many Walrus', a pencil sketch on paper, c. 1914 from the Eastern Canadian Arctic. Size: 20 x 26 cm. Royal Ontario Museum.

a variety of novel commodities. The women's sewing expertise was turned to use in the making of such saleable items as fully costumed dolls or the elaborate skin rug collected by I.O. (later Bishop) Stringer in the Herschel Island/Mackenzie River area during the late 19th century. In some instances, the outsider requested a particular item or provided the necessary materials for something special. This is the case with the various pencil sketches and drawings solicited and collected by a number of northern visitors. Explorers were aided by the accuracy and completeness of the maps they requested,[9] and the ethnologists' research was aided by their hosts' depictions of spirits and other creatures not visible in this worldly realm.[10] Robert Flaherty returned from his northern ventures with an impressive collection of pencil scenes, and the artist James Houston shared his sketchbook with an Inuit draftsman. The Inuit's ability to so successfully make use of an alien medium reflects their highly developed visual/manual coordination, their three-dimensional carving skills, their two-dimensional experience—dating back to prehistoric times—in the making of incised motifs on flat ivory and stone surfaces, and their adaptability to new media, new technology and new subjects.

Not all the craftsmen felt equally confident with the two-dimensional media, and in some cases the request for a pencil drawing might result in a carving instead. Mathiassen describes an incident involving Knud Rasmussen and the Iglulik shaman Aua, in which the famous explorer gave Aua a piece of paper and pencil and asked him to make a drawing of an episode the latter had been describing. 'Aua sat with the pencil in his hand for an hour without anything coming of the drawing; then he laid it down and said he would rather carve it in ivory, that would be easier. Six months later he produced the carving ... which is intended to illustrate the scene he described: A male walrus and three females drifting on an ice-floe, whilst Aua watches them from land through a telescope; his wife and child sit by his side'.[11]

Certainly most people seem to have preferred the traditional sculptural form, but even so they did not always restrict their choice of materials, size or subject matter to the indigenous or familiar. In his carving, Aua portrays himself using an imported piece of equipment, the telescope. Many of the implements brought north by the outsiders—particularly telescopes, rifles and certain tools—were of invaluable assistance to the Inuit in their day-to-day activities, and it was not long before these items were integrated into the culture and into the artistic subject matter. Just as he made tiny replicas of his own traditional equipment, the Inuit artist turned his

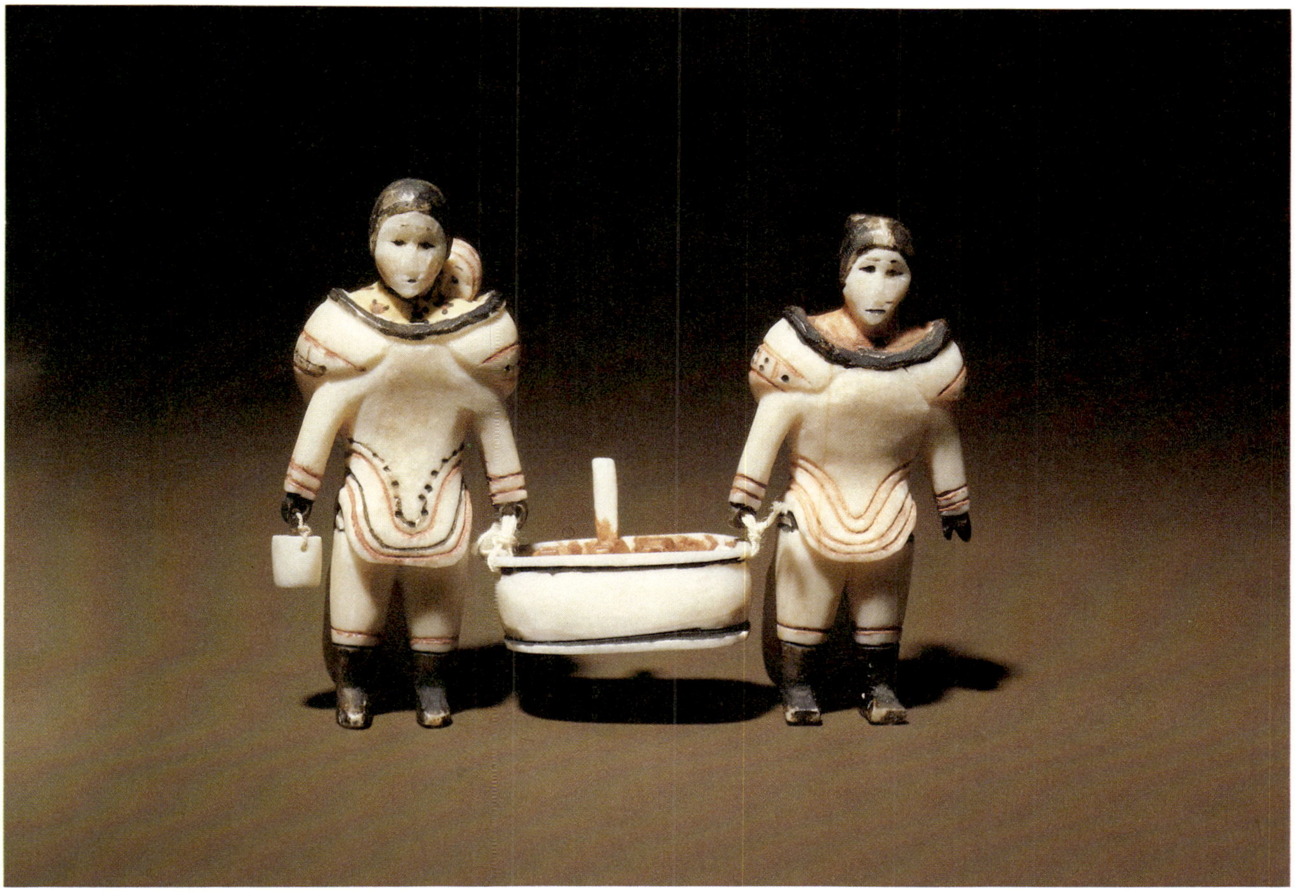

'Two Women Carrying Container'. Pre-1896. Carver unknown. Ivory with colouring.
Collected by James Wilson, Officer in Charge, Esquimaux Bay District, Labrador, 1892-1901.
Collection of his grandson, George S. Cotter.

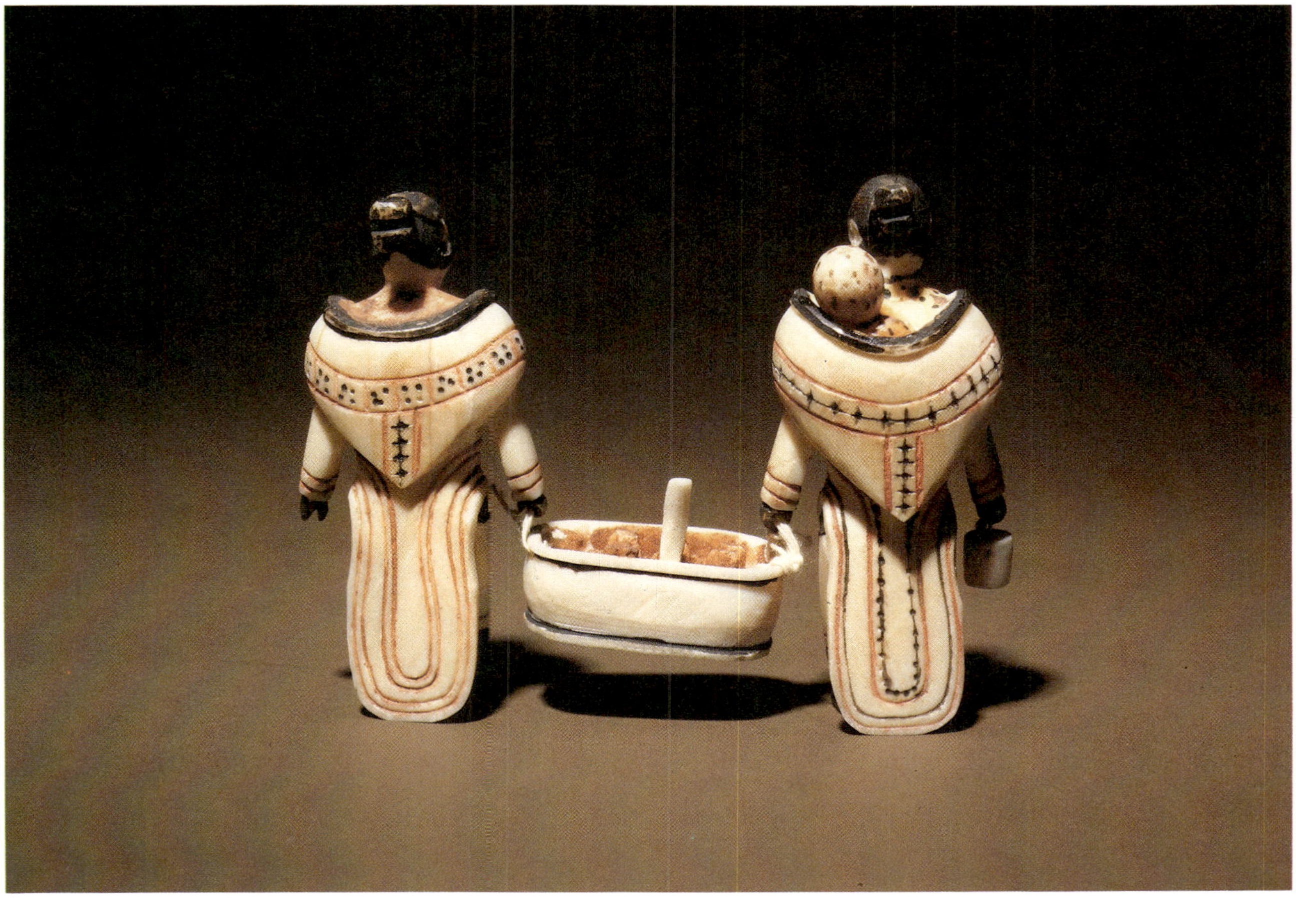

carving skills to the making of miniature models representing alien objects—many of which he had adopted for his own use, others which he saw the foreigner himself using. Thus we find carvings of such items as fox traps, saws, tools, axes, rifles, jack-knives, scissors, eating utensils and salt and pepper shakers.[12] Some of these carvings were very detailed and painstakingly elaborate replicas, such as the model primus stove and the whaleboat and ship models complete with rigging, sails, anchors and human occupants. The Inuit also recorded their new religion with carvings of Christ and the Madonna.[13] In addition to the rather extensive selection of trade models, the Inuit craftsmen also made carvings for the foreigners' own use or specifically intended as souvenirs. These include such items as letter knives, bookmarks, canes, cigarette holders, ashtrays, dice, brooches, rings, and the ever-popular cribbage boards.[14] Although many of these objects were made of ivory and remained on a fairly small scale, in keeping with traditional size and media, some of the works were of substantial dimensions and were made of stone or contained such unusual elements as cloth, string, beads and colouring.

Having examined some of the representative carvings and artifacts from the historic period, it is hard to reconcile their overall variety, quality, originality, quantity and technique with many of the statements made by northern visitors of the 19th and early 20th century. In general, these travellers were not impressed with the artistic accomplishments of their hosts, and they commented upon the decline in carving production and expertise. For example, Mathiassen states: 'On the whole the Iglulik Eskimos are not very skilful at carving: there are, however, exceptions ... but among the younger men this art is in a state of rapid decline.'[15] Franz Boas remarks that 'the artistic value of the old work made before white contact is considerably greater than that of the recent work of the natives of this region'[16] (west coast of Hudson Bay), and according to Jenness, 'carving in ivory had died out in many districts before the opening of this century.'[17]

Certainly, not all the observers were without praise for the artifacts which they observed, but the majority of comments were disparaging or negative, and at best unenthusiastic. Needless to say, there are uninspired and poorly carved works from the historic period as there are from any era, yet the evaluations made by the 19th and early 20th century writers seem unduly harsh—particularly when one views the actual artworks. The conclusions of these historic observers would necessarily have been influenced by certain factors such as the small sampling of artwork they individually observed, the particular tastes and views of their times with regard both to art and native populations, and their own presence in the North. The pressure exerted by their proximity could account for certain phenomena they observed; the crudeness of carvings may have resulted from the haste with which the items were made for trade on the spot; the subjects may have been influenced by their preferences in purchase; and the scarcity of objects may have resulted from overtrading or an unwillingness to co-operate, or secretiveness, especially with regard to religious artifacts. In addition, we should recognize that the specialties of these observers were not within the field of art or art criticism. Nevertheless, their conclusions have not been without influence in subsequent discussions of Inuit art, and one cannot ignore this influence or the contribution made by their observations. On the basis of increasingly available visual data, however, it would appear that the time has come to reassess the art of the Inuit made between the Thule and contemporary phases.

A review of historic period artworks indicates that their qualities have gone unrecognized or underrated in the past. As the pieces referred to here illustrate, the 19th and early to mid-20th century Inuit made a wide variety of artifacts, characterized by a sensitivity and feeling for media, design and colour, an attention to the significant and meaningful detail, ingenuity and imagination, as well as an overall technical expertise. Such characteristics are not unique to the historic period; they are equally prevalent in other periods of Inuit art history. We find, in fact, that the artworks made in the time span between the prehistoric and contemporary eras have a number of qualities in common with works made both before and after.

The similarities and continuities in subject matter, techniques, formats and meaning evident throughout the entire history of Inuit art make abundantly clear the very significant role of the historic phase as a link between the prehistoric and contemporary periods. Many artistic traditions from prehistoric times were maintained by the historic period artists, passed on to their successors, and have continued in use up until the present. On the other hand, external forces made the historic period one of change and adaptation; this state of transition, with new influences and elements, actually enriched and enhanced an already strong visual tradition. Artists of historic times adapted and utilized novel materials, subjects and techniques, and began to make artworks for a new purpose—innovations that were also passed onto succeeding generations. The historic period, then, can be characterized as one of transition on the one hand, and continuity on the other. ♦

Ernest Mayer

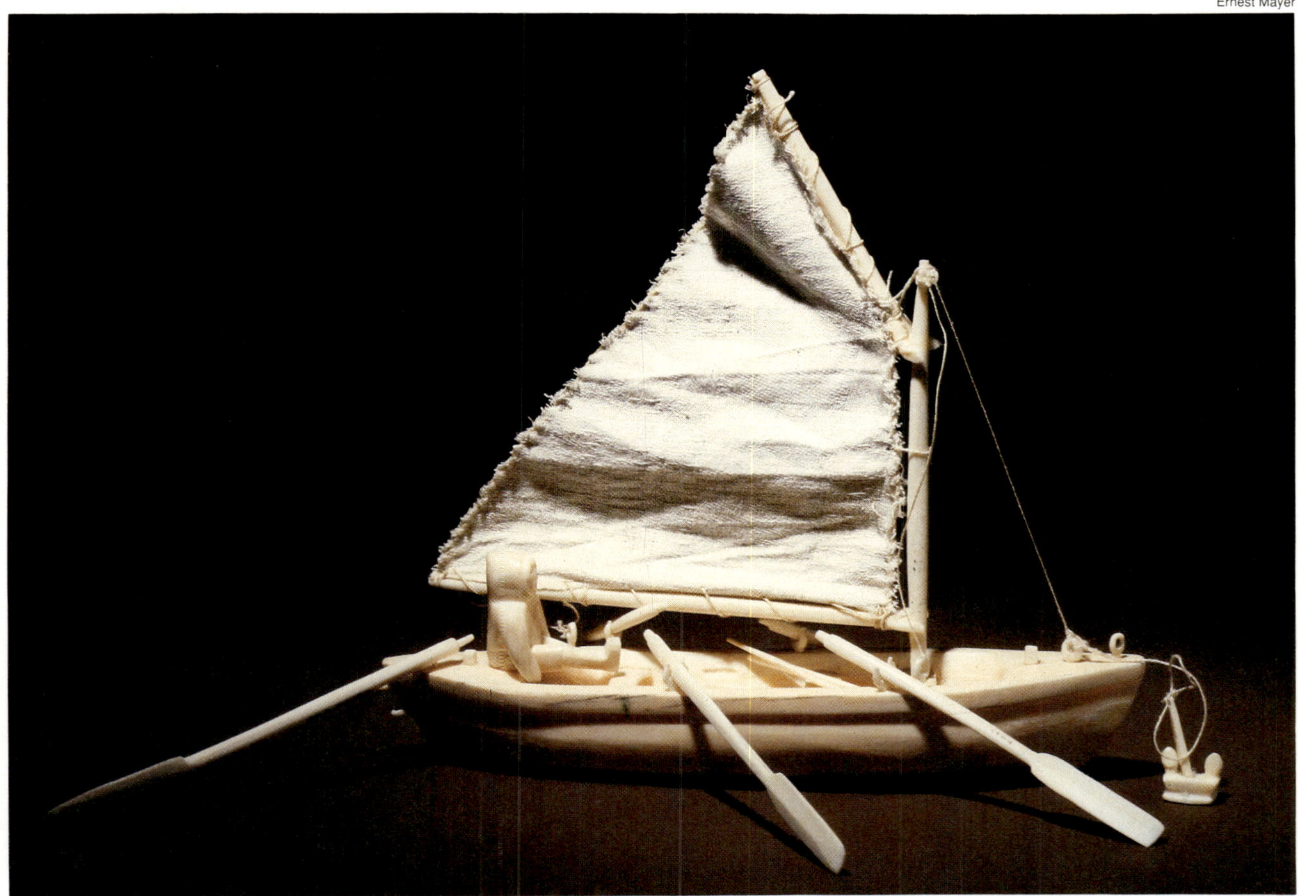

Whaleboat model in ivory, linen and string, c. 1945, from Repulse Bay. Height: 21.5 cm. Manitoba Museum of Man and Nature, Winnipeg.

Notes

1. For further information on the historic period, see Charles A. Martijn, 'Canadian Eskimo Carving in Historical Perspective', *Anthropos*, Vol. 59 (1964), pp 546-96 [text only] and George Swinton, *Sculpture of the Eskimo* (Toronto: McClelland & Stewart, 1972), pp 119-22 [text and some illustrations]. The *Sculpture/Inuit* exhibition catalogue (Toronto: University of Toronto Press, 1971), includes illustrations of a number of historic pieces.

2. For a more extensive discussion of this transition and the prehistoric period in general, see Robert McGhee, *Canadian Arctic Prehistory*, Archaeological Survey of Canada, National Museum of Man (Toronto: Van Nostrand Reinhold Ltd., 1978).

3. See W. Gillies Ross, *Whaling and Eskimos: Hudson Bay 1860-1915*, National Museum of Man, Publications in Ethnology, No. 10 (Ottawa: National Museums of Canada, 1975).

4. For additional illustrations see Jean Blodgett, *The Coming and Going of the Shaman: Eskimo Shamanism and Art* (Winnipeg: The Winnipeg Art Gallery, 1979), pp 166, 168, 170, 171, 192, 193; Franz Boas, *Eskimo of Baffin Land and Hudson Bay*, American Museum of Natural History, Bulletin XV (1901), p 107; E.W. Hawkes, *The Labrador Eskimo*, Canadian Geological Survey, Memoir 91, Anthropological Series No. 14 (1916), p 233; *Sculpture/Inuit*, illus. no. 30, 40, 41; and Swinton, *Sculpture of the Eskimo*, p 121.

5. See *Sculpture/Inuit*, illus. no. 74, 75, 84, 89, 129, 135, 149.

6. *Ibid.*, illus. no. 150, 151.

7. *Ibid.*, illus. no. 25, 55, 91, 94, 95, 227.

8. *Ibid.*, illus. no. 96, 233.

9. See, for example, Frank Speck, 'Eskimo Collection from Baffin Land and Ellesmere Land', *Indian Notes*, Vol. I, no. 3 (July, 1924), Pl. VI.

10. See, for example, the illustrations in Knud Rasmussen, *Intellectual Culture of the Iglulik Eskimos*, Report of the Fifth Thule Expedition 1921-24, Vol. VII, no. 1. (Copenhagen: Gyldendalske Boghandel, Nordisk Forlag, 1930).

11. Therkel Mathiassen, *Material Culture of the Iglulik Eskimos*, Report of the Fifth Thule Expedition 1921-24, Vol. VI, no. 1. (Copenhagen: Gyldendalske Boghandel, Nordisk Forlag, 1928), pp 104-05, fig. 60.

12. For additional illustrations see *Sculpture/Inuit*, illus. no. 90, 100.

13. See Jean Blodgett, *Looking South* (Winnipeg: The Winnipeg Art Gallery, 1978), no. 30.

14. *Ibid.*, no. 28, 29, 42, 45 (described in the catalogue but not illustrated.

15. Mathiassen, *Material Culture of the Iglulik Eskimos*, pp 104-05.

16. Boas, *Eskimo of Baffin Land and Hudson Bay*, p 460.

Whale Bone

By Jean Blodgett

Ernest Mayer

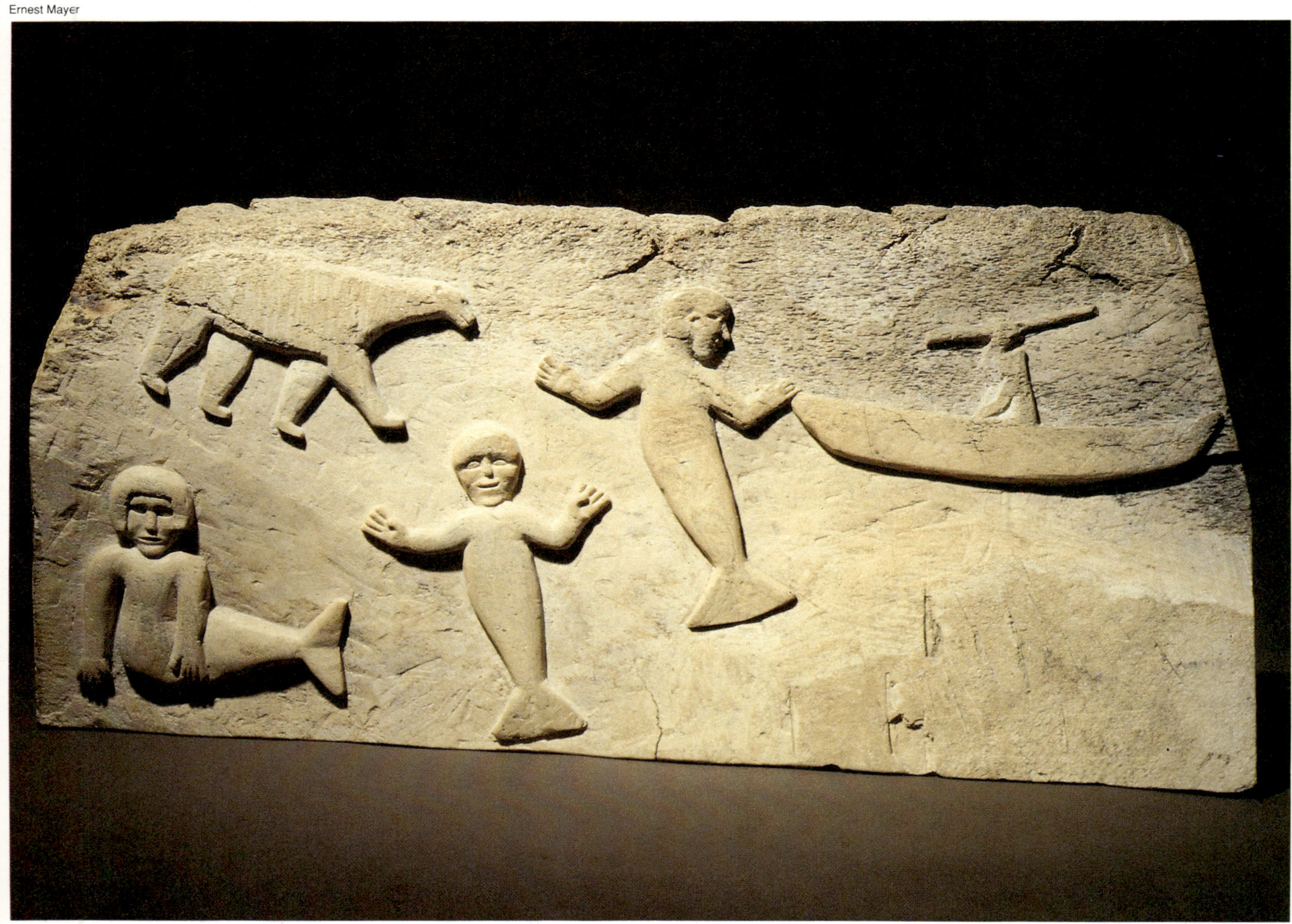

'Sedna Story' carved in whale bone at Pangnirtung by an unknown artist, 1972. From the Winnipeg Art Gallery Collection; donated by Ian Lindsay.

From *The Beaver,* Autumn 1982.

Model of a Thule culture house. Courtesy of the Canadian Museum of Civilization, Ottawa.

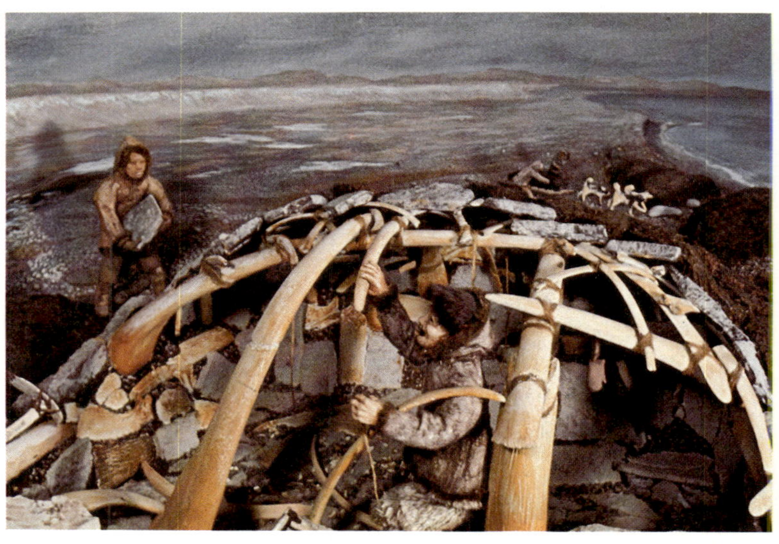

She held on to the gunwale; then the father took his hatchet and chopped off the first joints of her fingers. When they fell into the water, they were transformed into whales, the nails becoming the whalebone.'

The Eskimo of Baffin Land and Hudson Bay by Franz Boas.

AMONG THE MANY EPISODES in Eskimo* myths about the powerful sea goddess Taleelayo or Sedna is one where the goddess-to-be is thrown overboard from her father's boat as he tries to save himself from a raging storm caused by her deserted and angry bird husband. The young woman tries to cling to the edge of the boat only to have her fingers chopped off, joint by joint, by her frightened father. The fingers, falling into the water, become sea animals; the specific type of animal varies from story to story. In the version quoted above — from Cumberland Sound, an area historically rich in whales — the origin of baleen whales and whalebone is explained.

In legends, Taleelayo, no longer able to keep afloat, sinks into the water to reside beneath the sea from whence, as the sea goddess, she controls the animals so essential to the hunters and their families. Again in the Boas version, her submarine home is described as being 'built of stone and whale-ribs'. This description corresponds to the type of housing structure utilized by the prehistoric Thule culture Eskimos in Canada.

Unlike their predecessors of the Dorset culture who seem to have hunted only smaller game, the Canadian Thule Eskimos (c. 1000-1600) actively pursued the large bowhead whale. Armed only with their harpoons and riding in skin-covered frame boats, the Thule people undertook to hunt this great animal of the sea which is now (when still to be found) pursued in a more scientific and less dangerous fashion with such things as powerboats and harpoons with exploding heads. But the Thule Eskimos obviously had the equipment, expertise and courage to successfully take the bowhead whale, as the archaeological sites now so abundantly attest. Eskimos of the Dorset culture may have scavenged whales washed up onto the shore, but whale bone is not common as refuse at Dorset camp sites or as a medium for equipment and carvings, whereas the Thule Eskimos used the whale and its products extensively. Whale meat and oil were used for food and fuel, baleen was made into cups and containers, and strands of it were used for cordage and lashing. The whale bone was fashioned into toys and such tools and implements as knives, snow beaters, handles, harpoon heads, adze heads, picks and mattocks. From it the Eskimo also made shoeing for the runners of his sled.

Whole whale bones were used in the construction of burial cairns, meat caches and houses. The houses were made of sod, stones and whale bone, the latter acting as supports and rafters. According to Allen McCartney in his article in *Arctic* on 'The Nature of Thule Eskimo Whale Use', the typical Thule house, made with from 14 to 20 mandible rafters, would require the bones from seven to ten whales. Sufficient bones for all houses in a camp (up to 20 and more houses in the larger sites) would not have been taken in one season, but were acquired over the years. The Eskimos hunted whales only for the short time during the summer when the animals were feeding in open arctic waters; under their hunting conditions and with their type of equipment, it is most unlikely that they could have killed sufficient numbers to affect the overall whale population.

Whale bone was not a popular artistic medium with the Thule people; sculptures were primarily made of ivory. There are, however, several examples of implements decorated with incised scenes which show whale hunting in progress. These scenes depict men in umiaks (large frame boats covered with skin) in pursuit or actually having harpooned a whale. Perhaps best known of these is the ivory bow-drill handle found near present-day Arctic Bay and now in the Canadian Museum of Civilization, which is richly decorated with scenes of Thule Eskimo activity, including whale hunting involving several whales, umiaks and apparently an outrider in a kayak.

Incised decoration such as this was not unusual on functional equipment in Thule times, but Robert McGhee of the Archaeological Survey found an unusual specimen at the Brooman Point site on Bathurst Island in 1980: a whale-hunting scene

**Following current usage, the term Inuit applies to present-day Canadian Eskimos; the term Eskimo is used for anthropological and archaeological references.*

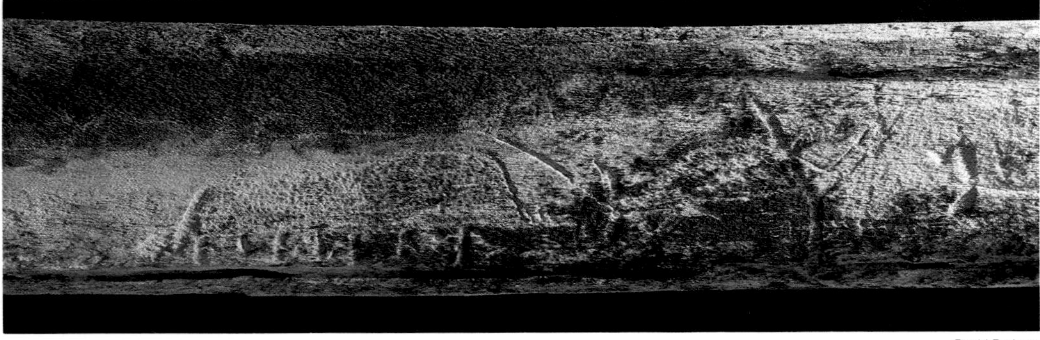

Incised whale-bone rafter from Thule house, c. 1100 A.D. Brooman point site, Bathurst Island. Length 122 cm.

David Barbour

incised onto a whale-bone rafter in one of the Thule houses. Presumably added to the bone once the house had been built, the scene, now vague and unclear, shows whale-hunting activity similar to that on the decorated implements. On the right, seven figures are shown in an umiak slightly above and behind the tail flukes of a large whale. Although not clear, it looks as if the whale has been harpooned in his centre back and the line from the harpoon head crosses the body, goes below the prow of the boat, bends and disappears into the bottom area of the scene — perhaps attached to a float that is no longer visible. Immediately above and to the left of this whale is another, more indistinct umiak with perhaps ten heads showing; to the lower left of this boat is a smaller whale, its tail flukes quite clear, but the body just rudimentarily defined with a line, and with some suggestion of a head. The shape of the head of the larger and more clearly shown whale is distinctively that of a bowhead. Also of interest in this scene is the use of hatching over the surface of the larger umiak, clearly distinguishing it from the surrounding area. Artistic devices such as this clearly set this scene apart from mere doodling.

After about 1600, changing climatic conditions affected the Thule way of life. Most significantly, with colder weather and increased pack ice, the whales could no longer reach many of their regular summer feeding grounds. Over the subsequent years the Eskimos adapted their hunting patterns to the resources available in their particular locale, moving frequently if necessary to pursue the game. Whales, where available, were increasingly hunted by outsiders — Europeans, British and New Englanders — often with Eskimo assistance. During the historical period, the Eskimos continued to make extensive use of whale bone and baleen, whether taken by themselves or outsiders, or simply recycled from older sites. In addition to the functions already outlined there is evidence that baleen was woven into mats for the sleeping platform and used for traps, fishlines and nets. Whale bone continued in use as shoeing for sled runners until sufficient metal was available — up to quite recently in some areas.

During this time, even with their burgeoning tourist market, the Eskimos did not make much use of whale bone as a carving medium. Ivory remained the favoured material until the late 1940s when, encouraged to use stone, the Inuit recognized its potential especially with respect to size and versatility. These are the very characteristics, along with availability, that first stimulated carving of whale bone. Throughout the contemporary period (1948 to present) stone has been the most popular material for carving, but poor quality or limited supplies in some areas have necessitated importation or the use of other media such as antler and whale bone. For example, the community of Spence Bay began flying in bone from the plentifully stocked Thule sites north of them to make up for the scarcity of stone in their own area. Until that time in the 1960s, whale bone had not been gathered or used for carvings on such a grand scale. However, a number of factors seem to have encouraged whale-bone carving in the late 1960s and early 1970s: the lack of sufficient stone in some areas to meet the increasing market in the South; several magazine articles with very positive commentary on the use of whale bone as an available, indigenous and appropriate medium for Inuit sculpture; and the tremendous success of whale-bone carvings in the marketplace. Seen as something distinctively Inuit, carvings of whale bone appealed to the collectors. This novel material, with its interesting natural shape, colour and texture, as well as the quality of carvings done by such people as Karoo Ashevak of Spence Bay, all helped to stimulate people's interest. Spurred on by the response in the South, carvers in communities like Spence Bay, Pangnirtung, Clyde River, Iglulik and Arctic Bay, with access to whale-bone depots, turned their hand to this exciting, newly rediscovered material. Even in communities with limited supplies sculptors were using some bone, and by 1975 more than a dozen communities were producing carvings made of whale bone.

Unfortunately far too often the gathering of this whale bone involved the disruption of Thule sites, since these camps provided not only large quantities of bone, but bone that was sufficiently aged for carving. Removal of these bones — by pulling and digging out or even sawing them off at the ground line — disturbed the prehistoric records and destroyed the layers of stratification so important to the archaeologists. As early as 1972 the Archaeological

Survey of Canada, National Museum of Man, instigated rescue projects to try to resolve the situation and in 1975 the National Museum and the Department of Indian and Northern Affairs jointly sponsored the Thule Archaeology Conservation Project to assess, among other things, the damage already done to sites. (For the report of this project see *Archaeological Whale Bone: A Northern Resource*, edited by Allen P. McCartney.) One partial solution tested in these operations was to turn over the no longer significant whale bone to local Inuit carvers once the archaeologist had completed his dig. The procedure obviously had its drawbacks for both parties, and the whale bone situation continued to raise questions in the North and the South of Canada about rights and priorities of the Inuit, the archaeologists, and everyone else involved.

In 1975 another factor was added to this situation from an unexpected quarter: the United States. During the 1970s Congress passed several acts which protect endangered species, including the Endangered Species Act of 1973. Enforcement agencies at first permitted importation of whale-bone sculpture as long as it was accompanied by a document from an archaeologist or other accepted authority verifying the age of the bone (since using bone from whales killed in prehistoric times would not endanger present populations), but in 1975 several shipments sent from Canadian Arctic Producers in Ottawa, one of the major marketing agencies for Inuit artists, to dealers in the United States were seized at the border. At that point Canadian Arctic Producers stopped all shipments of whale-bone sculpture to their dealers in the States as did the other Canadian suppliers, and tourists were advised against trying to take whale-bone carvings back home.

In the United States the Endangered Species Act is tied in with and used to implement (in the U.S.) an international agreement on endangered species, the Convention on International Trade in Endangered Species of Wild Fauna and Flora (CITES). Under this international agreement, which regulates trade in threatened plant and animal species in order to protect them from excessive commercial exploitation, participating nations require import and export permits for over 1,000 species, including baleen whales and their products (baleen as well as the bone). Permits have been and continue to be granted for the movement of Inuit whale-bone sculpture by the country of export — Canada — and all importing nations except the United States. In the United States, CITES permits are provided only for certain activities such as scientific or non-commercial exhibition purposes. At the present time, then, whale-bone sculpture may be imported into countries other than the United States as long as the appropriate CITES permits are obtained. (Check with the Canadian Wildlife Service; this system must also be used to export whale-bone sculpture from other countries back into Canada.) Import permits into the United States are very restricted and are determined by such factors as reason for movement, whether the sculpture was held in a controlled environment on the effective date of the Endangered Species Act of 1973, and so on, and I can only recommend a direct letter of inquiry to the National Marine Fisheries Service, United Stated Department of Commerce, for each individual case. Oddly enough, the United States still allows Alaskan native people not only to use whale products in their handicrafts, but to hunt actively limited numbers of this endangered species.

Ernest Mayer

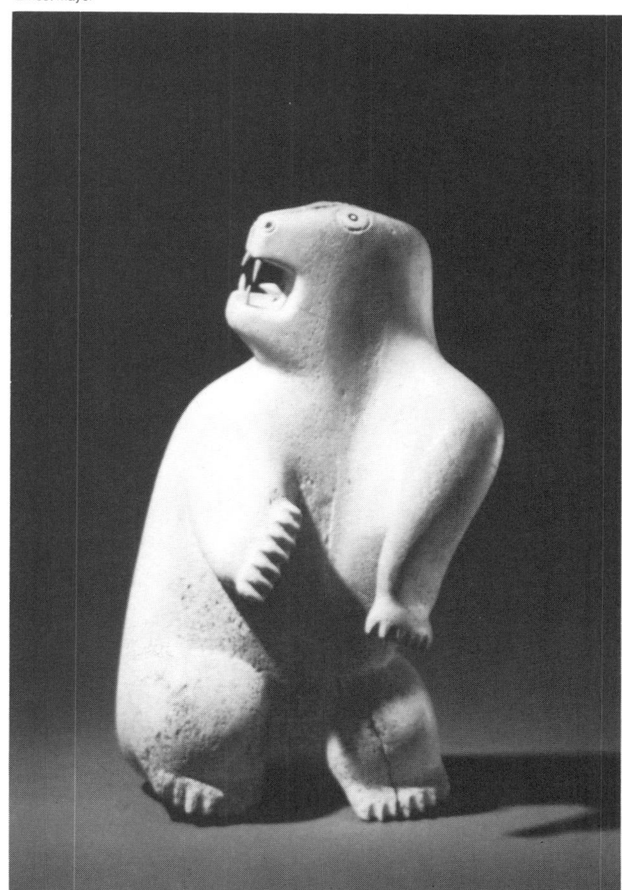

'Bear', 1973 by Karoo Ashevak (1940-1974) of Spence Bay. A work in whale bone, antler and stone.

The 1975 freeze on shipment of whale-bone sculpture into the United States caused quite a stir at the time, and was thought to have effectively curtailed whale-bone carving and with it the disruption of Thule sites. Pressure is still being exerted on the United States authorities through various channels to convince them to allow the importation of Inuit whale-bone sculpture, especially as the Endangered Species Act comes up for Congressional reauthorization this year. Even without the United States, however, it would appear that there is still a considerable market for whale-bone sculpture. Whale-bone carvings from places like Spence Bay, Pangnirtung and Clyde River are readily available

Ernest Mayer

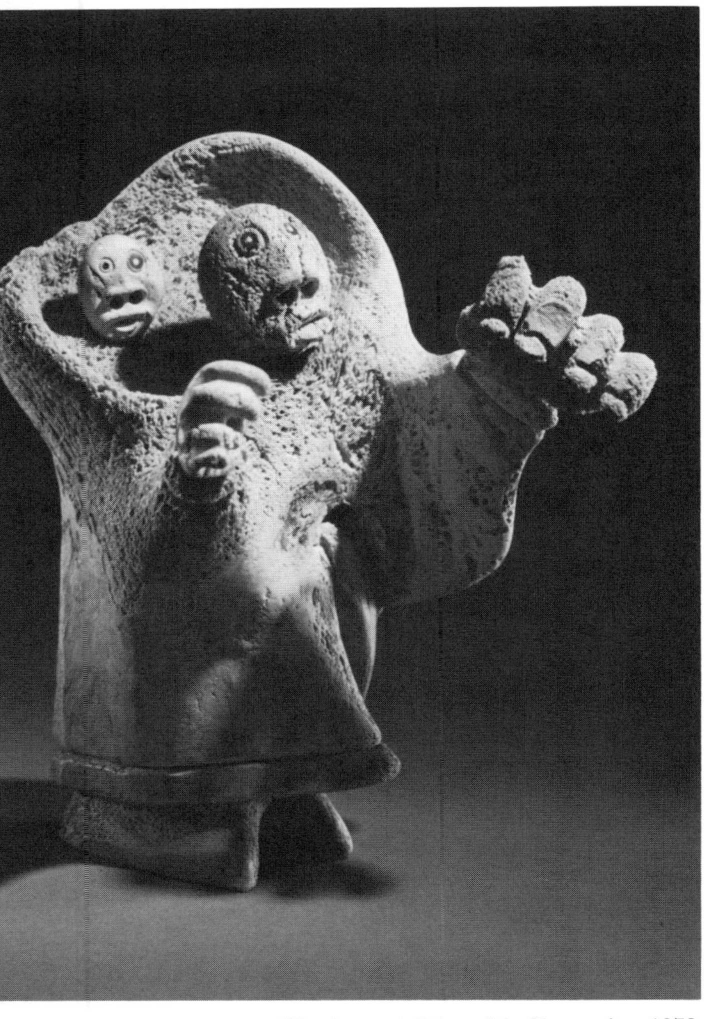

'Coming and Going of the Shaman', c. 1973. By Karoo Ashevak. Whale bone, antler and stone. From the collection of George Sutherland in Spence Bay.

Ernest Mayer

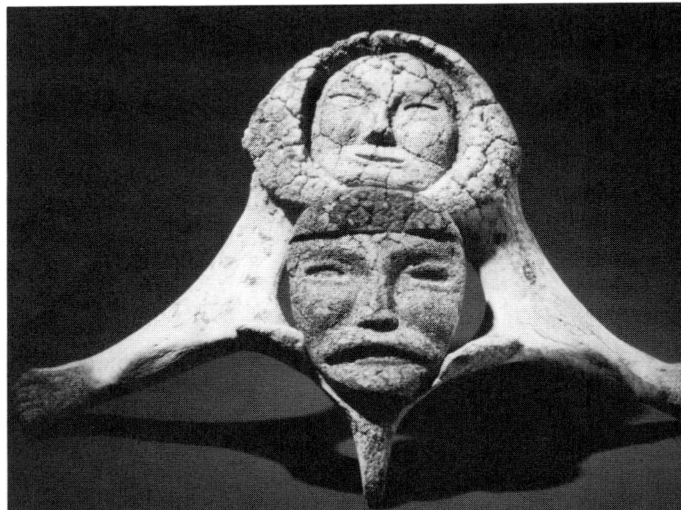

'Two Faces', c. 1969. By Joanassee Kakee of Pangnirtung. From the J. Twomey Collection, Winnipeg Art Gallery.

through Canadian Arctic Producers, although not in as great a number as previously.

That whale bone should continue to be a medium desired by some artists — and some collectors — is understandable considering its particular properties. Bones of the bowhead whale, such as the mandible, maxilla, skull, scapula and vertebra, provide the artist with an opportunity to work on a large scale with a medium that is naturally formed into interesting and suggestive shapes. Taking his cue from the shape of the bone, the artist may only work the surface enough to bring forth the form he sees there. Thus in Joanassee Kakee's sculpture, the body of the vertebra is carved into a face, the transverse processes become its arms with clenched terminal hands, while an added mask-like face rests in the opening of the spinal canal.

Other artists, like Karoo Ashevak, may have a sculptural concept first and then look for a piece of bone appropriate for their subject. His carving *Coming and Going of the Shaman* provides an outstanding example of how the properties and characteristics of whale bone can be effectively used by the sensitive artist. The title of this work is derived from Karoo's explanation that the sculpture represents the transfer of shamanistic powers, or the shaman spirit, from one shaman to another. The transference of powers is symbolically represented by the size and age of the two people. The larger head and hand are those of the shaman who is disappearing as his abilities pass to the appearing shaman, signified by the smaller head and hand. In keeping with his young shamanistic age, the novice's head and hand are not only smaller; they are of lighter-coloured, denser bone. On the other hand the sage and soon-to-be-eclipsed status of the knowledgeable elder is reinforced through the use of more porous, darker-coloured bone. The union of these two spiritual mates is conveyed by their sharing of one body, while the typical format of an Inuit mother with a child in her amautik relates to the older shaman's nurturing, instructing, empowering and spiritual raising of his offspring.

Karoo achieved the contrast of bone types in this work by adding the heads and the larger hand to the sculpture by pegging them into place. His technical expertise and delight with putting things together — and taking them apart — contributed to the complexity of his work. In Spence Bay he was recognized for his time-consuming and painstaking attention to details and finishing touches so evident in such characteristics as the inset eyes involving multiple rings in materials of contrasting colour.

Adding other media to the whale-bone sculpture is not unusual. Antler, ivory, baleen, stone and even wood may be utilized for contrasts in colour and texture. Yet these are generally restricted to minor touches which embellish the bone in a small but important way. In many cases the bone itself seems to be versatile enough. As seen in *Coming and Going of the Shaman*, bone may be of different porosity and colour. The texture of the bone naturally varies from the porous interior to the more solid exterior and this is further affected by external forces over the years, just as whale bone is bleached by the sun or dyed by the soil. The bone used in whale-bone sculptures can range in colour from white, to cream, to brown, to virtually black. Unlike whale bone, baleen is rarely used on its own as a sculptural medium. Instead it most often functions as an inset or attached accent on stone or ivory carvings, as well as on the whale bone. Slabs of baleen are sometimes used as the base or background for a scene of ivory or stone figures.

It is its size that sets whale bone apart from other sculptural materials. Structurally the bone enables northern artists to achieve, with a natural, indigenous medium, sculptures of a magnitude otherwise just not possible. But whale-bone sculptures are not always done on a large scale. Sometimes the artist will, for whatever reason, carve a small sculpture in bone that could equally as well have been made in another medium. Perhaps the bone was more readily available, or perhaps the artist wanted to take advantage of the natural colouring (as Alexina Panana Naktar of Repulse Bay has done in her charming *Mother and Child* made of whale bone with inset antler faces), or perhaps the artist simply preferred working with whale bone.

Not all sculptors like carving in bone. It may be preferable to very hard stone that is difficult to carve, but whale bone can be a tricky medium to work with. It may abruptly change from one consistency to another within one piece, and it may crack or split at any time. Such cracks, if they occur in the process of carving, may be integrated into the piece; at other times they can easily destroy the sculpture after hours of carving have already been spent. It is the structural tension and the bone's sensitivity to fluctuations in temperature and humidity that account for the cracks that develop in once-perfect pieces when they arrive in the South. Several Arctic Bay carvers, quoted in the book *We Don't Live in Snow Houses Now* refer to the difficulty of carving bone, and Oorebecca Issuqanqituq remarks: 'I like carving whale bone as well, although I didn't carve it often. The only people who do carve it are those who know which pieces of bone are good and which are not, and how to handle it.'

Another consideration with whale bone is that it must be aged for carving. Green bone is oily and smelly; it simply cannot be properly worked. This too explains the desirability of bone from Thule sites where it is available, accessible, well aged and bleached clean. Fresh bones from a bowhead whale, even if to be found at the present time, still would need considerable aging — some experts estimate from 50 to 100 years.

Although whale bone is usually associated with carving, especially large works, the West Baffin Eskimo Cooperative in Cape Dorset has, on several occasions, experimented with a whale-bone slab as a printing block. According to Terry Ryan the coloured background in the prints *Sea Sprite*

Larry Ostrum

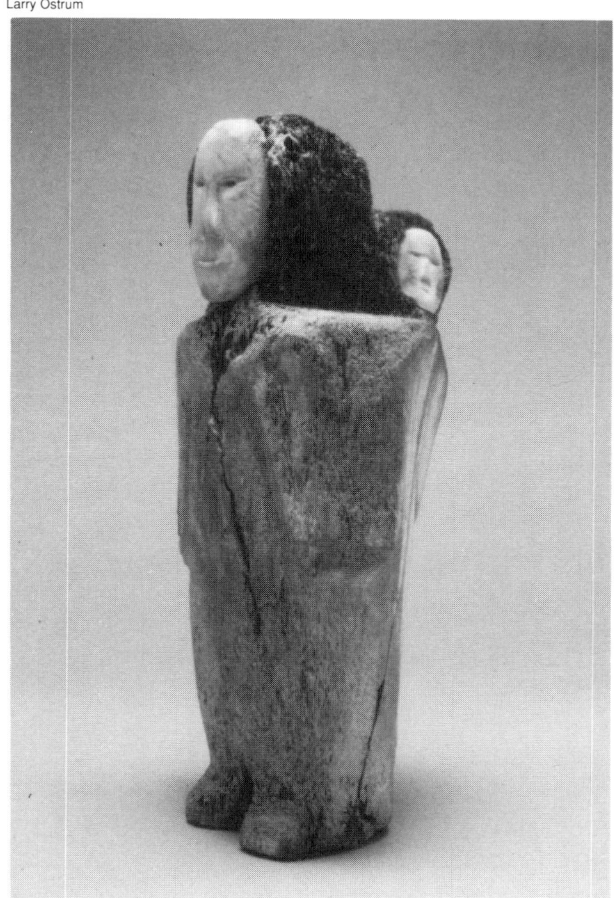

'Mother and Child', c. 1970. By Alexina Panana Naktar of Repulse Bay. Carved of whale bone with inset antler faces. In the collection of the Art Gallery of Ontario, a gift from the Klamer family.

Department of Indian and Northern Affairs

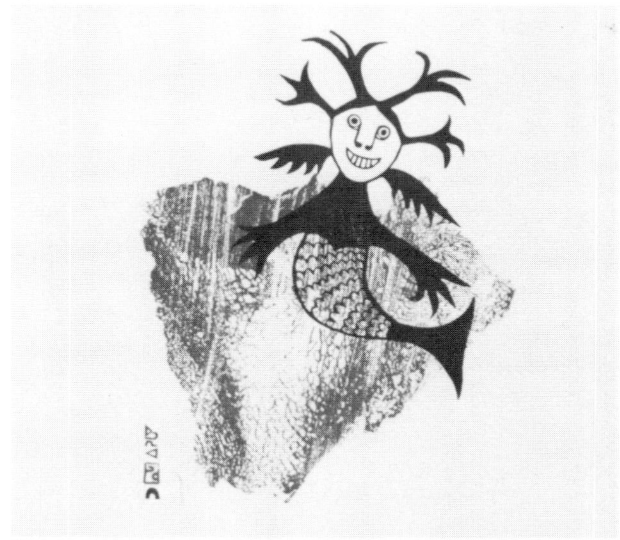

'Sea Sprite', 1961. A stonecut by Udluriak Towkee. In this print a whale-bone slab was used as a printing block for the coloured background.

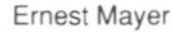
Ernest Mayer

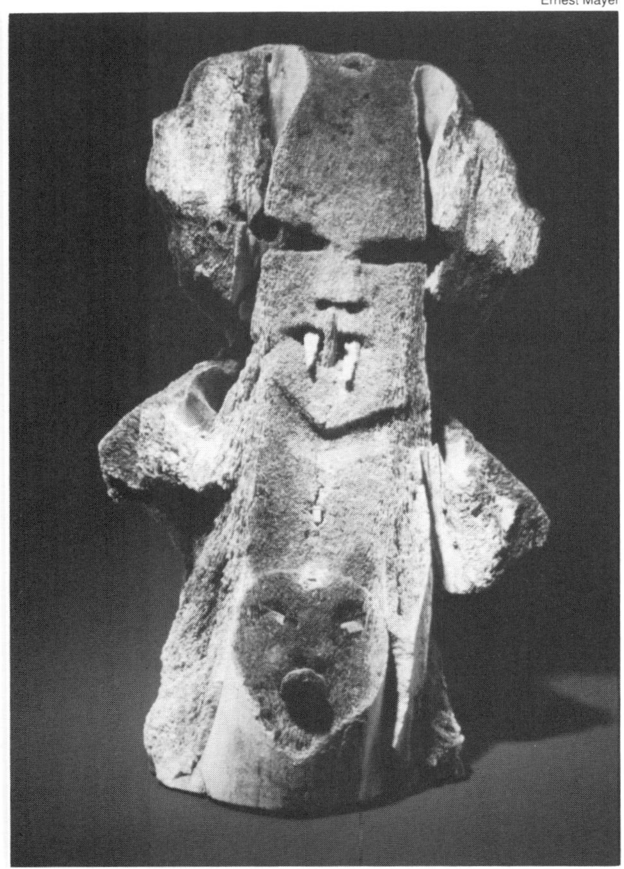

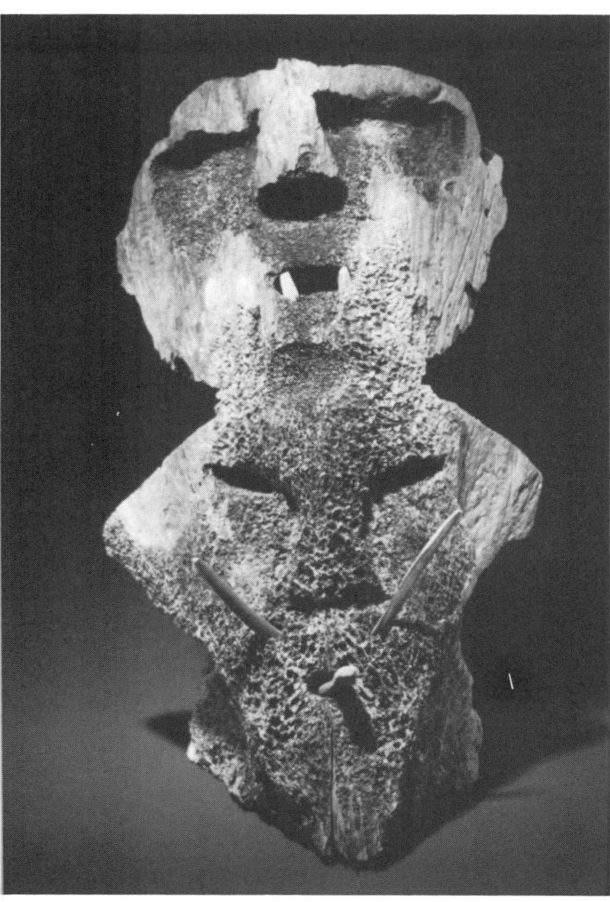

(1961/#73) and *Levilivela* (1966/#63) were printed from a flat piece of whale bone. For example, in making the former print, the printers cut the bone into a slab about two inches thick with a saw, inked the flat surface as they would a printing stone, placed the paper face down on it, and then rubbed the paper to transfer the ink onto it from the bone. Once this background area had been applied the image of the sea sprite was overprinted from a stone plate. A printed background, often of contrasting colour, was not uncommon in early Cape Dorset graphics, but it was normally applied with a paint roller.

In contemporary Inuit sculpture, the use of whale bone as a medium does not seem to have any symbolic connotations. Although a number of the carvings selected for illustration here tend to relate to shamanism, spirits or Taleelayo, many whale-bone works represent the everyday activities of animals and humans. Yet it is tempting to associate whale bone with spiritual representations, its qualities are so effective in suggesting the mysteries of the supernatural. Certainly the myth of Taleelayo, so closely associated with whales and sea animals is an appropriate subject to be relayed in bone, and Karoo Ashevak's carvings, so many of which were of shamanistic subjects, are not conceivable in any other medium. Shamans and Taleelayo, in fact, are subjects that are not unrelated in Eskimo mythology, for it was the shaman who had to intercede with the goddess in time of want, when animals were hard to find and difficult to catch.

Abraham Anghik, a young sculptor from Paulatuk now living in Vancouver, demonstrates this relationship in his impressive complex sculpture that so effectively conveys not only the essence and spirit of traditional Eskimo cosmology but basic universal concerns as well. The double-sided sculpture is formed from two bowhead skull caps hinged together. Sedna, a ripe, full female figure is opposed back to back with the sage and wizened shaman. Her side of the carving, especially her smoothly polished upper torso is of dense, white bone in contrast to the darker-coloured more porous and more textured surface on the side of the shaman. Sedna's torso is open and rounded, her arms formed by whales, her folded legs, walruses. Below and to her side are her father and her brother. United to the sea goddess but appearing on the opposite side of the sculpture is the shaman. The small heads above him represent his human charges, the animals beside and below him, his helping spirits. Both symbolically and in actual form the work signifies the duality of the universe; positive and negative space, fullness and void, male and female, land and sea, human and spiritual.

The front and back views of 'Shamans', 1970. By George Arluk of Rankin Inlet. Whale bone, antler and wood. From the J. Twomey Collection in the Winnipeg Art Gallery, with appreciation to the Province of Manitoba and the Government of Canada.

'Sedna and Angatkro with Familiars', 1981. (Page 37) By Abraham Anghik of Paulatuk. Whale bone, antler, ivory and grey stone. From the collection of John Adams in Vancouver.

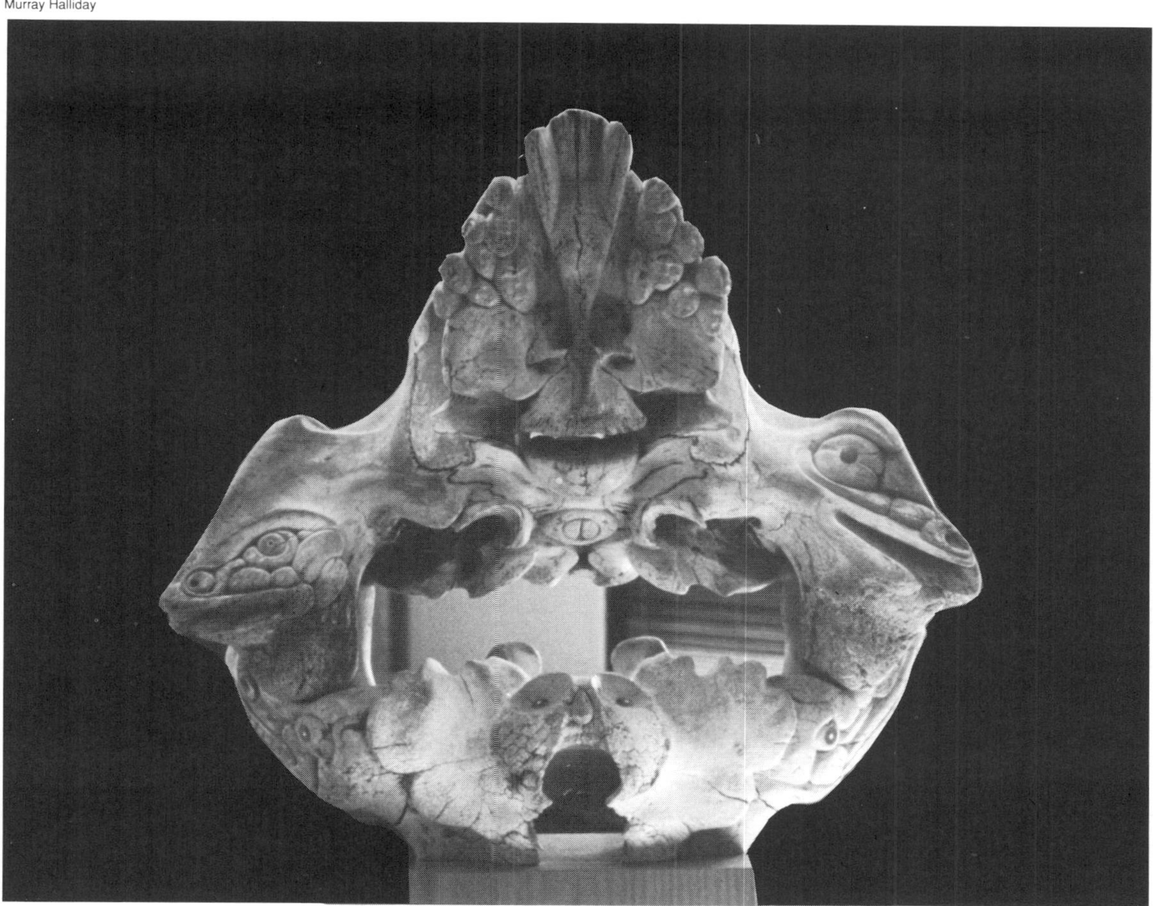

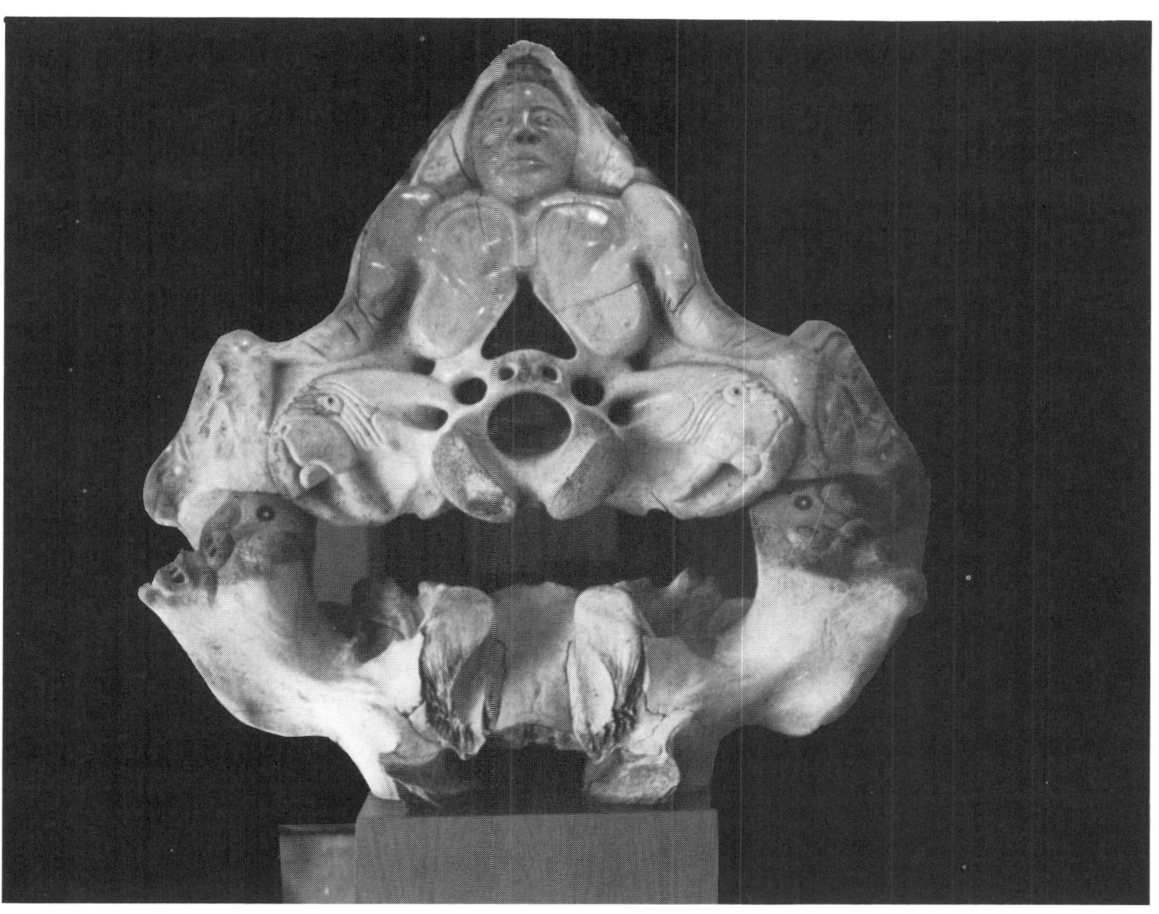

Parr

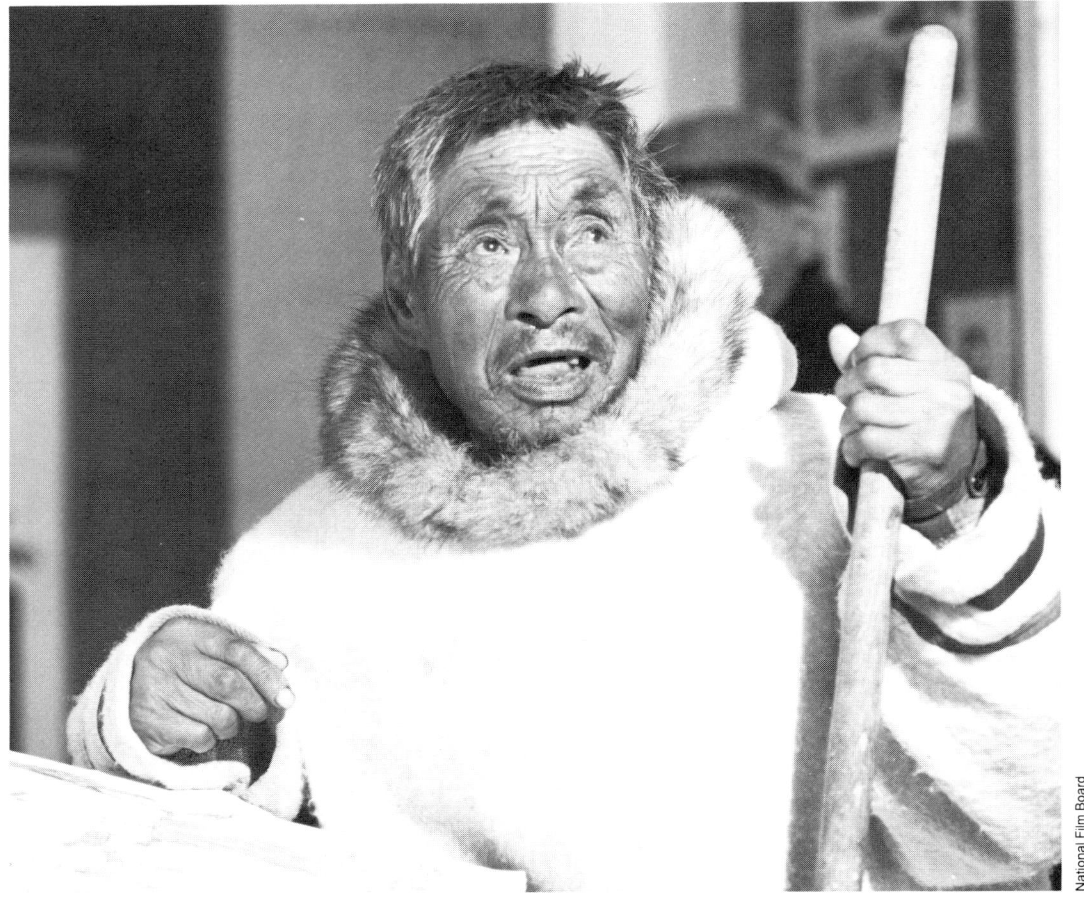

National Film Board

By Terry Ryan

ON MY ARRIVAL in Cape Dorset in 1960, Parr was already an elderly man. He had lived the greater part of his life at Tessikakjuak, an inlet on Baffin Island approximately eight miles north of Dorset Island. The area, one of considerable scenic beauty, had been for decades a popular and frequently visited fishing area. Parr and his wife Eleeshushe shared a home with Koviantilliak, their son, as was customary for those elders who were no longer able to provide the essentials required for everyday life.

Although the Cape Dorset print experiment was still in its infancy in 1960, there was a growing interest in and awareness of the graphic images emanating from the small workshop. In that location, all manner of activity took place: the purchase of stone sculpture and drawings, the cutting and printing of stone blocks, and experimenting in copper engraving.

In the spring of 1961, I approached Parr to ask him about his interest in drawing. He expressed reservations; however, I left him a large sketch pad and pencils. In the course of the following weeks, Parr filled the sketch pad with a myriad of images derived from aspects of the hunting culture which he had experienced. From that point on, Parr became a prolific and constant participant.

As his health failed, Parr settled in the village of Cape Dorset and visited the printshop almost daily with drawings. He used graphite pencils and later experimented with wax crayons, pens and pastels. Occasionally Parr would observe prints being pulled

From *The Beaver*, Autumn 1979.

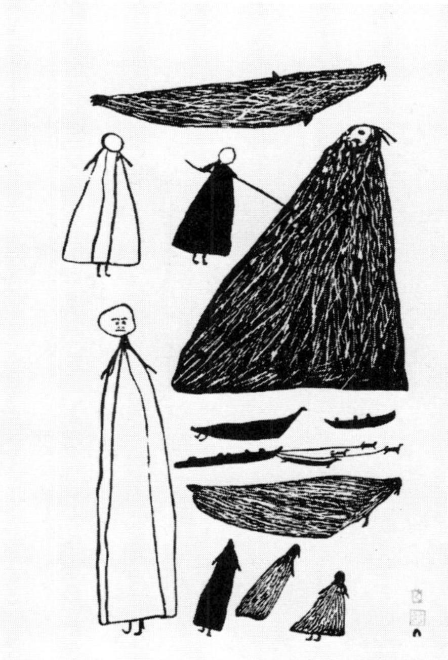

'Men and Walrus'. Stonecut, 1961.

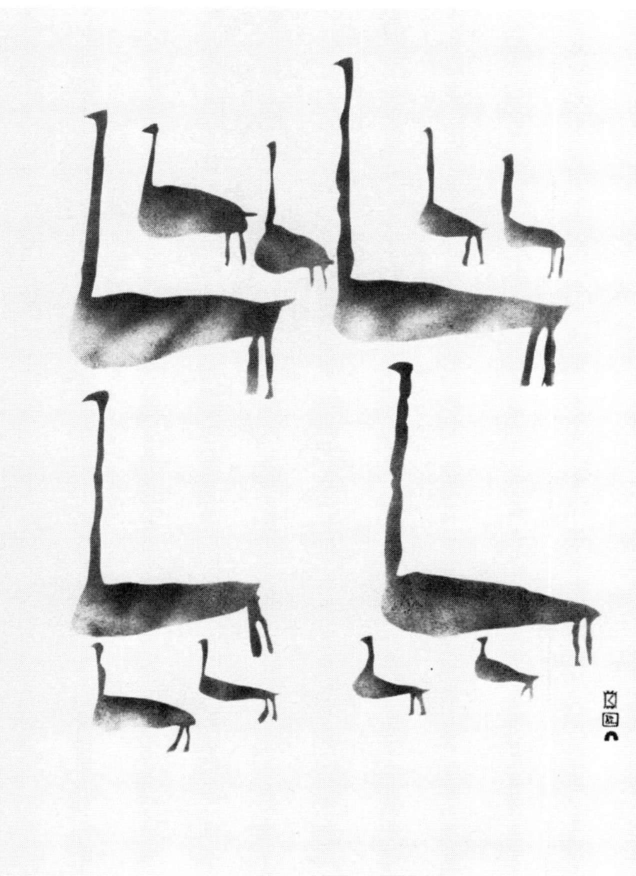

'Blue Geese Feeding'. Stencil, 1961.

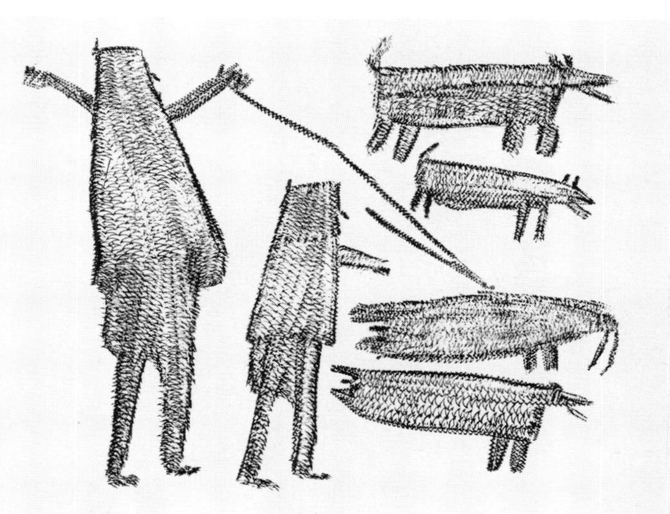

'Harpooning Walrus'. Engraving, 1963.

from the stone blocks. It obviously pleased him to sign his editions and to have people express interest in his work.

Parr found the medium of copper engraving a considerable chore; nor did he pursue the acid bath technique employed in soft ground etchings. After several plates had been proofed and editioned in this manner, Parr went back to drawing on paper.

As a younger man, Parr had suffered frostbite. As a result a portion of his foot required amputation. From that time on, he was obliged to walk with the aid of a staff. Small in stature and with white hair, he became a familiar figure, frequently wandering along the shoreline of the community of Cape Dorset.

Eventually, as Parr became incapacitated, he would send his drawings to the shops in the care of his youngest son Nuna or his wife Eleeshushe, who also was becoming a contributor to the annual graphic collection. Drawing in his small one-room house, Parr continued to record his memories of the past. He sat on the sleeping platform with legs outstretched to support his paper and diligently drew his images. In his personal style, he depicted those memories of a fading way of life—a life concerned almost exclusively with the hunt and survival.

In November 1969, Parr died in Cape Dorset. All of his drawing and print exhibitions were held after his death. He was never aware of the impact and importance of his art and his documentation of a vanishing culture. ♦

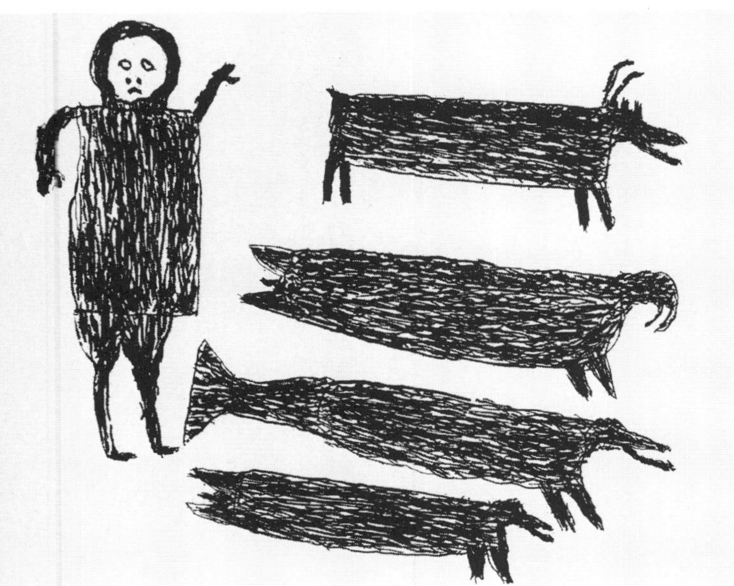

Untitled. Etching, 1962.

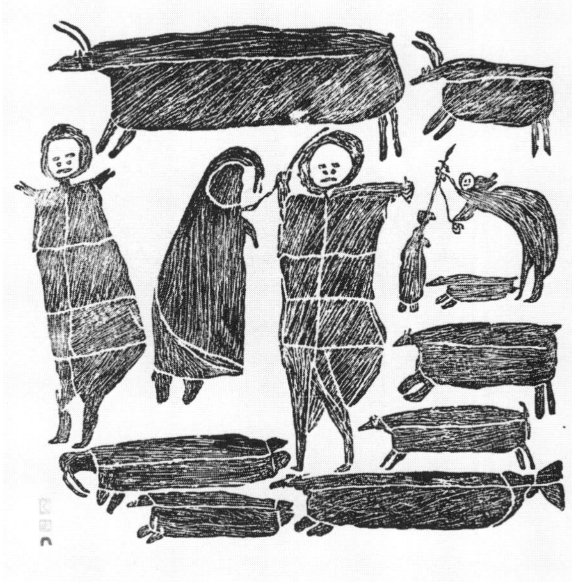

'The Hunters'. Stonecut, 1962.

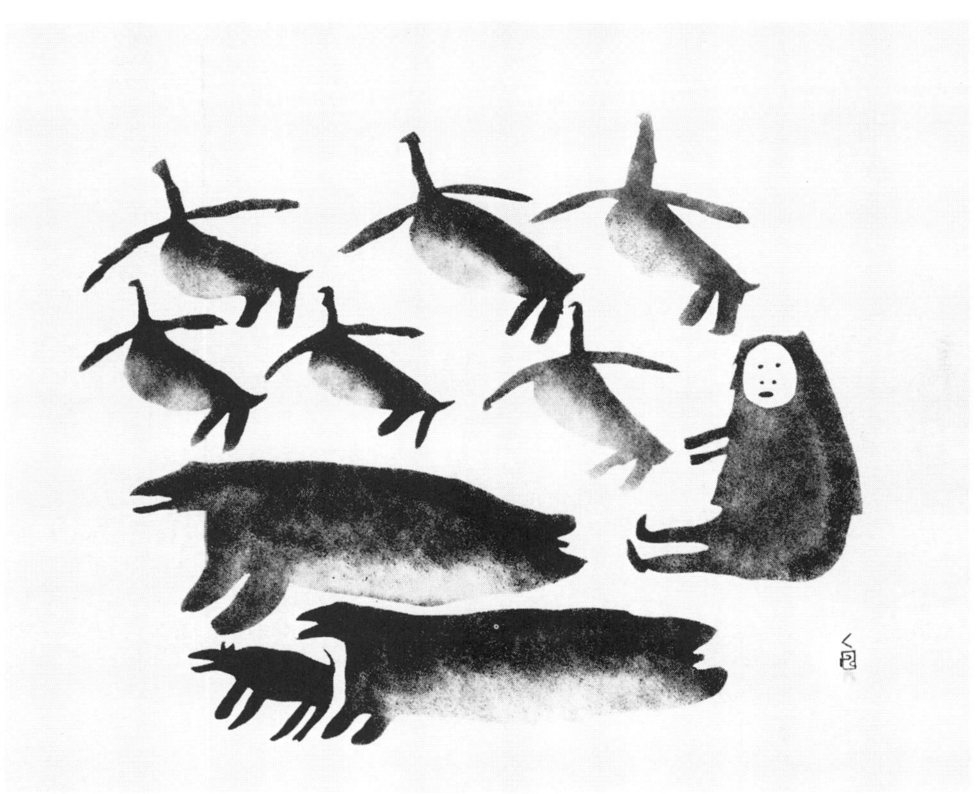

'Geese, Man and Animals'. Stencil, 1963.

'Children Chasing a Dog'. Stonecut, 1966.

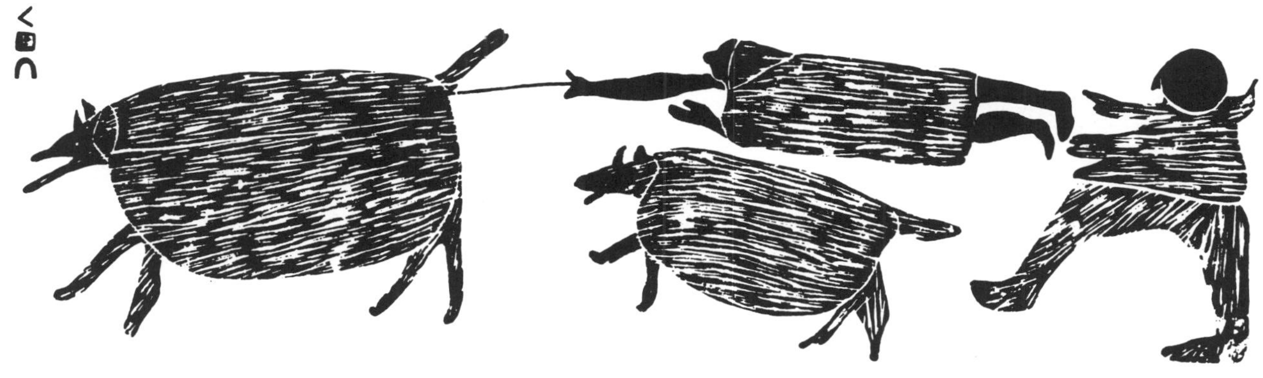

'Hunters'. Stonecut, 1970.

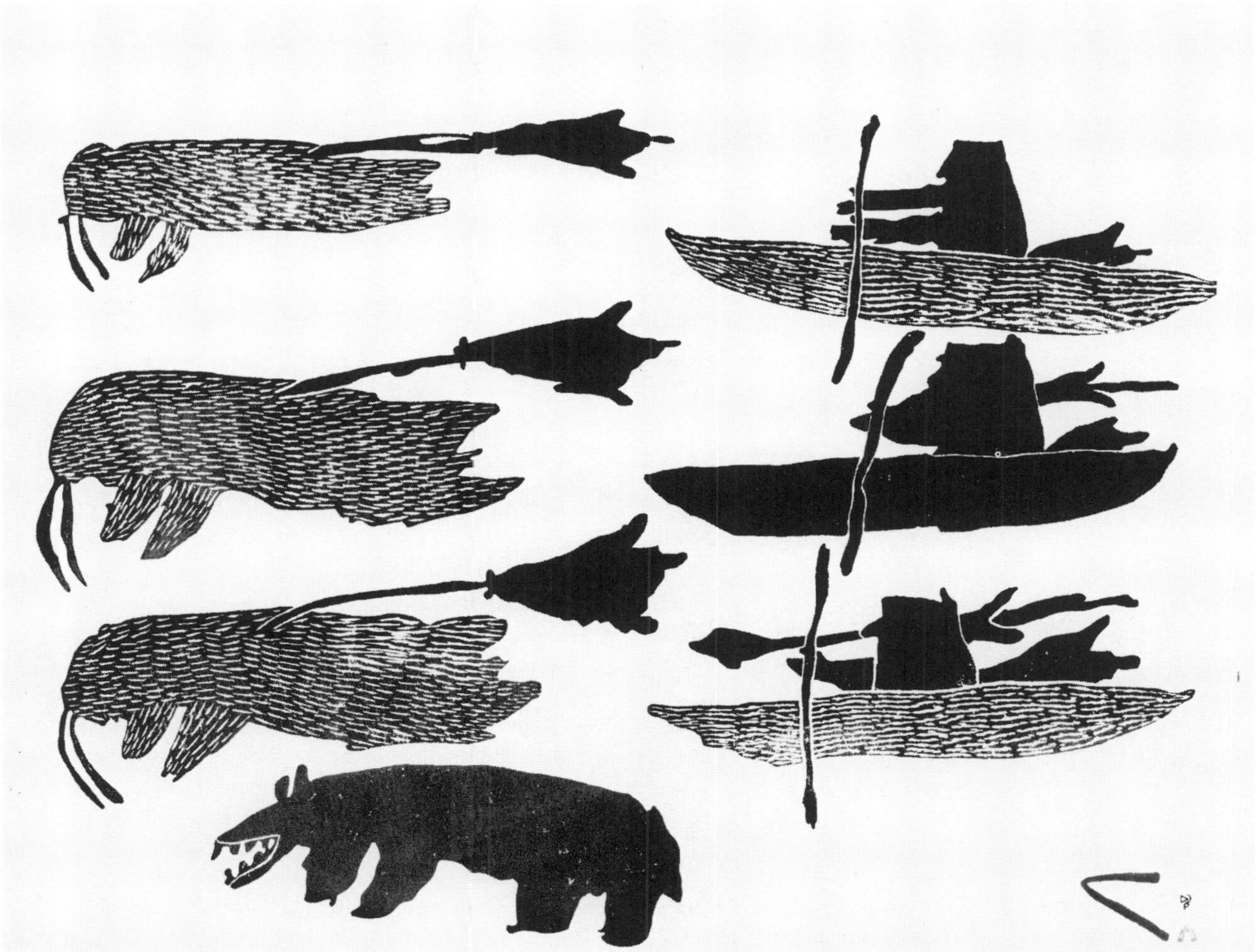

Osuitok Ipeelee

By Jean Blodgett

IN CAPE DORSET, a community of talented sculptors, the work of Osuitok Ipeelee clearly stands out. Carving steadily, thoughtfully and innovatively over the years, he has produced an extensive and exceptionally varied body of work, which cannot be easily typed or categorized by subject or format.

According to Osuitok, he was born in 1922 (not 1923 as most records indicate) at Neeouleeutalik camp, near Cape Dorset. He grew up living the traditional Inuit way of life on the land. In their search for game, his family travelled along the south coast of Baffin Island, east and west of the Cape Dorset area. At that time Inuit hunters also did some trapping to get pelts for trade, but prices were not good, and life was difficult. Osuitok recalls that 'everybody was struggling to survive'.

As a boy Osuitok acquired his skills in traditional Inuit fashion: by observation and practice. Just as he learned to hunt and survive by watching others and participating in daily activities, he learned to carve by watching his father Ohotok. Seeing his father make ivory carvings for sale to sailors on the supply ships that came north once a year made Osuitok 'curious and want to carve' for himself. At thirteen he began to make toys out of scraps of wood left over from packing crates from the ship's annual visits. 'So what I used at first was wood when I was very young, making my own toys.'

In his twenties, Osuitok began to carve in ivory, making sculptures for sale to the Roman Catholic missionaries in Cape Dorset. He clearly remembers the first carving he sold in the 1940s: a miniature fox trap, whose thin ivory elements bent to make the trap open and close. Osuitok made this carving on his own initiative, in the hope of getting something in return.

Having successfully traded the fox trap for food, he carved an ivory dogteam. He continued to make carvings for the missionaries, even duplicating a small crucifix in ivory at their request. When the Mounted Police, who periodically came over to Cape Dorset from their Lake Harbour detachment, heard about Osuitok's work, they too began asking for carvings. Of the works he sold to them he remembers a dogteam and an ivory tusk with incised scenes.

By 1951 Osuitok had established such a reputation for himself that he was described as the best carver on the south Baffin coast to James and Alma Houston. The Houstons had come to Cape Dorset to encourage the making of sculpture and crafts for sale in the South. Alma Houston writes of their first meeting with the artist:

> At last, we reached Itiliakjuk and there he was, a thin handsome man with a sudden, shy smile and beautiful, sensitive hands. His snowhouse was sparkling dry, its interior walls papered with fresh-looking pages from newspapers and magazines. We talked about our project; Osoetuk was quick in his enthusiasm. Caring greatly about his language and cultural heritage and, like his neighbours, experiencing hardship in gaining a living, he saw at once the possibilities inherent in the plan. He would help us.
>
> Winnipeg Art Gallery, *Cape Dorset* (1979) p. 14

Osuitok's association with the Houstons was to be a long and productive one. While continuing to make sculptures, which he—like other Cape Dorset carvers—now sold to the Houstons for shipment out to southern galleries, he went to work for James Houston, a job that resulted in his moving into the community of Cape Dorset in 1956 with his wife Nepeesha and their children.

It was a conversation with Osuitok that Houston credits with the beginning of printmaking in Cape Dorset. In his book *Eskimo Prints*, Houston describes how, in the winter of 1957, Osuitok's comments about the tediousness of painting the same sailor's-head trademark over and over again on cigarette packages led to a discussion of the printing technique. Houston's explanation of the process included a demonstration using ink, toilet tissue and incised designs on a walrus tusk Osuitok had just carved. This led to further experimentation and the subsequent establishment of the successful printmaking program that continues to this day in Cape Dorset and other northern centres.

Incising on ivory, such as on the tusk used by Houston to demonstrate basic image transfer, is

In October 1984, the author interviewed Osuitok at Cape Dorset. All quotations and information attributed to the artist are from these personal interviews, translated by Letia Parr and Jimmy Manning.

Jimmy Manning

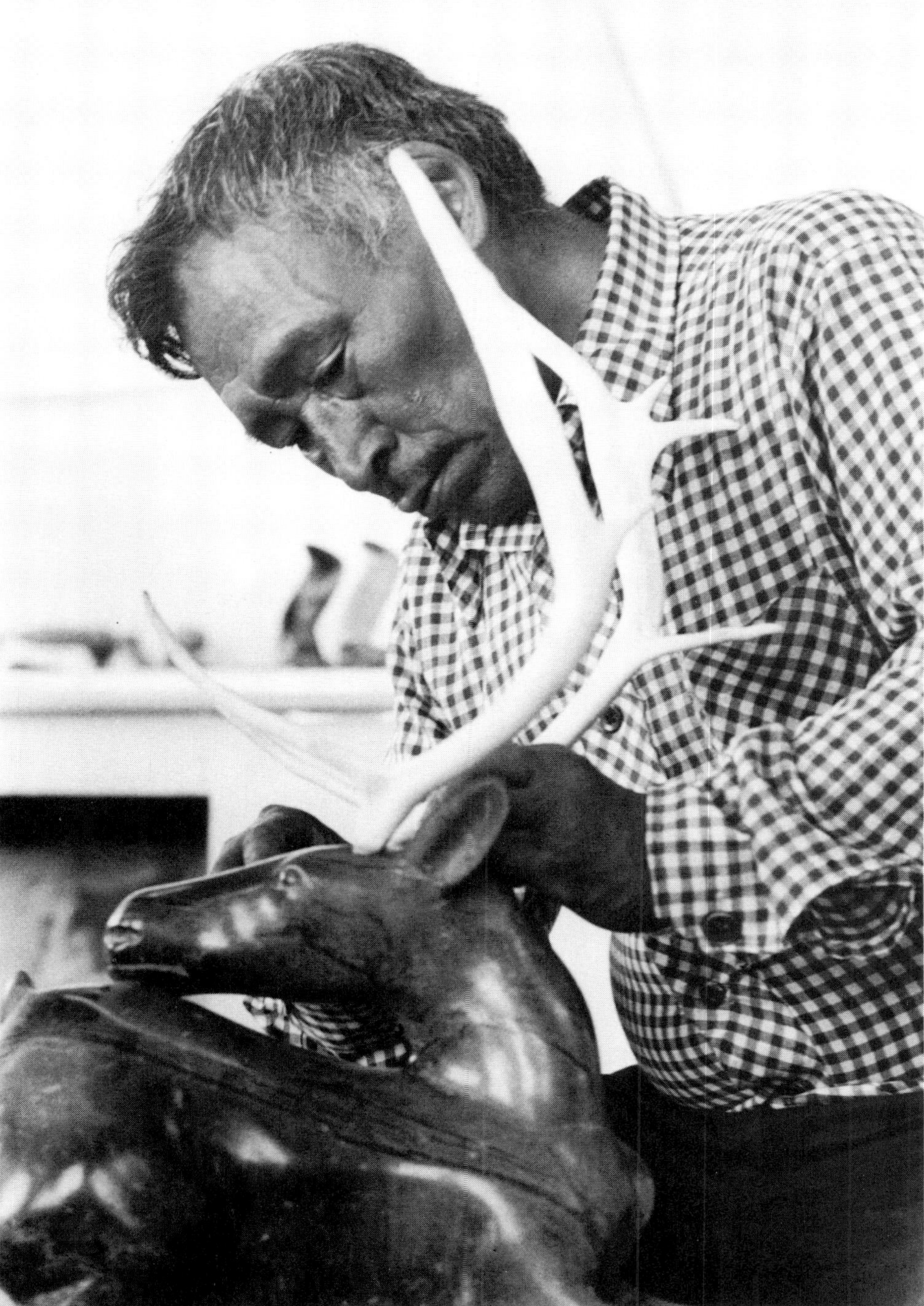

Osuitok Ipeelee with his carving of a caribou.
Cape Dorset, 1983.

essentially a two-dimensional technique more like drawing than sculpting. In fact the artist may actually draw out the design before incising into the flat surface of the smoothed material.

'If I'm going to do incising on ivory or horn,' Osuitok explains, 'I draw it in with a pencil first and then I do the incising on top of the pencil. Once I've done the drawing and I'm doing the incising, if I think that this part is too large or too small, then I adjust a bit.'

After doing the incising he uses ink or a moistened pencil to fill in the lines.

Osuitok's own experience with graphic techniques dates to the 1940s when he began drawing and incising on ivory. During this time he also did some watercolour painting. Osuitok does not remember where he got the box of watercolours and says that his few paintings were just experiments. (Peter Pitseolak's paintings, done as early as 1939 with watercolours given to him by the present Lord Tweedsmuir, may have inspired others in Cape Dorset to try this new medium.) Osuitok recalls, 'In earlier days even before Jim Houston I used to watercolour. By the time of Jim's arrival I already had

Indian and Northern Affairs, Ottawa

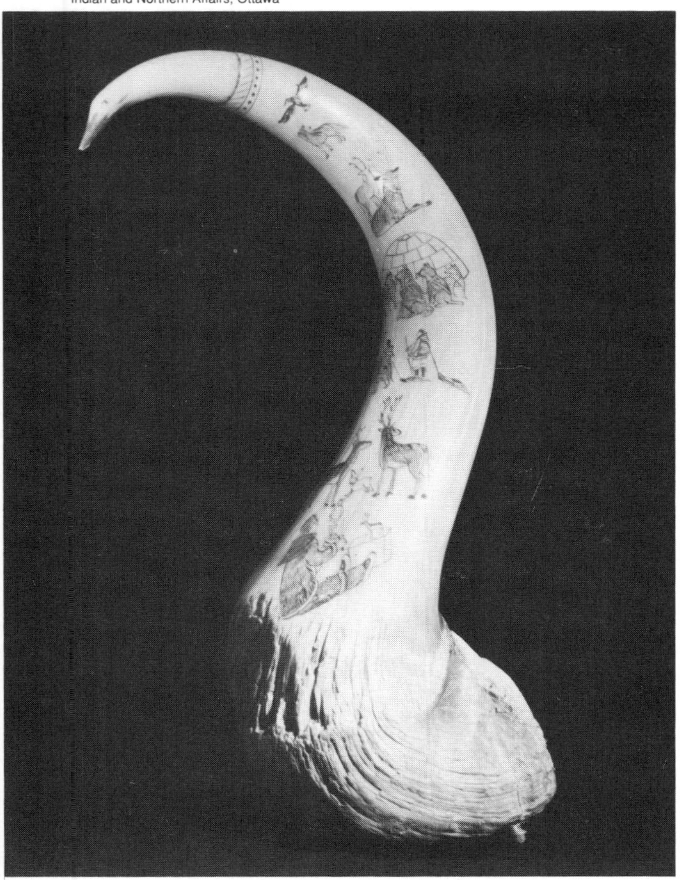

Incised musk-ox horn, 1953. Musk-ox horn and blacking, 42.0 x 18.5 x 20.0 cm. Canadian Guild of Crafts Quebec: Permanent Collection.

an idea what a drawing or painting would look like.' Houston, for his part, remembers that when he first met Osuitok he saw reproductions of drawings of animals and birds from books by Dewey Soper, the naturalist who travelled Baffin Island in the 1920s, up on display in the family dwelling. Osuitok participated in the new printmaking venture in Cape Dorset by contributing four images that were made into prints. In the first set of graphics released in 1958, two prints, *Musk-ox* and *Weasel* are attributed to Osuitok. These may have been derived from the designs on his incised tusks, or even from pencil drawings, since the new printmaking program's need for designs had resulted in an increasing number of people taking up drawing.

The two animals in these 1958 Osuitok prints are somewhat soft and cute, not the assured, decisive forms characteristic of his style. It may be that Osuitok's original images were adapted for the prints by Houston or the printshop personnel, a practice not uncommon in the early days of the program. In the first official catalogued Cape Dorset collection in 1959, there were two additional Osuitok prints: *Four Musk Oxen* and *Owl, Fox and Hare Legend.* These were printed by Iyola, who recalls the original pencil drawings; to make the *Four Musk Oxen* (see page 59), the original single animal motif was simply repeated four times to make the print image.

Since 1959 there have been no further Osuitok prints. Unlike many of his fellow Cape Dorset artists, Osuitok did not continue to contribute drawings to the burgeoning printmaking project. He stopped at that time, he says, because he was not paid enough for his drawings. But he had other reasons too.

> Maybe why I don't draw is because if I start to draw I think I would want to do it non-stop. But right now I would rather do carving. You know, when I carve for three full days—what it usually takes me to do a carving—after working three or four days my eyes are very tired and I sometimes wonder if I started drawing they would get worse. Working on soapstone right now, I don't have any problem other than my eyes. My arms are pretty strong yet. I don't know how long I'll be able to carve, because I don't know my future. But I think when I reach a point where I start to get tired from working on soapstone, maybe I would turn back and start drawing, because in drawing your arms don't really work hard.

In the 1950s neither his strength nor his eyesight were a concern for the young Osuitok. With the Houstons' encouragement and a steady market for his sculpture, his work flourished. He began to carve primarily in soapstone, although he continued to use ivory as well as trying other media. James Houston supplied him with several musk-ox horns—a medium he had not used for carvings before—and in working one of these horns, Osuitok incised the scene of a seated Inuk sculptor with his knife, work table and carvings of a caribou and a human figure. Osuitok says that the scene does not represent himself but is intended to show the way Inuit people carve. Nevertheless, it does convey a sense of personal interest, and certainly carving was to become an increasingly significant part of Osuitok's life.

In January 1952, four carvings by Osuitok, or Oshaweetuk B as he was then called, were shown in the 'Eskimo Art' exhibition held at the National Gallery of Canada in Ottawa. This was the first documented showing of Osuitok's work in the South. In 1955 another exhibition at the National Gallery, 'Eskimo Sculpture', included six Osuitok works. The majority of items in that show were collected in 1954 for the federal government. Although none of the Osuitok sculptures were illustrated in the catalogue, the entry for one work in the exhibition list seems to correspond to the sculpture of *Woman's Head* in the collection of the Canadian Museum of Civilization.

Also in 1955 Osuitok was involved in a major carving project in Cape Dorset: the making of an official mace for the Council of the Northwest Territories. Working from a basic outline sketch sent to them from Ottawa, a team of craftsmen under the direction of Peter Pitseolak and Osuitok, with advice from James Houston, made an elaborate ceremonial mace using primarily indigenous materials and themes. According to Osuitok, who was in charge of the carving of the ivory and bone elements, Houston asked that hunters and animals be carved on the whale bone section just under the musk-ox horns, but the other areas were left to Osuitok's discretion. In addition to the bas-relief animals, hunter, and mother and child carved on the main band, there are rings of whales, fox pelts and seals. The fine carving and careful arrangement of these motifs show Osuitok's hand.

In 1959 Osuitok was asked to work on another commission: a carving of Queen Elizabeth to be presented to her on the occasion of her visit to Canada. In carving this sculpture, Osuitok followed the advice and suggestions of James Houston, who requested the work. The generalized facial features reflect the fact that Osuitok did not have a photograph to work from. Nevertheless, the sculpture is a striking one, done with considerable care and technical expertise. Attached to the main stone body are whale bone hands (one subsequently damaged), feet and head, the latter surmounted by a delicate copper crown with fluted edges which caused Osuitok no end of trouble.

Unlike other commissions that Osuitok has received, or his own work, the sculpture of Queen Elizabeth represents a subject foreign to the artist. (While the concept of the mace was an alien one, the motifs carved on it were not.) In his work Osuitok depicts subjects that are known to him through personal experience. The animals and humans of his earlier carvings, especially caribou, musk-oxen, birds and women, are subjects that he returns to over and over again throughout his career. In fact, certain subjects may be the focus of his work for a particular length of time.

> It's always different in different years. Last year I did mostly birds, very few human figures. It's because the human figure to me is the most hard work. I haven't given up on human figures. Maybe next year, if I'm still alive, I will do more human figures than birds. So my system works: in different years mostly birds or mostly humans, and so on.

Since he is an Inuk hunter, the animals of his environment are particularly meaningful to him and an obvious source of inspiration for his sculpture. Working and reworking these subjects, Osuitok shows solid, bulky, shaggy musk-oxen; elegant, gentle caribou positioned at rest or rearing up on hind legs; lordly polar bears; massive walruses; and a tremendous variety of birds—birds with their wings spread, birds with their prey, birds balanced on one leg, birds laying eggs, birds with their chicks. Sometimes he chooses to represent only the head of the animal, concentrating the essence of the creature in a portrait-like bust. Sometimes, but not very often, the animal subject is shown together with a human figure. There are, for example, several versions of a hunter wrestling with his walrus prey, the man dwarfed by his huge opponent.

Representations of men, such as these hunters or

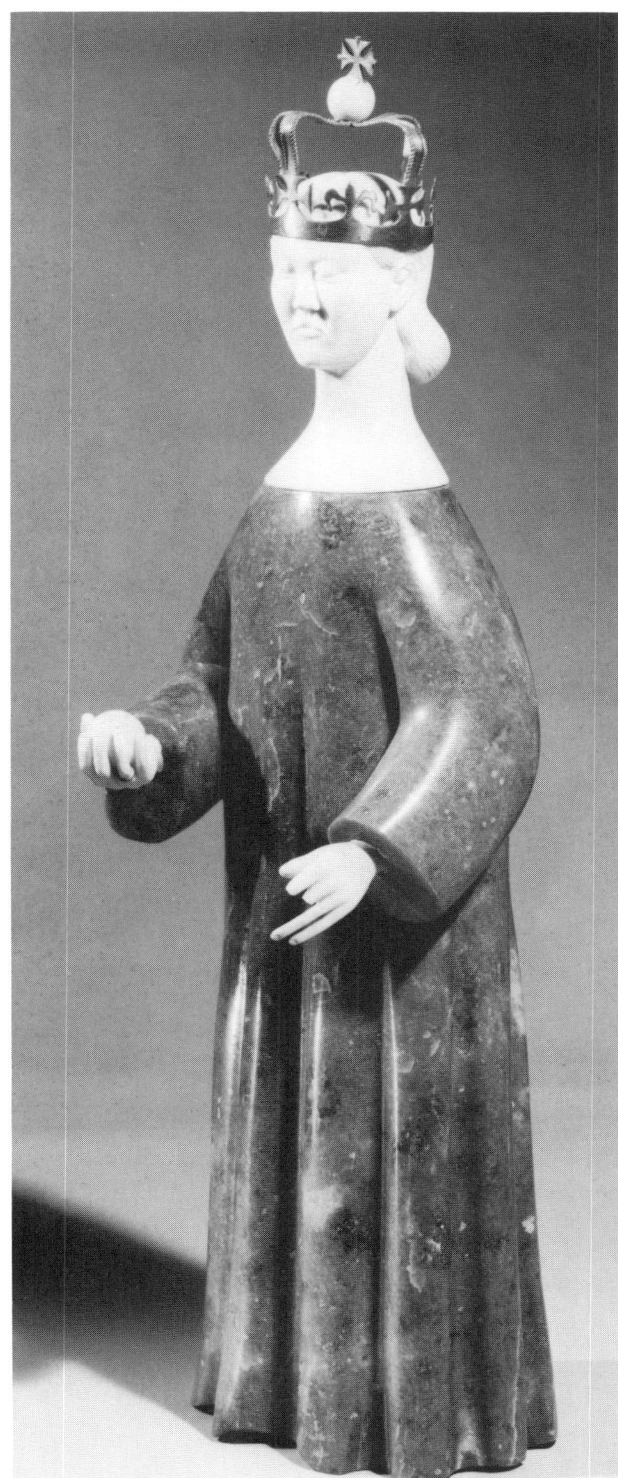

'Queen Elizabeth II', 1959. Green stone, whalebone and copper, Measurements unknown. Copyright Reserved to Her Majesty Queen Elizabeth II.

Indian and Northern Affairs, Ottawa

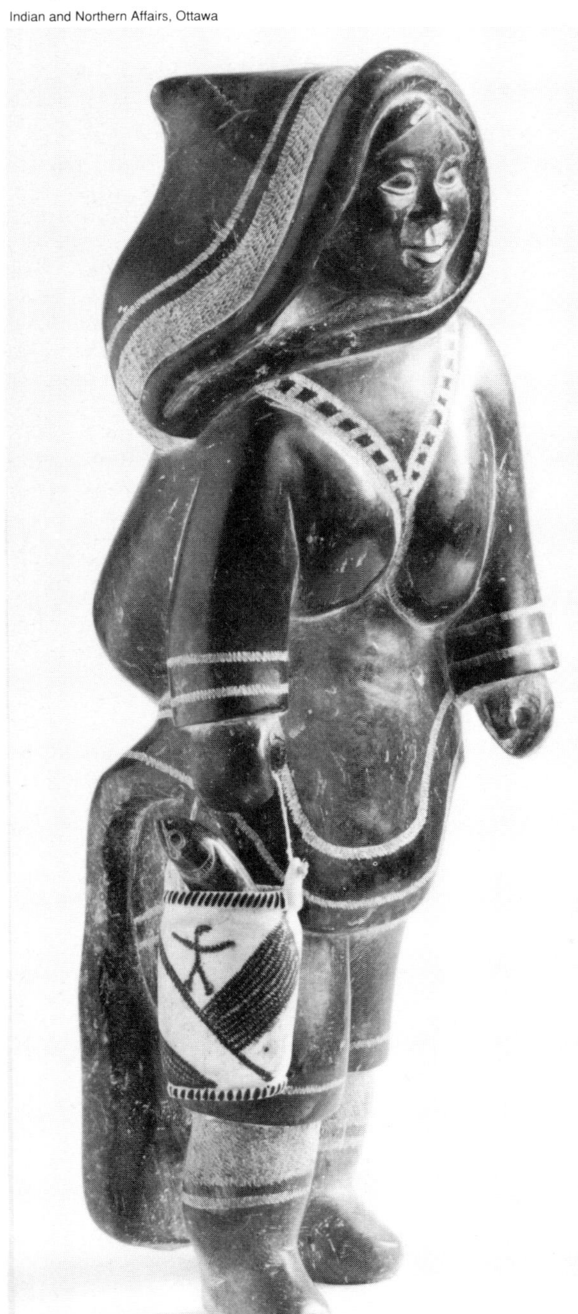

'Fisherwoman', 1963. Green stone, bone, blacking and string, 46.9 x 16.0 x 14.7 cm. Toronto Dominion Bank Collection, Toronto

the rare drum dancer, are far outnumbered by those of women. His representations of the female range from portrait busts with delicate facial features, long eyelashes, pert noses and elaborate braids, to the buxom figures of his fisherwomen. He pays tribute to the Inuit woman's ability to fish, sew and care for children, and he frankly admires their physical form. While he does not recall ever carving a nude, he has done a number of sculptures of women showing bared breasts. He not only just likes breasts; for him breast feeding is like a miracle. 'The babies are healthier. It's just amazing how children grow after they've been breast fed.'

Osuitok's appealing, realistic female forms have been known to prompt other Cape Dorset men to admire their beauty to the point of joking about marrying them. Jimmy Manning, of the West Baffin Eskimo Co-operative in Cape Dorset, tells how one of Osuitok's carvings of a woman done in white stone, on display at the Co-operative, became dirty around the nose from being touched by so many people.

In his carvings Osuitok claims he is just representing Inuit people, not specific individuals, even though the completed image may seem to resemble a particular person. While many of Osuitok's sculptures show the people and animals he knows from his day-to-day life, there are also some works in his *oeuvre* inspired by traditional Inuit beliefs. The sea goddess Taleelayo, the mythological creature with mermaid-like body who was believed to control the animals that people hunted, is a popular subject for Inuit carvers. Osuitok has done a number of representations of the sea goddess, taking special delight in carving her long flowing hair.

The traditional Inuit belief in transformation—the ability of animals to change into humans, and humans to change into animals—has also inspired Osuitok in his work. In discussing one carving of a seal-woman, he told how in his youth while out hunting with his father he saw three seals turn into humans. 'I know it's not just a fairy-tale story that animals can turn half-people. I've actually seen it happen.'

People, too, could change form. Shamans especially were known to have this ability, and Osuitok heard about his own father being seen as an animal. Osuitok has identified several of his carvings as representations of shamans. In one sculpture, a female shaman with a seal head and human body is dressed in the traditional Inuit woman's parka, or *amautik*, in the back pouch of which she carries a small seal. Discussing this transformed shaman and child he explains:

> Shamans when they were just about to die would give, or pass on, their power to a daughter or son or whomever and that person would become very sick, almost die, when the power was going into their heart. I have watched someone trying to give power to a daughter and I thought

Erik Dzenis

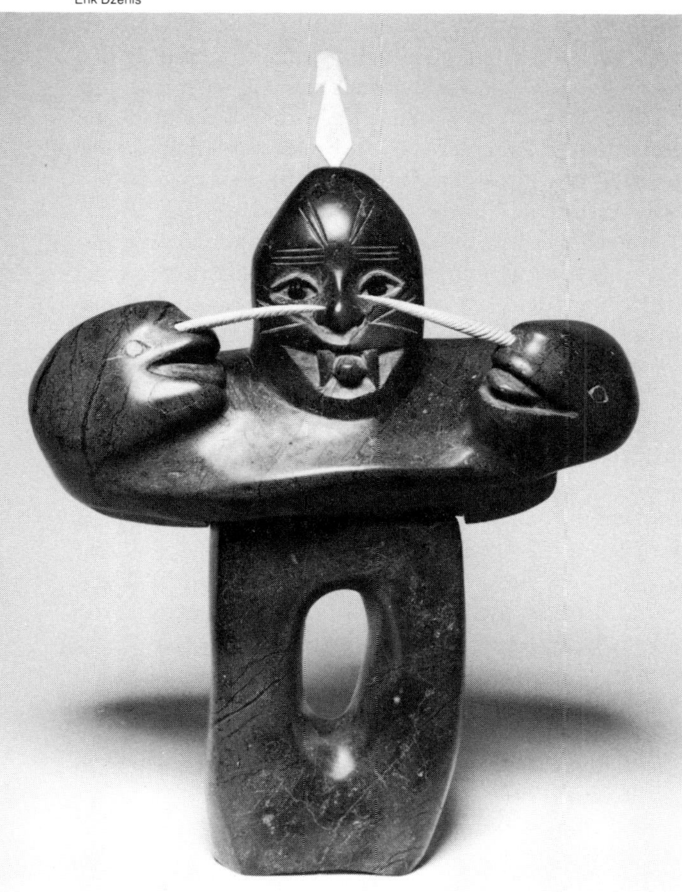

'Shaman', mid 1970s. Green/black stone, ivory, bone and blacking, 19.0 x 33.0 x 12.7 cm. Collection: M. F. Feheley

In 1983 and 1984 Osuitok made two versions of a harpoon-shaped carving. In discussing this *Harpoon-Head Figure*, his explanation reveals the multiple layers of significance and reference in the work.

The reason I made that figure was a man was called a man because he was always successful, a good hunter, if he had harpoons (before we had guns). The harpoon tip was the major equipment that men used to hunt, and with that harpoon head he was always successful if he was lucky. Using a harpoon you're always a good hunter, you always get a seal or whale or walrus because when you harpoon it, the harpoon head stays in. It doesn't let go—it's opposite from a bullet.

When you hit a seal or whale or walrus, with a bullet, even if you're a good hunter sometimes the animal sinks and you lose it. But if you were using a harpoon you get it. So I made the harpoon-shaped figure carving.

While I was making that I was thinking to put maybe a peg that represents the shaft of the harpoon but I thought if I put that it was always going to fall down.

You know sometimes you look at a harpoon head and it sometimes looks like a woman with the amautik because it has a little thing at the back. Then I thought to myself maybe if I put legs that piece is going to be safer. When you look at a harpoon head it is shaped like that, there are holes on the side; it looks like there are supposed to be arms sticking out there. But as you can see there are no arms but just the shape; the thing here is the shape of the hood of a woman and then this part here for the flap of the parka.

'Harpoon-Head Figure', 1983. Green stone, Height: 40.6 cm. Private Collection.

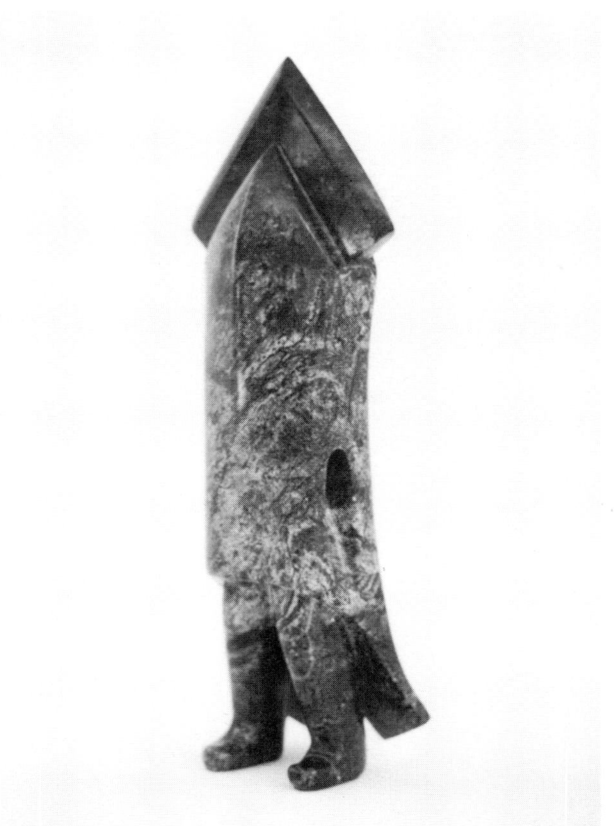

Leslie Boyd

the daughter was going to die when the power was going into her.

Osuitok made one sculpture entitled *Shaman*, because, he says, he wanted to try carving a shaman. His depiction of the figure utilizes several shamanistic characteristics. The shaman's upper torso changes into matching narwhals, his hands becoming their heads. In his mouth, on either side of his protruding tongue, are tusk-like teeth, often part of the shaman's transformation process (the performing shaman might insert ivory tusks—made-up teeth Osuitok calls them—into his mouth). The harpoon head in the figure's forehead, visually corresponding to the tusks of the two narwhals, relates to the shaman's ritual use of a harpoon to stab himself and thus demonstrate his supernatural powers. Osuitok also explains that the symmetrical markings on the shaman's face are not tattoos, since men did not tattoo themselves: 'I just put them in so that the carving looks better.' While his explanation makes the marks purely decorative, he may have unconsciously been recalling facial markings on certain shamans. Peter Pitseolak in *People from our Side* tells of a shaman who had 'three marks on his cheek for killing ghosts'.

Also the harpoon head was used as a weapon for shamans. A shaman used to stab himself with the harpoon.

For a long time I had in mind to carve this. As I said before, I keep filing things away. And a right time came and I carved it.

In contrast to such works rich in traditional content, Osuitok may also concern himself solely with form, to the exclusion of any representative subject at all. He has made two versions of a twisting, rising shape, which is non-representational but reminiscent of a growing form. 'I think it would be very beautiful to see, even though it's not an animal, just a structure.' Osuitok explains another carving, which to the observer may look somewhat like a bending whale tail.

This carving isn't really anything. I just carved it the way it is. I can't tell you very much because it's just a figure. I made this carving to make it complicated. It looks very simple and yet it's complicated because you really can't tell what it is. It's not a whale flipper; it's just a carving.

While Osuitok generally concentrates on one or possibly two main motifs in a sculpture, he also carves in more complex formats. Over the years he has expanded and developed the technique of incising multiple scenes on ivory. While continuing to make incised ivory tusks, he has also worked pieces of antler—some as much as a metre in length—by incising and carving bas-relief motifs. Osuitok describes working on a tusk or horn: 'If I am going to do incising I start from the bottom and work up towards the tip because there's more space at the base to begin.'

In 1977 Osuitok was given a narwhal tusk to carve for his forthcoming solo exhibition at the Waddington Galleries in Toronto. Narwhals are not plentiful in the Cape Dorset area, and this commission gave Osuitok the opportunity to work on an entire tusk on his own. On one side he carved, in relief, various arctic animals, their individual stance and character clearly portrayed even on this diminutive scale.

On the other side of the tusk, Osuitok has incised rather than carved out even more complex animal and human motifs, including a fish weir, a rock-pile fox trap, and a hunter in his kayak. Within this long, narrow, restrictive format, Osuitok has created a rich and animated scene. Showing different subjects, different poses and different activities, he has used various types of incised lines and amounts of inking to indicate texture, space, ground area and motion; showing, for example, the ripples in the water caused by the dipping kayak paddles.

One of the motifs on the tusk is a man seated on

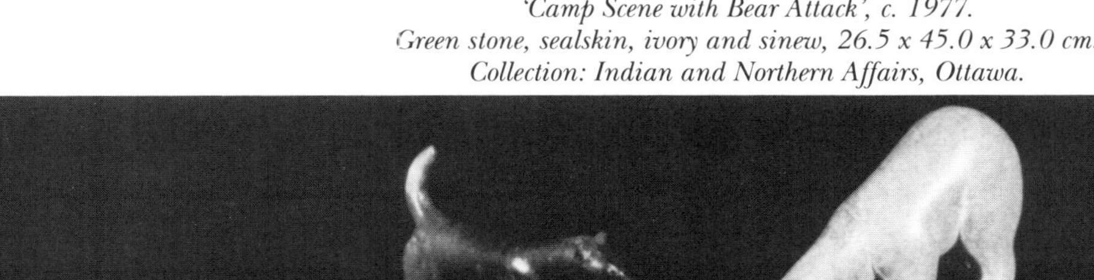

'Camp Scene with Bear Attack', c. 1977.
Green stone, sealskin, ivory and sinew, 26.5 x 45.0 x 33.0 cm.
Collection: Indian and Northern Affairs, Ottawa.

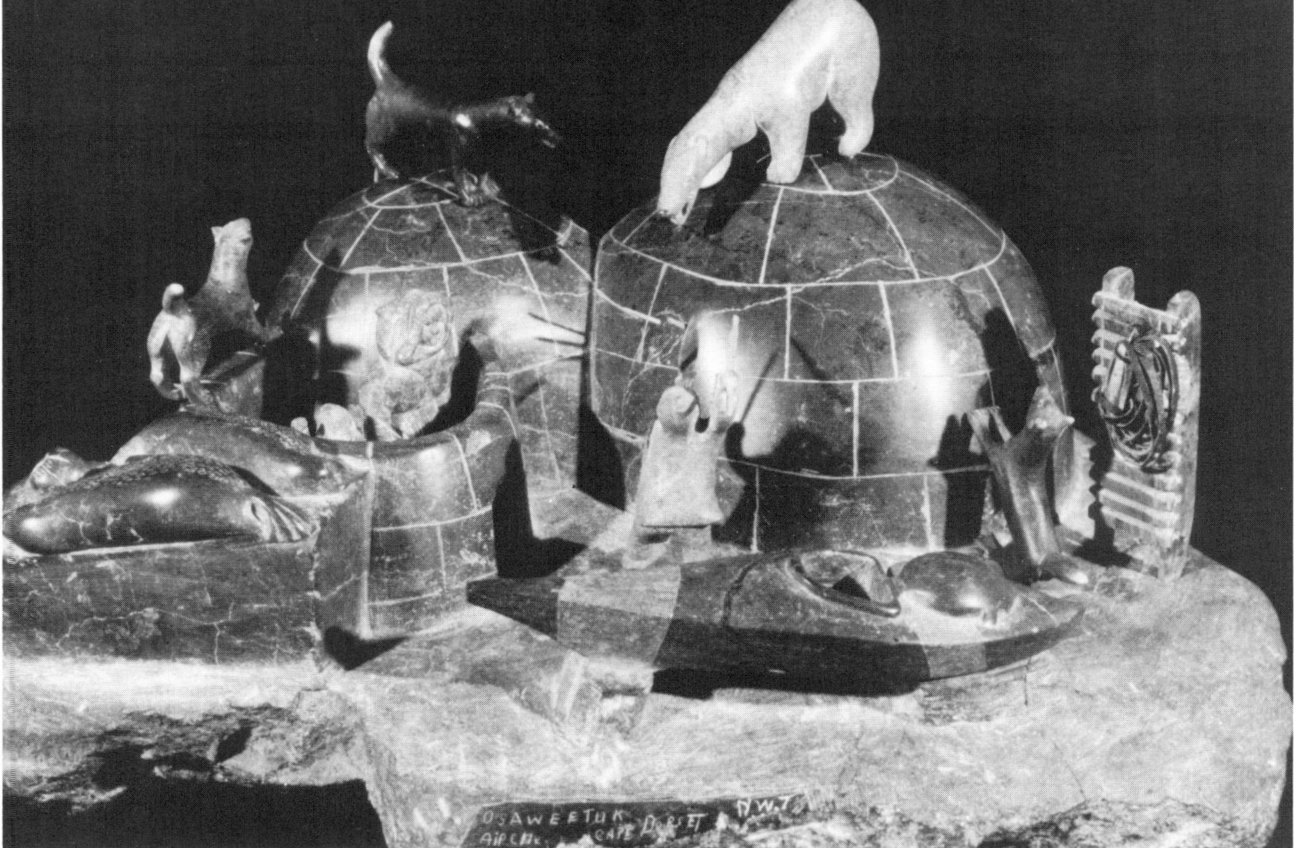

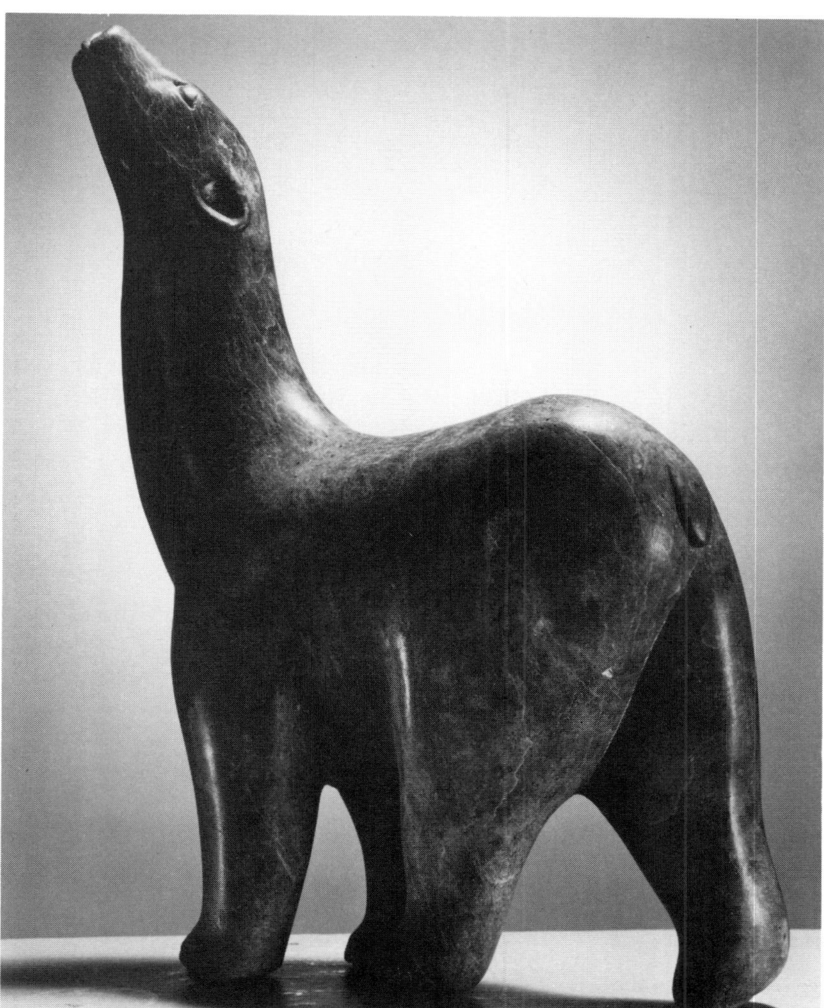

Larry Ostrom

'Bear Spirit', c. 1969. Green stone, 40.5 x 31.4 x 10.5 cm. Art Gallery of Ontario, Toronto. Gift of the Klamer Family, 1978.

an inflated sealskin paddling his way over the water: probably a representation of Taktillitak, a local hero who escaped from a small island on a sealskin float. This representation of Taktillitak seems to be the only subject that comes close to fulfilling the original commission, which was, according to Osuitok, to illustrate legends or stories. Instead Osuitok has concentrated on showing traditional everyday activities, documenting the old way of life so that, 'when I'm not around our grandchildren will know what we were up to.' The first sentence of the accompanying syllabic text incised on the tusk explains the sculptor's subject and intent. 'This is how we used to be before the white man came to our land.' The text goes on to tell how husbands and even women used to hunt in winter and summer.

Osuitok usually supports his incised antler ivory pieces with a stone base which, in turn, is carved with various motifs. This base, as carefully done as the rest of the work, reflects Osuitok's belief that a carved base looks and supports better than a flat unembellished one.

Osuitok may also incise or carve multiple scenes entirely in stone. Some of these are scenes of a degree of complexity that only an accomplished carver like Osuitok would dare to attempt or be able to execute successfully. He may combine individual human and animal motifs in elaborate interlocking forms, the heads and bodies arranged vertically one above the other in totem fashion, or extending off at various angles. There are also complex camp scenes, complete with dwellings, equipment, animals and people, that show remarkable workmanship in the carving and detailing.

In a large stone sculpture now in the Canadian Museum of Civilization, Osuitok has carved and incised animal and human motifs, including an *umiak* (sealskin passenger boat) under sail, as well as a female face, breasts and a skull. The quantity and quality of detail in this work is particularly impressive considering the hardness of the white stone. Sculptures carved in this local stone by Osuitok and other Cape Dorset artists are usually more basic forms, with minimal detailing and surface definition.

In discussing the various stones available to him, Osuitok has described this white stone as the hardest kind to carve. 'It takes patience, a lot of work and a lot of courage.' Another undesirable stone is a dark green-black type with bits of hard rock in it. 'It's one of the worst kinds a carver would want to carve, like the white one. Those two are the kinds a carver is not really happy to work on.' The early stone, he says, was not very good. Its hardness restricted certain features; for example, he thinks he probably did not carve ears on the *Woman's Head* in the collection of the Canadian Museum of Civilization, because the stone was too hard. Osuitok prefers the light green stone that, 'when you get it really smooth, it looks glassy. From my experience, it's the best kind of stone you can carve.'

While Osuitok has worked primarily in stone since the 1950s, he continues to use a number of other media for the body of the work and for additional detailing. These include wood, ivory, copper, musk-ox horn, narwhal tusk, whale bone and antler. Supplementary materials are sensitively and appropriately used: actual antler for the antlers on a caribou, or ivory for the tusks of a walrus. Contrasting colouration is achieved with such materials as pencil, ink, and white glue. Even more inventively, Osuitok will burn the tips of the carved antler and bone horns on his musk-oxen to give the horns the distinctive darker colouring at the tip 'to make it more real'.

Osuitok's early carvings, done primarily in ivory, were made at a time when, he says, there weren't many tools and those they did have weren't very good. But even with better tools, he prefers working in stone.

> Ivory tends to crack and that's why I don't carve it more. It's not as much fun as carving soapstone because it is so hard and it breaks easily. Working on ivory is tiring and the ivory will crack when it dries and if that happens it would be embarrassing.

As for musk-ox horn, this material, he says, 'is softer than ivory tusk and therefore harder, or more difficult, to work on. When you are doing the edging you can easily slip.'

To work these different materials Osuitok uses chisels, files and various other commercially available tools, many of which he modifies by softening them with a blowtorch and shaping them to suit his needs. Handles are added; files are sharpened to points; separate pieces are lashed together to make implements with various functions.

For Osuitok the quality and availability of stone are paramount concerns. If he has money for gas for his boat, he may go the long distance to get the stone himself, or he may buy it from the co-operative or from other carvers. Once he has the stone, Osuitok must match up his ideas for carvings with the materials at hand. He explains the process.

> How I work is that I have to think first, and then I have to look at the stone next to see if it's going to suit my imagination.
>
> It takes time to think about what I'm going to carve. If I take a piece of stone and haven't thought about what I'm going to make, then it takes me longer to decided what to make. What I do is I look through the stones, the rocks, and then sometimes they are ready to be chopped into shape. Some are easier than others; it depends on how the stone was taken out of the ground. I look at the stone and then I think about what to make of it. Usually three days before I start shaping it.
>
> When I do carvings, most of the time I try and have the stone more like talking to me, to tell me if it will work this way.

Osuitok then thinks of what he is going to carve ahead of time and assesses his supply of stone to see if his idea can be realized. Sometimes it cannot, so he files the thought away for future use.

> Working as a carver, the way I see it is, it's hard work, because for me I have to think ahead of time what I will be doing out of that soapstone. Sometimes it doesn't always work. When I see the soapstone right away I know that it's not going to work, the size or whatever. In many cases I would file my thought that wouldn't work for that stone. I just file it away in my mind and then when I get the proper soapstone, one that is a good size and is going to work, then I continue.

Sometimes he may wait for some time before circumstances are appropriate for him to carve the sculpture he has in mind. One work that he says he hopes to do before he dies was inspired by a dream about a polar bear with shining eyes. 'But I would need a very nice soapstone and it would take a long time to do.' Osuitok's plans to carve some pinkish-white stone that he has into a non-representational twisting sculpture have been held up because he does not have the dark green stone he wants for the base.

When asked where he get ideas for his work, Osuitok replied:

> I can't really tell how I get my ideas but when I think they just come to my mind. Getting other people's ideas is not right if you are going to be a carver. I can only tell that I work hard getting my ideas, I don't know where from. But as I said, I keep filing my ideas and I still have them. I can't really tell you more about how I get my ideas.

But, as Osuitok explains, having ideas and finding the appropriate stone, is only the beginning. And Osuitok's realization of his subject does not involve models or sketches, but his imagination and memory. 'No, I don't go to look for a caribou so I can make a copy of it. I just use my imagination.' To complete a work successfully, a carver must fully realize his ideas.

> When you're a carver, if you get your idea of what you're going to make, you have to follow each step by looking at your imagination. If you do that, it's going to be a perfect carving. And it's going to be a finished carving. For instance, if a particular piece had, let's say, eight different steps, and I only did six steps and then started to hurry, I don't think that would really be a good carving. But if I had ten steps, ten thoughts, and if I did them all, it's going

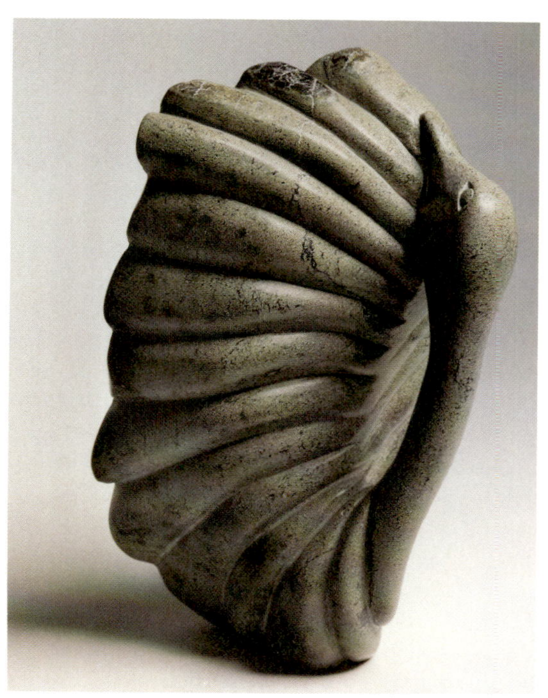

Erik Dzenis

'Preening Bird', late 1970s. Green/black stone, Height: 23 cm. Private Collection.

'Caribou Head', c. 1970. Green stone and antler, 54.7 x 31.5 x 45.6 cm. Art Gallery of Ontario, Toronto. Gift of the Klamer Family, 1978.

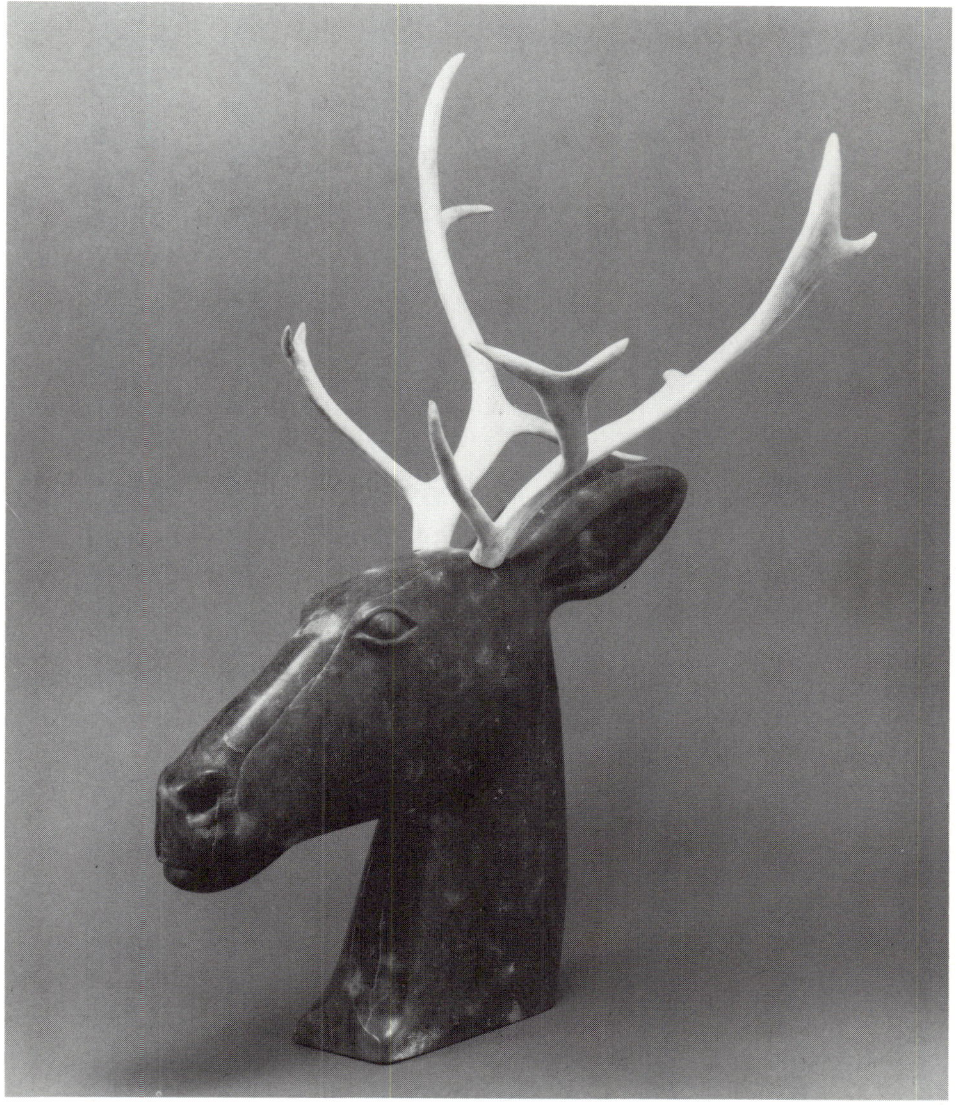

Art Gallery of Ontario

to be a good carving. And you're going to finish it and you're going to finish your thought. Sometimes when I have to finish a thought on a carving, sometimes I don't eat at all. When I do the carving step by step, it's not hurried but I'm anxious to finish it.

Finalizing a sculpture, realizing it in its entirety, requires concentration and a place to work undisturbed. Because of this, and the stone dust, Osuitok generally works outside, either in the open when weather permits or in a small tent or hut.

If I had a great thought yesterday and I started to work at home the noise would bother me, people would bother me. So a lot of times I will take my piece and walk away from the house and not really hide but just go away and try to work alone, because working alone will work with what you had in mind yesterday. If people bother you all the time, your thought is going to go away eventually.

The time Osuitok requires to finish a carving depends on such factors as its size and complexity, but three to four days is about the average, he says. The carving *Fisherwoman* in the Toronto Dominion Bank Collection, a piece with a lot of detail, took him about a week to complete. In addition to the incising on the main figure of the woman, Osuitok made and decorated the traditional-style container she carries. Like the bags that women used to make of square-flipper sealskin 'with a fancy design', this bag is decorated with a design 'to make the carving look better' and black marks imitating the stitches. Inside the woman's bag is a delicately carved fish. In spite of the fact that the fish is barely visible, Osuitok has taken great care to carve it and to add the laboriously incised tiny markings. For Osuitok such detail is very important. Details are part of the total statement, one of the steps in carving, as he would say. The really successful finished carving is a resolved, complete statement. Detail work helps realize the final sculptural form, making it 'as if it were real'.

Works from the 1960s, such as *Fisherwoman*, have particularly fine detailing. But throughout his career, Osuitok has effectively used different types of incised markings to simulate texture and colouration, showing fur trim on parkas, scales on fish, feathers on birds, ripples in water, or the hair on musk-oxen, sealskins and humans. The degree and type of detail depends in part on the type of stone he is using. The green stone that he likes is 'the best kind; you can get a lot more detail out of it when you're carving it.'

While Osuitok does not do as much incising now as he did in earlier carvings, he continues to do various other types of detailing and fine carving. The main sculpture, and any implements, inset eyes or other elements added to it, are made with great attention to both overall form and finishing details. In the carving *Sea Goddess* made in about 1983, for example, the texture and thinness of the two braids belie the fact that they are carved out of stone. Great skill has gone into the sculpting of these braids, the equally thin flowing front fins and tail, the delicately modelled facial features, and the balance of the goddess's arched body.

Balance is another technical concern that has preoccupied Osuitok over the years. 'To me that's the most important part—the most important thing in carving—the balance. You have to really know how it's going to work; if you don't you are going to end up with a problem.' Osuitok's birds in particular, cantilevered off to one side or dangerously top heavy, are balanced on very fine points. Using a smooth piece of wood, levelled by means of a cup filled with water, Osuitok finds the balancing point for a sculpture and establishes the base for it. Rather than trying to make the stone base totally flat across the bottom, he hollows out the center into a concave shape. The sculpture rests more stably, he says, on the outer edge of the base.

Such precarious balance adds to the sense of movement and tension in Osuitok's sculptures. Elements in a work are caught in mid-motion, or extend off to one side, or seem suspended between impossible points. Much of this effect is achieved in the interaction between stone and surrounding space. Osuitok not only carves the piece of stone; he extensively utilizes the actual space around and within it. Elements rising up and out at various angles extend the sculptural impact into the area beyond the actual sculpture. Spaces within the carving, between wings, beaks or other features, emphasize the relationship between the positive and negative, between mass and space. Sometimes the sculpture is almost flat, the more two-dimensional effect highlighting the silhouette of the image.

Osuitok's different ways of treating the space in and around his sculptural form are only one aspect of his inventive and experimental—yet always accomplished—style. Osuitok works and reworks subjects, often returning to old favourites, but also trying something new he has thought of. He is particularly adventuresome in the actual carving; continually trying new things, pushing both his material and himself. His consummate technical abilities enable him not only to attempt the seemingly impossible with the stone, but to accomplish it with great success. There is tremendous variety in shape, form and style: the realistic, the expressive, the elegant, the open, the compact, the stylized. Osuitok himself discusses this variety in relation to a sculpture made in 1984 of a stylized human figure.

As I was saying before, sometimes I like to do different things. Doing that, maybe they would be more appreciated. For that particular piece I just told myself, oh let me think of something else, and then I started it and it became that way. Going back and looking at different pieces, it's very interesting because you go back and see what you've done in different steps.

Before, when I wasn't that old, I thought that the days were all the same during the week, but as I get older I can

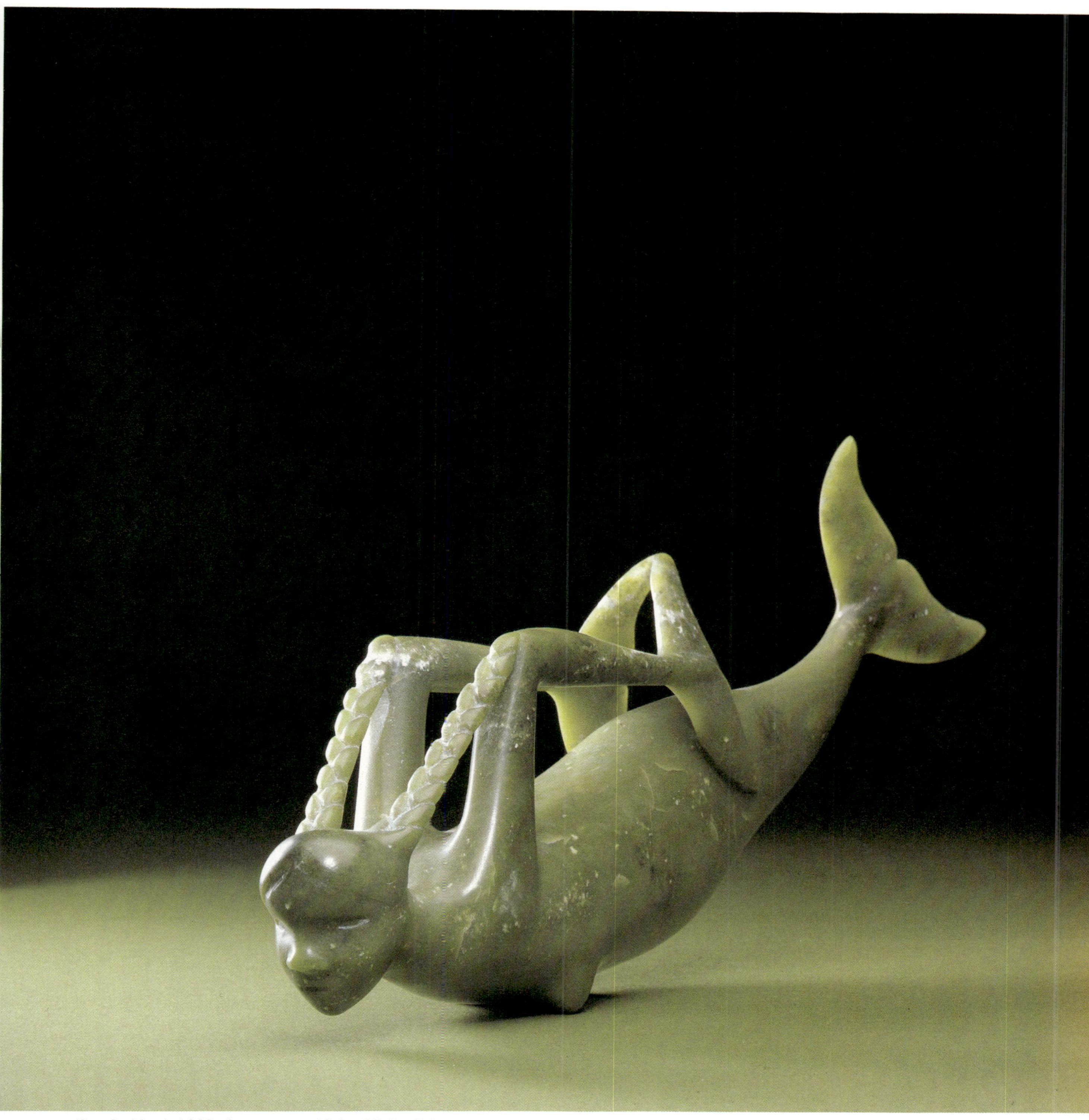

'Sea Goddess', 1983. Green stone, 13.0 x 35.0 x 7.0 cm. Private Collection. Photograph: Courtesy of Joseph Antonitsch, Inuit Galerie, West Germany.

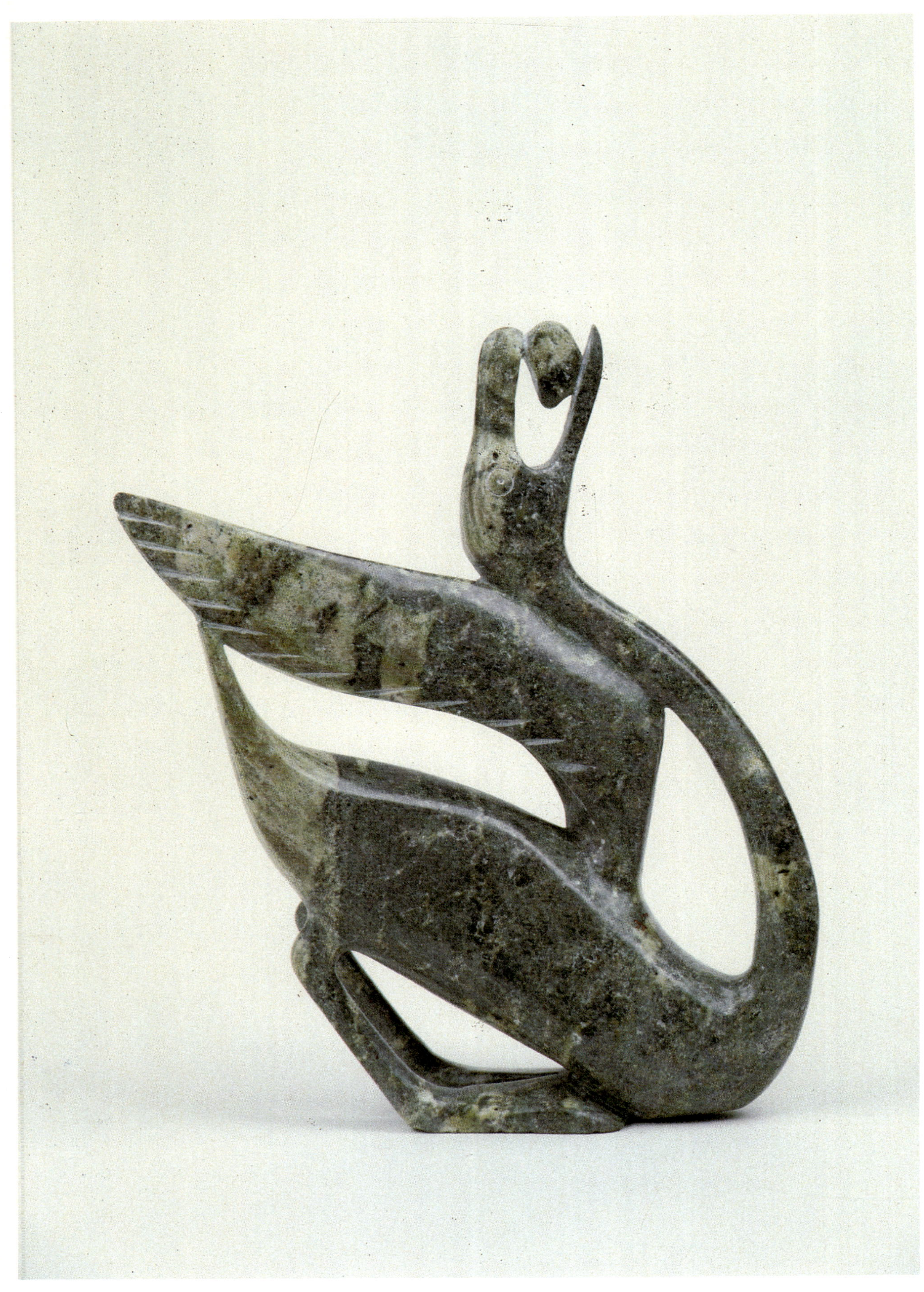

Osuitok Ipeelee

see that days are different. Because in some days you think differently and then the other days you think of something else. That is why I'm doing different things.

The unstandardized nature of Osuitok's work sometimes makes it difficult to identify yet another of his sculptural styles as actually his. Dating his sculpture can also be difficult because of his varied and changing styles. Only the rare sculpture has a date written on it, and generally Osuitok himself cannot establish specific dates for earlier pieces. He does sign his work, however, especially since the early 1960s, generally using syllabics and sometimes Roman letters. The signature itself has changed over the years because, as he says, his name is 'not really resolved'. Although he now uses the name Osuitok Ipeelee, earlier works may be signed Osuitok Ohotok or Osuitok Ohotok Ipeelee, the name Ohotok coming from his father.

Just as Osuitok learned carving from his father, several of Osuitok's own sons have established reputations for themselves within the younger generation of Cape Dorset sculptors. Tukiki's stylized, abstracted forms have been included in exhibitions in the South and were featured in an article by John Robertson in *The Beaver* magazine. Sangani's carvings, done in a more representational style, are characterized by considerable skill, sensitivity and promise. Osuitok describes Sangani as a very good carver. 'He can be a better carver than his father.'

Since the 1952 National Gallery exhibition, Osuitok has been included in a number of group exhibitions nationally and internationally. He has also had six one-man shows in Canada, the United States and Germany. Osuitok himself has travelled extensively, not only for exhibition openings but also for business, personal pleasure and reasons of health. He has been to Australia, New Zealand, the U.S.S.R. and cities in southern Canada.

Osuitok's commissioned works have included several sculptures made for specific occasions; he has also been asked to build traditional *inukshuit*. The *inukshuk*, a rock cairn often made in the shape of a human being, was used as a marker or directional aid in the arctic landscape. Osuitok has built three *inukshuit* in Cape Dorset to be shipped out and assembled in the South: in Toronto, Ottawa, and Strasbourg, France. In 1973 Osuitok was elected a member of the Royal Canadian Academy of Arts.

In discussing his carvings, Osuitok has said that he works hard to obtain his ideas. Clearly he works equally hard to realize them. He plans his work, thinking ahead of time about his subject and ideas, and if necessary filing away his thoughts for future use. In choosing and carving the stone, he is sensitive to its inherent weakness and potential, recognizing that the stone may not always be equal to his intent. But if this stone is not adequate, another surely will be, since in an Osuitok carving anything seems possible. New ideas are explored, new ways of carving are tried, new formats are utilized. Osuitok moves from subject to subject, from form to form, creating a richly varied body of work. Yet Osuitok's strength is not just his variety and his innovativeness but, more importantly, his ability to carve new ideas and new configurations successfully. Following his imagination through, step by step, he realizes his sculptural intent in its full entirety. Modestly assessing his abilities, Osuitok reflects:

For my work I don't come out saying I'm a great carver; I can do this, I can do that. No, it's not like that. I'm just happy, I'm proud of myself that I'm able to think and I'm able to carve what I can. ♦

'Bird', 1982. Light green stone, 30.5 x 29.5 x 7.7 cm. Collection: Mr. and Mrs. Samuel Sarick.

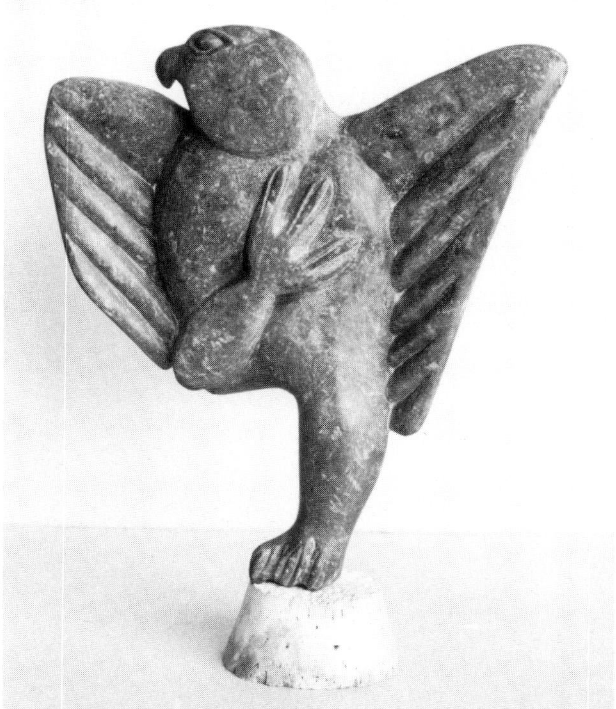

'Hawk on One Leg', 1968. Green stone and whalebone, 49.0 x 41.0 x 12.0 cm. MacMillan Bloedel Limited, Vancouver.

The author wishes to acknowledge, with deep appreciation, Osuitok's significant role in this project, particularly his thoughtful and conscientious participation in our interviews. Thanks, too, to the translators Letia Parr and Jimmy Manning. As usual Jimmy went out of his way to be of assistance. I am also grateful to the many individuals who, by their co-operation and helpfulness, contributed to this article, especially Ray MacSkimming, Terry Ryan, Pat Feheley, Lesley Boyd and Max Dean.

Pitaloosie is among the artists whose works are much sought after. Her 'Bird of Sargo' priced at $125 in the 1972 collection sold for $1,175 by silent auction in Hamilton 18 months later.

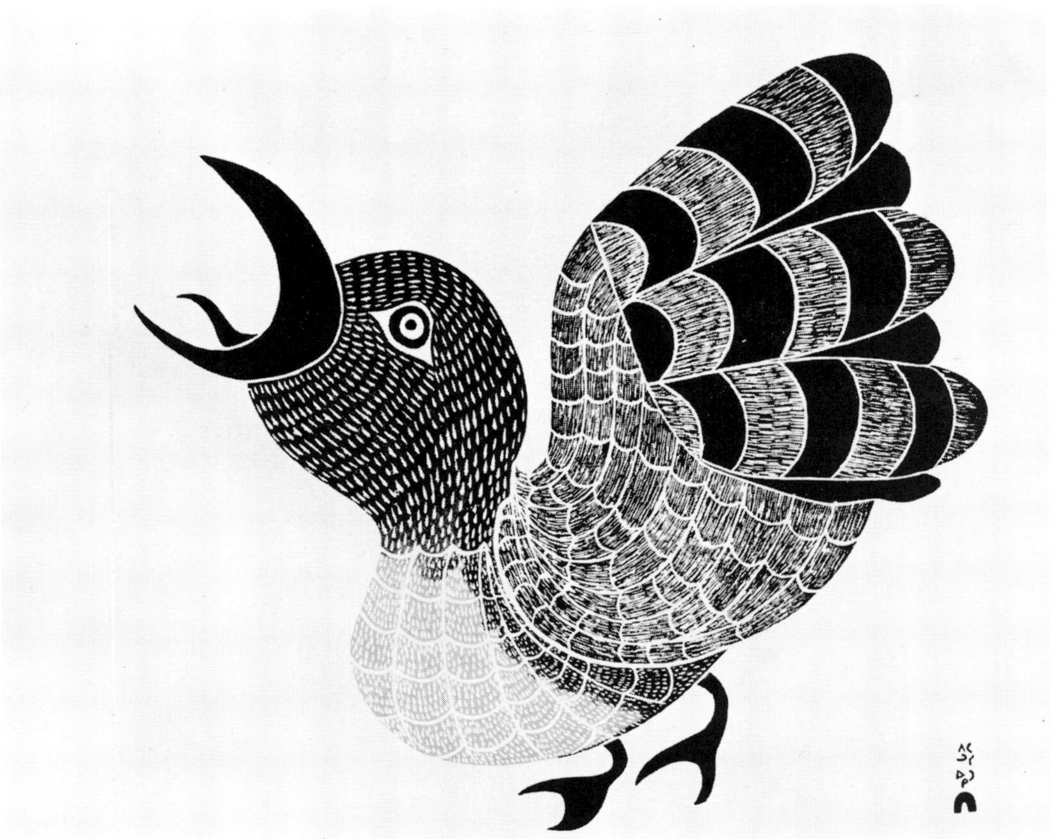

The Cape Dorset Prints

By Mary M. Craig

EACH YEAR A DATE in early November is chosen as the official day when the annual collection of Cape Dorset prints goes on sale in some fifty galleries in Canada and the United States.

As the day begins the Inuit artists in Cape Dorset on West Baffin Island sleep on, their creative exuberance stilled and their minds and bodies at rest. Not as peaceful is the scene on Georgia Street in Vancouver, Dresden Row in Halifax, or Elgin Street in Ottawa. There, at midnight, lines begin to form outside the doors of darkened galleries where a selection of the prints will be offered.

Those who are experienced in obtaining their first choice of the prints are warmly dressed and carry thermos bottles, blankets, and folding cots to sustain them through the cold hours of early morning. Conversation is at a minimum. Each is silent about the print he has in mind. He may have seen it at a non-selling preview the previous day or he may have heard from a friend who attended the official opening in a distant city that an outstanding print by Kenojuak or Lucy, Kananginak or Pitseolak is offered in the year's collection. Whatever the incentive, lines form and wait for the doors to open. Other collectors rise at 3 a.m. and use bedside telephones. Their calls are timed to reach dealers in New York, Vancouver, Winnipeg, Los Angeles or Frobisher Bay just as the sale begins.

From *The Beaver*, Spring 1975.

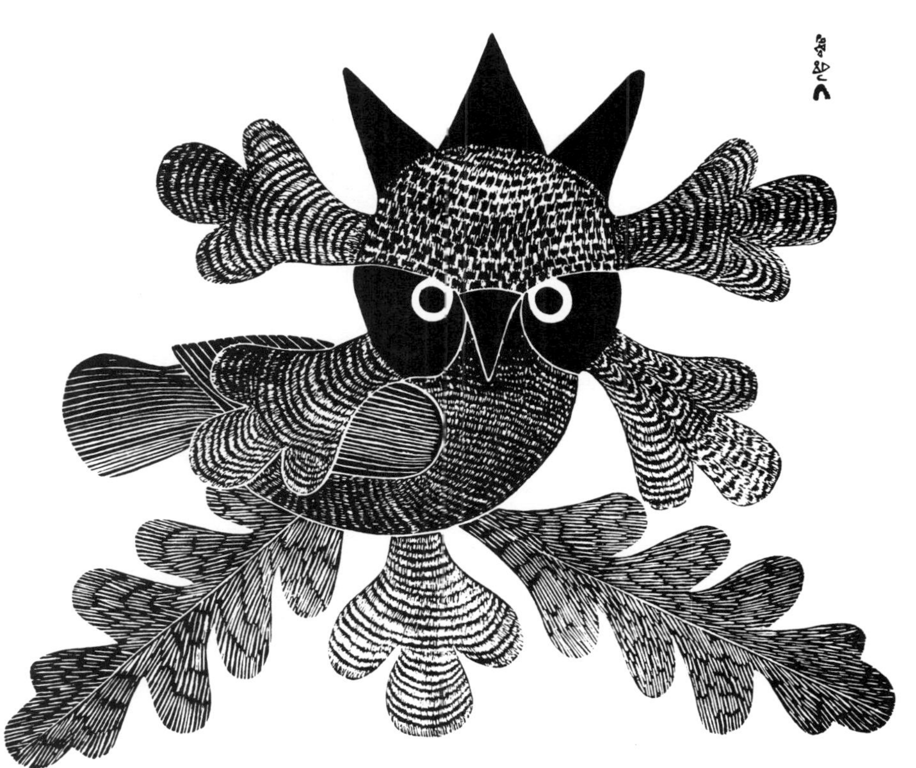

Kenojuak preferred this print 'Festive Bird' 1967, to her famous 'Enchanted Owl' 1960, which traded hands in Calgary in 1974 for $35,000.

Each year fifty numbered prints are pulled from the design cut into a slab of stone; then the block is scored or broken. Franchised dealers are limited to one complete set of the prints except for the Canadian gallery that is selected annually to hold the official opening. This gallery carries two sets of prints; it previews all others by a day, or if the opening is an evening event, by one night. Most galleries have to set systems guaranteeing the fairest distribution possible. A popular way is to allot numbers to the customers according to their positions in the line-up. The holder of number one has the first and his only choice. Complications set in as the prints dwindle and choice becomes limited.

Between 1959 and 1974, Cape Dorset produced more than 48,000 prints under 1,058 titles and catalogued in 15 editions. (Five prints in 1960 did not appear in that catalogue.)

These figures do not include the uncatalogued collection that James Houston assembled at Cape Dorset during 1957 and 1958. These first prints were small, simple designs by artists whose names became established in subsequent years: Pootagook, Oshaweetuk (now spelled Osuitok), Kananginak, Luktak, Iyola, and Mungitok. The artist Kudlalak, whose designs *Canada Goose* and *Geese Rising* were included, died shortly after the collection was introduced.

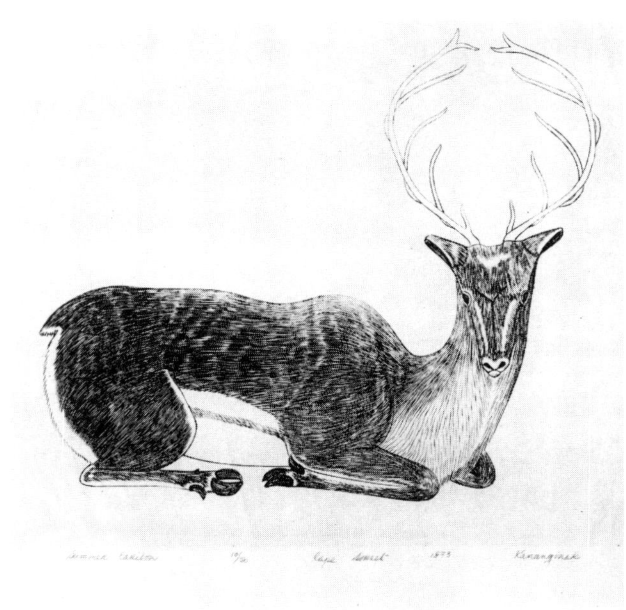

Virtually all fifty copies of 'Summer Caribou', an engraving by Kananginak, were sold on opening day 1973. Its value doubled the next year.

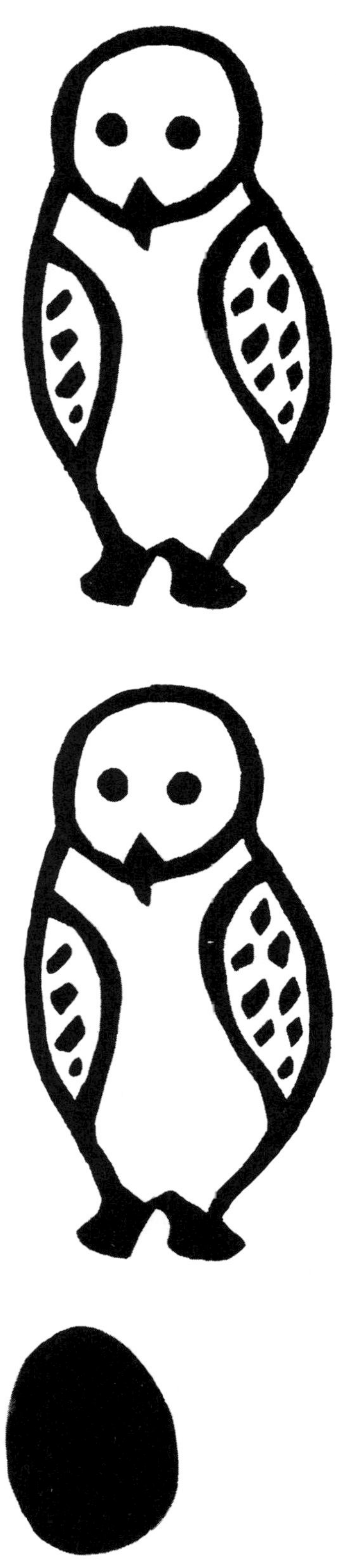

The stone block for the print 'Snowy Owls and Egg' by Iyola was one of the first made. Alma Houston who has this section of the block (shown horizontally below) in her possession believes that it was cut in the fall of 1957, although prints were not taken from it until 1959. Once thirty prints were taken, the block was broken. 'Snowy Owls and Egg' valued at $1,800 - $2,000 in 1975, is held by both the National Art Gallery in Ottawa and the Museum of Modern Art in New York.

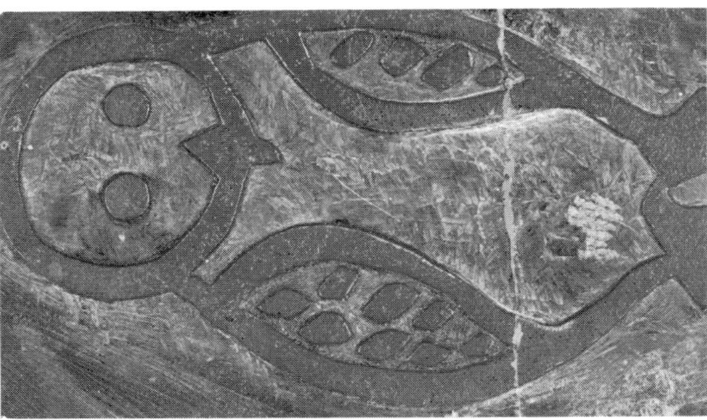

Twenty designs made up the 1957-58 collection; thirty prints were pulled of each, after which the stonecut or sealskin stencil was destroyed.

In December 1958, the Cape Dorset prints went on sale at the Hudson's Bay Company store in Winnipeg. Thirteen designs were offered 'matted ready for framing'; prices ranged from $5.00 for *Woman and Dog* by Iyola and *Two Loons* by Luktak, to $12.50 for *Hunters on Ice* by Mungitok and *Caribou and Young* by Kananginak.

These small rare prints are often unrecognized by dealers and collectors today. They seldom change hands although it is reported that a complete set of the collection was sold in Vancouver in 1974 for $55,000. This is not an unrealistic figure; some owners of the unusual little prints have refused $2,500 each for them.

In 1974, again in Vancouver, the 1959 collection of Cape Dorset prints—forty-one in all—sold for $74,000. This again was a modest price when the prints that make up the collection are considered. These included a stencil by Niviaksiak *Man Hunting at Seal Hole*; this print alone brought $5,200 at an auction at Christie's, Montreal, in October 1974. Seven other works by Niviaksiak, of equal if not superior merit, were in the 1959 collection. The first print by Kenojuak *Rabbit Eating Seaweed* appeared in 1959. The great Pootagook was represented five times; one of his prints *Joyfully I See Ten Caribou* is now in the National Gallery of Canada. The intriguing linear abstract *Division of Meat* by Tudlik is also a National Gallery acquisition. Kananginak was represented by three prints; Oshaweetuk's beautiful stencil *Four Musk Oxen* appeared in a small edition of thirty and the *Sea Goddess*, Taleelayo, was shown in print form, probably for the first time. There were also stone rubbings in editions of ten.

The following year's collection included eleven prints by Kenojuak including *The Enchanted Owl*. Originally priced at $75.00 *The Enchanted Owl* changed

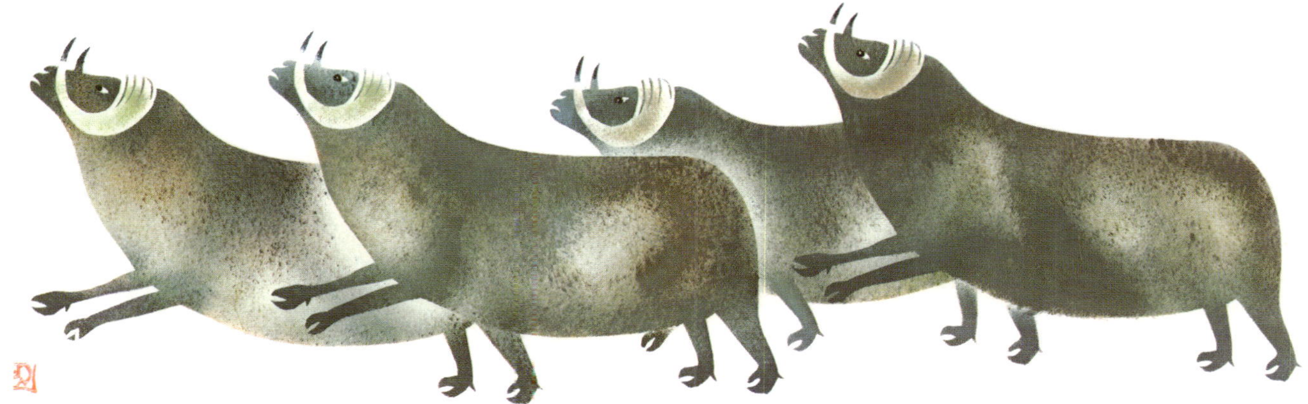

'Four Musk Oxen' by Oshaweetuk 1959, sealskin stencil in a limited edition of 30, was valued in 1975 at $3,000. Latterly, on his carvings, Oshaweetuk uses the spelling variant Osuitok.

hands for $5,000 in 1969, for $7,000 in 1971, for $10,000 in 1973, for $12,000 in 1974 and again the same year for the staggering sum of $35,000 in a private sale in Calgary, Alberta. One wonders how many of the original fifty prints of *The Enchanted Owl* are extant and what prices they will bring in future years.

It has to be noted that these high prices are not realized by the Inuit artist or the co-operative but by fortunate or astute collectors. This is the name of the game, and it is in no way peculiar to Inuit art.

The year 1960 introduced two more great ladies—Lucy and Pitseolak. It marked the dawning of the brief and brilliant career of the old hunter Kiakshuk who was in his seventies when he started to draw. He died five years later and his last print appeared posthumously in 1967. Kiakshuk's lifestyle, his profound, intimate knowledge of the land and ancient ways is comparable to the late Parr's whose prints distil the Inuit vision. A collector given opportunity and inclina-

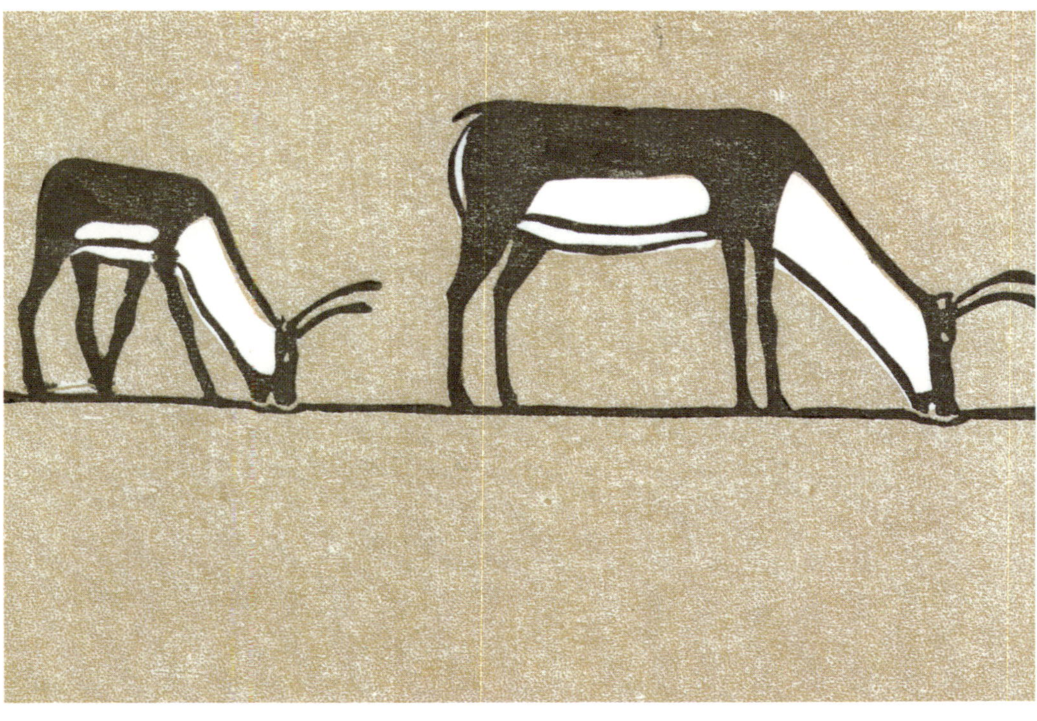

This rare and simple print 'Summer Caribou' by Pootagook, the great and powerful leader of the Dorset people until his death in 1959, was the first print made at Cape Dorset. A stonecut measuring 6" x 4", it was printed in a limited edition of 30. In 1975, the owners of this print refused offers of $2,500 for it.

tion could have purchased all seventy of the 1960 prints for $2,070, the total of their initial prices.

The following year, eighty-three prints could have been purchased for $3,184. These would include Lucy's *Large Bear* owned by the Tate Gallery, and Parr's first stencil print *Blue Geese Feeding*.

The engravings introduced in 1962 and 1963 for the most part failed to excite buyers, but connoisseurs did not pass them by. Ten years were to elapse before the general collector became aware of them and they gained just recognition. They have not escalated to the extent of the stonecut prints and stencils although the 1962 and 1963 prints are worth eight to ten times their original price.

The first attempt at copper-line engraving by an Inuit is attributed by James Houston to Iyola, and by Terry Ryan to Kiakshuk. This is the process of incising lines on a copper plate by means of an instrument called a burin or graver. Parr and Kenojuak and her husband, Johnniebo, briefly used the soft ground etching technique. In this case the image is bitten into the plate with acid; a less precise effect is produced because the line quality cannot be diminished or increased gradually.

Between the years 1964-65 (catalogued together) to 1974 a number of artists produced prints that could be classified as 'sleepers'. Ulayu, for example, who showed several charming prints in the 1964-65 collection including *I Saw a Strange Bird* would be surprised to hear that her 'Bird' was priced at $1,000 in 1975.

The year 1966 was a brilliant one with Parr, Kenojuak, Lucy, Pitseolak, and Kiakshuk all represented. Two prints issued that year clearly bear the symbol or chop of Pootagook. The great leader died in 1959; the 1966 signature was that of Iyola's wife, Pootogook. The symbols for their names linearly presented are identical, but in the structural designs adopted by the West Baffin Eskimo Co-operative, the distinction is clear.

The earlier catalogues usually reproduced exact information on the logos of the artists and printmakers—a valuable reference once the prints have been dispersed.

In the centennial year, 1967, a portfolio of six engravings by Kenojuak was issued on the advice of the Eskimo Arts Council. With an introduction by James Houston, a portrait and a biographical sketch of the artist, this collection was originally priced at $400. However several of the engravings had been separately dispersed, reducing the folio edition to 45. In 1974, five of the set sold separately in Winnipeg for $300 each.

In 1967, the decision was made, with some trepidation, to price a Kenojuak print at what seemed a whopping price—$95. The chosen print *Composition* sold in Calgary for $3,500 in 1974. Other Kenojuak prints, including the one that is her personal favourite—*Festive Bird*, sold the same year for prices ranging from $1,200 to $1,800.

In conjunction with Canada's centenary, the National Gallery celebrated the first printmaking years

Tudlik was 72 years old and nearly blind when he produced 'Seal Thoughts of Man' in 1959. At this time he was internationally famous for his carvings of owls.

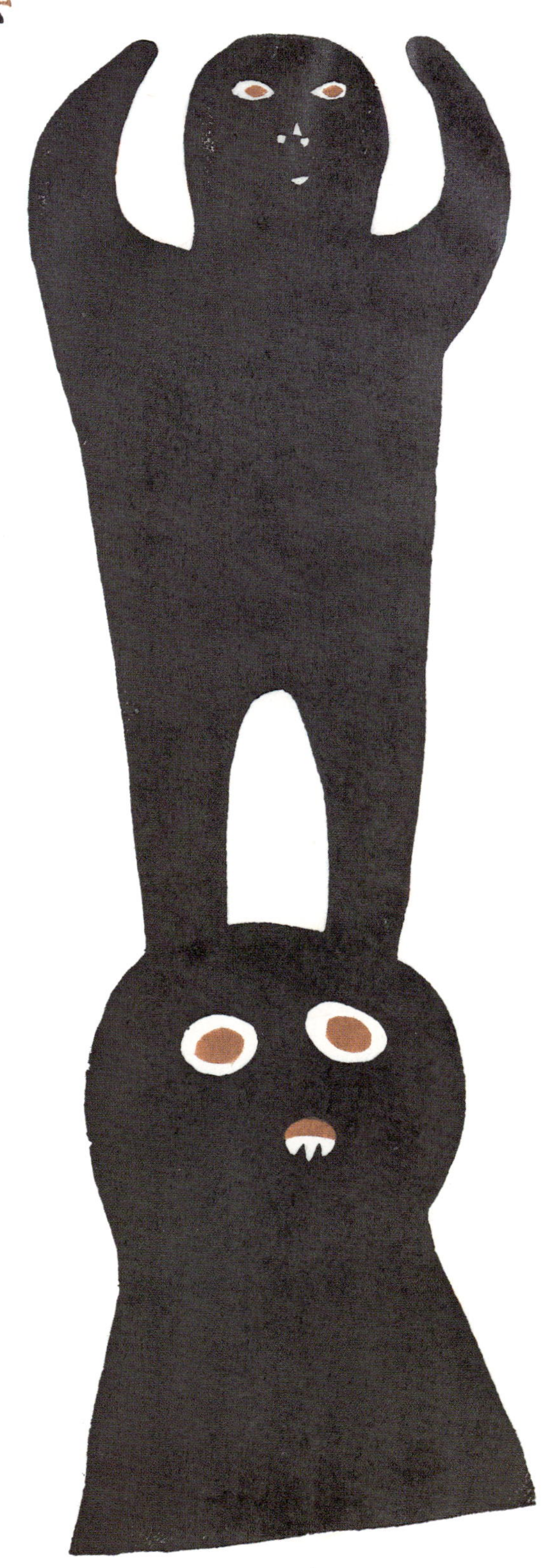

Eegyvudluk and author Mary Craig watch as Iyola prepares to ink the stone for Kenojuak's 'Night Hunter'.

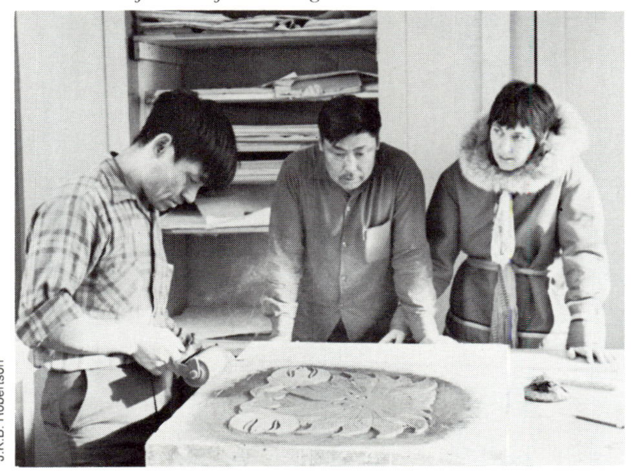

J.K.B. Robertson

Kakulu, whose print 'Reflected Images' was included in the 1974 collection, is young and talented.

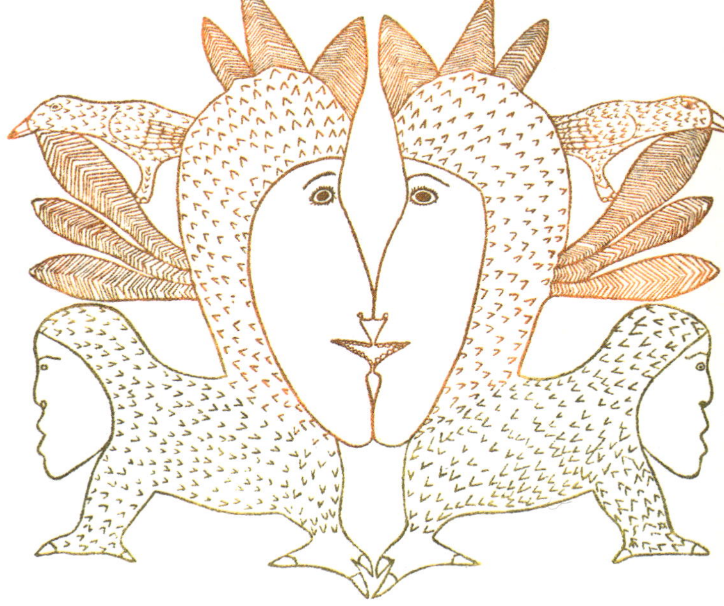

'Mother Birds Protecting Young' a sealskin stencil by the famous and prolific Pitseolak, from the 1961 collection.

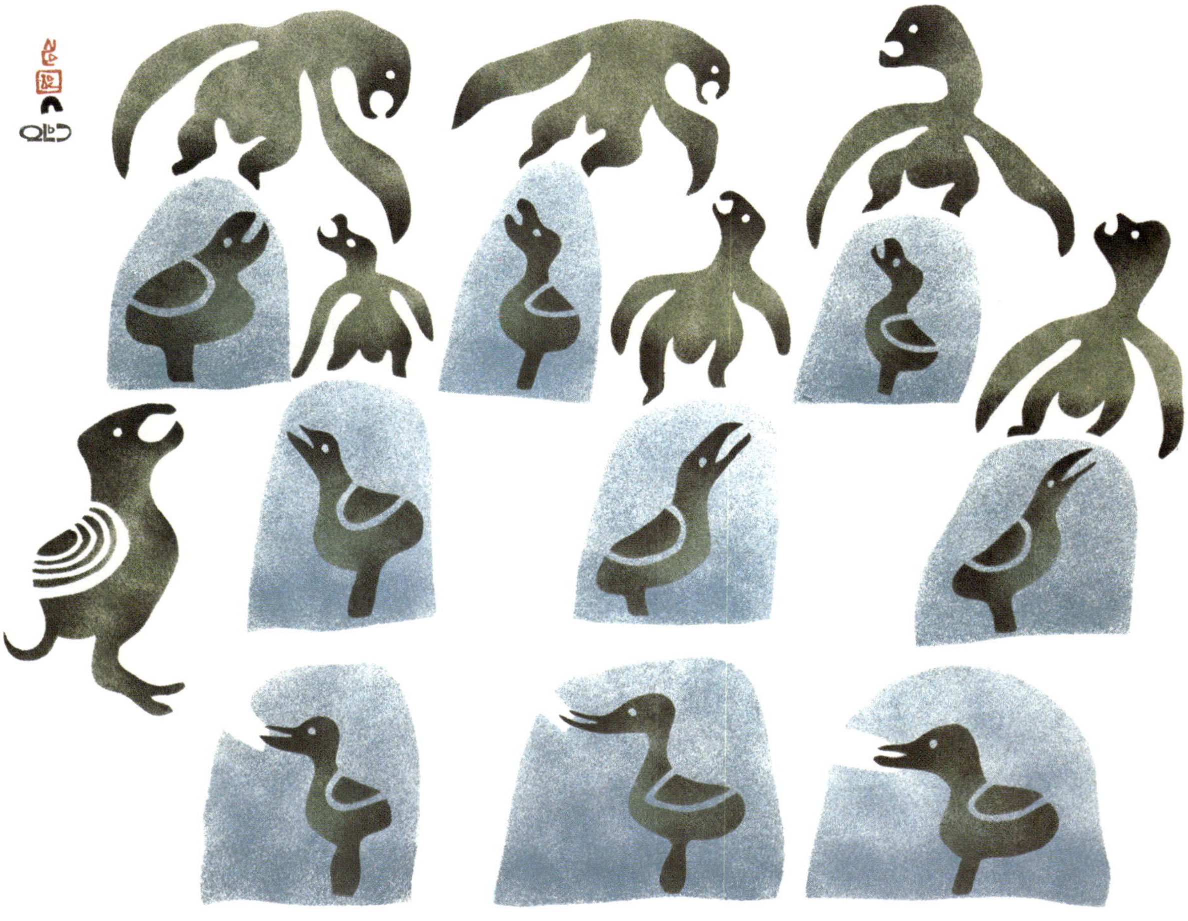

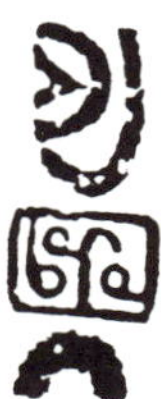

In this signature the symbols are those of the artist Pootagook and below, the printmaker Kananginak. The igloo is the mark for prints from the West Baffin Eskimo Co-operative.

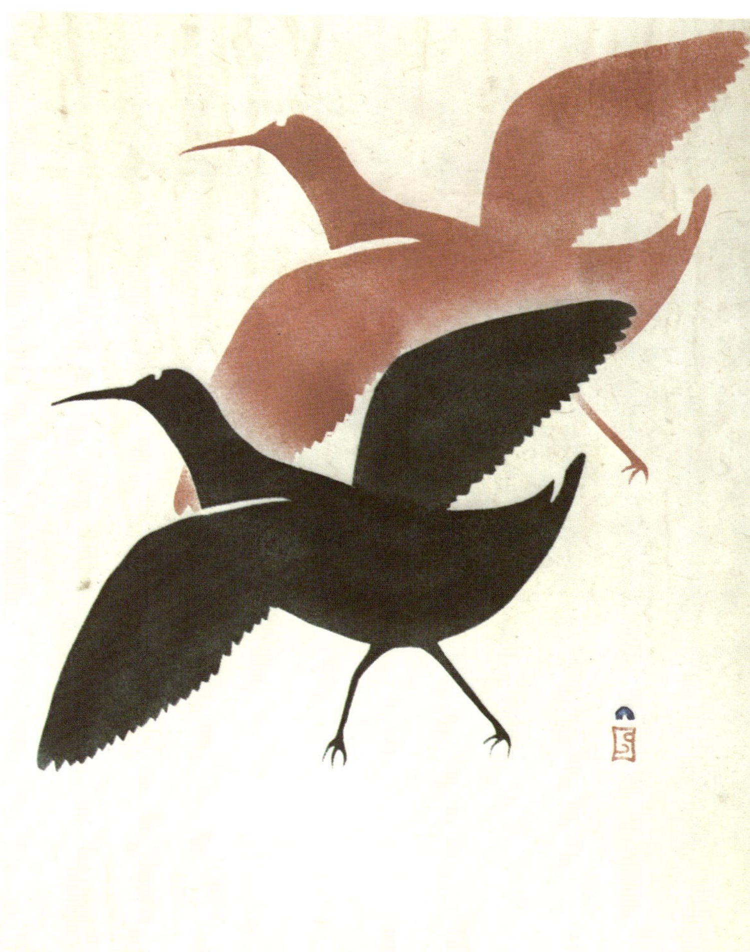

'Arctic Shore Birds', a sealskin stencil by Luktak 1959, is valued with others from the collection of this year, at $2,500.

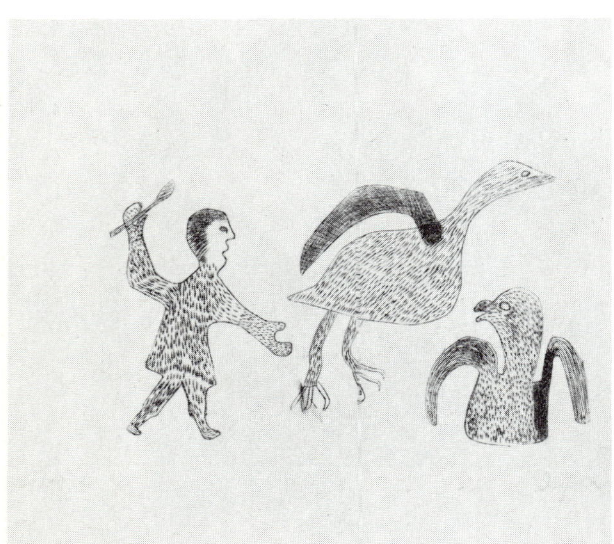

In 1962 the copper engravings were included in the collection. This one, by Iyola, is believed to be one of the first.

Eegyvudluk pulling Kenojuak's print 'The Owl', 1969.

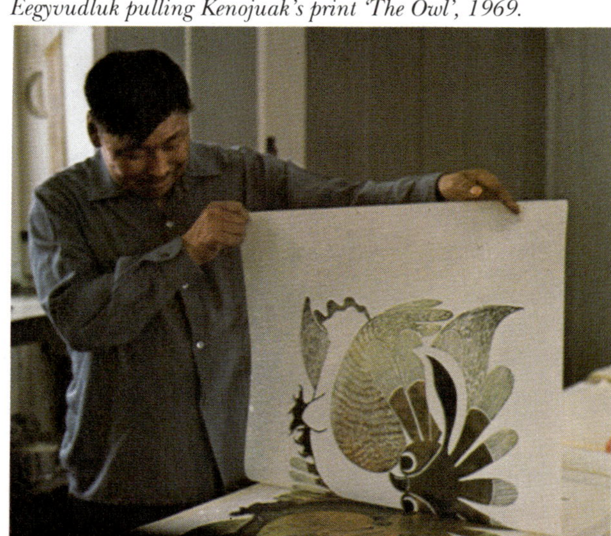

with a circulating exhibition 'Cape Dorset - A Decade of Prints and Recent Sculpture'. In the foreword to the catalogue, James Houston wrote, 'Whether the coming generation will be encouraged to carry forward their natural artistic heritage remains the question to be answered in the future.'

Part of that future has now passed and we have part of the answer. Some of the older artists—Lucy, Pitseolak, and Jamasie—are still with us, perennially in demand. Pudlo has joined these pace-setters with *Umingmuk* in 1970 and *Long Journey* in 1974. Parr is gone but *Hunters of Old* was issued posthumously in 1974 at $800, an unprecedented price for a new release. It traded quite blatantly within hours for double that figure. Kananginak, who was 40 on New Year's Day and Kenojuak are still in their creative prime.

Other older people, Ikayukta, Kingmeata, and Keeleemeome, whose talents lay dormant for the greater part of their lives have shared their dreams with us in their latter years. Time will limit their contribution as, sadly, it has for Eleeshushe, Anna, and Peter Pitseolak. Ningeeuga, not young herself, is perhaps following the example of her mother, Anirnik, in showing us glimpses of the many-faced spirits she knows so well.

The young, but not the very young, are still attracted by printmaking as a means of expression. Pitaloosie (Pauta's wife) first appeared in 1968. Her works are much sought after; *Bird of Sargo* produced in 1972 brought $1,175 by silent auction in Hamilton eighteen months later. Sorosilutu and Kakulu are both young and talented.

In Cape Dorset, stonecut printing and engraving have rival interests to lure away young creative minds. The stone lithograph will appear in the near future; animated film making, tapestry weaving, jewellry making and typography are all being taught in the community.

The selection of prints for the annual Cape Dorset collection is approved by the Eskimo Arts Council. The blind stamp of the Council appears on each print as well as the signatures of the printmaker and the artist in syllabics, and the igloo, the mark used by the West Baffin Eskimo Co-operative for prints.

A suggested retail price list accompanies each new collection. At the time, each dealer is asked to withhold the prints from the public until a specified date. It works well for the artist when prints are launched simultaneously and at the same prices. Dealers who ignore the price list, who ask higher prices, or who sell before the launching date can only be considered exploitative. On the other hand, to price excessively at source would be equally exploitative.

To the artists themselves, printmaking remains a curious and exciting facet of their lives. One April day in 1968 that wise old lady Pitseolak, in a conversation with Alma Houston and Oshaweetuk said 'Sometimes I would laugh to myself; I am making my living with paper that tears, and I depend so much on it!' ♦

Anirnik, born in 1909, began to draw compositions from the spirit world in the 1960s. In 'Spirit with Sea Animals' the spirit wears a pointed gnome-like hat.

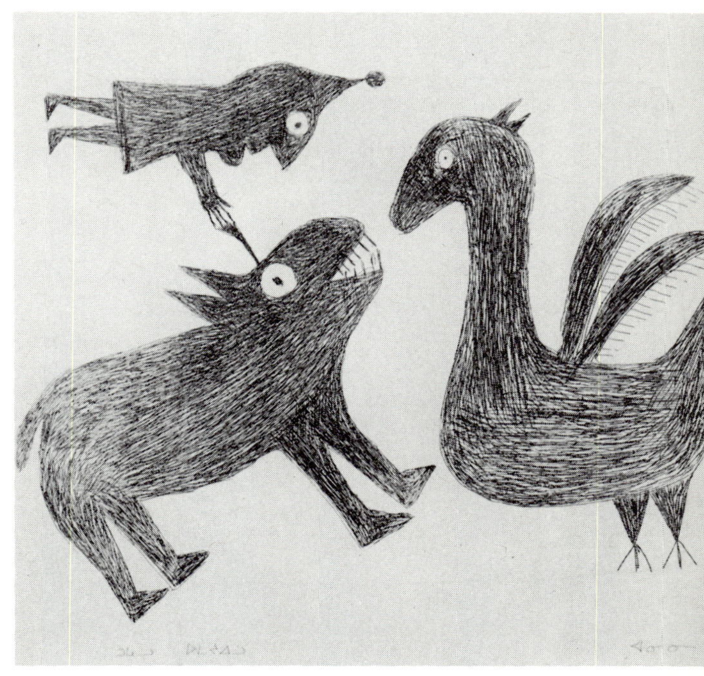

'Two Caribou' by Pauta contributed to the brilliance of the 1967 collection. Originally priced at $75, its value in 1975 ranged from $1,200 to $1,500.

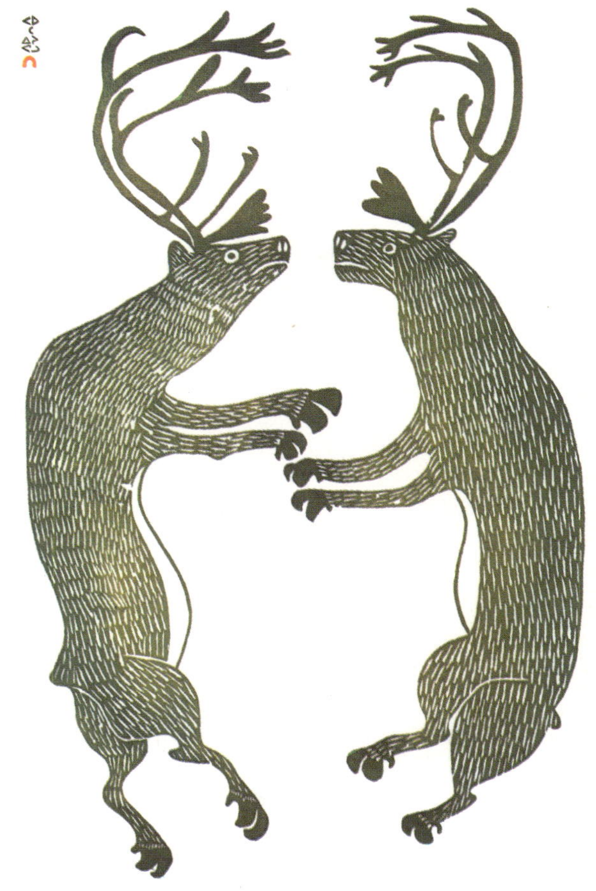

P. Murdock

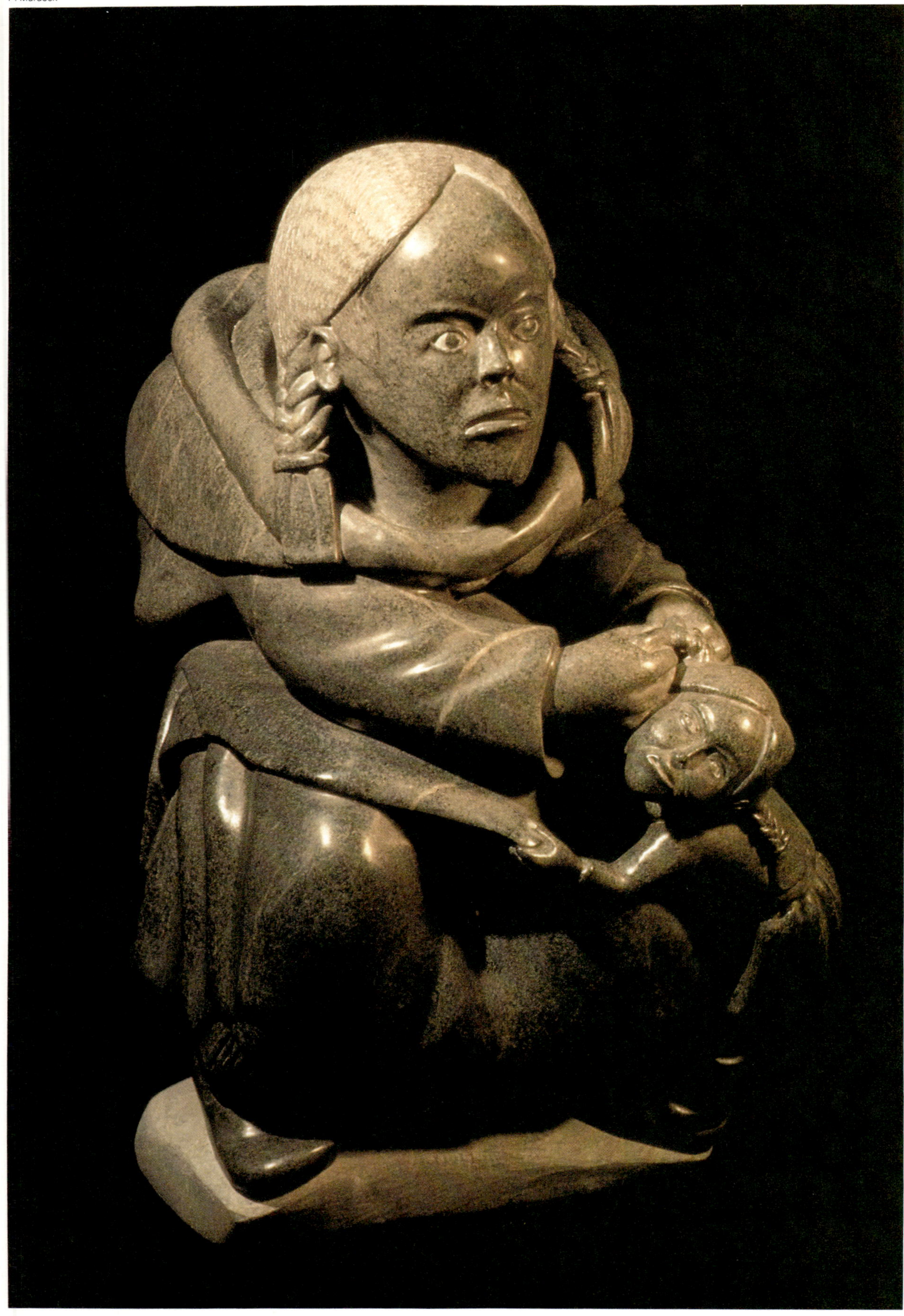

Based on interviews with the Iyaituk brothers, in Ivugivik, 1984.

'Woman Braiding Child's Hair', undated.
Nutaraaluk Iyaituk, Soapstone.

The Iyaituk Brothers

Nutaraaluk and Mattiusi

By Marybelle Myers

IN 1980 WHEN I WAS WORKING on the exhibition 'Things Made by Inuit' I was so taken with the work of Mattiusi Iyaituk, a young Inuk from Ivugivik in Arctic Quebec, that I used his sculpture *A Young Hunter's First Catch* on the cover of the exhibition catalogue. At a time when many of the older Inuit artists were dying, it was exciting to see young talent developing in new directions. As Mattiusi says, his style is 'modern'. Other Inuit might say that his work is as good as, but different from the work of previous generations.

His older brother, Nutaraaluk, an equally talented sculptor, works very much in the old style. Together the Iyaituk brothers make a fascinating subject; for, in spite of their shared history and continued collaboration, they are a study in contrasts.

The work of Nutaraaluk exemplifies the Povungnituk ideal of technically refined realism (his first carvings were sold to the Hudson's Bay Company in Povungnituk). Born in 1943, Nutaraaluk typifies the generation of Inuit who came to manhood on the land but are now committed to an urbanized lifestyle forged in the late 1950s and early 1960s, in which carving supplements hunting as the principal means of livelihood.As Nutaraaluk says, 'I was not born to be a carver but I became a carver.'

Indeed, for people like Nutaraaluk, carving has come to have a significance akin to hunting: both are integral to survival, culturally as well as physically, in a way that wage labour can never be. Inuit sculptors can participate in the modern wage economy and continue traditional practices since carving is easily combined with seasonal hunting activities, can be done anywhere and doesn't depend upon imported skills and materials.

This is a way of life under threat, given the present softening market for Inuit sculpture. Previously the Inuit-owned co-operatives (which, along with the Hudson's Bay Company, are the principal purchasers of carvings in the North) would buy virtually everything an Inuk produced; this felicitous arrangement has had to be discontinued in the face of growing inventories at the southern distribution agencies: La Fédération des Coopératives du Nouveau-Québec in Montreal and Canadian Arctic Producers Limited in Winnipeg. In Arctic Quebec, where the co-operative movement has always been strong, the situation is being dealt with by paying carvers an advance at the time of purchase (a maximum of $35 except for the occasional major piece which will bring an advance of $200) with the intention that when and if the carving sells, the artist will receive his fair share.

The Arctic Quebec solution is particularly difficult for carvers like Nutaraaluk who was used to receiving several thousand dollars for his larger carvings immediately upon completion; but it is the co-op's way to equalize losses as well as gains. This drastic measure to reduce the cost of financing inventories cannot fail to have an effect upon the quantity and the quality of sculpture being produced. Nevertheless, Nutaraaluk, for one, continues to put all his energies into his carving, in the firm belief that things will improve.

Mattiusi, for his part, is a success story for the 1980s. Seven years younger than Nutaraaluk and educated in English at the Churchill Vocational Centre in Manitoba, Atuarniq High School in Great Whale River (grades 10 and 11) and Quebec High School in Quebec City, his approach to his life and art is completely different from Nutaraaluk's. In his sculpture, he combines the 'modern' (his word) abstracting of form with the traditional technique of bone inlay, just as in his life he combines modern wage labour as a policeman with the traditional pursuits of hunting, fishing and gathering. He seems to have the best of both worlds; he is as able to address a seminar in Pennsylvania as he is to harvest country food.

Mattiusi is not as dependent upon the traditional life as his older brother and therefore considers carving to be something of a sideline; for, like ever-increasing numbers of Inuit, he has more options than do people like his brother. As Nutaraaluk points out, there are only two options available to the older Inuit: hunting and carving. Only the latter generates the cash needed to pay for hunting equipment and gas, for housing, clothes and telephones. But it is no longer possible to survive only by hunting, and it appears that the second option may be threatened.No wonder Nutaraaluk said, when asked what he would like to say to the people of the South, that he would ask them to buy his carvings if possible, because he doesn't want to throw his life away.

It is impossible to write about Inuit artists without writing about hunger and suffering, for this was the reality until very recently. Probably no adult Inuk has escaped the experience of great physical deprivation. The Iyaituk family, living in igloos just north of Povungnituk at Cape Smith (now named Akulivik), had a more difficult time than most. Subsisting mainly on sea mammals, they moved up and down the east coast of Hudson Bay from Gillies Island north to Cape Smith. Sometimes they moved inland in pursuit of caribou. The four older siblings died from starvation and exhaustion in their attempts to find food for the family, leaving Nutaraaluk as the oldest son. They died, he says, when 'they were old enough to go by kayak.' He also says he prefers not to talk too much about past hardships, possibly because it would seem too much like boasting in the face of present success or because it might invite a reversal of fortune. Nutaraaluk says merely, 'My father tried very hard to live and hunt for his children.'

The outstanding shared characteristic of Nutaraaluk and Mattiusi is their competence in everything they choose to do. Visiting their sister, Sarah, who is a teacher, one steps over eiderdown drying on the rocks, obtained by Mattiusi. Her freezer is full of birds and muktuk that Nutaraaluk provides, and she wears a duffle baby carrier that Mattiusi, adapting a design from Pangnirtung, sewed himself. One of the two large Peterhead boats on the beach belongs to Nutaraaluk. Both brothers command high prices for their sculpture.

No doubt this competence comes from having to scramble against real odds; but the blindness of their mother, Lucy, was also a factor. Because of her handicap, the children achieved self-sufficiency at an early age. Nutaraaluk says she had pain in her eyes for a long while and, one day, after being hit in the face with hailstones, the pain increased until she went blind. That was in 1951, when Nutaraaluk was eight and Mattiusi only one. 'She could no longer walk outside without help, although she could manage to do a few household chores such as looking after the pots,' Nutaraaluk says. 'It was hard for the family because we were young. My sister and I had to work and sew the holes in our pants. Our mother gave us instructions. After a few years of her being blind, I had to clean the seal myself and dress it up.'

It is not surprising, then, that Mattiusi knows how to sew. 'I learned to sew from my mother,' he told me. 'She would start me off and I would finish it myself.' He considers it a useful skill to have; for, 'whenever we go hunting, it seems there is something to sew.'

The Iyaituk competence also comes through the paternal line. Around 1955, the remaining members of the family moved into Ivugivik where food was more plentiful. They were close to starvation when they arrived but they soon established themselves. Markusi, the father, who had a talent for carving, used to sell his work to the Hudson's Bay Company in Povungnituk in order to get bullets and tea. In Ivugivik, he continued carving until 1965, when he was hired as a janitor and handyman by the Quebec government. In 1968, he was described as 'one of the wealthiest Eskimos in Ivugivik—paying for his three-bedroom house and for an 18 horsepower motor.'

Lucy died in a house fire a few years ago, and Markusi's activities are now somewhat restricted since he wears a pacemaker. He has moved in with his daughter, Sarah, and her children.

Like everyone else in Ivugivik, the Iyaituks have a camp ten miles or so outside the settlement during the summer. They remain a closely knit unit, looking after each other and working together. Mattiusi and Nutaraaluk go together to get soapstone and draw on a common stockpile for their carvings. They often carve (though not necessarily together) in Nutaraaluk's 'carving house', starting a piece outside with an axe and finishing it inside.

On the day that I arrived in Ivugivik in the summer of 1984 Nutaraaluk arrived back from summer camp with twelve carvings, ranging from small (for him) to medium-sized ones. All were of animals: bears, fish, birds. He prefers to carve large. As he puts it, 'There's a difference in how you handle the big ones and the small ones. The big ones feel better in my hands. I like to carve something that will not move away when I put more force on it.'

In spite of its pictorial qualities, his work cannot be categorized as realistic. La Fédération des Coopératives du Nouveau-Québec refers to it as 'imaginative realism', a phrase that captures the larger-than-life quality of his work. This is a trait Nutaraaluk shares with other carvers from the

Povungnituk area where he first started carving, selling his work to the Hudson's Bay store while Peter Murdoch was manager.

Nutaraaluk describes his approach to his work: 'What I see around me is what I carve. I have seen many bears, but I don't carve the actual bear; I carve the feel of the bear. I wouldn't want to carve from a live model. I carve from my head.'

The hardest part of making a carving, he says, is thinking about it. When asked whether the block of stone suggests the shape to him, or whether he starts with a preconceived idea of what he wants to make, he says: 'I find the time to think ahead of what I want to make. I look for the stone and make what I want. I stick to my idea regardless of the stone—but I also try to find the appropriate stone.'

He starts by working outside with an axe, to get the form of the sculpture. Then come files, coarse to fine, still working outside, or in a small tent when he is at camp. The chisel is next, followed by a tool he made 'according to his own need' to smooth away file and chisel marks, and to do the final shaping. He has to buy new tools frequently, as they become blunt. Finally comes polishing with sandpaper and water. Nutaraaluk's sculptures are always highly polished, testament to hours of labour. Before all this comes the search for soapstone. Although he prefers above all to work with green stone from Cape Dorset, he is content to use local stone which is still plentiful around Ivugivik but is hard to quarry. He takes several men out in his Peterhead to get the stone, investing considerable labour and expense to obtain the raw materials for his soapstone art. The work is dangerous as well; in Inoucdjuac recently, a man working in a quarry was crushed to death when the stone collapsed on him. As Nutaraaluk told me, 'If you came with me to dig out the soapstone, you would know it is very hard. It is cold here in the winter and sometimes the stone cannot be cut out because it is so hard. We could use dynamite but that ruins the soapstone which, being soft, cracks easily.'

Carving is part of the rhythm of Nutaraaluk's life: 'If we hunt in winter, my ten-year-old son and I, we're waiting for the seal to come up and my son circles around the hole on the ice so the seal will come up and we will be able to eat. After I come back from hunting, I start to carve.' He learned both skills from his father, through observation. 'I never really paid attention to what he was doing but, one day when I was about 14, I began to realize that if my father died, there would be no one to help me. I would have to be able to support myself.'

He is speaking, of course, about the time when the survival of the Iyaituk family was at stake; the first association that Nutaraaluk made with carving was that it could be used to buy bullets, to get food. Carving was, then, part of the strategy of physical survival, and this fact is a continuing inspiration for Nutaraaluk, although carving is an activity for which he has great natural talent and which provides him

Marybelle Myers

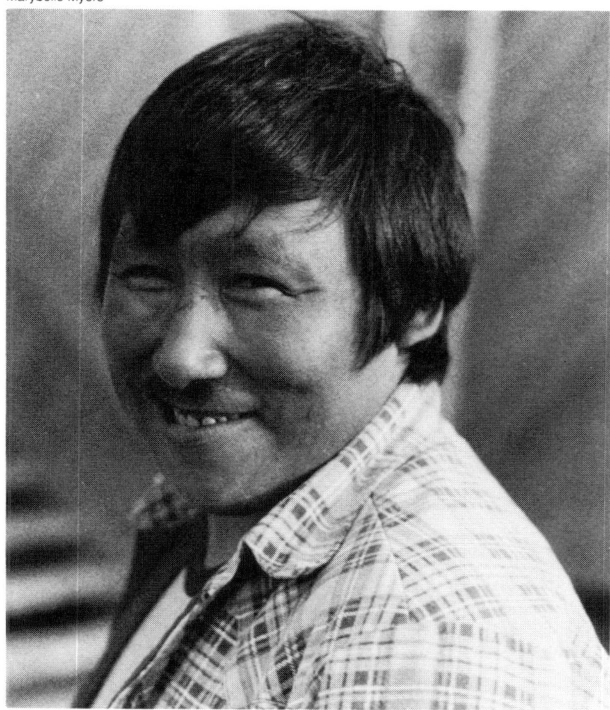

Nutaraaluk Iyaituk, carver and hunter, outside his home in Ivugivik, Arctic Quebec, 1984.

with satisfaction as well as cash.

The importance of a financial return should never be downplayed; indeed, given the present situation of low cash advances, Nutaraaluk is preoccupied with how he is going to manage. It is tempting, he says, to go around the co-operative and sell directly to white people, but he wants to resist this temptation; he knows that although it would serve the purpose of getting him more ready cash, it is not a solution in the long run.

For Nutaraaluk it isn't a question of being able to look after his immediate personal needs. Even more important is the preservation of a market for carving, so that the Inuit can continue to live more or less as they are now. In fact Nutaraaluk, recently elected a director of La Fédération des Coopératives du Nouveau-Québec, voted in favour of reducing payments on carvings until the market improved. Even though he says that he had little choice in this, since 'carvers even more famous than I voted for it', he signals his support of the move. 'If people stop buying carvings, the way we live will pass away. We'll not be Inuit any more. The only two activities Inuit have now are hunting and carving, but we can't earn our living just from hunting—pay rent on our houses, pay for our phones and gas for our boats and snowmobiles. It is only with carvings that I can buy something from the co-op. I feel tired, trying to make carvings so cheap, but I can't give it up because it's my life, the only way I can live.'

The system in Arctic Quebec of making only a nominal down payment to carvers is particularly trying for Nutaraaluk. Previously he was in a good cash position—able, for instance, to pay $30,000 for

Peter Murdock

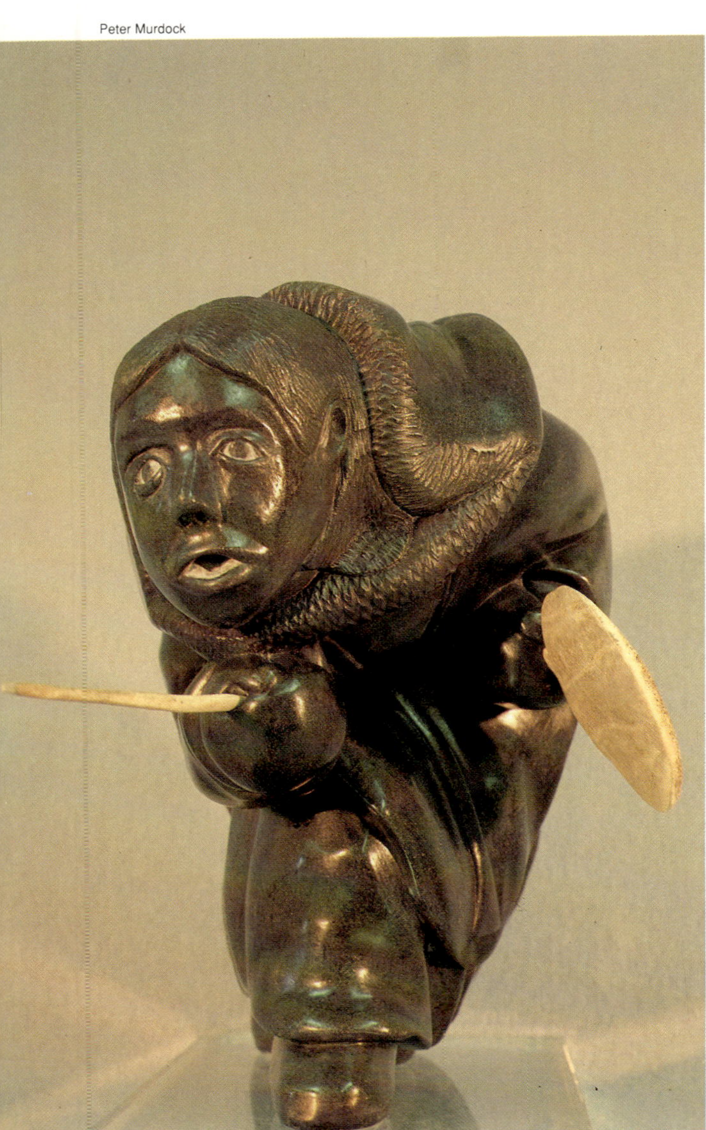

'Woman Drummer I', 1979. Nutaraaluk.
Soapstone, ivory and whalebone, 48 x 30 x 35 cm.
Collection: Nova Corporation, Alberta.

his Peterhead, which he purchased second-hand in Cape Dorset. Now he can hardly afford to finance trips to get soapstone.

It isn't that he needs cash to buy food; he needs it to buy gas and equipment, so that he can obtain his own food from the land, as well as stone to carve, so that he can, in turn, buy gas and equipment and so on. With typical foresight, a current project is to build up his dogteam which is cheaper to use than gas for his snowmobile.

Retreat to the past is the only real option for someone like Nutaraaluk. As he says, 'I have no possibility of getting any other job except as a carver. Younger people who speak English can get jobs but I have absolutely no other choice. As long as I can carve, I am happy. Now I am working hard for less, but I don't want to stop. Some people have stopped carving and now get welfare; they get more money each month from that than I get from carving. I know I could get welfare if I stopped carving, but it's too important to me. I don't want to let it go, even though it means that my life is harder than the lives of those who get welfare or have jobs.'

While it is clear that one reason for the success of carving is its fit with the Inuit lifestyle, Nutaraaluk makes the connection more eloquently than most. 'Sometimes I go on the FM radio, talking to people about the future of all our children. I would like Inuit children to be able to live by carving because this is the only way we will be able to keep our Inuit life. My dream is to have someone who could translate my words into French, so I could go on the television to tell the Quebec government the harm that welfare is causing. People stop carving because they can get welfare. And people accept money from the Hunter Support Programme (one outcome of the James Bay and Northern Quebec Agreement, which provides hunters with a monthly stipend to spend a specified number of days hunting on the land), not realising that they are throwing their lives away. It is so easy for those people to hunt, although hunting is hard work! You Whites have different lives from us. I couldn't live in the South because I get hungry for what we eat. Even when you come here, still we are separated. I see some Inuit trying to get into the White way of life. I'm trying to call them back to the Inuit way. I'm not doing this just because of myself and my family but for all Inuit.'

These words are from a man who lived in an igloo until he was 14, hunting by kayak and dogteam. Those indelible early experiences, when keeping alive took virtually all of one's thought and energies, are still very much in his memory. Indeed, Nutaraaluk has a prodigious memory, able to recall being on his mother's back and even the day of his birth: 'There was a light on my mother's belly and I had to urinate. After I came out, I was very cold and since I wasn't breathing, I was set aside on the bed of willow branches while they looked after my mother. But the pain of the branches made me cry and someone picked me up.'

At his least inspired, Nutaraaluk turns out technically accomplished, but, for him, prosaic pieces. At his best, his work is compellingly tactile. He carves with his hands as much, perhaps more, than with his eyes. When I watched him working, it is obvious that he was reading the surface of the stone with his hands the whole time, enveloping rather than merely holding the rock. He likes to carve large sculptures because 'the big ones feel better in my hands.' Usually his pieces are freestanding, but occasionally he carves a base, following the practice of many contemporary Inuit carvers in Arctic Quebec. Sometimes this practice is aesthetically effective, as in *Woman Braiding Hair* and *Woman Drummer I.*

Nutaraaluk's preferred subject matter is women and bears. Usually, the women are engaged in some household task—dressing skins or braiding a child's hair. Although he works with massive forms, he pays meticulous attention to detail, particularly in his human figures and the depiction of hair, fur and other trim and the folds of a garment. Occasionally he incorporates other substances, such as caribou antler, into the figure. In contrast, his animal figures rely on simple lines with a minimum of detail; he does not attempt to show the fur of the bears nor the scales of the fish, although he has, on occasion, provided detailing of a bird's wings.

The most outstanding feature of Nutaraaluk's female figures is the invariably anguished faces. Even the woman braiding the child's hair is frowning, leading inevitably to speculation that, consciously or not, the model he had in mind was his blind mother. In fact, in this carving the gaze is directed away from the child and the task at hand. Nutaraaluk tells me, however, that he was not carving with anyone particular in mind.

In contrast to the seriousness with which he treats female figures, he takes some licence with his bears, incorporating some of the humour for which he is noted among his townsmen. He has carved dancing bears and also a small bear which, he says, can walk: 'I noticed that most carvings don't move. They just sit there on the shelf. So I made a bear that can rest in either of two positions—just touch it and it walks!'

Nutaraaluk has not yet had a solo exhibition of his work, perhaps because his sculptures are huge and relatively expensive. Four pieces from a private collection in New York were featured in a group show at the Zimmerly Museum in New Jersey in December 1984. Apart from one piece in La Musée de Civilisation in Quebec City and two in corporate collections, his work resides mainly in private collections.

Mattiusi learned to carve by watching Nutaraaluk. Their styles were similar at first, but Mattiusi has now developed a style that is uniquely his. As he says, 'I also learned a few things on my own.' Nutaraaluk, who didn't think it was good that Mattiusi was copying his style, really likes his brother's work, so different from his own. 'It feels to me,' he says, 'as if you are looking at those things from a distance; for example, a real owl from a distance.'

Mattiusi sold his first carving when he was around 14. 'I took a piece of soapstone and started to file on it while my brother was carving. I kept on filing my stone and decided I would make a bird's head. It so happened that Saima Luuku, who was working at the co-op in our settlement, said that I could sell it. My carving was about one inch high and looked like a raven's head. I had not intended it to be that, but that is the way it turned out. That raven's head opened the door to soapstone carving for me.'

It was not until almost fifteen years later (1978-79) that Mattiusi attracted attention in the South with his distinctly personal style. Until then, as he says, 'I was just making ordinary carvings unlike the ones I am making now. I started carving in this manner five or six years ago. I was making a little man and carved it the usual way on one side, but then I got lazy or something, I guess, and just made shapes on the other side. I didn't think it was good enough to sell so I just kept it at home on my shelf. But Peter Ainalik who is now the purchase manager for the co-op told me that the people in the South would like that carving. It was later, when I heard people talking about old carvings, that I started using bone with the soapstone, sometimes ivory, but not often because ivory can't be sold in the States. I guess that's how I developed that style of making abstract shapes and using bone faces.

'I decided to make a simple carving with no details but with a face and boots made of ivory. The figure was holding a fishing line with a fish at the end. This is the way I have been making my sculptures ever since—simple, no details, with bone faces and tools.'

Marybelle Myers

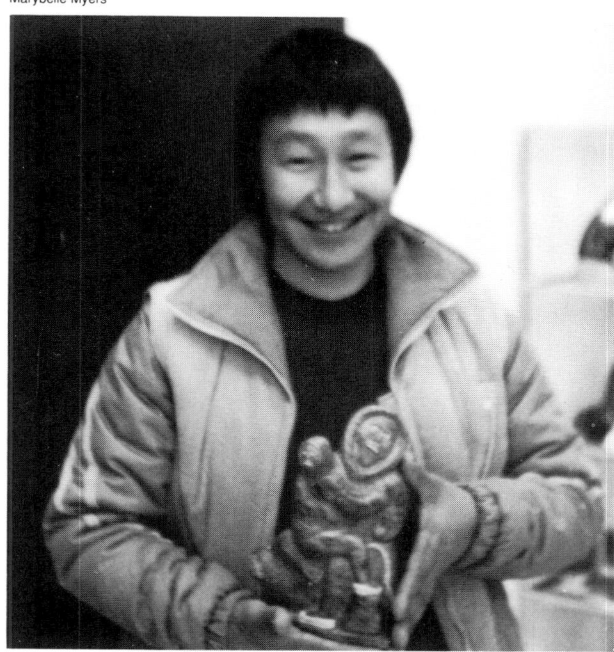

Mattiusi Iyaituk, Ivugivik, 1984.

When asked about his approach to his work, Mattiusi replied, 'Sometimes I get an idea first of what I want to make and I shape the stone into what I have in mind. But sometimes I start chipping and the idea comes.'

He adds, 'Sometimes I leave carving for a few months or days. It's like anything else, when you run out of ideas, it's better to leave it for a while.'

Interestingly, Mattiusi has a habit of making for his family and friends, carvings of things they are frightened of, a sort of inverse talisman. He made a bee for his brother-in-law who is frightened of bees. Similarly, he made his wife, Lydia, a shrimp, 'Because,' as she told me, 'I'm afraid of live shrimps.' Carved in ivory, it is coloured with marking pen and has rope antennae. This shrimp resides in Mattiusi's private collection, housed on the lower shelf of his television stand, which he has lined with red flannel

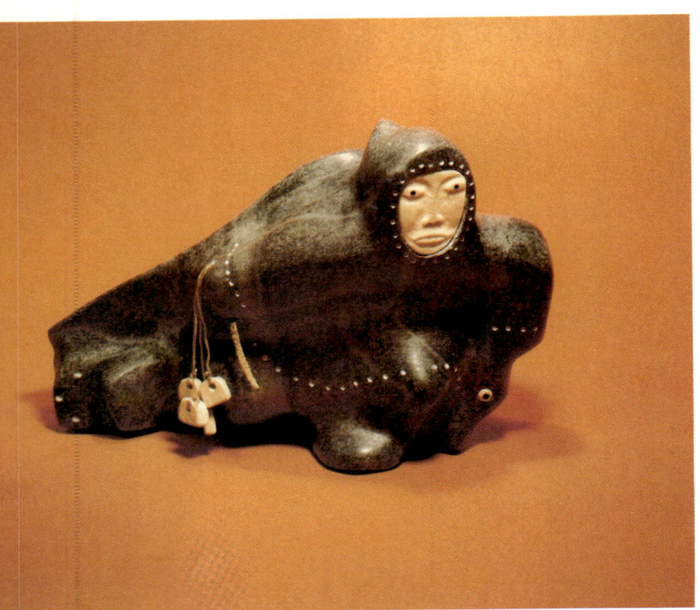

'My Grandfather Catches his First Swan as a Boy', undated, Mattiusi. Soapstone, caribou antler and sinew, 19.2 x 25.7 x 18 cm. Private Collection, San Francisco. Mattiusi: 'Before they had shotguns, they used toggles — but not exactly like this. They would use rocks.'

and illuminated with a light from above. Here he has an assortment of artifacts (a bone needle, pot shards, a handle for a bow drill, harpoon heads) which he has found. He also has carvings, mainly ivory miniatures which have personal significance for him: a ring he made for his little son, a miniature (1" x 2") soapstone *kudlik* containing wax and a wick that can be lit, an ivory puzzle, a fragile ivory chalice, an ivory cup with a handle and several tiny creatures besides Lydia's shrimp. Scattered throughout the house are other personal carvings: a soapstone caribou that he started in Toronto but never finished and, in pink onyx, an egg cup with an eye sitting in it and an ashtray with three eggs. The onyx was a gift from Ted Leishmann, manager of Arctic Showcase in Toronto. While visiting Toronto, Mattiusi had admired an onyx sculpture in the Gallery Phillip and said he'd like some onyx to carve. He also used the block of onyx to carve a walrus which he entitled *A Walrus in a Sunset.*

Mattiusi has a great sense of fun, in spite of his shyness which, he told me, was the consequence of his being sent in 1961 (when he was ten or eleven) to hospital in Clearwater, Manitoba, to be treated for tuberculosis. As he said, 'I had no contact with home for one whole year and I felt really lost. I made some friends after the first few weeks so it wasn't so bad, but there were only people from the Northwest Territories in that hospital and when I finally got home I was only able to speak the Northwest Territories language [dialect]. People always laughed at me, so I stopped talking and have been shy ever since.' It is somewhat ironic that while Nutaraaluk fantasizes about being able to communicate to the South about the vital importance of carving to the Inuit way of life, Mattiusi, who can move with relative ease between the two worlds, for that very reason does not quite share Nutaraaluk's passion about carving. He says: 'Yes, it matters. If I should get tired or quit my job or get disabled and can't work anymore, I would have to carve. I've never thought about it the way Nutaraaluk does, but although I used to say it was my hobby, when I think of it, it's really more than that.'

Mattiusi proves Nutaraaluk's point; it is because he has more choices that carving is a fall-back position for him. He is a constable with the Quebec Provincial Police, having completed training courses in Nicolet and Rouyn-Noranda. Although Lydia says, 'He's more a hunter and a carver than a policeman,' Mattiusi says he likes the job because it gives him 'freedom of movement.' He does worry, however, when shooting is involved. He has a billy stick but no gun, for 'to wear one would be to invite others to wear one as well.' There is a small jail in Ivugivik—an abandoned matchbox house with the best view in town and two cells. It is not used often, but when it is, Mattiusi and another man spell each other off as guards. Lydia agrees that although 'he didn't look for

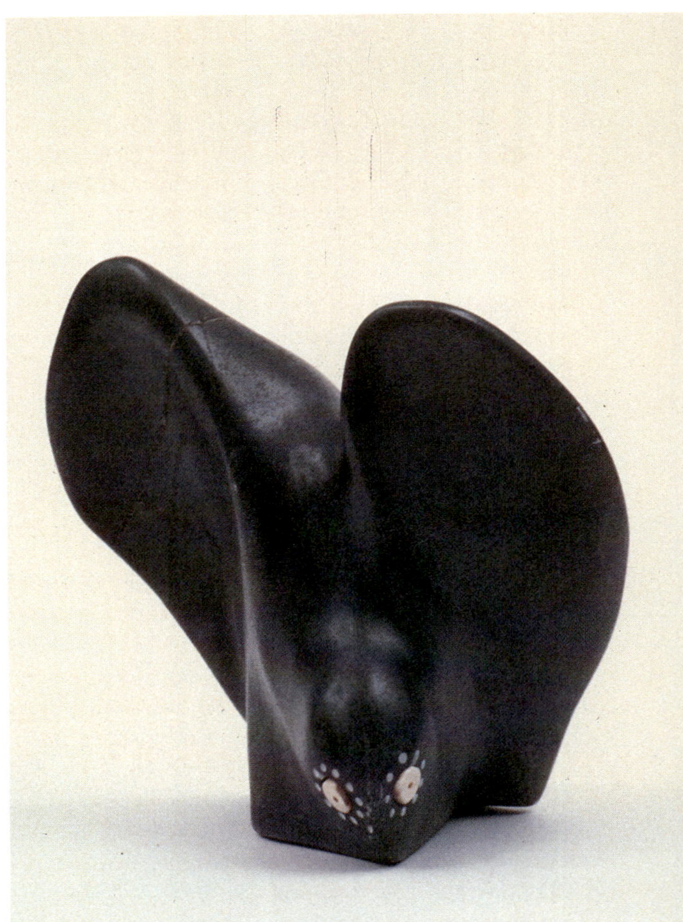

'Bird', 1982, Mattiusi. Soapstone and ivory, 27 x 30 x 17 cm. Collection: Mr and Mrs Samuel Sarick, Toronto.

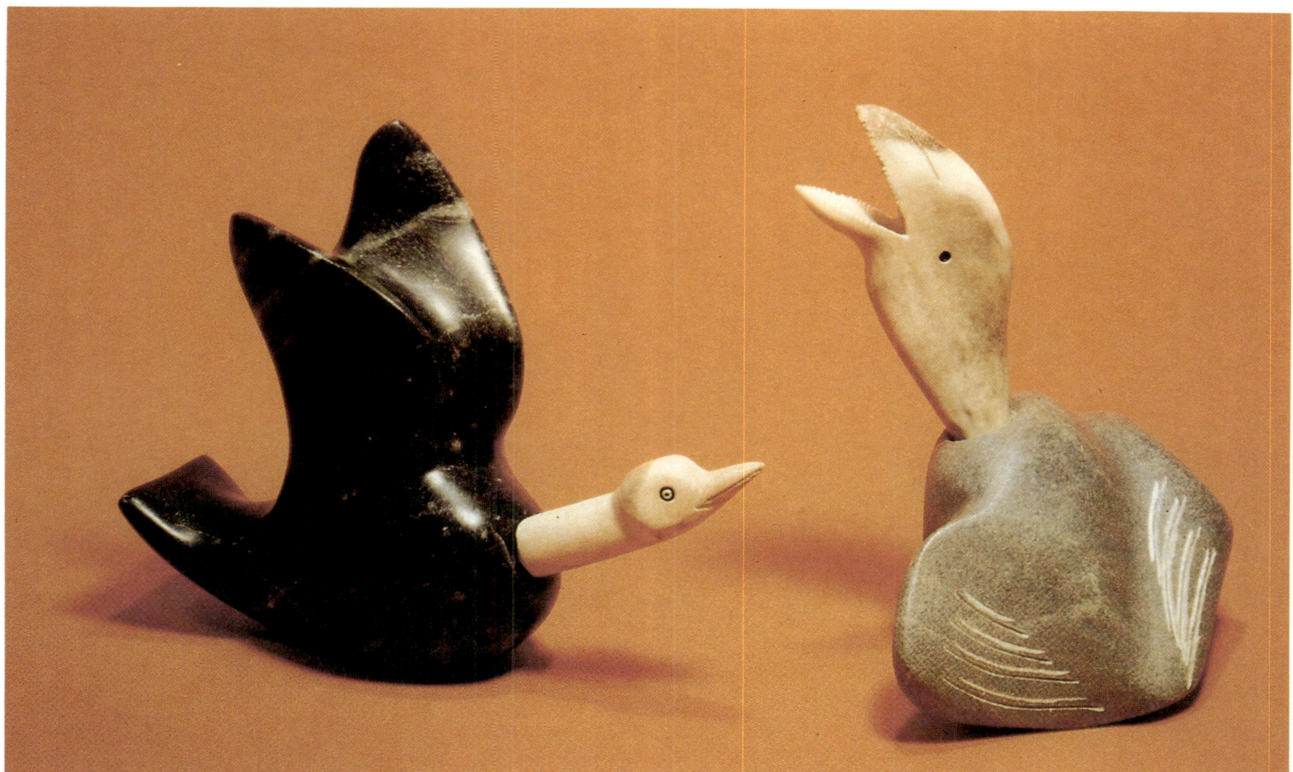

'Flight', Mattiusi. Soapstone, caribou antler.
Collection: Images of the North, San Francisco.
Mattiusi: 'These two birds were not carved as a set.'

'Hungry Bird', Mattiusi. Soapstone, caribou antler.
Collection: Images of the North, San Francisco.
'This is a baby bird ... the teeth are carved right on the bone with a file.'

the job, he doesn't really mind it. The freedom is okay,' she says, 'but the hard part is that you know everybody, how they are, their lives.' Inuit policemen in small villages are sometimes called upon, of course, to deal with members of their own family who break the law.

Even though it is clearly dangerous work, he has a strong social conscience and feels he has a duty to be a policeman ('Somebody's got to do it'); similarly, he considers that even though 'I know that if I want to, I can market my own carvings, it would be selfish of me to sell directly.' For this reason, he continues to support the co-op, although he is approached frequently by people wanting to buy his work directly. Although she has four children ranging in age from one to ten, Lydia also contributes to the household income through her job as Air Inuit agent, issuing tickets and keeping the community informed about flight arrivals and departures. She also helps Mattiusi 'polish and finish his carvings with sandpaper in water. When I see that he's tired but wants to finish it, that's when I help him.'

Mattiusi's sculpture embraces a wider subject range than the work of his brother. An undated biographical statement from Arctic Showcase in Toronto says that Mattiusi's early carvings were all in ivory and then, 'for a few years he seemed to be in a rut, "pot-boiling" one stone kayak after another. It wasn't until the renaissance of the inlay technique that he found the right combination for his fertile imagination.'

Now his subjects are varied and, in spite of his being at home in the modern world, usually drawn from the past. 'I wouldn't put a speed-boat or a ski-doo in a carving.' Ironically, in spite of a style which he and others in his village refer to as 'modern' his subject matter is invariably based on his early history—those first five or six years when he lived in an igloo north of Povungnituk. He prefers to draw on everyday scenes from life at that time—so different from his life now in a house that has been renovated by a recent government project, with running water, a washer and dryer and, as in most houses in Arctic Quebec, the television usually turned on as a backdrop.

There is some controversy surrounding this attitude. Many Inuit believe that in order to sell in the South, carvings must depict the traditional arctic lifestyle, as if it hadn't vanished—as if all Inuit still hunt animals by dogteam and live in igloos. In reality, this culture has been overlaid with a lifestyle seldom depicted in art. Mattiusi says that he has thought about incorporating some elements of his present life into his work, but 'I don't know how to explain it—I just think something might be wrong with them. I make a lot of things for myself and my family but never sell them.' Mattiusi considers his best sculpture

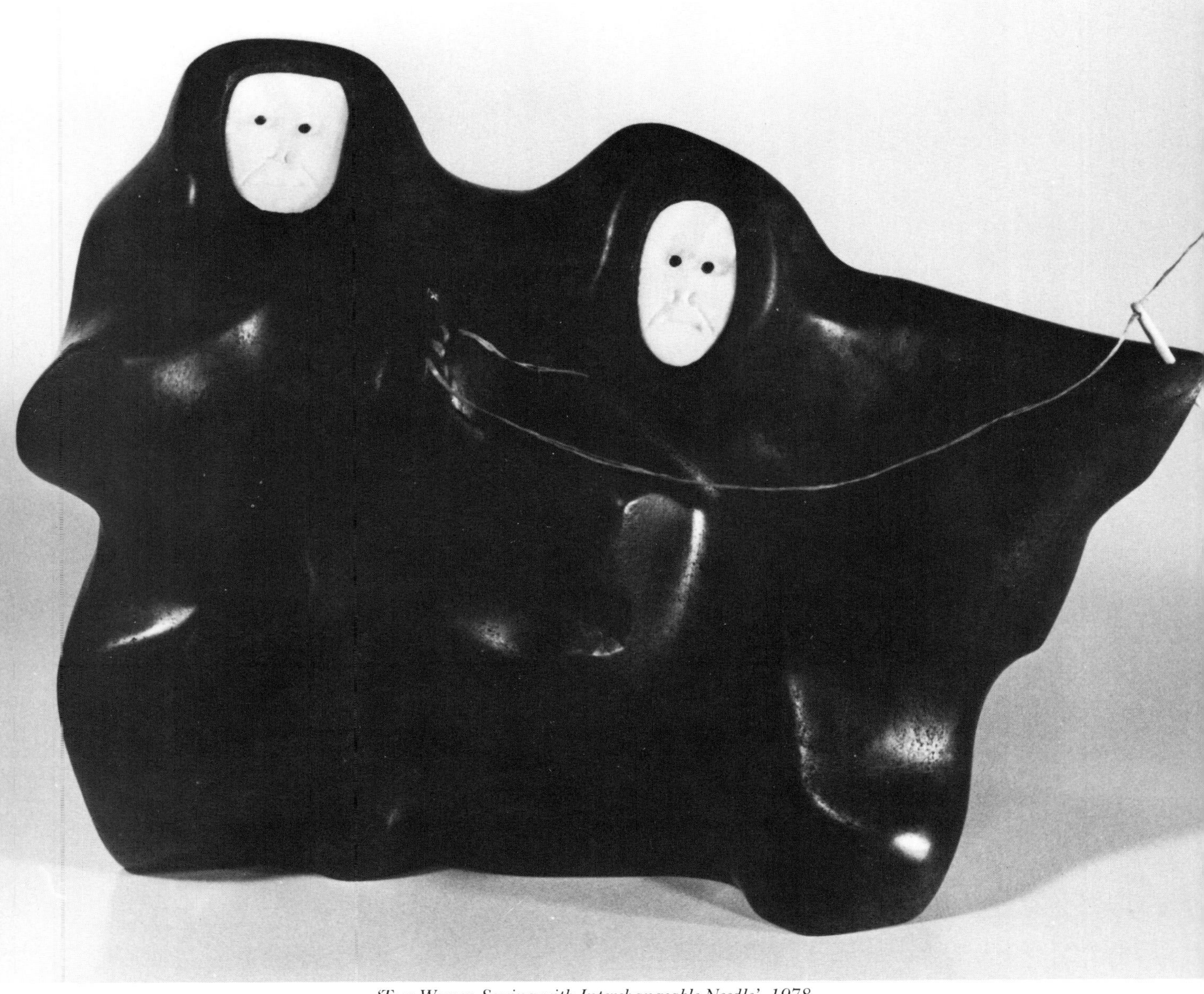

'Two Women Sewing with Interchangeable Needle', 1978.
Soapstone, caribou antler and sinew, 22 x 27 x 16 cm. Collection: D. Stillwell.
Mattiusi: 'Women used to sew together. When making the skin of the kayak they never worked alone.'

to be *The Dream*, but it is not clear whether this is because 'everyone says this is the best' or whether he really has some personal attachment to it. It appears to have been named rather impulsively. Its purchaser asked Mattiusi what it was and 'I had to say something so I said that it was "The Dream" because I had carved a little man asleep in the igloo, and outside there were all kinds of shapes.' Mattiusi is the only Inuk I know who gives titles to his carvings, usually incising them in English on the bottom of the work. He explained that when he started carving, 'People asked me to write down what it was, and I used to do this on a separate piece of paper. These got lost or mixed up, so I later started writing right on the carving itself.'

Shamans have been the subject of only three of his sculptures. Generally he deals with the more prosaic events of life, as indicated by some of the 'story-titles' he bestowed on his work:

> This man was hunting on loose ice. As soon as he caught some seals, he hurried towards solid ice. He didn't even take time to remove the harpoon head from the last seal he caught. Suddenly he met a polar bear. He is trying to hide behind a huge block of ice. He is very frightened but still he won't let go of the seals.

Clearly, Mattiusi experiences these sculptures in much the same way as novelists 'live' their characters. His grandfather, Pita Quiluqi, figures in many carvings; yet his grandfather died before Mattiusi was born, so that he has only heard stories of him.

The fact that Mattiusi now incises his titles on the

'A Dying Bird', 1980.
Soapstone and caribou antler,
15.4 x 33.3 x 17.9 cm.
Collection: Indian Affairs
and Northern Development.
Mattiusi: 'I have heard that people
in the South don't like carvings of
things dying. The rock looked like
a dying bird to me so I chipped
away at it until it looked
like a bird.'

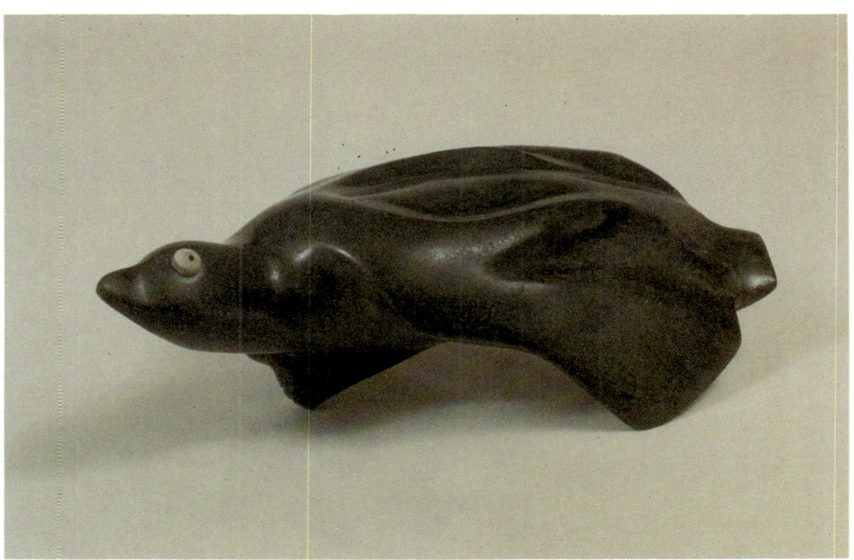

base of his carvings means, of course, that they are shorter, more like conventional titles than the information that was written on the accompanying piece of paper. Now his titles are, for instance, *Shaman Performing his Rituals* and *Family*.

The hallmark of Mattiusi's work is innovation. As he says, 'As far as I can remember, I always liked doing things and making things for myself. I used to make my own toy boats and tried some strange ways to make sleds, like the one I made with a ski in front for driving; it did not work very well.' He uses mixed media: soapstone with caribou antler or ivory inlay. He also incorporates materials such as sinew. Eyes are made with drawing ink. Whereas Nutaraaluk carves hair or fur into the stone, Mattiusi has revived the practice of using dots to suggest parka trim. These are done with a drill, 'an electric drill or bow drill, depending upon where I am working.'

Another very important contrast between the work of the two brothers has been drawn to my attention by Werner Zimmermann, an artist who worked as an advisor to the Pangnirtung printshop. While Nutaraaluk's work is all on the surface of the stone, Mattiusi's sculptures have an inside as well as an outside. His faces of caribou antler or ivory are inserted into the stone, drawing the viewer inside the work. Indeed much of the action in the sculpture is hidden, the bulges in the stone giving only a hint of what is going on inside. This effect is clear when one looks at Mattiusi's carvings. *A Young Hunter's First Catch* works because, through consummate skill, Mattiusi has managed to convey the impression of real, living people. The faces are buried in the stone, which undulates with life.

The faces of Mattiusi's sculptures are invariably realistic, while the rest of the carving is stylised. Like those of Nutaraaluk, these faces are usually grim, but this is typical of Inuit sculpture: a contrast to south-

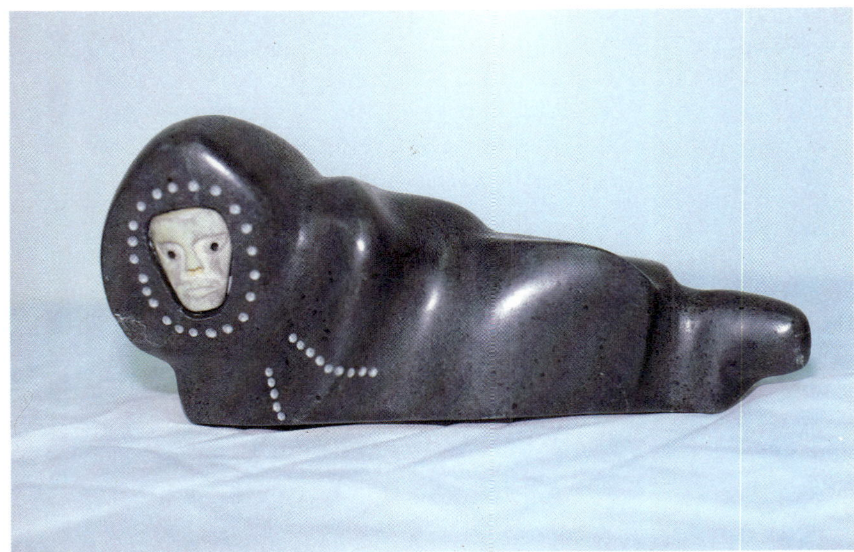

'Woman Resting', 1976.
Soapstone and caribou antler,

Collection: Miss Boyadjian, Toronto.

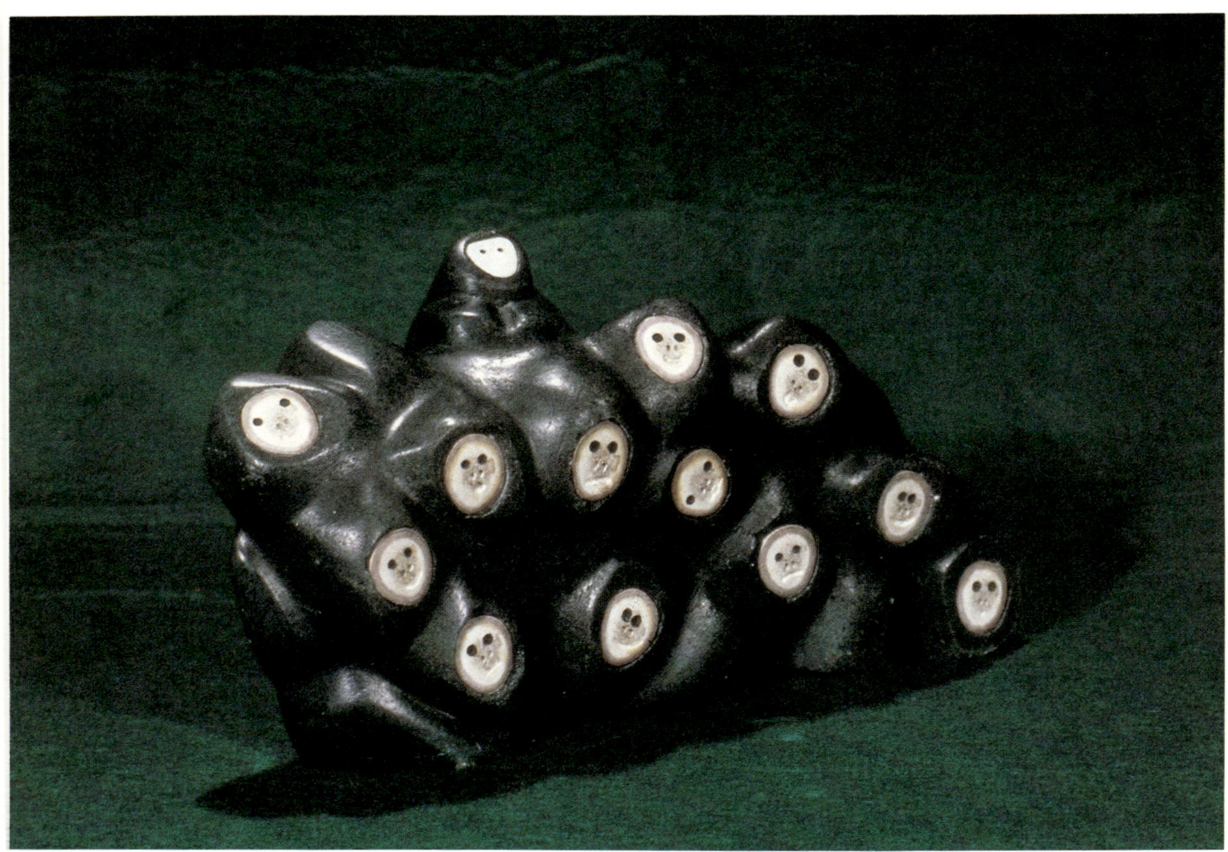

'A Young Hunter's First Catch', 1979.
Soapstone, caribou antler and walrus ivory,
18.5 x 34.5 x 11 cm. Collection: Things Made by Inuit,
La Fédération des Coopératives du Nouveau-Québec.

Mattuisi (from text of 'Things Made by Inuit'): 'The small ivory face at the top represents a boy who has returned home with his first seal. Below him, symbolized by caribou antler faces, are all the women of the village, happy to share in the feast.'

ern stereotypes of the happy Inuit. I mentioned this to Mattiusi who said he's never thought about it. But 'It gives me an idea. I'll try to make a happy carving.'

In 1981 Mattiusi attended a one-man show of his work at the Images of the North Gallery in San Francisco. He, with his wife Lydia, also attended the Third Conference of Canada's Peoples—Cultural Contributions in York, Pennsylvania in 1983 where several of his carvings were on exhibit; in spite of his reticence, he successfully responded to questions at the seminar and was a 'great hit' according to conference co-ordinators. In August 1984, Mattiusi was awarded a Canada Council Explorations grant so that he could produce work for a solo exhibition based on his own conception.

Seven years of varying opportunities have made a world of difference for Mattiusi and one might hope that his is an example of the direction other Inuit youth may take—carving not so much from necessity as inclination. But then, he was born in a snowhouse and influenced by parents and siblings living very much in the old style. He has the same roots as his older brother Nutaraaluk, and without that early training and experience he might not have been able to straddle the two worlds so comfortably. It is the younger people, born in settlements and unable to live on the land, who are struggling to find a purpose in their lives. Fortunately for both Nutaraaluk and Mattiusi, they have clear goals and the resources to achieve them.

Author's note: Since this letter was written in November 1984, Mattiusi has had a highly successful one-man show at the Canadian Guild of Crafts in Toronto. He has resigned his position as police officer and now spends all his time hunting and carving.

Nutaraaluk continues to carve and, happily, sales have improved in the South and the Inuit are now receiving larger advances for their work. The two brothers recently purchased a new Peterhead boat, larger than the one they had, and when I spoke to Mattiusi on August 8, 1987, by telephone, they were planning a trip to Cape Dorset for soapstone. ♦

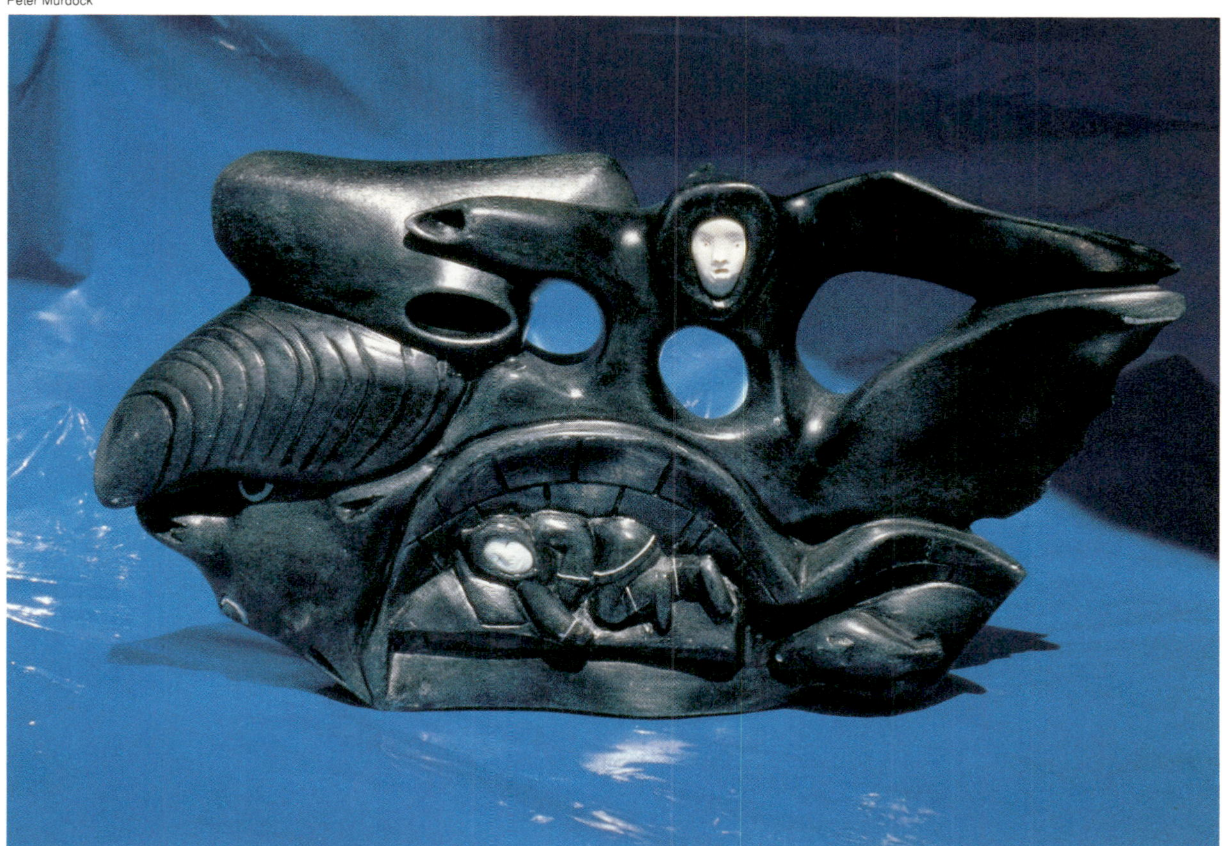

'The Dream', (front view above), 1978.
Soapstone and ivory, 22 x 42 x 8 cm.
Collection: Dorothy McDaniel.

Mattiusi: 'This man was hunting and he had to haul a seal all the way home. He got tired, went to sleep and had those dreams.'

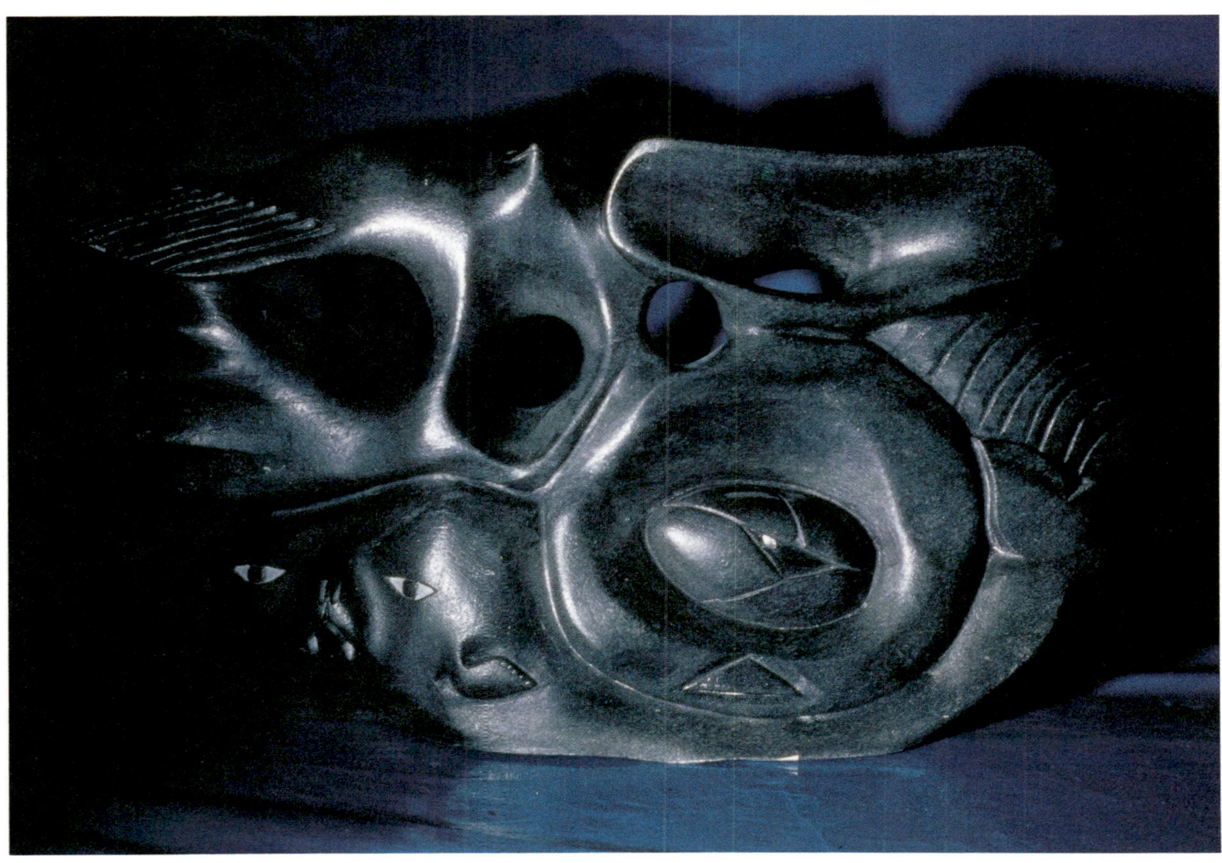

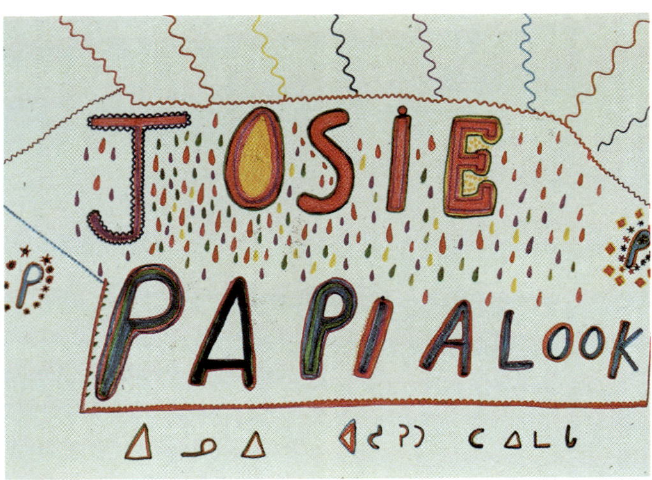

By Marybelle Myers

INDIVIDUALITY IS NOT THE SHIBBOLETH to Inuit that it is to some Southerners. Since no Inuk willingly makes himself conspicuous above his fellows, in life or in art, it is hardly surprising that Inuit art tends towards a common style. Collectors with even a little experience can usually pinpoint accurately the region or village where a particular piece was produced. What is surprising is that, in spite of the value placed on homogeneity of the group, some Inuit have managed to sustain a strongly individualistic style in their everyday life and in their work. Josie Papialook, or Paperk as he was earlier called, is a sculptor and graphic artist, one of those individuals who, drawing his imagery and his strength from Inuit tradition, sees things differently than his fellows and unabashedly follows his bent.

George Swinton has referred to Papialook's work as 'decorative realism'; it could also be called 'naive realism', for he is an ageless child, at once both mystified by and unafraid of nature. Knowledge comes to him through all of his senses—hearing, seeing, feeling—and, unlike more conventional folk, he does not distinguish among them. It makes sense to him to include both tangible and intangible elements in his pictures since both are features of what he knows to be reality. Speech and motion patterns are as real to him as the beings generating them and it doesn't occur to him not to draw the chatter and the footprints of his creatures. Similarly, he gives shape to the surrounding air and the movements people and animals make as they walk, fly or swim through it.

Although Papialook is an eccentric in a village of carvers committed to a technically flawless rendition of reality, he, of course, draws on the same cultural consciousness as do his contemporaries. Born inland from Povungnituk around 1918, he lived the 'Old Way' for most of his life and has first-hand knowledge of the hunting camps where people lived in igloos and hunted by kayak. In spite of times when food was scarce and death by starvation a likely outcome, life 'on the land' was more comprehensible to Inuit than it is now in towns. Beginning in the mid-1950s, Inuit abandoned their family-based camps and moved into administrative centres. The closest centre to Papialook was Povungnituk where, since the death of his wife, Martha, in 1978, he has lived with Peter, a son now in his late twenties. He used to have 'lots of relatives' he says, but 'they're all dead now'. His mother died when he was quite young but when his father died Josie was old enough to bury him.

Papialook doesn't live the life of a bachelor by choice. When I saw him in 1978, he told me of an unsuccessful overture he had made to the father of a young girl from nearby Inoucdjouac. Lucy caught his eye while she was visiting in Povungnituk and, deciding that she would make a good wife, Papialook pursued the project, following her on the plane back to Inoucdjouac. This is the way he tells the story.

'With all this white hair, I must be pretty old. But I don't get the pension yet. I tried but I couldn't get it. I also tried to get a new wife but didn't succeed. I went to Inoucdjouac, trying to get a new wife, a nice young girl.

'I didn't ask her. I was arguing about it with her

The title design is by Josie Papialook.
Photographs by the author.

From *The Beaver,* Summer 1982

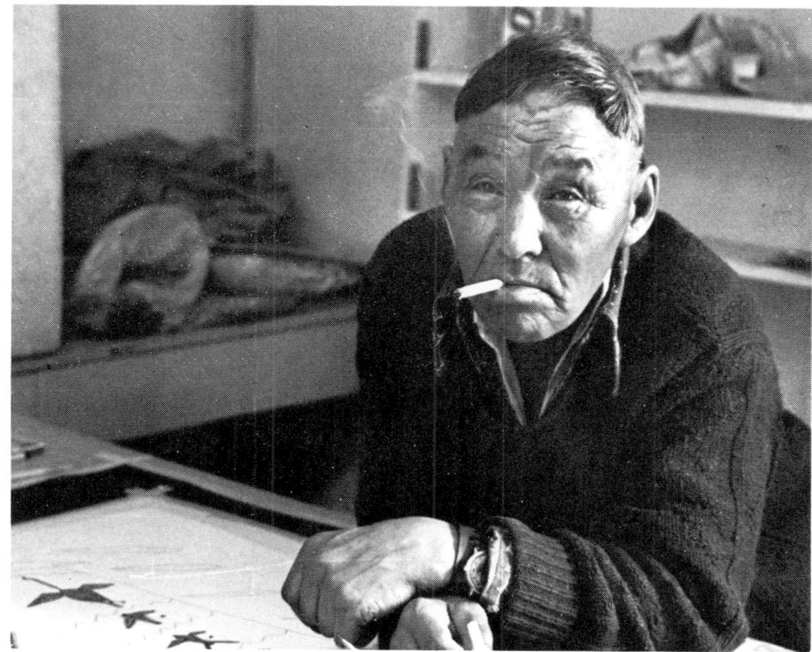

Josie Papialook (also called Josie Paperk in the Povungnituk print catalogues), sculptor and graphic artist, in the Povungnituk printshop.

father on the plane. I followed that girl all the way to Inoucdjouac. When we got there, I went to her place but I left the next morning while everyone was still asleep. I gave up because her father didn't want me. I came back to Povungnituk without a wife.'

'Have you given up?'

'I haven't given up but I just don't know where to look. It's really bad in my house with no wife. It wasn't so hard to find a wife in the old days.'

Everyone laughs when Josie tells this story. Well liked, he is considered something of a joker in his village. Like a child, he is always responsive to silly jokes. Like all jokers, however, he appreciates the seriousness of humour.

Whatever else it may be, carving for Josie is a handy way to supplement his income:

'I earn my living by carving and welfare. I wanted a canoe once and I walked off to find some stone. I used to just stop and carve right on the spot whenever I found stone.'

Certainly, although it portrays many of the same elements, the humour and the choice of birds and small animals as subject matter, Papialook's carving plays a secondary role to his graphics. Stone is obviously a clumsier medium for him but, in spite of its restrictions, he manages to imprint the Papialook style. A favourite theme in sculpture is fish with funny snouts, and birds of wistful appearance. Often, the birds are on a base decorated with finely scratched flowers or footprints, and the fish on a bed of waves. Occasionally, he carves figures or masks but these are less successful than his small creatures.

Although Papialook used to spend a lot of time with some of the great carvers in Povungnituk—Davidialuk and Joe Talirunili—he acknowledges no influence:

'Nobody taught me how to carve. I learned by myself. One time, I just sawed off a piece of very hard stone and started carving.'

Papialook sculptures, always small, can be held comfortably in the hand. Like his late contemporary, Talirunili, Papialook doesn't hide his lack of technical finesse. Imperfections in the stone are not carved away but circled in case anyone should miss them. Occasionally, he even carves stitches around a flaw in the stone as one would sew a patch on the knee of trousers. The bottom of the carvings are usually adorned with his signature, 'Josie P. Papialook', a version of his name which he adopted a few years ago. His name and signature require some explanation.

Without his doing, his name has been variously spelled. Until 1966, it was commonly rendered as 'Papi' or 'Puppy' which is more phonetically apt than 'Paperk' (meaning tail) which came into usage in print catalogues in 1966. In the late 1970s, he began signing his prints and carvings, 'Josie P. Papialook' with the middle initial usually circled. 'Papialook', literally translated, means 'Big Tail'. The change was made, Josie says, 'because my father's real name was Papialook'. The middle initial 'P' is one of those things which struck his fancy and was adopted as his own. It is a take-off from the copyright sign © which Inuit were advised several years ago to incise into the bottom of their carvings to thwart reproduction. By 1978, and in his drawings particularly, Papialook began to display a fascination with his name, sometimes utilizing it as the sole image in his drawings.

Some highly embellished renditions are enclosed in an arrow, an idea he picked up during a trip south when he observed that 'white men draw arrows to show you which way you're going'.

He once painted his name in all its splendour on the water tank sitting on the counter in the printshop. The tank already had a big 'P' (for Povungnituk) stamped onto it and this served as all the inspiration Josie needed to set to work on yet another name drawing. He once said that his best art consists of writing his name in the snow because 'it goes into the air and stays forever'.

It is my impression that Papialook's carvings are more of a personal joke than a labour of love. Paper and ink, however, opened a whole new world to him. He is best known to collectors as a graphic artist and his love of the medium is obvious. He was one of the first people in Povungnituk to become involved in printmaking although, in the last few years, drawing has become a preferred activity. Undoubtedly this preference is due to the fact that drawing, being a freer medium, allows for the expression of a naturally flamboyant nature. It also allows for greater sociability. After Martha died, Papialook was lonely and his productivity declined. He began going to the printshop every day. He couldn't carve there, of course, because the dust would have gotten into the ink. He tried printing some of his own stonecuts but candidly concluded that he is 'too messy to print a whole edition'. Eventually, he set up shop in a corner, leaning on a counter and drawing for hours on end.

Papialook approached printmaking and, later, drawing, in his typically ingenious way, establishing personal conventions in subject matter and style right at the beginning. Although his drawings are more far-ranging in subject matter than are his prints and carvings, birds remain a favourite theme in all media. There is no mystery about this choice of subject. With typical candour, Papialook says, 'I like to draw birds because I'm not very good at drawing a man'. He claims that he takes pains to achieve a realistic portrayal of whatever he draws even though his unique perceptions of reality obscure this avowed concern with accuracy. He often draws a bird with one foot visible or a bird with one wing, 'since the other one is behind him'. Untutored in perspective, these 'realistic subjects often appear to be balanced on one foot or aerodynamically unsound. Occasionally, he resorts to symbolic representations of real objects. An igloo may be depicted by a grid containing a coiled sealskin rope. A box drawn around the image or a solitary figure may represent a tent.

When describing the subjects of his work, Papialook invariably uses the historical present tense as in, 'This woman is going to put a sealskin out to dry and after that she is going to eat the fish.' He sees his drawing not as completed action but as dynamic, all parts related in some kind of imminent action.

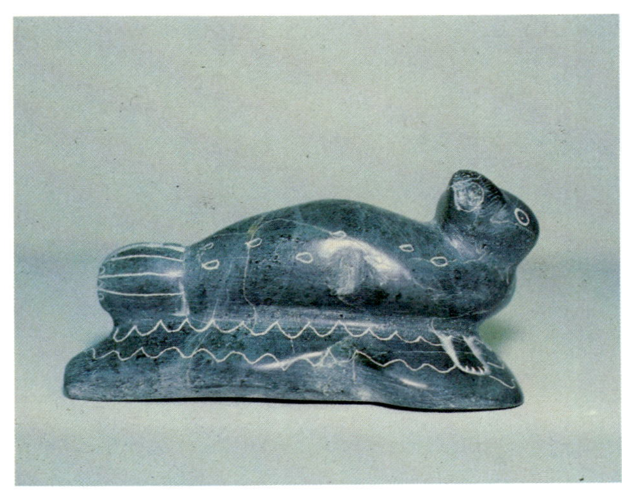

'Seal Floating on a Bed of Waves'. Sculpture by Josie Papialook.

The stars around a figure's head indicate 'his really cold breath' but 'he doesn't go into the igloo to get warm because he doesn't like the people inside. Also, it's too dark in there and he likes the light.'

In a 1965 print, *Bird Hunting* (Povungnituk 1965) the bird has been drawn outsize and the fish in its stomach. I did not discuss this print with him but feel sure that he would say, 'The bird has just eaten a fish' or 'I know that birds eat fish.' Our conception of realistic portrayal would be to show only the exterior of the bird; to show, in other words, only what we can see with our eyes. Papialook, however, sees no reason to exclude certain knowledge even though it cannot, at that moment, be perceived visually. This may make good sense since paper and ink do not mimic the reality of life but merely represent it. We can write 'The bird ate the fish' in letters which convey information. Why not in pictures? Wasn't that the first use of pictures?

The presence of moving 'wind' is one of the profound realities of Papialook's existence and he includes it in all of his graphic work with a few exceptions. The 1962 stonecut print *Building a Snowhouse* (Povungnituk 1962), is a crude first attempt at printmaking. As was customary in early prints from Povungnituk, all of the action is contained within the stone, the image being merely incised and the outer edge of the stone left for printing. In a forerunner of what later became a Papialook hallmark, he has portrayed the wind by vague, wiggly lines. In the same year, in what must surely have been a later attempt at the same theme, he has achieved a more complex wind-pattern in *Building an Igloo* (Povungnituk 1962). Here, the wind pattern may be general or emanating specifically from the man. This print also contains another Papialook convention, the engraving of the footprints of his subjects 'to show how they got there'. In a much later drawing (1978) he showed not only the footprints his bird subject made as it walked but

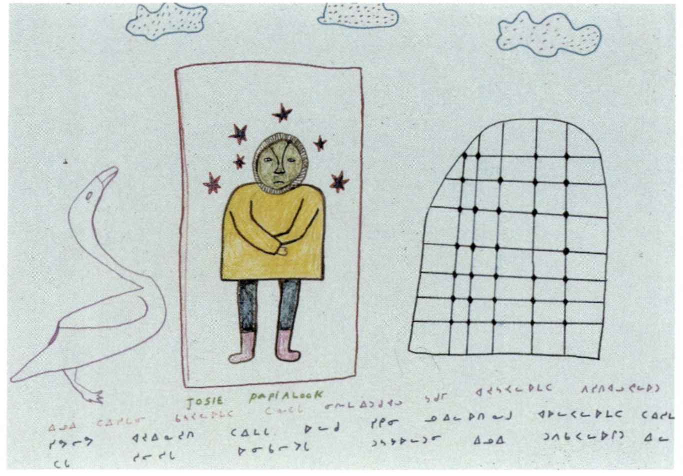

In this drawing by Papialook, the stars around the figure's head indicate 'his really cold breath'; the box drawn around him may represent a tent. The artist's work has been exhibited by The Canadian Guild of Crafts in Montreal, The Raven in Minneapolis and the Marion Scott Gallery in Vancouver.

Papialook was the first artist at Povungnituk to decide the colours for his stone engravings. Below is his engraving 'During the Time it Blows, Kopinuak, the Songbird, Flies'. Povungnituk, 1978.

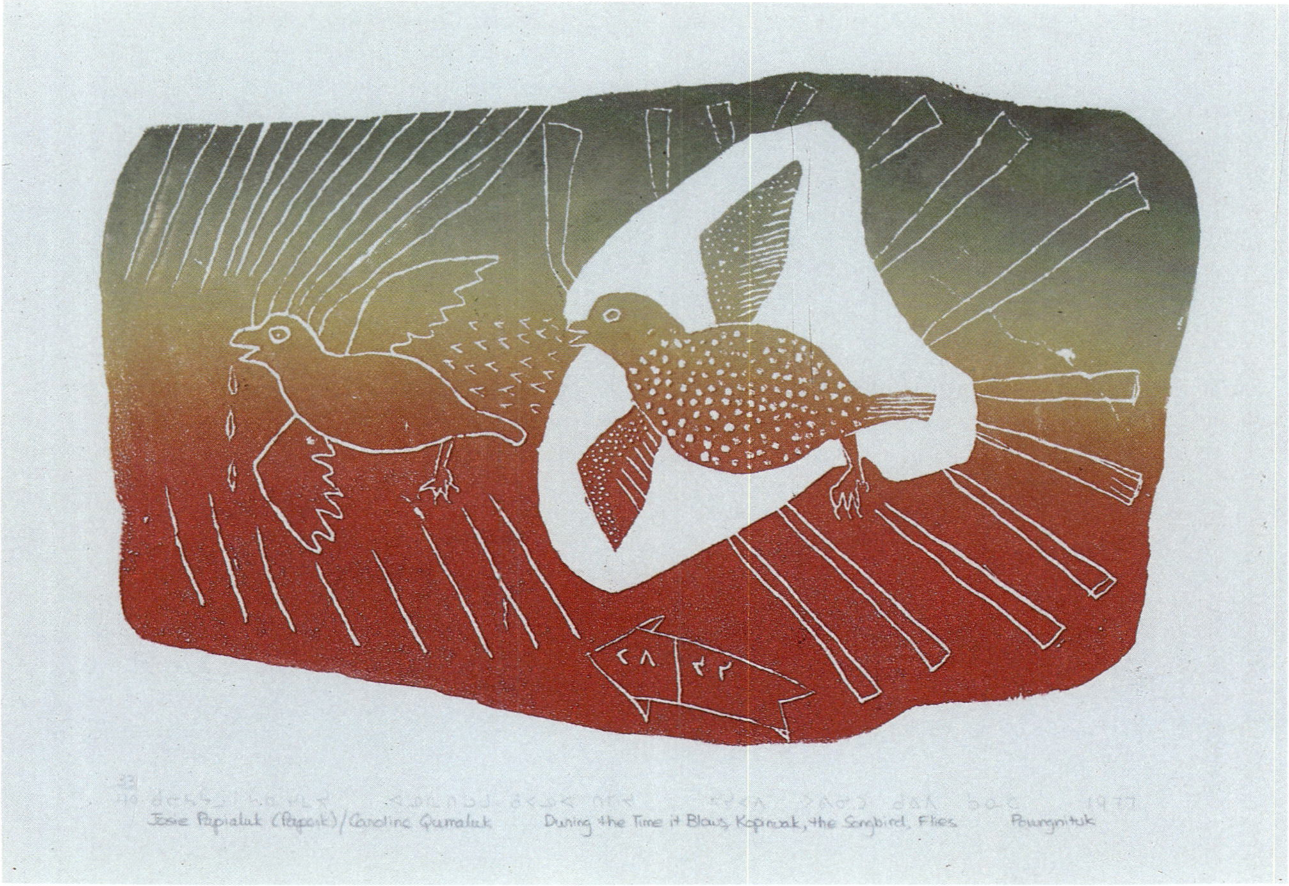

also included the marks it made when it scraped to a stop, 'the scratches from the wings when he landed'.

His drawing of motion cannot be reduced to a formula although the more intense the action, the more intense the rendition. The wind is, he says, always different colours and shapes.

'There are all different kinds of wind. Yes, all different kinds. Some very strong and some not strong enough. Sometimes, it makes clouds and rain. It is also all different colours.'

'Where does the wind come from?'

'I think the wind comes from the clouds. I don't believe it comes from the ground. But I *do* believe winds come from up high. There are, however, some winds which are close to the ground.'

'Where does it go?'

'I can't imagine what happens to the wind when

it leaves the ground. I really don't know where it goes. I feel it all around but I cannot find out where it comes from and where it goes.'

'Have you ever seen the wind?'

'Yes. I see it almost every day. I feel it strongly. That's how I see it. Not with my eyes but with my hands and face. The wind is different all the time. It never stays the same. That's the way it is. My younger brother died one time when the wind caused drifting snow. That was a long time ago when we were hunting on foot together and a big storm came. It was sad. I almost froze my hands at that time, digging in the snow which was piled up by the wind.'

There is even, Paperk says, air or wind under the water, causing it to move and to form waves.

'I think there must be wind under the water. Also, I think there is wind under the ice because when you cut a hole through the ice a lot of water wants to come up.'

In a 1978 drawing, *A Bird We Never Saw*, Papialook has drawn the creature's breathing in a leaf-like

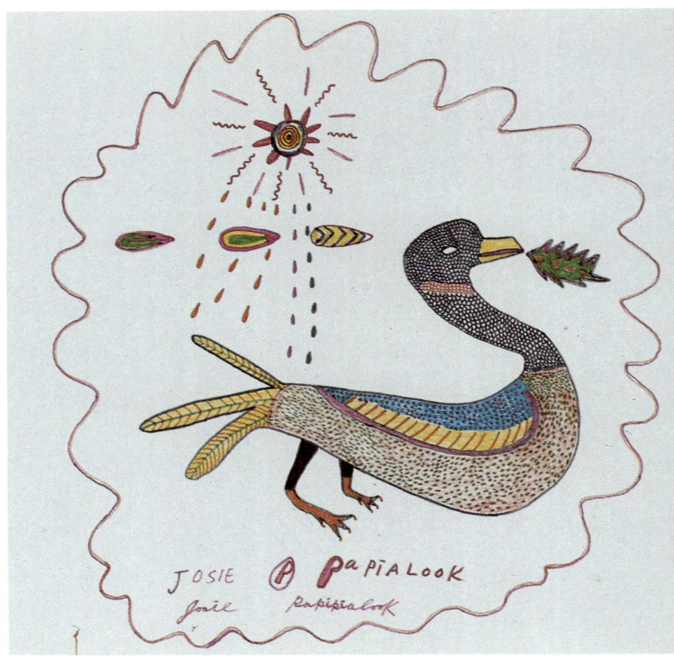

'A Bird We Never Saw' by Papialook. In this 1978 drawing, purple and blue lines represent the wind coming from the sun. The orange and blue drops are 'tears'.

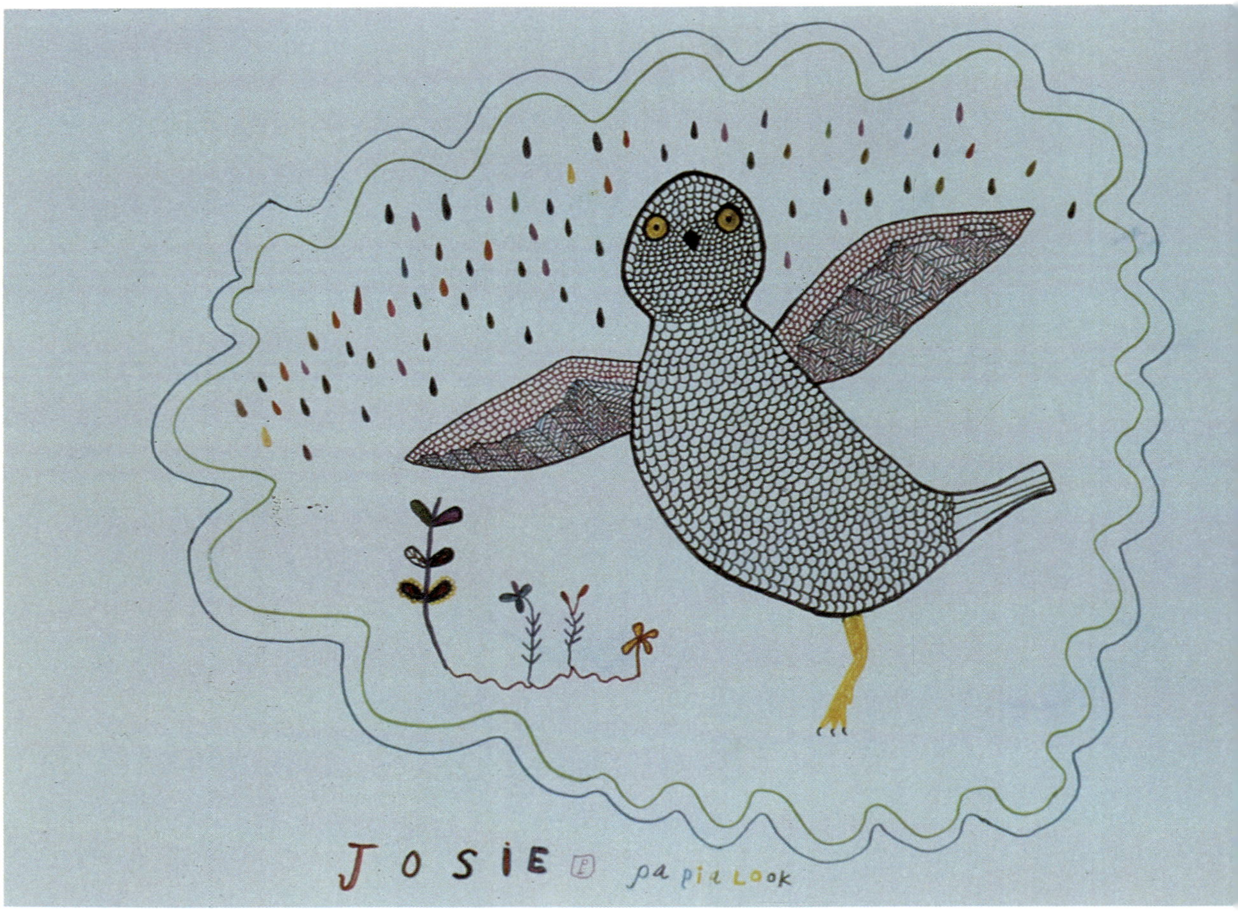

Papialook's drawing of a bird flying in the rain and surrounded by a circle of the wind.

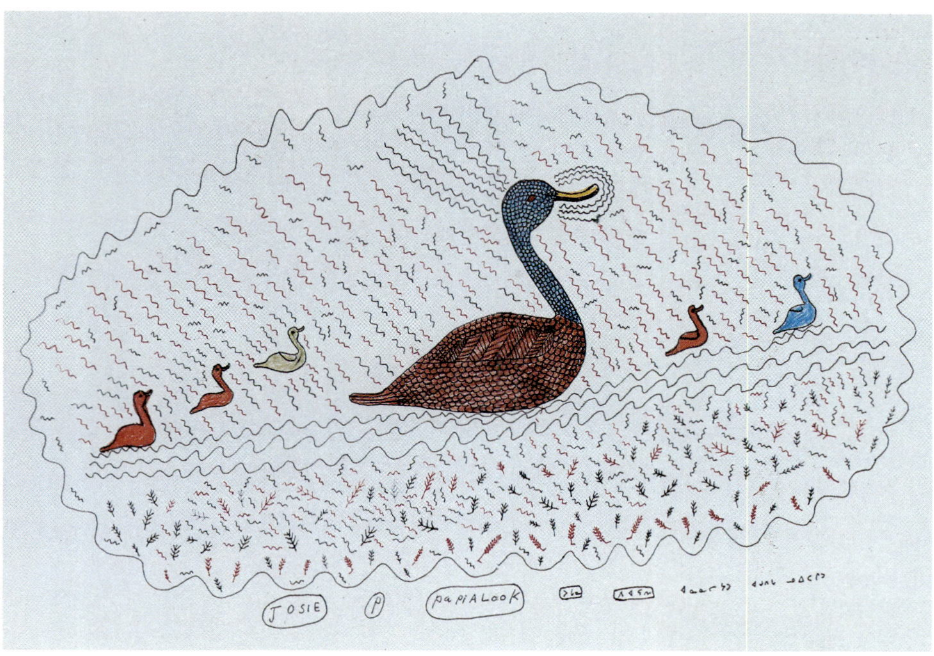

The depiction of wind, rain and sound, are hallmarks of Papialook's graphic art.

configuration with the three colourful feather-like shapes behind the head representing the breath 'going out behind him'. The dazzling motif in the upper right is the sun, engaged in a dynamic of its own while the straightforward purple and blue lines represent the wind coming from the sun. The orange, purple and blue drops are 'the tears from the sun as it sighs and cries towards the land'.

The wind is always present in his work, often encircling the image, and it is tempting to draw an analogy to the Povungnituk tradition of leaving the edge of the printing stone as a boundary for their engraved images. The only motivation for this appears to be a desire to show all of the elements. Things don't just float in nothingness. They are contained in an atmosphere, or a stone block.

Papialook does not separate himself from his work. Like a child, he is the centre of his own universe and the subject of much of his graphic work. In 1978, he drew two curious self-portraits in which he has red hair and tattooing, a practice formerly indulged in by Inuit women who pulled soot-blackened needles under the skin. Predictably enough, Papialook's townsmen and admirers find these so-called portraits outrageously funny. Apart from the self-portraits, it appears that Papialook is the subject of several of his drawings and prints. The 1964 catalogue included a poorly engraved print called *Fishing*. The interesting thing about this work is the appearance of an enigmatic face on the lower right. It has been carved in such a way as to utilize the outer edge of the stone as the boundary of the face. It may have been that the shape left after carving the main image suggested itself to Josie as a face or, it may be, in view of his lack of distinction of gender, that this is intended as a self-portrait.

Mask imagery pops up from time to time in his work and, always, the faces are tattooed. In the early years, the mask is secondary to the main action, brooding over it as an outside observer. Later, it becomes central as in *Face*, a full-blown portrait surrounded by barely incised creatures — a fish on the left, a bird and a seal on the right and all with their motion-specific indicators.

This print, incidentally, reveals a new interest in colour for Povungnituk printmakers. It was printed in orange, black and yellow, colours which would have been chosen by the shop manager and Annie Amamatuak who did the actual printing. At that time, the artist who did the drawing and/or the stonecut had no input to the actual printing. For fifteen years, the printshop had been dominated by four or five women trained to ink and pull the prints. Artists would cut their stones and bring them to the print-shop to sell and that was the end of their involvement.

Interestingly enough, the colour used in *Face* could as easily have been chosen by Papialook himself. It is quite in keeping with the choices he made for prints catalogues in 1978 when Werner Zimmermann, a consultant who worked with the Povungnituk printshop for two years, encouraged the artists to provide critical input to the printing of their work. Josie was the first to come in to decide the colours for his stone engravings. With no hesitation, he chose rainbows of primary colours—melding bands of orange with red and blue with green. These two stones had already been proofed in black and the difference between those and the proofs pulled by Josie in colour was dramatic. A sure instinct had guided him to colour which enhanced rather than smothered his imagery. This was a taste of what would soon, in his felt-pen drawings, appear as an obvious inclination towards flamboyant colour. In contrast to the drawings, many of his early prints appear drab and heavy. This is undoubtedly due to the solid dark inking which deadened the essential gaiety of his imagery. Josie put it simply: 'Colour makes my prints look better.'

Apart from the lift provided by his choice of buoyant colour, the Papialook prints in the 1978 collection are noteworthy for their improved technique. *Whistling Swans with Their Young on the Ground* is a very fine print, conveying a new feeling of precision. One stencil was included in this collection, *A Duck with Outspread Wings*. It was cut by Leah Amituk from a drawing by Josie and although it is recognizable as a Papialook bird, it seems rather bare without his customary accessories, footprints and movement indicators. It has a distinctly unfinished quality, as often happens when the work of one artist is interpreted by another.

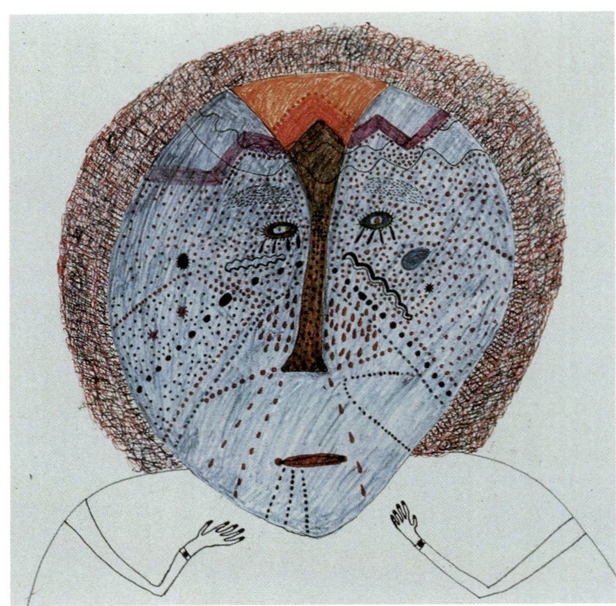

A curious self-portrait, with the tattoo marks that were fashionable with Inuit women of earlier generations.

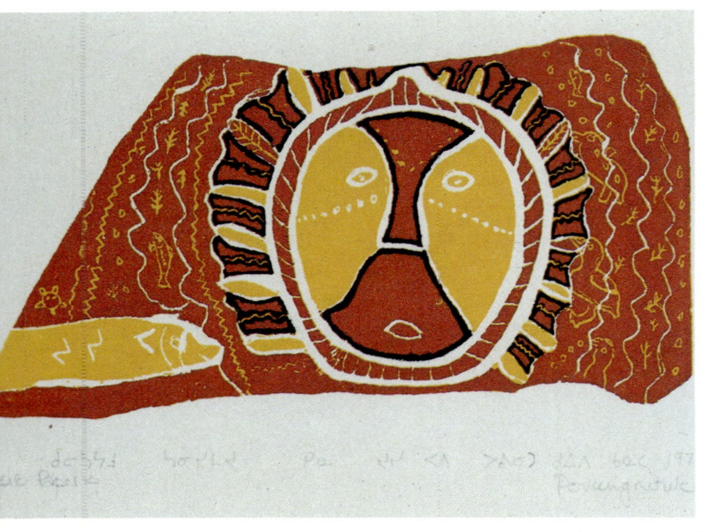

'Face', a portrait surrounded by a fish (left) and a bird and seal (right), with their motion indicators. Povungnituk, 1975.

Seagull Singing, which was cut by Papialook himself, is a genuine departure or rather, an aberration in style. Here, he has completely and uncharacteristically freed the image from the stone and made the sound and motion patterns as well as the footprints, more precise. This print was made after a workshop conducted in the community by Bob Paterson and it may be that it is evidence of an outside influence or, at least, a different attention to technique. Whatever it was, it was only temporary. *Making a Snow House* signals a reversion to earlier themes and styles. Once again, the figure is in partial relief with the shape of the stone left to contain the imagery.

In *Fixing an Igloo in Winter* (Povungnituk, 1980) Papialook has, I think, been more successfully interpreted by Josie Sivuarapik, a young newcomer to printmaking. Although the print, a combination serigraph and stencil, is quite unlike any of Papialook's previous work, it is uncannily his. The feeling is his, although the rendition could not be.

Colour can bring a print to life but so can titles. The selection of titles was always rather tricky since Povungnituk prints arrived in the South with only syllabic titles and rarely was there an Inuk available to translate. The necessity of rushing into print with the catalogue in order that the prints could go on sale within a few months of their receipt meant that there was little time to seek out a proper translation. Titles were bestowed, often, by reference to the obvious action. Needless to say, discrepancies occurred because what was obvious to the Inuit artist might not be so obvious to the non-Inuit observer. It was often the case that the real meaning of a work would be obscured by a safe but lacklustre title such as *Man and Bear*. Sometimes, an Inuk would later comment on what was really going on in a particular print or translate the syllabics and the whole thing instantly took on a new life. I remember that in 1976, Ali Tulugak, a very competent translator, was available for translation. Consequently, some 1976 prints, particularly those of Josie P. Papialook, were rendered infinitely

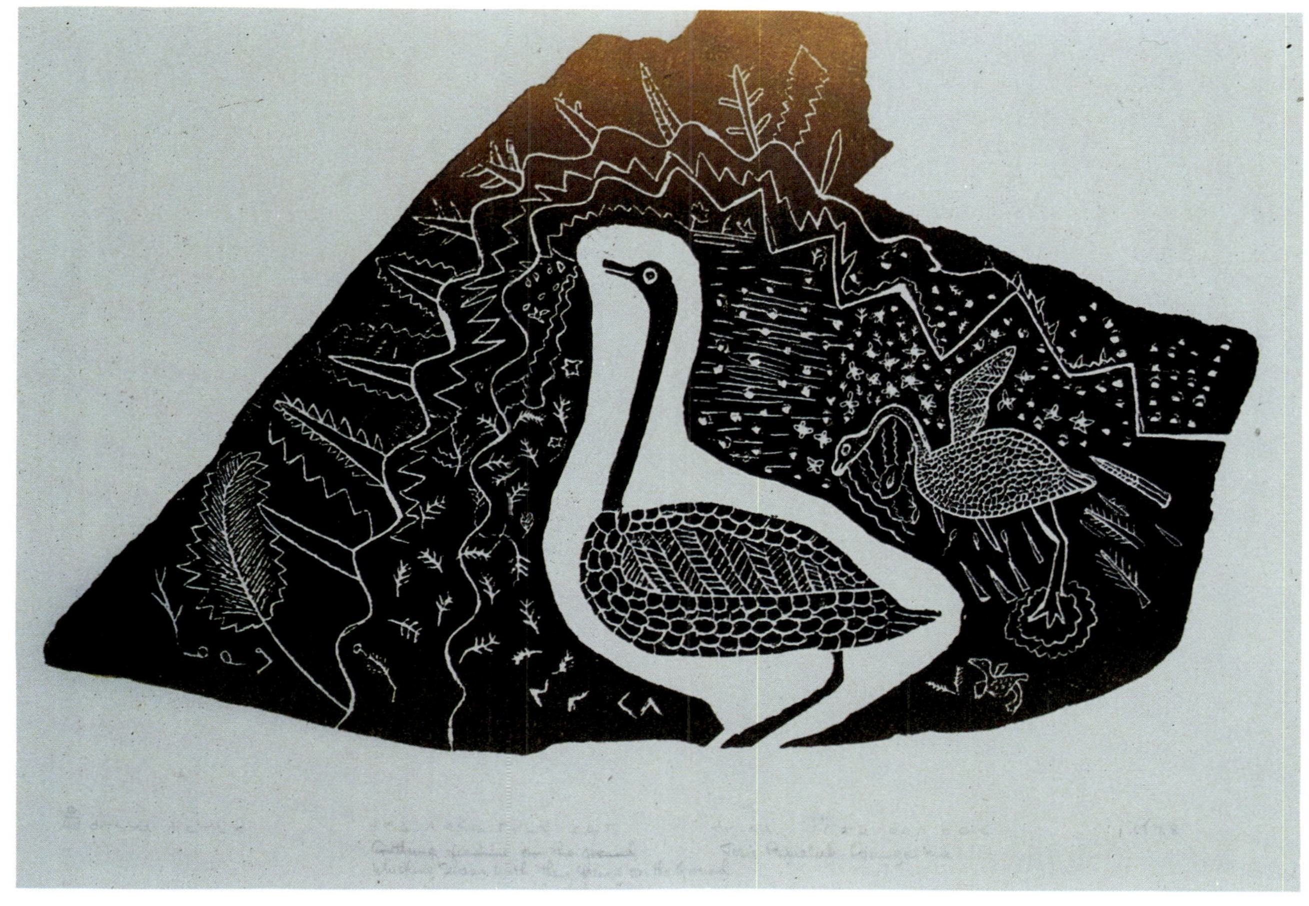

'Whistling Swan with Young on the Ground'. Povungnituk, 1978.

more appealing. Compare *Man Opens His Arms to Nature* with *Fishing* or *Face.* The 1976 titles of Papialook's prints are, I think, more in keeping with the artlessness of the images.

So much about Josie Papialook is paradoxical—an old child, a serious joker, a simple sophisticate. He may be taken on one level, as the town joker, fun to laugh with and at. On another level, his simplicity masks a sophisticated philosophy. He could well be enjoying some cosmic joke which eludes the rest of us—his name becoming the air; the wind connecting everything; he is part of the wind; therefore, he is the connection. Certainly, he cannot be dismissed as a mere joker.

I asked him if his pictures were meant to be serious or was he trying to make us laugh. He says he's being serious. He's 'trying to help the printshop'. Maybe he thought that was the right answer or maybe that is really, his intention. At any rate, his efforts to 'help' have not gone unnoticed. The year 1979 marked the twentieth anniversary of the first arctic co-operative and Josie was awarded a gold pin by the Povungnituk co-operative in recognition of his efforts. I heard about it from Ali Tulugak who said that Josie had 'fumbled his speech', saying, in effect, that he was very glad he used to be starving to death. 'It came out sort of silly', says Ali, 'and made everyone laugh'. A serious joker.

But, above all, Papialook is an original man. Like Sisyphus, he sees humour in the seriousness of life. An ageless child with a child's fascination with a universe which sometimes nurtures and sometimes batters. A universe whose most unfathomable spaces are not so awesome that they cannot be drawn, given form. Josie doesn't know that air has no shape. He doesn't know that it has no colour. He doesn't know that you cannot see the wind. ♦

At first Inuit carvings of Christian subjects were stiff and unexpressive. Now, works full of energy and emotion demonstrate the strong integration of Christianity into Inuit life.

Christianity and Inuit Art

By Jean Blodgett

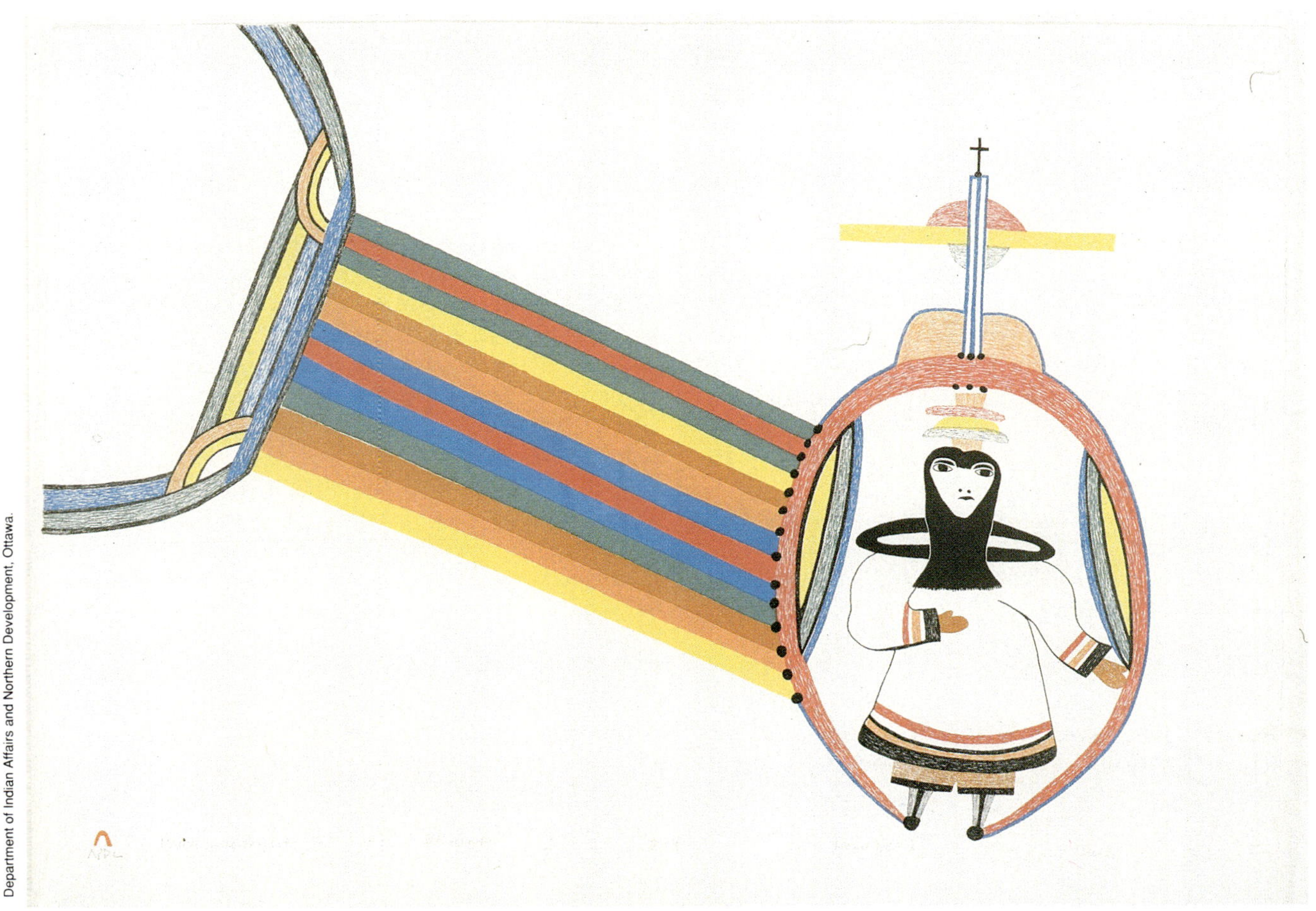

Department of Indian Affairs and Northern Development, Ottawa.

The 'prophet' descends, as others in the North these days, in a brilliantly coloured helicopter. 'Arrival of the Prophet'. Lithograph by Pudlo (1916-). Cape Dorset, 1983. 56 x 78.5 cm.

From *The Beaver*, Autumn 1984.

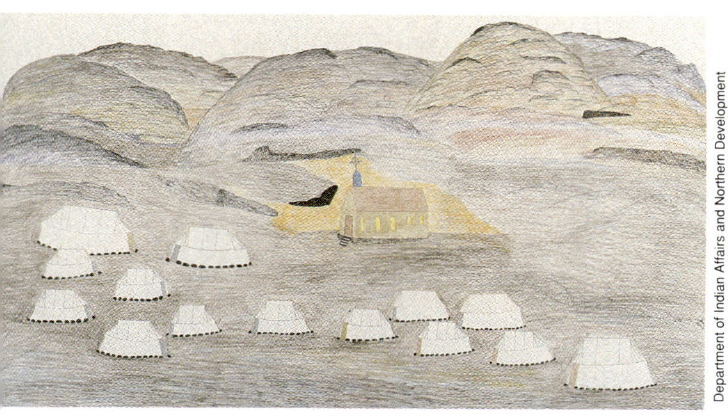
Department of Indian Affairs and Northern Development

'Cape Dorset Anglican Church, 1956-1965'. Drawing with coloured pencil and felt-tip pen by Etidlooie Etidlooie (1910-1981), Cape Dorset, 1980-1981. 56.3 x 76.2 cm.

THE IMPORTANCE OF THE CHURCH in the Canadian Arctic is indicated by the northern saying that the Hudson's Bay Company's initials, HBC, stand for 'Here Before Christ'. While the Company's presence in the North seems to go back to time immemorial, the church seems to have been there for almost as long. Missionaries followed hard upon the heels of Company traders—if they did not actually precede them—into remote areas, and their influence throughout the North has been just as pervasive.

Moravians established their first permanent mission in Labrador in the late 1700s; Roman Catholic and Anglican work, begun in the mid to late 1800s, has been particularly active from the turn of the century on; recently the Pentecostal movement has become yet another major religious force in the Arctic. Over the years conversion to Christianity essentially replaced the traditional Inuit religion. The new religion seemed to affect all aspects of life just as the old religion had: impatient explorers record how their Inuit guides would not travel or do any other work on Sundays, missionaries tell of extensive Christmas celebrations with people from surrounding camps, and printed translations of the Bible first introduced a system of writing for the Inuit language.

This new religion also had its effect on traditional artistic practices, but not as great an effect as might be expected. The arrival of missionaries in the North did inspire some representations of Christian subjects. For example, Inuit in the Chesterfield Inlet area, where the Catholics established a mission in 1912 and a hospital in 1931, made ivory carvings in the first half of this century of standard Christian subjects such as the crucifix, Christ, and the Madonna and Child. The technique, material and size are comparable to other contemporaneous carvings from the area, but the subject matter is decidedly alien. Not only are the figures foreign in appearance and dress, they are stiff and unexpressive. Obviously copied from some religious source, the subjects lack conviction. Whatever the religion of the unknown makers, these works are not inspired or inspiring but they are important documents, since representations of Christian subjects were not common at the time. Of these, many are to be found in the collections of religious organizations, suggesting that the majority were made at the request of missionaries.

These early missionaries did not provoke an outpouring of Christian carvings, nor did they substantially reduce the number of artworks inspired by traditional religion. While missionaries worked hard to get people to give up their traditional religious beliefs and practices, they do not seem to have specifically addressed the topic of religious art. Perhaps unaware of the strong traditional link between religion and art, they did not consider art an important issue. It may be too that the Inuit, trying to survive in a harsh environment, continued to make use of traditional religious objects even though ostensibly now Christian.

Another major consideration, probably the most influential factor in the proliferation of traditional religious subjects and the small number of Christian ones, was the burgeoning commercial market for Inuit art. Missionaries were just one early wave in a flood of outsiders into the Arctic. These visitors collected souvenirs and artifacts in increasing volume, and Inuit began to make more and more items, especially carvings, for sale or trade rather than for their own use. Under these circumstances, Inuit continued to represent traditional religious subjects for a number of reasons. It may be that as Christians making carvings for someone else, they were representing a subject that was no longer spiritually meaningful to themselves. Or, whatever their beliefs, they may have simply treated the subject as something to carve like any other familiar topic. Or they may have been reacting to encouragement from a market that was collecting objects representative of another culture. As such, the objects would be expected to reflect traditional Inuit values not imported ones, such as Christianity.

This last factor continues to be a major influence in the field of Inuit art. While contemporary Inuit artists may choose to document their old ways for reasons of pride and sense of heritage, they are also under considerable pressure from the market place to represent traditional subjects rather than more currently relevant ones. Artworks showing shamans, dog sleds, or igloos are more popular than those of Christ, snowmobiles or pre-fabricated houses. Whether as a result of saleability or the artist's personal preference, shamanistic and mythological subjects far outnumber Christian ones in contemporary Inuit art.

If Christianity has not inspired a great number of artworks, it has inspired a group of varied, innovative and creative pieces. Taking this inspiration in its broadest sense some of the works document churchmen and the church's presence in the Arctic. Etidlooie of Cape Dorset, for example, in his 1980-

Office for Educational Practice, University of Guelph. Courtesy of Macdonald Stewart Art Centre

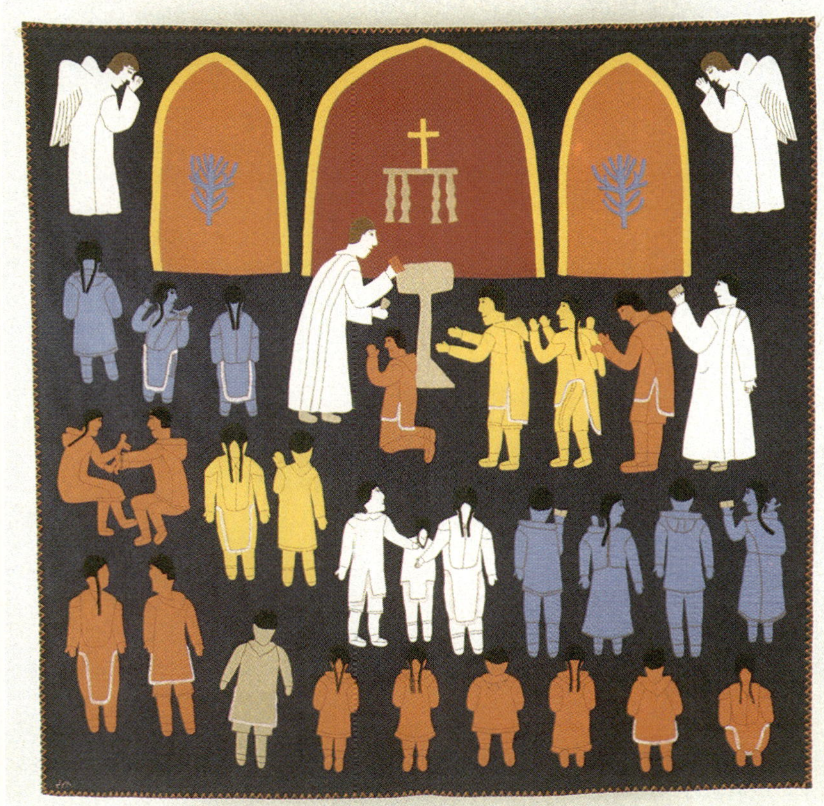

'Scene'. *Wall hanging in wool, felt and embroidery floss by Mary Yuusipik (1936 -) of Baker Lake. 147 x 149.4 cm. Gift of Donald Harvie, Calgary, to the Macdonald Stewart Art Centre, University of Guelph.*

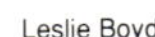

Leslie Boyd

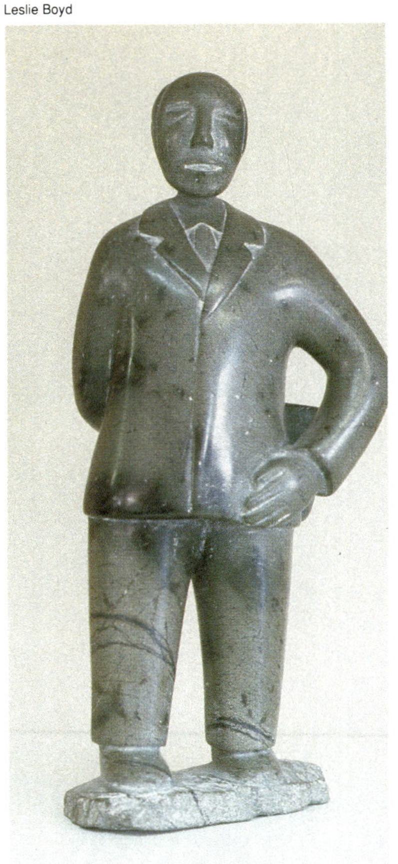

'Missionary' *Carving in green stone by Ovilu Tunnillie (1949 -), 1981. Collection of the West Baffin Eskimo Co-operative, Cape Dorset.*

Jean-Pierre Roy

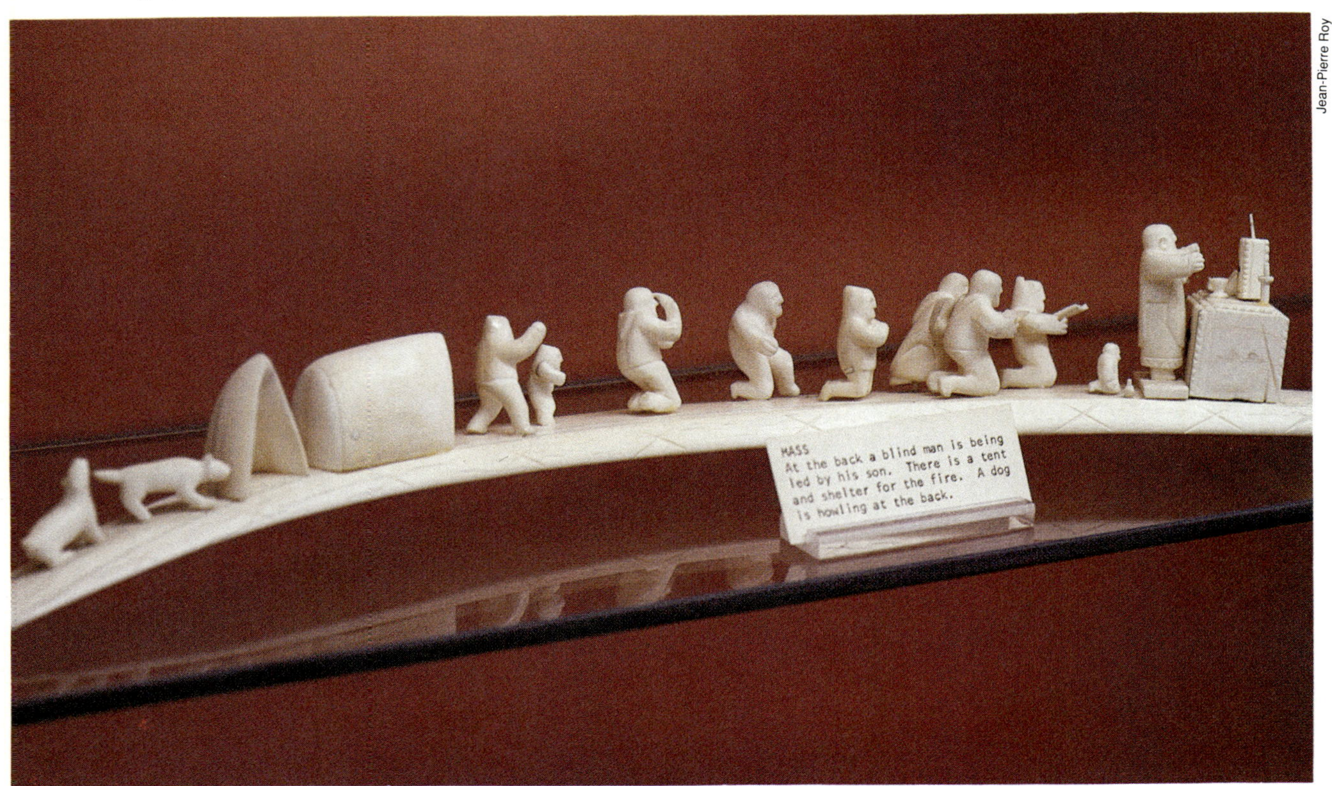

'Mass'. *Carving in ivory by Antonin Attark (1909-1960) of Pelly Bay, c. 1954. Length 45.7 cm. Collection of the Eskimo Museum, Churchill.*

81 series of drawings illustrating the history of his community shows the local Roman Catholic and Anglican churches in the early days not long after they were built. The Anglican church, the only permanent building in the valley at the time, is set in a densely coloured summer landscape, surrounded by the white tents of Inuit families. The Catholic mission, built on the other side of the community near the Hudson's Bay Company buildings, a few of which are included in the drawing, is shown in a snowy winter scene. A team of sled dogs is tethered outside the mission, and oil barrels—ubiquitous in the North at the time and used as colourful accents by Etidlooie—dot the landscape.

Also from Cape Dorset is Pauta's 1963 carving of an unidentified priest. The bearded figure, dressed in vestments, stands with arms raised to the side, hands outstretched in the gesture symbolic in Christianity of gathering people to the church. In contrast to the welcoming—if stereotyped—gesture of Pauta's *Priest* is the stiffly formal *Missionary* made in 1981 by Ovilu Tunnillie also of Cape Dorset. The rigid frontal stance, the severe, almost blank facial expression, the coat and tie, as well as the unfriendly position of the figure's arms—one akimbo, the other holding a book, presumably a Bible, behind his back partially hidden from our view—all create a distance between us and this man of God. While the artist may be depicting the clergyman's awkwardness in a strange environment, it is more likely that she is making a comment about outsiders in the Arctic. A younger artist, Ovilu has done other carvings making even more pointed statements about changing social conditions in the North, such as her sculpture of a white man bottle-feeding alcohol to an Inuk. Her carving of the *Missionary*, then, is more than likely not just a document of the church's presence in the North, but a comment about it.

Other representations of local clergy include the circa 1955 sculpture of *Frère Henri, an Oblate Missionary* by Antonin Attark of Pelly Bay and, from Repulse Bay, another community with a strong Catholic following, John Kaunak's *French Missionary Paddling Kayak*, 1960-66 (both in the collection of the Winnipeg Art Gallery). Kaunak's missionary, a small torso in a fully equipped traditional kayak, is somewhat dwarfed by his impressive, elongated vessel. Only closer examination reveals that the figure in the cockpit is a bearded, balding non-Inuit. While Kaunak was probably representing a particular missionary his overall presentation is more general than Attark's in his carving of Frère Henri. In this small stone bust the artist has sensitively portrayed a man he must have known well. Done with great feeling for his subject, Attark's sculpture is an intimate portrayal of a relaxed Frère Henri, shown with his hands clasped behind his head.

The Eskimo Museum in Churchill has several other carvings by Attark relating to Christianity. Of particular interest is his portrait of *Pope Pius XII*. The half-figure carved in white ivory, with attached papal accoutrements in contrasting colours, sports a pair of green plastic sunglasses. In a complex composite work titled *Mass*, Attark shows a gathering of Inuit in church. Moving from left to right, small ivory figures are shown entering, crossing themselves, and then kneeling in front of the altar where a priest officiates. Elements such as the tiny objects on the altar, the naturalistic poses of the figures and the presence of small children make the scene real and meaningful—meaningful to us as it obviously was to its maker.

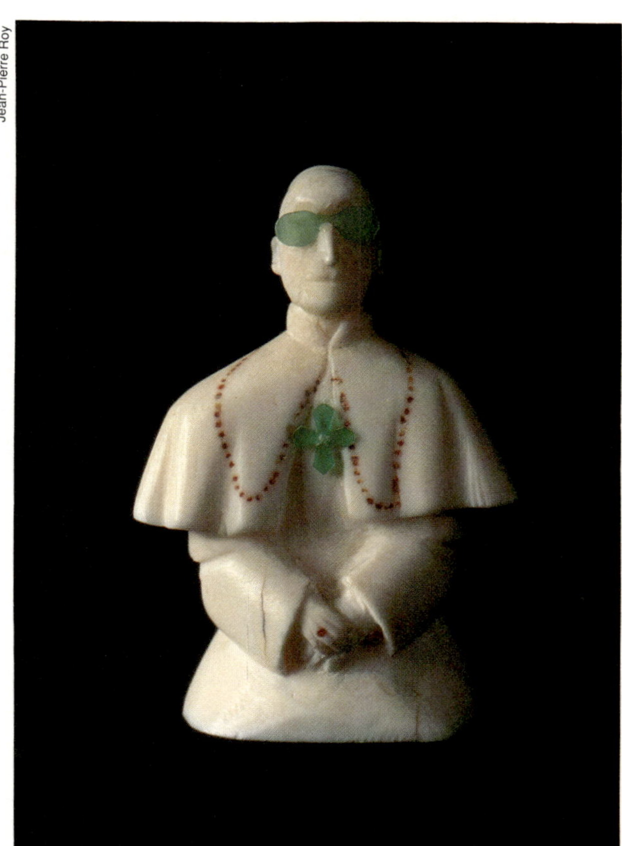
Jean-Pierre Roy

'Pope Pius XII'. Carving in ivory, plastic sun glasses, by Antonin Attark (1909-1960), c. 1954. Height 8.9 cm. Collection of the Eskimo Museum, Churchill.

Worship and church gatherings have inspired other artists too. Like Attark these artists document not only the churchmen but Inuit as practicing Christians. The late Ennutsiak of Frobisher Bay did carvings showing a row of seated Inuit figures holding open Bibles or hymnals as though in church. A sculpture by John Polik of Eskimo Point titled *Singing Psalms* shows a group of twelve figures being led in song. The singers, some holding hymnals, their leader and an additional figure all made of antler are pegged to a base.

Working in sculpture, the artists are somewhat restricted by their media, although both Polik and Attark, by pegging individual elements onto a base, have achieved complex grouped scenes. Seamstresses making wall hangings, on the other hand, have the advantages of a larger format, a wide range of colours, and the potential for finely sewn details. In a hanging now in the collection of the University of Guelph, Yuusipik of Baker Lake shows a church interior crowded with people. The congregation of men, women and children fill the lower two-thirds of the scene; some kneel, some stand, some hold open books, their colourful clothing contrasting with the white vestments of the two churchmen. The central clergyman, holding a book with embroidered syllabics reading 'to baptize the Inuit', baptizes the kneeling figure in front of him. Above are three arches, the central one housing an altar and cross. Flanking the arches are two angels, whose corner positions and bowed heads add to the orderly, worshipful air of the hanging.

Angels, a particularly popular subject in contemporary Christian art, appeared early in the Cape Dorset print collections: there was *Angels in the Moon* by Natsivaar in 1960 and *Fallen Angels* by Pannichiak in 1961. In the late 1960s Pudlo's interest in the formal possibilities of the angelic subject resulted in a series of drawings and several prints, *Arctic Angel* and *Winter Angel,* in 1969. But angels were not the only Christian subject to catch Pudlo's attention. His prints have also represented the *Ecclesiast,* 1969, the *Esigajuak* (Roman Catholic Father), 1973, and the *Arrival of the Prophet,* 1983. Christian motifs appear in non-Christian and even shamanistic prints too. In the *Long Journey* of 1974, Inuit figures wend their way along a winding path up the hill to a church. In both *The Igloo Builders* and *Thoughts of Home* from 1975 there is a small cross in the center between igloos and tents, and in the print *Shaman's Dwelling* of the same year a cross-like form rises above the central structure. In *The Seasons* of 1976 a cross flanked by two loons rises above the roof of a rounded building with a cross inside, possibly St Jude's Cathedral in nearby Frobisher Bay.

Pudlo's treatment of his Christian subjects is consistent with his overall artistic approach. Like secular or traditional religious subjects, they are drawn and redrawn as he works through the various forms or they are integrated in with other motifs as part of an image where visual effect not narrative accuracy is paramount. Even the prophet arrives in a brilliantly coloured helicopter; colours, balance of composition and helicopter subject all typically Pudlo. What may seem like disrespect is just common sense (and artistic licence)—after all everyone these days travels by plane and helicopter in the North.

In Pudlo's print *Shaman's Dwelling* a cross-like form is shown together with an igloo identified by the work's title as a shaman's dwelling. Kukiiyaut of Baker Lake, in a 1976 untitled drawing inspired by personal family history, shows her shaman grandfather and his two helping spirits confronted by an angel and Jesus Christ. Conjunction of Christian and shamanistic elements like this within one work is rare. While many artists represent both Christian and shamanistic subjects, they generally do so in separate

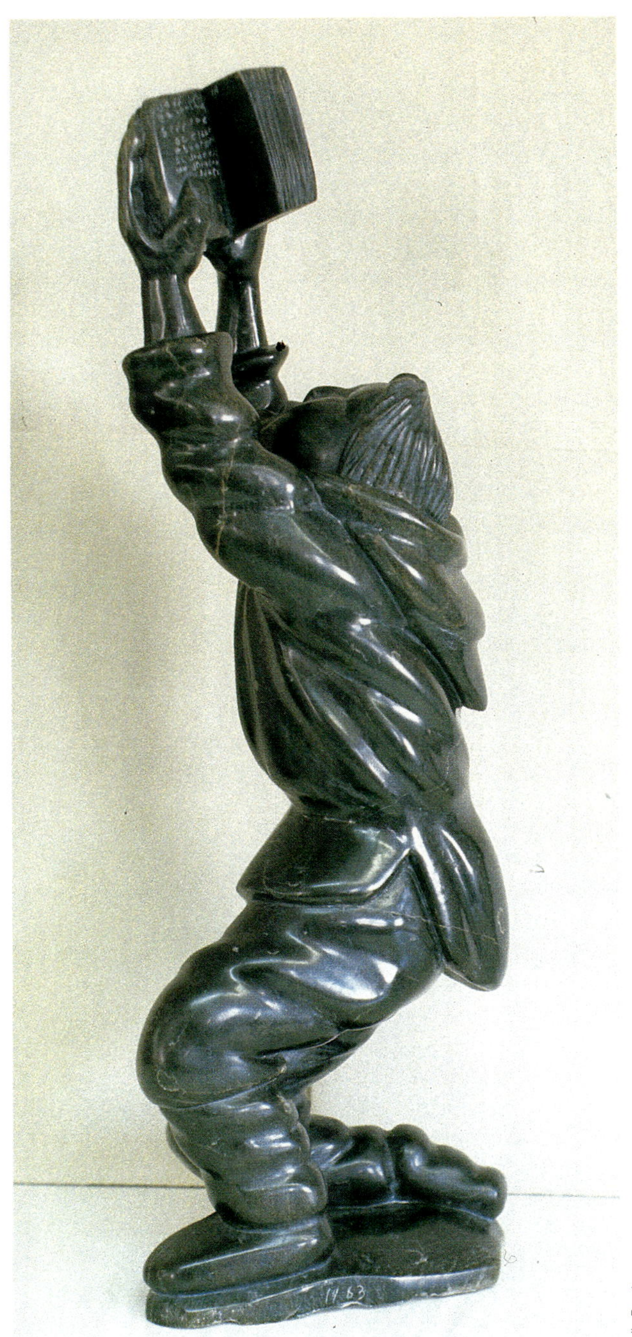

Leslie Boyd

'Figure with Bible'. Carving in green stone, 1983, by Kiawak Ashoona (1933-) of Cape Dorset, who was converted to the Full Gospel Church. Collection of the West Baffin Eskimo Co-operative, Cape Dorset.

works. Sculptor Marc Tungilik of Repulse Bay, for example, in a recent exhibition had individual works representing—among other subjects—a priest, angels, shamans and spirits.

Tungilik first started carving at the encouragement of Oblate missionaries. Father Franz van der Velde records how in 1945 he asked the artist to copy a small bust of Christ. The resulting ivory miniature now in the Eskimo Museum in Churchill shows the head of Christ crowned with thorns. Depiction of Biblical figures such as this Christ or the early

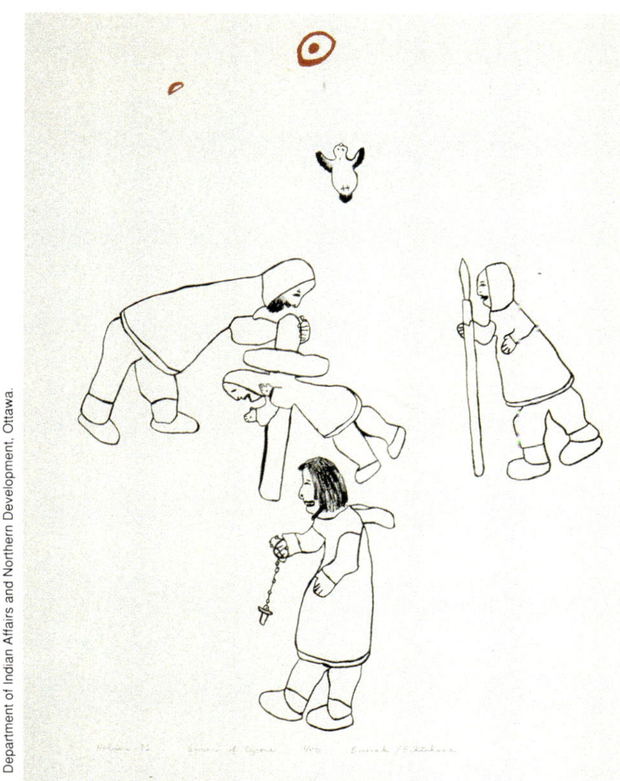

Department of Indian Affairs and Northern Development, Ottawa.

'Simon of Cyrene'. Lithograph by Mark Emerak (1901- 1983) of Holman Island, 1983. 50.5 x 39.5 cm.

twentieth-century Christ and Madonna and Child from Chesterfield Inlet referred to earlier are not common and seem to result from requests rather than the artist's own initiative. Local clergy, community church buildings, Inuit worshippers and angels are much more prevalent. Contemporary works representing individual Biblical figures such as a carving of Mary Magdalene and one tentatively identified as the *Madonna and Child* by Irene Kataq of Repulse Bay and that of *Moses* by Kabubawakota of Cape Dorset are few in number. Kabubawakota's *Moses* is a dynamic, expressive figure in swirling robes, his long-fingered hands holding aloft the tablets, but often the carvings of Biblical personages seem remote and foreign presumably because many were done on request and as such may have been copied.

Artists depicting Christian subject matter may depend on standardized western prototypes, especially for Biblical individuals who are known to them through the illustrations provided in material such as religious comics, books and posters brought to the North. But depictions of subjects personally meaningful to them can be as expressive and effective as any of their work whatever the subject, as we have seen in the pieces by such artists as Attark, Ovilu Tunnillie and Kabubawakota. That the Christian subject is meaningful to the artists may result from visual variety and interest (Pudlo), cultural concerns (Ovilu Tunnillie), personal associations (Attark), or religious conviction. While this latter quality is difficult to identify, some works definitely result from the artist's religious beliefs. In 1983 Kiawak Ashoona, a well-known Cape Dorset sculptor who regularly depicts traditional subjects, carved a sculpture of a *Figure with Bible.* On bended knee, the man holds high an open Bible on which are incised, in syllabics, passages from John (1:1-2; 3:5) and I Corinthians (2:21-22). Inspired by Kiawak's recent conversion to the Full Gospel Church the sculpture is full of energy and emotion; the figure upward-thrusting, the clothing agitated, it is an impressive testament to Kiawak's faith in his new religion.

Kiawak's figure dressed in modern Inuit clothing, like the depictions of Inuit in church, clearly demonstrates the integration of Christianity into Inuit life. Their new religion is now culturally meaningful to people in a real and significant way. This is not to say that only the devout represent Christian subjects but that Christianity is now an important aspect of northern life. While we cannot presume to assess the artists' religious convictions, we can see that they have a thorough knowledge of their subject matter. And their depictions of these subjects, often interpreted in a very personal way, make the Christian incidents even more relevant to themselves as Christians in the Arctic. This is certainly obvious in a type of Christian representation we have not yet discussed, the depiction of specific Biblical episodes.

The 1983 Holman graphics collection included a print by Mark Emerak entitled *Simon of Cyrene.* Mentioned only in passing in three of the four Gospels as the man who helped Jesus carry His cross, Simon was not a major Biblical figure. But the episode—and its implications of a bystander (representative of mankind) helping the Saviour—is accorded the importance of a station in the Stations of the Cross. This devotion has never been depicted in prints from Holman or any other Inuit community, although Edith Iglauer in her book *Inuit Journey* mentions having seen photographs of sealskin tapestries from Holman, made under the supervision of Father Tardy, that illustrated the Last Supper and the Stations of the Cross. Father Tardy, an Oblate missionary, is a long-standing and important figure in the history of the community of Holman and its graphics program. Through him, Emerak would have had access to religious information and illustrations, the source of inspiration for this print and other drawings he has done of Christian subjects.

But here Emerak's view of the episode is a decidedly personal one. On the one hand we have accuracy in the representation of Christ, a small bowed figure struggling with His cross, assisted by a powerful but gentle-looking, bearded Simon, as well as the use of religious symbolism in the two red orbs in the upper part of the image (the only bit of colour in this otherwise black print) that surely represent the sun and the moon. These two heavenly bodies—significant in Inuit mythology—are standard symbols in Christian art indicating, in scenes of the Crucifixion, the sorrow of all creation at the death of Christ. On

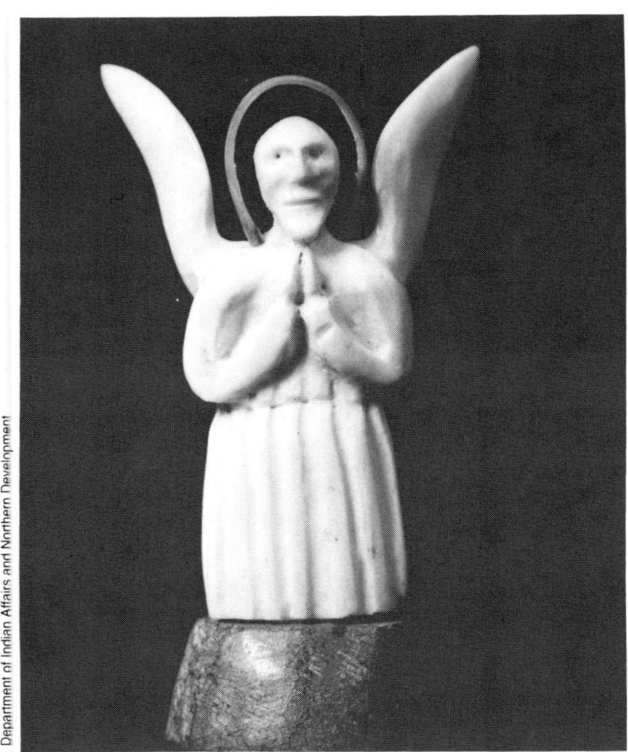

Department of Indian Affairs and Northern Development

'Angel'. Carving in grey-green stone, ivory and musk-ox horn by Marc Tungilik (1913-1986) of Repulse Bay, 1982. 7.3 x 4.0 x 2.5 cm. Collection of the Department of Indian and Northern Affairs.

the other hand, we have some variations from the original version: the Saviour, on his way to be crucified already has the nail wounds in his hands—perhaps as a timeless attribute or to clearly identify Him in the scene; the dove overhead, if symbolic of the Holy Spirit as it usually is, is not associated with this episode—although it could be included here for additional symbolism; the figure in the foreground holding a rosary—a form of devotion not instituted until the thirteenth century—may play an auxiliary devotional role or simply represent a modern worshipper. Finally we also have the intrusion of some purely local influences: the figure to the right, surely a Roman soldier, carries an Inuit spear; all the figures are dressed in Inuit clothing, and the plump dove looks rather like a snowy owl. Clearly Emerak's image was not slavishly copied without thought from some religious manual. He has not only adapted a Biblical event into a setting and style typical of Inuit prints, but he has considerably enriched this deceptively simple-looking scene with various Christian elements and symbols.

If Emerak has the people in his Christian scene wearing Inuit clothing, Nanurluk in a wall hanging made in 1976 seems to have moved Biblical events from the Holy Land to the shores of Baker Lake, N.W.T. Surrounding a map of the Baker Lake area are a number of Biblical episodes. Moving clockwise from the mid-left these are: Mary Magdalene washing Christ's feet and drying them with her hair, Christ appearing after His Resurrection and showing the nail wounds in His hands to doubting Thomas, Christ carrying the cross, the Crucifixion, Jesus and the Child(ren), and David and Goliath. These events, from both the Old and New Testaments, are not presented in any particular order, but such is often the case in Inuit art in representations of other events such as traditional legends and stories. Artists, and storytellers for that matter, do not necessarily follow a chronological order or strict time sense in presenting the episodes making up their narrative. (We could also apply this to Emerak's version of Simon of Cyrene.)

Nor should we too literally interpret the central map in this wall hanging, showing in some detail Baker Lake with its islands and tributary streams. Certainly several of the mourners at the Crucifixion actually overlap the edge of the map. But in view of Nanurluk's general style and on the basis of works by her and other Baker Lake seamstresses in which maps or Baker Lake souvenir medallions are shown in conjunction with other subjects, it is probable that the map is not identifying the location of the Biblical events. The two may not be unrelated, however; perhaps the artist is formulating an association between Christian worship and her native area, establishing Christianity within the context of modern Inuit life. This would tie in with the participation of the Inuit couple in the lower right who, having stopped their dogsled, their backs to us, intently observe the Biblical events taking place in front of them.

In contrast to the Emerak print where all the figures are dressed in Inuit clothing but, like so many contemporary prints, no landscape setting is indicated, Nanurluk suggests a pictorial space by the arrangement of scenes and the orientation of the Inuit couple. In addition she has represented the people and their clothes in a fashion consistent with reality or standard religious illustration. The Inuit couple is dressed in parkas; the Biblical figures wear robes, tunics and loin cloths—Goliath even has a pair of lace-up sandals. While the faces of the two Inuit are not visible, the faces of the Biblical figures are Caucasian, and Christ has long flowing hair and a beard.

Another Baker Lake artist, in fact Nanurluk's mother Jessie Oonark, has done a number of works related to Christianity. One of these, a print in the 1984 Baker Lake collection, shows Christ on the cross. To either side of him, on a bold ground line midway up the image, are two figures; one kneels while the other, a Roman, drives a nail into Christ's hand. Below stand six mourners touching the Saviour's feet and weeping in despair. The Roman and the mourners are all dressed in Inuit clothing. A devotional-like piece, the title of the print identifies Christ as the *Giver of Life.*

In a drawing of *The Last Supper* Oonark's depiction of clothing, facial features and beards of the figures as well as the setting with background draperies and a Roman column show little Inuit

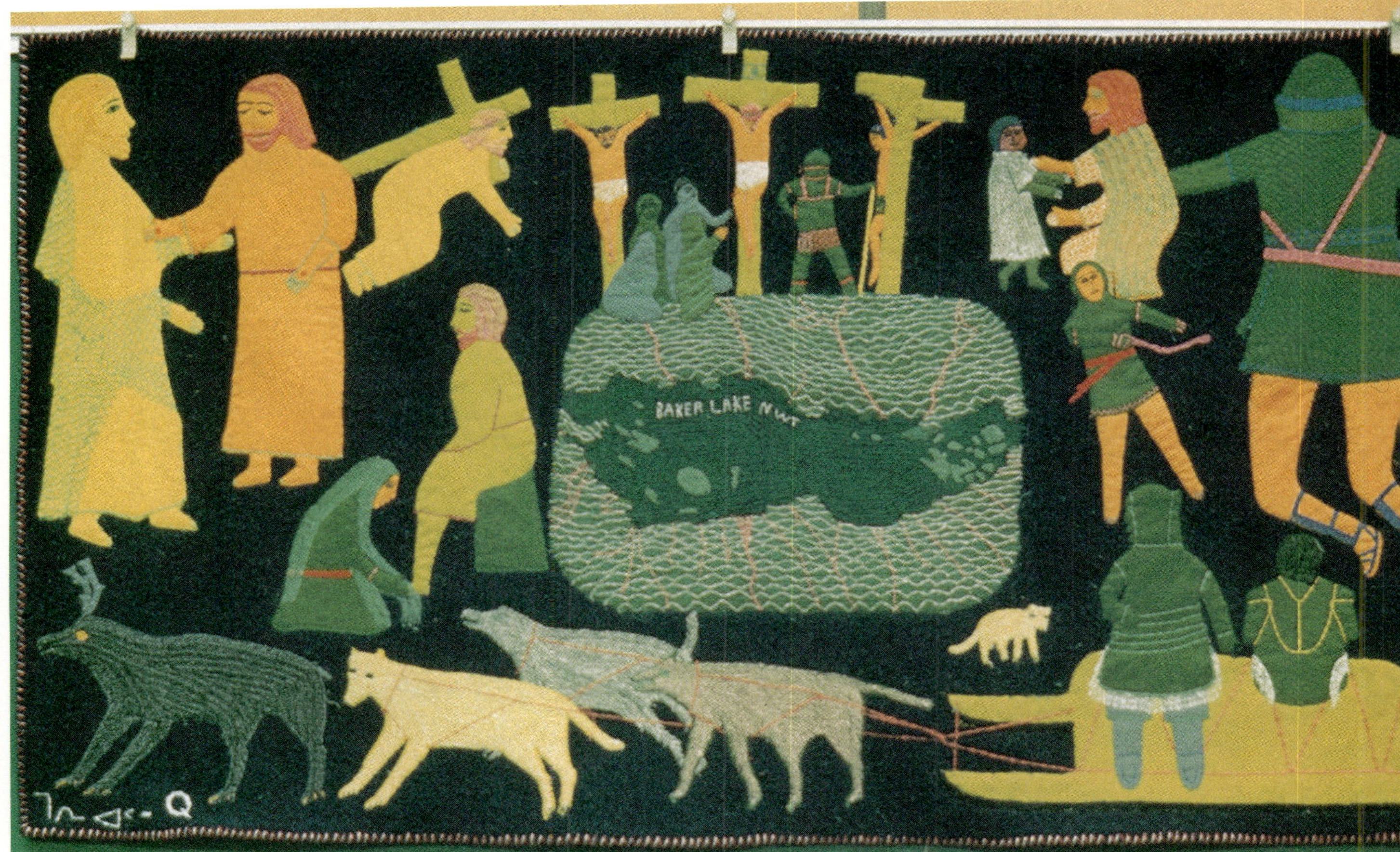

Untitled. Wall hanging in duffle, felt and embroidery floss by Miriam Nanurluk Qiyuk (1933-). 1976. 75 x 136 cm. Collection: Anglican Church, Baker Lake.

influence, but more often she combines Inuit and Christian figures or motifs. Sometimes the integration of the two makes it difficult to identify the subject with certainty. This mixing of imagery and content is not unusual in the work of prolific, creative artists like Oonark who follow their visual instincts and seemingly unconsciously depict a tremendous range of subjects from the everyday to the spiritual, from traditional to western.

Oonark's monumental (over four by six metres) wall hanging in the National Arts Centre in Ottawa, for example, illustrated and discussed in Peter Mellen's book *Landmarks of Canadian Art*, combines traditional and Christian motifs. In the midst of a richly varied scene of traditional Inuit life is a central figure that 'probably represents an angel, or the Virgin, with the other figures bowed down in worship around her.' Another Oonark wall hanging, now in the collection of the Art Gallery of Ontario, shows Inuit figures, abstract shapes and what appears to be Moses with the tablets. The central figure in the upper rectangular area, Moses holds the tablets above rounded mounds that may symbolize Mount Sinai. Attention is focused on him by the use of colour, the orientation of the figures on either side of him and the placement of the shapes and heraldic dogs above. The figure of Moses is echoed by a figure immediately below him who stands on top of an arch. A typical Christian form, the arch holds four kneeling figures symmetrically arranged on either side of a column of triangular shapes. The format and upward movement of this scene are reminiscent of those representations in religious paintings showing deceased Biblical and saintly figures carried up to heaven by angelic escorts. In addition, the triangular shapes line up with and lead to the figure on top of the arch and through him to Moses above, establishing a strong central and hierarchical relationship.

The Christian interpretation of untitled works such as this wall hanging is suggested by the content and format of the actual work, comparison with titled works, and recognition of the fact that Oonark was a devout Christian. She has done religious works on her own initiative and on commission. Oonark was one of the Canadian artists asked to illustrate the *Sunday Mass Book* published by the Canadian Catholic Conference of Bishops in 1976. Her drawing *Waiting for the Lord* shows Christ, His body positioned as though on the cross, seemingly weightlessly suspended above a group of people; in the mid-upper right is an angel.

Commissions such as this account for some of the religious art made by Inuit artists. But even more significant in recent years is church encouragement,

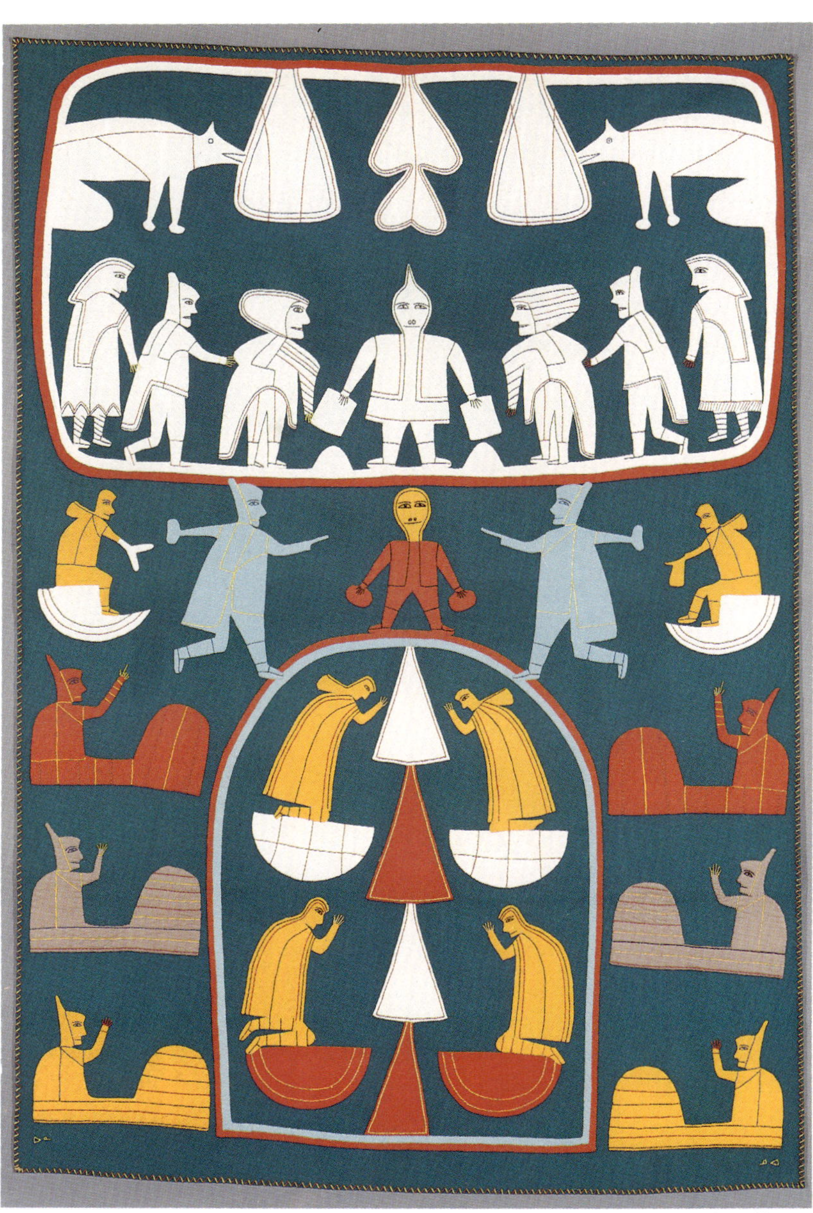

Untitled. Wall hanging in wool, felt and embroidery floss, by Jessie Oonark (1906-1985), c. 1974, 212.0 x 144.0 cm. Collection of Art Gallery of Ontario.

James Chamgers

and Inuit initiative, in decorating local churches, especially within the last 30 years or so, as more and more communities have acquired permanent buildings and as the Inuit have become increasingly active participants in their local church affairs. Religious art is one of the few types of contemporary art that the Inuit make for themselves and keep in the North. Churches may be adorned with wall hangings, woven tapestries, sealskin altar cloths and floor coverings, ivory crosses, soapstone fonts and carvings, even, at St Edmunds Anglican church in Great Whale River, an oil painting (showing Peter faltering as he walks on the water)—all made by local Inuit.

The richness, variety and creativeness of church decoration is exemplified by St Jude's Cathedral in Frobisher Bay. Here in an igloo-shaped structure, two sleds in the traditional style turned on edge serve as Communion rails; another sled, standing on end, acts as pulpit with the microphone concealed behind a harpoon head; woven grass baskets serve as collection plates; two narwhal tusks form the cross over the altar; six wall hangings, made by seamstresses in (moving from left to right) Eskimo Point, Coppermine, Povungnituk, Iglulik, Baker Lake and Inoucdjouac, are full of traditional Inuit and Christian subjects and symbols. In an article in a 1972 issue of *The Arctic News* devoted to the subject of the new cathedral, some of the women explained the significance of their panels. The hangings illustrate Christianity in the North with images of specific meaning and symbolism. For example, in the Povungnituk panel the dogteam shows that Inuit used to go long distances to understand about the faith; the rainbow shows the love of God (God's covenant to Noah), and the flowers relate to growing in faith like a flower. In the Iglulik panel, people from different places and in different dress demonstrate that 'God placed His servants in different places, all belong to one God'.

Barbara Lipton

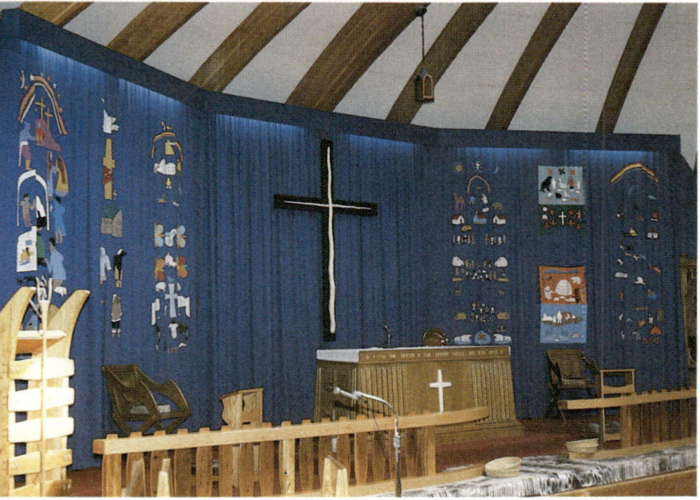

St Jude's Cathedral in Frobisher Bay, 1984.

George Hunter

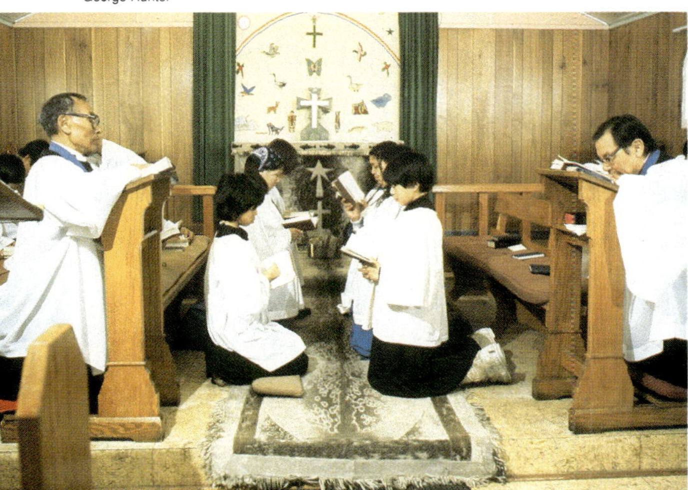

St John's Anglican Church, Cape Dorset, 1978.

'Merry Christmas'. Carving in red and grey stone by Simon Qamanirq (1953-) of Arctic Bay, c. 1965. 7.5 x 8.0 x 0.6 cm. Collection of Images Art Gallery Inc., Toronto.

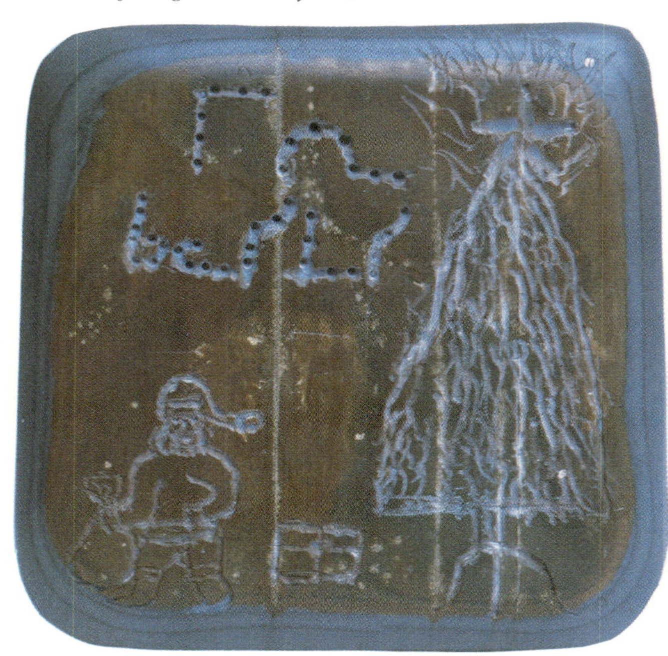

Michael Neill

Finally no discussion of Christianity in the Arctic would be complete without mentioning Christmas. Christmas has become as popular in the North as it is in the South. In the old days there was sufficient ice and snow cover by December to travel by dog sled and people could again go to the closest trading post and mission—the two institutions often being located at the same place. Missionaries usually made an event of the occasion. Reverend Peck at the mission station of Blacklead Island in recording the Christmas of 1895 tells how a large number of Eskimos gathered at the mission for celebrations lasting over a period of several days. There were services, a 'magic lantern lecture' showing scenes from Christ's life, and the distribution of prizes to children for school attendance, behaviour and cleanliness. In addition, gifts were exchanged, refreshments provided and a Christmas tree (made from the hoops of a flour barrel and decorated with coloured paper) displayed.

Peter Pitseolak in recording the history of people in his area tells of gathering in Cape Dorset to celebrate Christmas with dances and races on the ice. Robert Flaherty, the film maker, spent the Christmas of 1915 on the Belcher Islands. His group's party, with Santa Claus, gramophone music and a Christmas tree made of spruce boughs (brought from Great Whale River) decorated with brightly labelled empty fruit cans, was attended by local Inuit including one Wetalltok who recorded the event in a drawing now in the Royal Ontario Museum in Toronto. A more recent Inuit artist, Simon Qamanirq of Arctic Bay, has done his own version of a Christmas greeting card. A thin slab of stone, incised on both sides, shows Santa with his pack and a Christmas tree with a gift-wrapped present beneath. Phonetically spelled out syllabics—the system of writing originally introduced by the missionaries—is 'Merry Christmas'. ♦

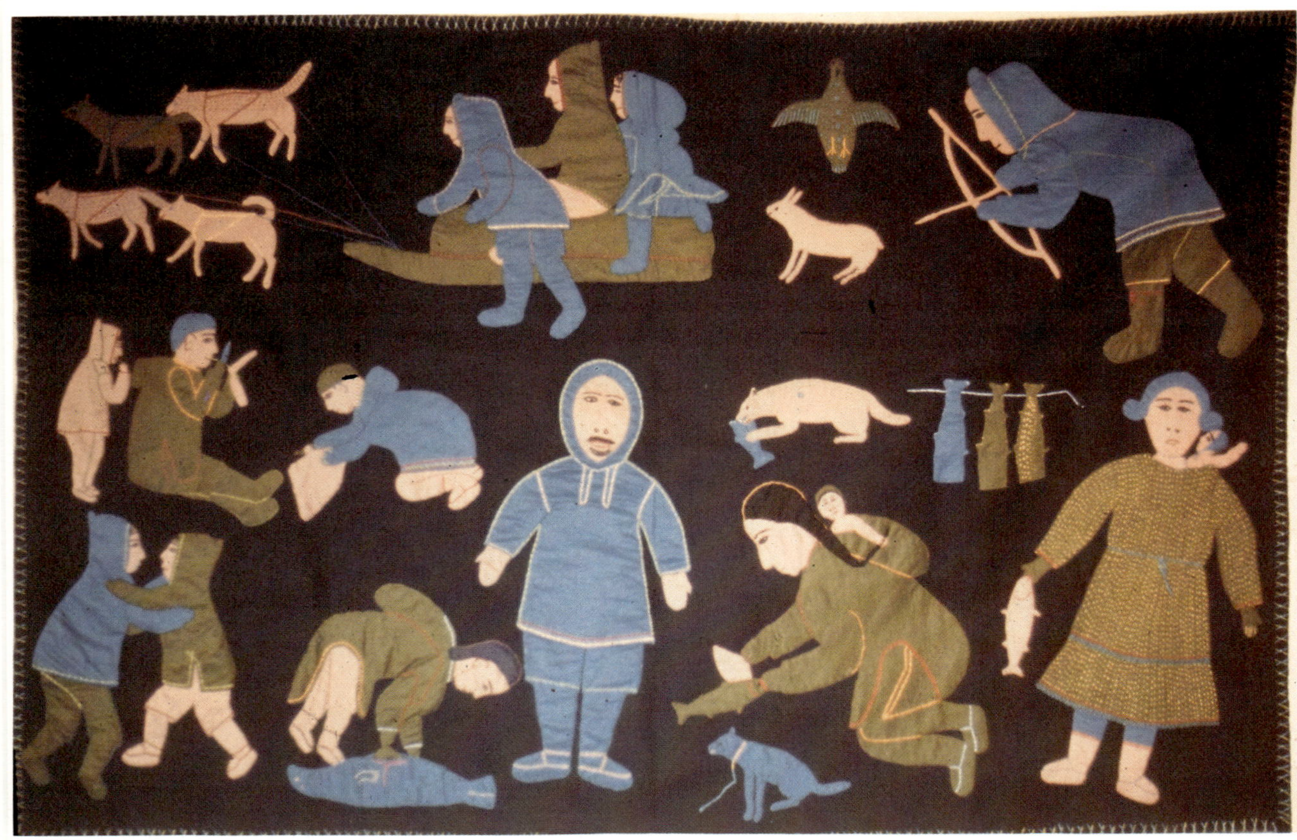

Wall Hangings from Baker Lake

By Sheila Butler

ALL THE WALL HANGING ARTISTS in Baker Lake learned to sew from their mothers while living in igloos or summer tents on the land. They first sewed caribou skin clothing, using caribou sinew for thread.

'Inside a snowhouse there is not much light, and it is cold with frost on everything that you are working with,' recalls one artist, Nancy Kanayuq.

Although the families with school-age children no longer spend the entire year on the land, many leave the settlement in the summer to live in tents and fish and hunt. The women all take some sewing with them, and Aqnaquinnak, Tuu'luuq, Tatya and other Baker Lake women have made beautiful wall hangings while out on the land in their summer tents. The older woman, Marion Tuu'luuq, wife of the artist Anguhadluq, remembers the old life very well indeed.

'Snowhouses were cold, your hands were cold, the skins were tough and hard, but there always seemed to be enough space. In the old days we had an old woman who lived with us and she sewed our caribou skin tents.' Tuu'luuq well remembers the hardship of the old life. 'I have sometimes wished that I were a fish, then my life would be lively and full of fun.'

In July 1969, when we arrived in Baker Lake to attempt the introduction of printmaking, there was a sewing project in the community. Sponsored by the federal government, this project was separate from the craft shop, housed in another building, and concerned with garments only. It was primarily a machine-stitched, factory-oriented operation. No wall hangings were being made at that time. Owing to various marketing problems and difficulties arising from the women's dislike for the factory system, this sewing project was shut down in the early spring of 1970.

The opportunities for employment for adults in Baker Lake were extremely limited and so the closing of this project was a blow to the women of the community who depended on their sewing abilities to bring a little extra income to their families. Soon,

---

Photographs by Jack Butler

From *The Beaver,* Autumn 1972.

many women were coming to the craft shop, standing patiently, rocking on their heels to soothe the babies they carried on their backs. An Inuit sense of propriety demanded that they wait quietly for a suitable interval before asking their question. Their question was translated for us. 'We want something to do. Is there something that needs to be done?'

At that time our budget was stretched as far as seemed possible just to pay the printers and sculptors, and although we hated turning these women away, we could think of nothing to suggest. Not so easily discouraged, most of the women returned in the next few weeks with various sewn items for sale—traditional caribou skin boots, duffle socks made from blanket-weight wool fabric purchased at the Hudson's Bay Company store, women's outer garments or amautiks with the pouch for carrying babies on the back. As far as our budget would permit, we purchased the best of these items with craft shop funds and sold most of them to the non-Inuit residents of Baker Lake who needed the warm arctic-style clothing. The women's amautiks were especially in demand by women who had small babies, since without a 'back-pack', they were doomed to months of staying indoors. Prams or strollers are a physical impossibility for mother and child alike in Baker Lake. The huge snow drifts and high winds and sub-zero temperatures prohibit the use of such commonplace southern methods of baby transportation.

Among these useful and beautiful articles of clothing, we purchased some small, charming, stitched and appliquéd pictures, made from scraps left over from the cutting of garments. These first tentative efforts were repetitive animal patterns and scenes of

Wall hanging (p. 94) by Kanayuk, 1971.

In a flowing horizonless composition by Naomi Ityi, below, animals mingle with the men who depend on them for food and clothing.

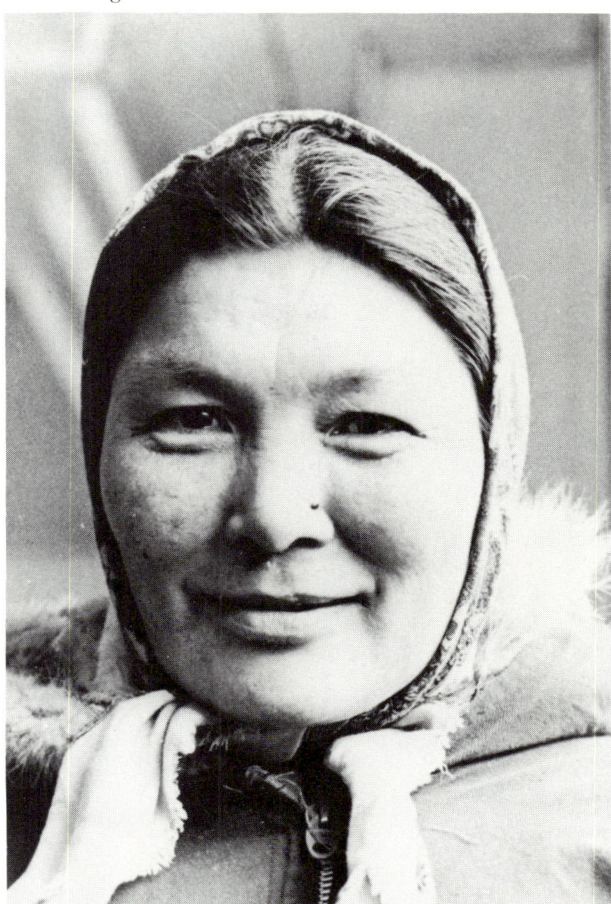

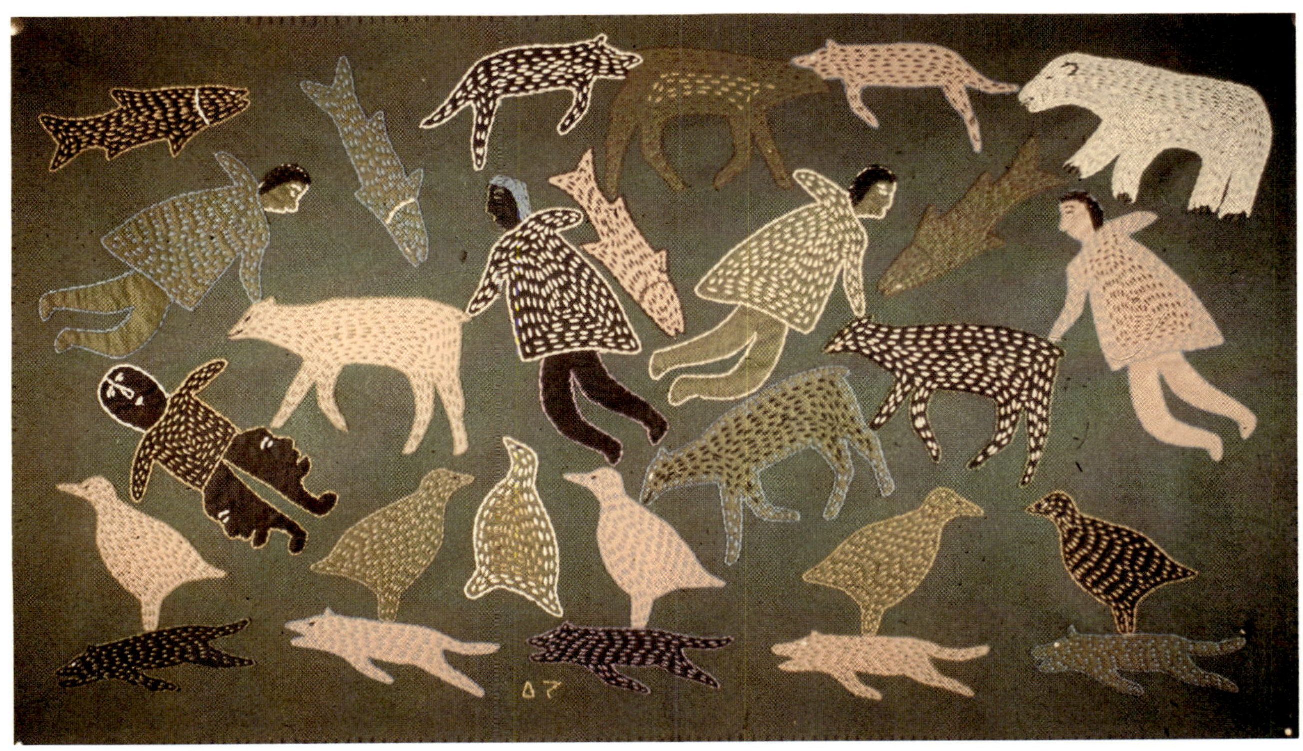

Irene Avaalaqiaq gives substance to the fantastic creatures of her imagination. These beings suggest interdependence and harmony between man and animal as one form melts into another, the strong stripes unifying them into one.

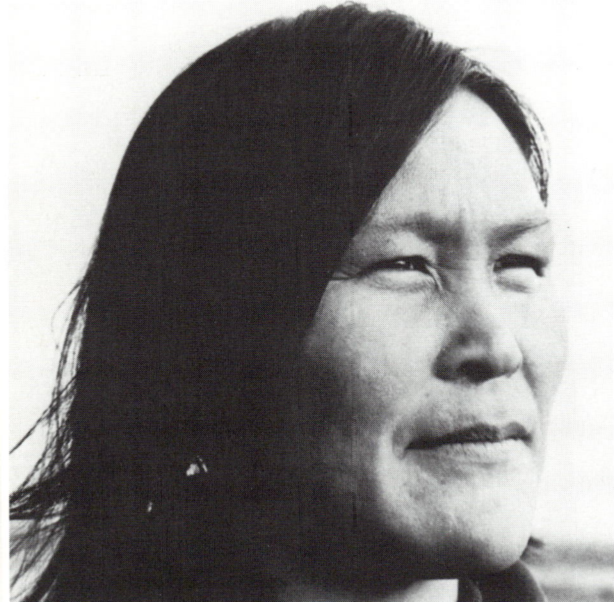

traditional Inuit life on the land. One of the first women to bring these small pictures for sale was Naomi Ityi. She stitched some of her own design and used pencil drawings by Ittuluka'naaq as the source of the design for a few others. Ittuluka'naaq, now deceased, was too old at that time to be able to sew well. Soon we were treated to our first sight of the wall hangings by Jessie Oonark.

Oonark was then, and remained until her death in 1985, one of the most accomplished of Inuit artists. Word soon travelled around the settlement that we were paying better and better prices for these interesting appliquéd pictures, and soon more and more women were bringing them to the shop. We called them wall hangings and we learned that the Inuit ladies had a word for them—*neevingatah*—and that they had made similar pictures in 1966 and 1967 when the first Baker Lake sewing project was managed by Elizabeth Whitton, the Anglican missionary's wife. Mrs Whitton remembered vividly an early wall hanging by Oonark's daughter, Victoria Mamnguqsualuk, depicting the changing seasons in the Arctic.

The idea of designs cut from one fabric and appliquéd to another piece of fabric was of course not new to the Baker Lake women since this is the method of decoration for their traditional skin clothing. In decorating the caribou skin clothing, geomet-

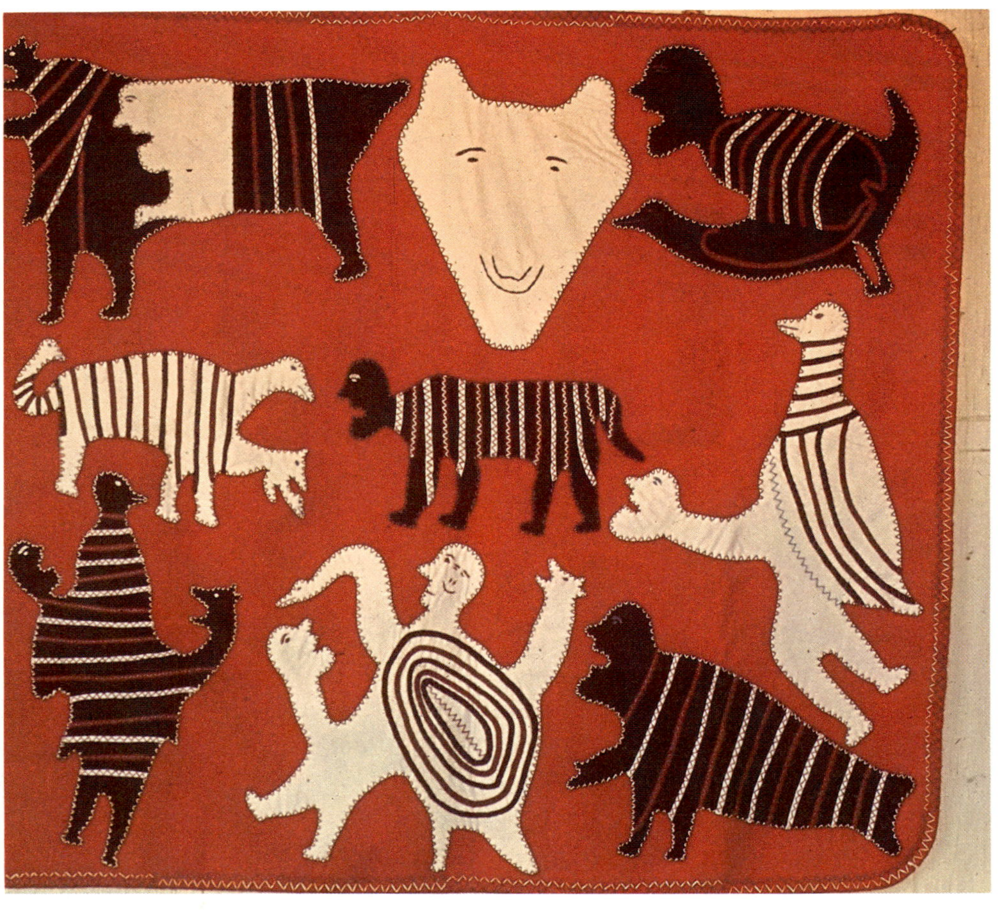

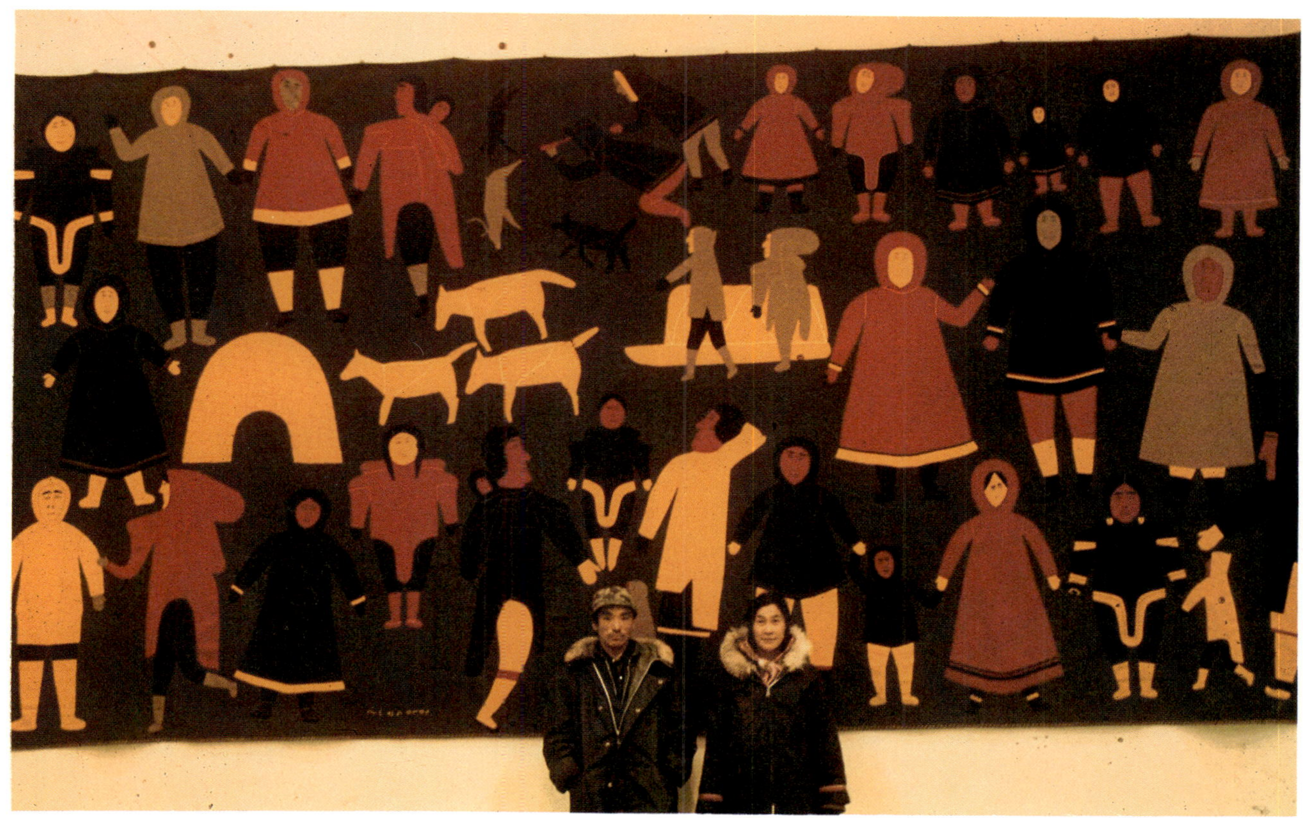

Rita Aviliayuk and her husband stand in front of her immense hanging in the gymnasium of the Baker Lake school.

ric designs are cut from the white belly fur of the caribou and set into the main portions of the garment which are made from the brownish-grey part of the caribou fur. The technical difference between this and the sewing of the wall hangings is that the cut pieces for the hangings are sewn down to a rectangular, uncut backing, whereas the cut pieces in the skin sewing are set into matching cut-out areas in the garment. The only exception to this distinction is that Oonark, in some wave of nostalgia I suppose, sometimes reverts to the methods of skin sewing in her wall hangings and laboriously cuts corresponding holes in the backing, setting in the matching designed pieces cut from another colour.

As the number and quality of these small hangings grew, we wanted to provide better materials, and particularly some larger pieces of fabric for backing to give enlarged scope to some of the breathtaking designs. When the garment sewing factory had closed, much of the inventory of fabric had been stored in the upstairs loft of the craft shop. So, using melton cloth or the lightweight wool fabric called stroud, we cut larger backing sizes and smaller pieces to be used for cutting the figures. We gave this cloth, along with several colours of embroidery floss, to the most promising of the wall hanging artists. The use of new large pieces of cloth rather than scraps, expanded the creative possibilities and heightened everyone's enthusiasm. We gave little in the way of aesthetic criticism but simply suggested that maybe a decorative border could be added, or more in the way of decorative stitching. Of invaluable assistance was Ruby Angrna'naaq, the young Inuit woman who was at that time acting as our secretary. She did the vital job of interpreting in most of our conversations with the wall hanging artists, none of whom spoke English.

Using, as we did, material that simply came to hand for the first large hangings, the range of colours was rather limited in the earlier work. The backings and the figures were made of the same weight of cloth, the available colours being red, white, or navy duffle cloth, or red, white, yellow, tan, green, or black melton cloth. By the late summer of 1970, the wall hangings looked promising and we had made quite a dent in the inventory of stock left from the old sewing project. Large quantities of supplies come into Baker only once a year, when the ice has melted sufficiently in late August to allow a ship to enter Baker Lake from Hudson Bay via Chesterfield Inlet. When the time came to order things for sea-lift in the summer of 1970, we had confidence enough in the hangings to order a large supply of many colours of felt to be used for the cut figures, more melton cloth for the backings, and an array of many, many colours of embroidery floss. This was a further incentive to the talented seamstresses, one of the high points being the production of an immense hanging, approximately 12 feet by 20 feet, by the young woman Rita Aviliayuk. This large scale is even more remarkable when you consider that the entire work of cutting and sewing was done in a very tiny three-room house in the midst of Aviliayuk's family of three small children and a continuous stream of visitors, relatives, and friends. In fact, the artist was never able to see the entire hanging because her house was too small to hold the work unfolded. She saw it section by section, with finished portions being folded up as work progressed. The only wall in Baker Lake large enough to hold this hanging was in the newly constructed school gymnasium. So when it was completed we took it to the gymnasium for the first viewing. The hanging seemed so right in the setting that teachers and students worked to raise money and subsequently purchased Aviliayuk's large hanging for the Kamanituak Public School in Baker Lake. It has remained permanently on the wall where it was first hung.

Aviliayuk's working conditions are the rule, not the exception, in Baker Lake. All the hangings are made in the artists' own homes. The backings are cut at the shop, and the felt cut into 1/8 and 1/4 yard pieces. All other cutting and all designing and sewing are done at home. Although their homes are tiny, they prefer to work there, for the majority of artists have several small children. A cottage industry enables mothers to keep an eye on the children and earn money at the same time. Baker Lake mothers are traditionally permissive in their methods of child-rearing, so some of the women prefer to sew late at night when the children are sleeping, rather than reprimand them for interfering. Many of the women sew while sitting on a bed or cot, reminiscent of the old life when women sat on the snow sleeping platforms in the igloos to sew. Oonark, for instance, always worked this way.

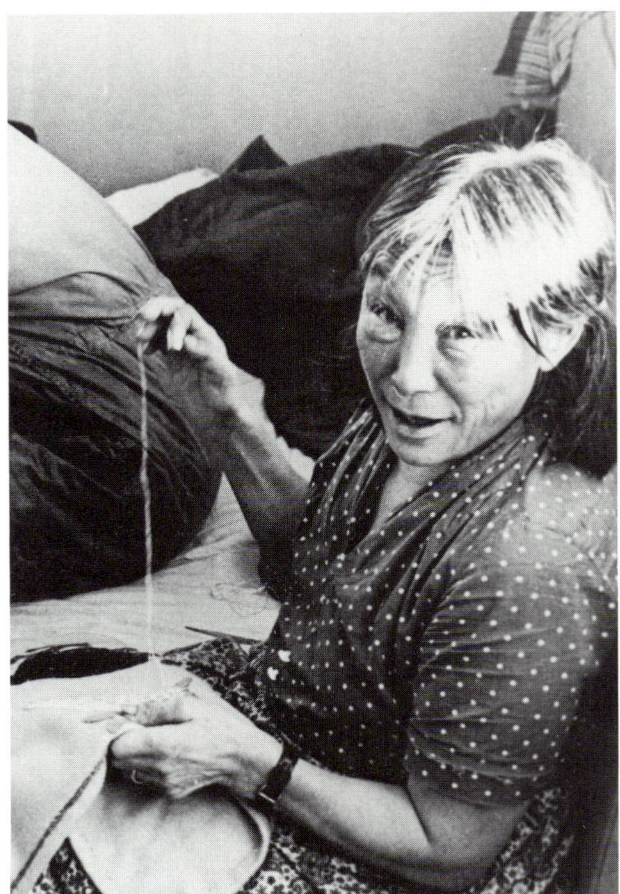

Elizabeth Angrnaqquaq, and below, the detail from one of her hangings.

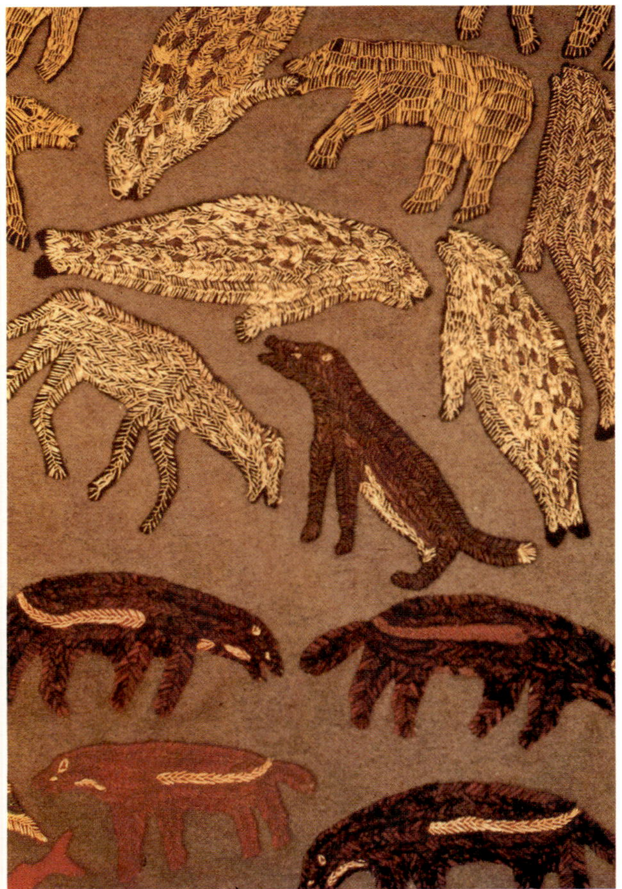

In the spring of 1971 the Baker Lake sewing shop was opened again as an industrial project of the Northwest Territories Government. This time we rejected the factory system, emphasizing instead the strength of the Baker Lake women in the area of exclusive hand-crafted sewing. The making of wall hangings was transferred from the craft shop to the sewing shop at that time, with twenty women working regularly on hangings of high quality. Given the extra shop space and materials, we were able to enlarge our scope and begin to make hand-made clothing, beautifully decorated by the same women who made the wall hangings. Now they worked both on clothing—parkas, mitts, vests, hats—and on hangings, and were pleased with the variety of work to be done.

The backbone of the operation of the sewing shop was a young man named Harold Etegoyok. He did all the cutting of garments and wall hanging backings, most of the paper work for the shop, and all of the interpreting for us in our conversations with the artists. All the day-to-day management of the shop—including packing, shipping, and sales—pricing the

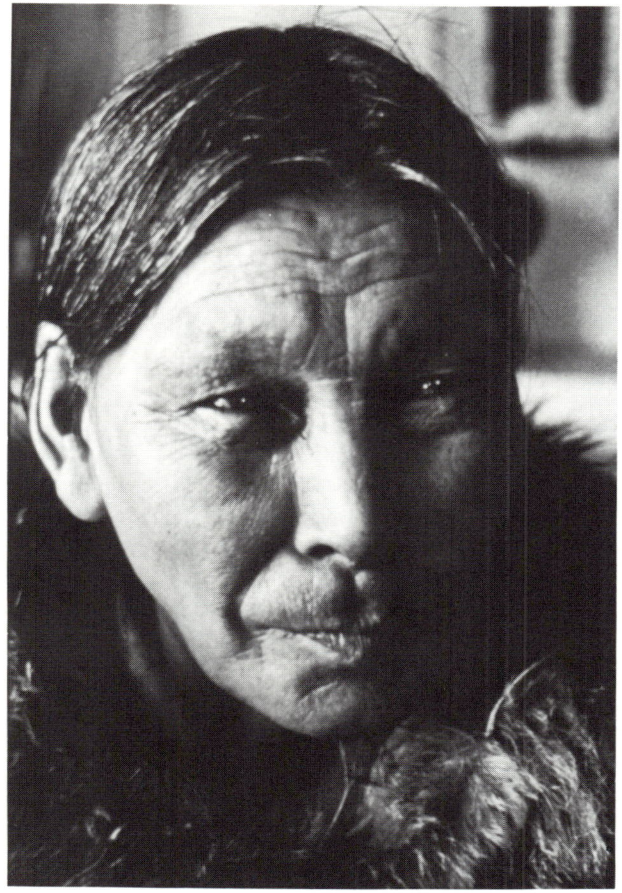

Jessie Oonark c. 1971 (left) and below her wall hanging, 'Figure in Striped clothing', 46.3 x 44.5 cm. Collection: Winnipeg Art Gallery; donated by Mr. and Mrs. K.J. Butler.

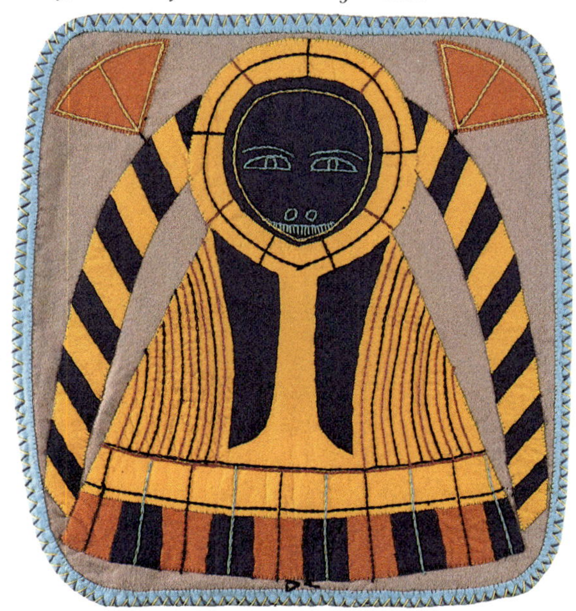

WAG: Ernest Mayer

work, and paying the artists was Harold's responsibility and this was as important to the making of the hangings as the sewing.

Harold Etegoyok's mother, Elizabeth Angrnaqquaq, sews some of the most beautiful hangings with the arctic animals of land and water as her subject matter. Using an over-all pattern of stitchery to achieve the effect of a true furry animal texture, Angrnaqquaq's designs show an anatomical and textural understanding of the creatures she portrays. The game management officer in Baker Lake was particularly impressed by the reality of the animal life in Angrnaqquaq's work.

In southern Canada, Jessie Oonark is the best known of the Baker Lake artists, and by far the most prolific. She has had a one-woman show of her hangings and also of her drawings. Alternating between sewing and drawing, she worked constantly and divided her earnings among her adult children (most of them artists in their own right) and her many grandchildren. There is an emotional intensity about Oonark's strong two-dimensional, shape-oriented style, reminiscent in many cases of ancient Egyptian tomb painting. It is important to note that elements in many of her designs which appear to be simple geometric shapes are actually severely elegant stylistic representations of objects vital to the old Inuit culture. Circles are more than circles—they are drums, the symbol of the drum dance, the central ritual in the ancient shamanistic hunting religion shared by our long-ago European ancestors. An ancient part of us responds to Oonark's circles. Similarly, in the many-figured hanging with the sun face, we see that Oonark gives prominence to the triangle with one rounded side, the woman's knife. This and the needle were the woman's most vital tools, without which she and her family could not survive. A contemporary note is introduced by the snowmobiles which have generally replaced the traditional sleds and dogteams.

Despite the joyous elements and colours in all the many hangings, the evidence is there too, of the incredibly harsh aspects of the old life on the land. Death by starvation or disease was a constant threat and no Inuk wants to return completely to the old ways. The new danger is that the Inuit people will lose touch completely with their cultural roots, their language, and their way of life and will have little with which to replace the loss. The Baker Lake people were, in traditional times, among the most isolated of Inuit groups, but they have now accepted twentieth-century technology with all its accompanying changes. While there is concern for the economic future of the growing community, there is hope too, through the innate artistry and determination of its women who continue to create Baker Lake wall hangings. ♦

The Care of Fine Prints

MOST OF THE STONECUT PRINTS and stencils from Cape Dorset and Baker Lake are printed on Japanese rice paper which is in fact made of mulberry bark. The lithographs are printed on conventional European printing paper. The enemies of these works of art on paper include dust, air pollution, excessive heat and humidity, and *all* light.

The one safe matting board for the prints is a high-grade cellulose obtained from cotton fibres. It is called 'Museum Board', 'All Rag Board' or '100% Rag Board'; it comes in white and off-white only. A four-ply thickness (1/16 inch) provides enough depth to give a print freedom for the slight buckling that can occur with changes in atmospheric conditions and, when framed, allows air to circulate as a buffer against condensation on the glass. A high-grade watercolour paper will do if Museum Board is not available. All other mat boards, including those with a facing of rag stock, contain harmful chemicals which migrate to the print, staining and eventually destroying the paper.

Just as important as the quality of the mat board are the methods and materials by which the print is attached to it. The margins of the print must never be trimmed. The size of the paper and the position of the image on it are part of the artist's original concept. Sometimes the margins are folded to accommodate a visual preference but this impairs the pristine quality of the print.

Under no circumstances should prints ever be drymounted. This process, which attaches a print to its backing like wallpaper prevents the paper fibres from expanding and contracting in response to atmospheric changes. But more important, it incorporates a foreign material which, once again, spoils the original concept. The glue in drymount paper is another abusive agent.

Prints should be attached to their backing at the upper corners only, by hinges made of good quality gummed paper (stamp hinges), pure linen gummed tape or Japanese paper applied with a vegetable paste. Pressure-sensitive tapes—scotch, masking and brown wrapping tape—and synthetic glues or rubber cement all have destructive properties and should never be used. A gummed cloth tape is best to attach the front of the mat to the back.

A thin piece of mat board hidden beneath the inner edge of the frame serves the purpose of a visible mat if the latter is not wanted. These handmade papers have at least three uncut or deckle edges. Often it is a shame to cover them.

In framing prints, plexiglass may be considered rather than glass. It does not condense moisture as easily as glass; it is lighter in weight, less breakable, and can be obtained with additives that filter out the ultra-violet rays. Plexiglass, however, scratches easily, attracts dust and is expensive.

The choice of a frame is a personal matter. The important thing is to ensure an adequate seal between the frame and the back board to prohibit entry by dust and other pollutants.

A word of warning: not all framers follow these procedures. If in doubt, do the vital steps yourself.

If you plan to store your prints, it is preferable to do so in a hinged mat and back. If not matted the prints must be separated by layers of non-acid paper. Storage cases must have less than 65 per cent humidity to prevent the growth of mould. Mould feeds on the paper fibres, weakening the sheet, so frequent examination is recommended. It is important to chose a good quality storage case made of non-acidic material.

Dust, too, contains a large amount of air-borne mould spores. For this reason, cellulose acetate, with its dust-attracting static electricity, is not recommended as a permanent covering.

Provision for the free circulation of air also inhibits the growth of mould.

All hung prints are subject to deterioration, given time. One must find a compromise between enough light for proper viewing and not too much to hasten the action of deterioration. Excessive heat will shorten the life of paper. It is not a good idea to hang a print over an active fireplace or radiator.

City dwellers face the added hazard of air pollution. A major component of smog is sulphur dioxide produced from the combustion of fossil fuels. If absorbed by paper it converts into sulphuric acid, causing discolouring, embrittlement, and finally, disintegration. Adequate sealing of frame and back board is essential.

The dangers resulting from excessive humidity have already been discussed. Outside damp walls, as found in old stone houses, are unsuitable environments for the hanging of prints.

Restoration is not for amateurs. Consult museum experts. Be aware that amateur restoration is sometimes carried out by framers without proper qualifications or knowledge.

Fine prints do require special care. Owners of Inuit prints have the dual responsibility of protecting a personal investment and preserving a great cultural heritage.

Mary Craig. 1975. Updated, 1988, in consultation with Mary De Grow of Winnipeg, Conservator of Works of Art on paper.

The First Printmaking Year at Baker Lake

By Sheila Butler

FIRST ARRIVAL IN THE ARCTIC can be a disconcerting experience—as unreal as a dream of flying to the moon.

In the summer of 1969 my husband, Jack, agreed to accept, on a temporary basis, the appointment as craft officer to the Inuit community of Baker Lake, 1,000 miles north of Winnipeg. On July 1, he and I and our five-year-old daughter arrived in Baker Lake and, save for the fact that we three could huddle together, we would have been blown like straws in the wind and would very likely have made a hurried departure.

Just the experience of changing in Churchill from a normal southern flight with standard passenger seats and smiling stewardesses to a genuine WW II DC3 with a few seats for the paying passengers—the rest of the space taken up with cargo, cases of bread and apples, oil drums which made loud and unsettling noises upon take-off and landing, all tied down with large ropes; the pilot a harried-looking gentleman in an old leather sheep-collared bomber jacket which obviously was of the same vintage as the aircraft; the 'stewardess' a teen-age boy who helped to sling aboard the mail bags and other cargo and later brought us paper cups of instant coffee or pop—gave us the ominous feeling that we had bitten off more than we could chew, and in a way, we had.

The only other passengers on the flight from Churchill to Baker were some construction workers who had obviously plied themselves with strong

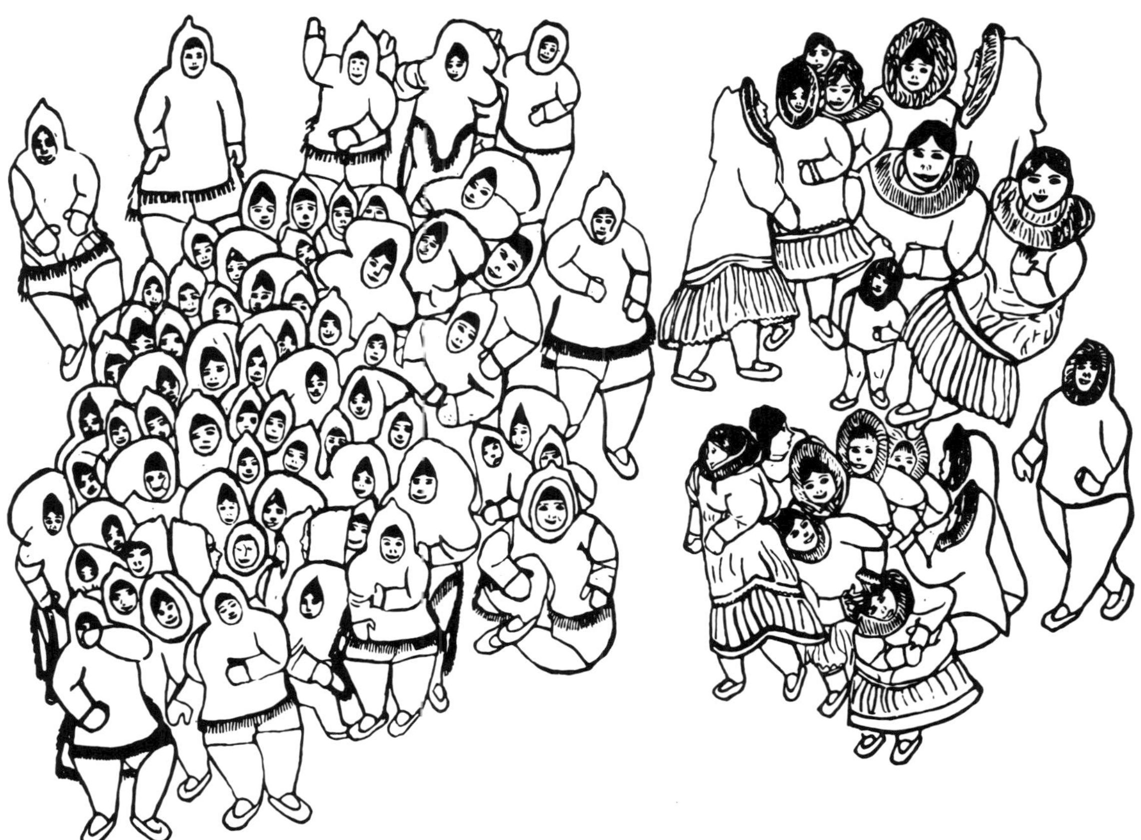

'Celebration': a stonecut by artist H. Kigusiuq and printer Iksiraq. Prints are from the Butler collection and are reproduced with permission of the Sanavik Co-operative Association.

From *The Beaver*, Spring 1976.

spirits in order to withstand the rigours of the journey. One voice in particular rose in argument with a fellow passenger so that several minutes before our landing in Eskimo Point, the previously described harried pilot had to come back and threaten to radio ahead to the Royal Canadian Mounted Police detachment. Fortunately the threat was sufficient deterrent and the trip proceeded uneventfully until we at last climbed out onto the wind-swept gravel pad used as a summer landing strip in Baker Lake. We were met by the Acting Area Administrator for the federal department, Jerry Tanner. He loaded us into a truck for the short run into 'town' and introduced us to one of the local nurses and the R.C.M.P. officer, who were also in the truck. All three of them welcomed us cordially and it was not until many months later that Jerry confessed that the pilot had radioed ahead to say that he had a potentially unruly passenger aboard. Baker Lake had experienced a succession of rather unfortunate craft officers and Jerry, expecting the worst, was sure that the 'unruly passenger' could be no other than the new craft officer, my husband, Jack Butler. So the R.C.M.P. officer and the nurse, armed with a tranquilizing needle, had come prepared to wrestle Jack to the ground if necessary. By the time we heard this confession we had also heard the Inuit recite their succession of craft officers in much the same way that I remembered reciting the succession of the Kings of England in a high school history class. 'One man drink too much and they take him out. One man draw a big penis on the side of his house and the nurses give him a shot and they take him out. One man punch his fist through the Area Administrator's door...' By the time we had put in our first winter in Baker the behaviour of the previous unfortunates sounded like quite rational responses to the cold, the isolation and the Kafkaesque frustrations of functioning in a government bureaucracy.

Fortunately in one area at least we were all prepared. We were both professionally trained and practising painters and printmakers. And we had seen a great deal of Inuit art and loved what we had seen. Our first introduction to visual work by Canadian Inuit, Cape Dorset prints, came from Professor Douglas Wilson with whom we studied as undergraduates at Carnegie-Mellon University in Pittsburgh, Pennsylvania. Under his excellent instruction we were enabled to enlarge our limited vision and to admire those forms of non-western art which have mistakenly been called 'primitive'. Later, in 1962 as a graduate student at the University of Illinois, my husband met Professor George Swinton who had come down from the University of Manitoba to search for new additions to join him on the faculty. My husband accepted Swinton's offer to his first teaching position and so we came to Winnipeg, which seemed the 'Far North' at that time, and at the same time a little closer to Inuit art. We soon became acquainted with the Swinton collection of Inuit sculpture and in 1964 we saw for the first time a show of original Cape Dorset prints, our previous experiences having been reproductions in books and catalogues. We were overwhelmed by the exhibition from which we purchased a small print of a walrus hunt by the artist Parr. Another large print which I remember clearly from that show in 1964 was a stencil image of a direct frontal view of a rabbit, *Running Rabbit* by Pudlo, 1963. Previously I had never thought that such a complete and vivid image could be possible with simple stencil technique. The memory of this great print influenced me deeply as I began to work with the Baker Lake people to produce stencil prints of their own.

Our return to Canada in 1969 was again at the invitation of George Swinton. We had written telling him that we intended to try Canada again, this time with the idea of becoming Canadian citizens and of settling down permanently. We were considering Vancouver and we asked George to let us know of any employment possibilities that he might be aware of. Working for the industrial department of the federal department of Indian and Northern Affairs in the Arctic was one possibility we had not thought about. Baker Lake is a long way from Vancouver and we thought that we were going to Baker on a temporary basis, just to fill in until they found someone to take the position permanently.

In June 1969, George reported on our appointment to the Chairman of the Eskimo Arts Council, George Elliot, stating that the appointment was 'short-term only'. He added that he had spent a full three and a half days with Jack to help prepare him for Baker Lake—all that was possible under the circumstances.

In all the talk of hiring there was never any discussion of my role in the ensuing employment. We went to Baker knowing that we would work together on the project but at that point no one was willing to discuss the possibility of my being hired. Since we were intending to go to Baker only on a temporary basis until they found a permanent craft officer it did not seem worth arguing about. So for the first two months in Baker, I worked without salary.

When the first group of prints was acclaimed by the Canadian Eskimo Arts Council and we decided to stay in Baker, we were able to negotiate my hiring, but a contract at much less than half Jack's salary was the best we could do—even though we shared the same duties, shared equal responsibility for aesthetic decisions and put in the same number of hours. My contract did not cover attendance at conferences in Churchill or Yellowknife and when it came time to attend openings of Baker Lake prints in southern cities, only Jack's way was paid. The conference issue was particularly troublesome. Since I was not able to negotiate my own contract in person without paying the return fare to Churchill my contract terms were discussed with my husband. There seemed to be nothing I could do except to accept this arrangement

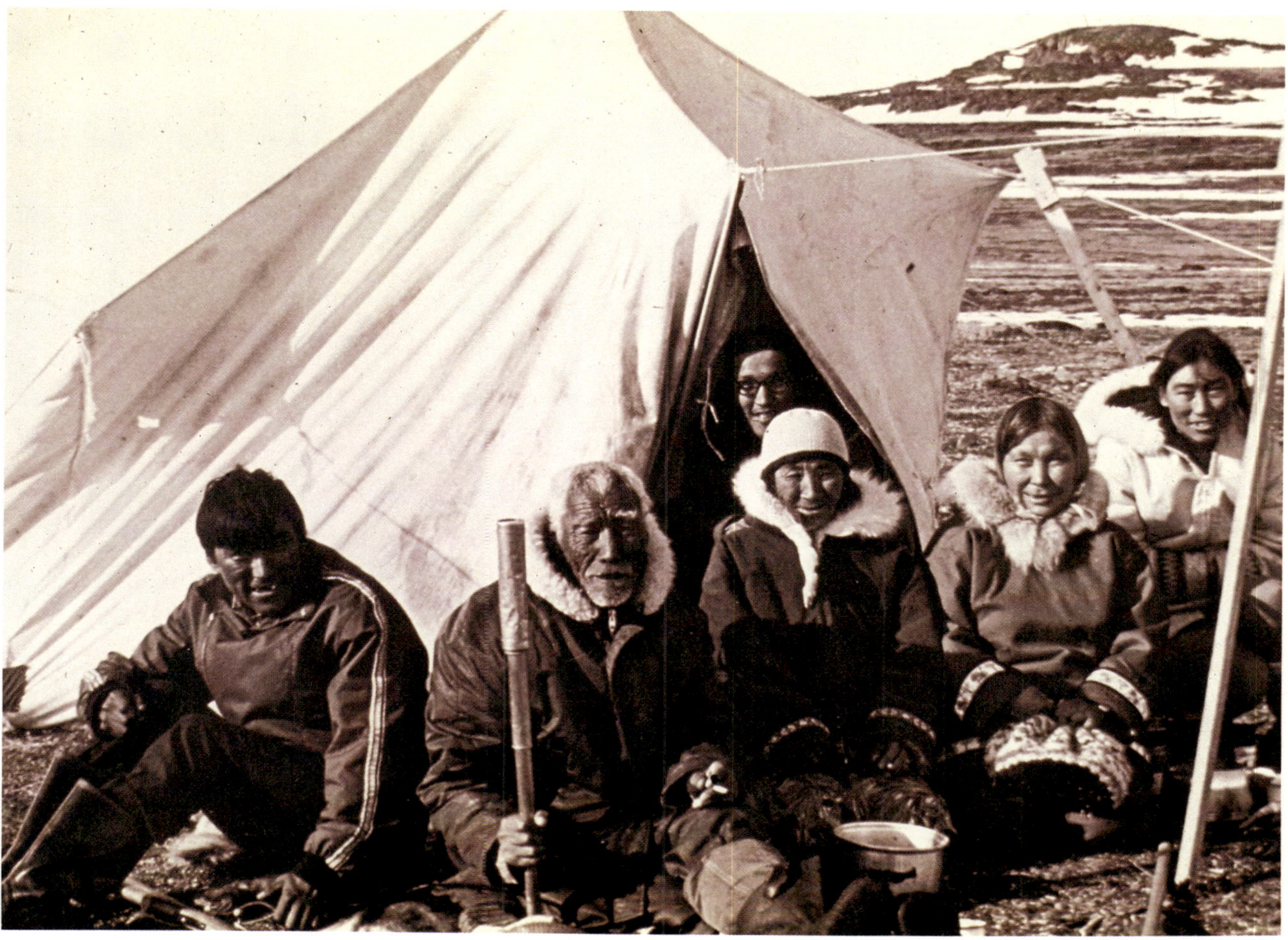

A group of Baker Lake artists: Thomas Iksiraq, Luke Anguhadluq, Marion Tuu'luuq, Jessie Oonark, Phillipa Aningrniq, in front of Anguhadluq's tent at the Prince River.

if I wanted to continue to work with the Baker Lake artists, and I did want to continue.

Our first summer in Baker was difficult although the first-hand contact with the Inuit artists was instantly rewarding. We had shipped a trunk of bedding and clothing more than a month in advance of our departure from Pittsburgh. Naively we assured ourselves of its imminent arrival each day. Experienced northerners know better than to expect any form of shipping or communication to function as planned and our lost trunk was our first lesson, although many more advanced lessons were soon to follow. We had not yet been reimbursed for our travel and so with dwindling funds we purchased some indispensable rubber boots for sloshing through the summer mud, some blankets (we did without sheets), and whatever food was available. No one had warned us about the summer shipment, but here again we learned a lesson. The Hudson's Bay Company store had only the strangest assortment of food items left at this time of year, because they were waiting for their annual stock of supplies which would soon come by sea during the one time of the year when ships have access to Baker Lake. The sympathetic nurses gave us some canned goods from the odds and ends left in the nursing station storeroom and we had peculiar meals of canned spinach, canned wieners, stale crackers and other oddments. By the end of July we had no margarine or butter, no canned or powdered milk, and no toilet paper, but lots of canned spinach.

My husband had purchased a parka in Winnipeg but my daughter and I waited vainly for our winter coats packed in our wandering trunk. Having come from the 95 degree swamp-like humidity of a Pittsburgh summer with air full of reddish iron-ore dust and sulphur fumes, the Baker Lake summer felt chill. I then learned that sewing clothes is not just a romantic old Inuit tradition but is still an indispensable part of arctic life. My child was cold, there were no children's parkas left at The Bay, it would take too long to order one from Winnipeg, and I was too new on the scene to know any Inuit woman well enough to ask her to make one for me. So I borrowed an Inuit-made child's pullover duffle parka, made a paper pattern from it, purchased some wool duffle cloth and a strip of fur from the Bay and somehow put together with hand stitching a rather lumpy little parka that seemed to ride up a bit strangely in the front. But it was warm and served well during that whole first winter in Baker. When my daughter grew out of it I gave it to an Inuit family where it made the rounds for a couple of winters more.

We were at first mystified that so many of the 'white' houses were vacant and worse yet, for us, the craft shop was almost deserted too. We had not been aware that this was a community where many of the white residents—the entire staff of the school for instance—are away on holidays for all or much of the summer. Many of the Inuit families also leave the settlement to live on the land for the warmer months of the year. It was the worst time possible to come in and try to begin a new project. Fortunately we were too inexperienced to know this and so we began to spend all day, every day in the shop, talking to anyone who came in, usually through the services of the secretary and interpreter, Betty Amarouk, who showed up one day, mercifully speaking English. She had worked with the previous craft officer and was somewhat reserved with us newcomers. We had no idea how she was interpreting our remarks to the few people who came in to sell carvings when they heard that some new 'Kabloonas' had opened the craft shop again. Having come from a big city we were at first alarmed by the appearance of many of the young Inuit. It was summer and many were wearing leather jackets and riding Hondas, looking to our urban eyes frighteningly similar to gangs we had seen on the streets of New York. Had we come all this way to get caught in the cross-fire of a 'rumble'? It did not take long to get beyond surface appearance to the astonishingly gentle nature of the people we were to work with, and our fears subsided.

A few people at a time continued to drift into the shop, some to sell carvings, others just to have a look at the newcomers. Given the language barrier, the best way to raise interest in printmaking seemed to be to make some prints. So we rummaged through the odds and ends of supplies left from previous failed efforts to introduce printmaking to Baker Lake. We did not have everything we needed but using what came to hand, Jack started to make a stonecut and I started to make some stencil prints, using drawings from a few sketchbooks we found stored in the loft of the shop. The stencil technique is an exceedingly simple method which has since been used with great sensitivity by the Baker Lake people to produce astonishingly varied results. The stencils are cut from a heavy, slightly transparent waxed paper. The stencil paper is placed over the drawing to be used. The drawing shows through the transparent stencil paper so the particular areas to be printed are traced with pencil onto the stencil paper. Then the drawing is removed and the traced areas or lines are cut out using an Exacto knife.

The first Baker Lake stonecut print was 'Trout' by artist Iksiktaaryuk and printer Kaluraq.

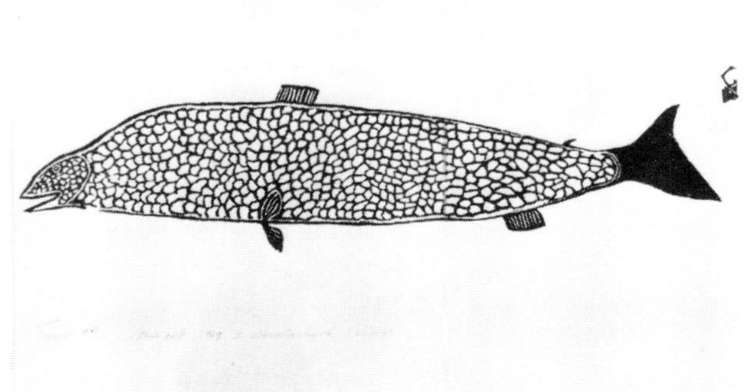

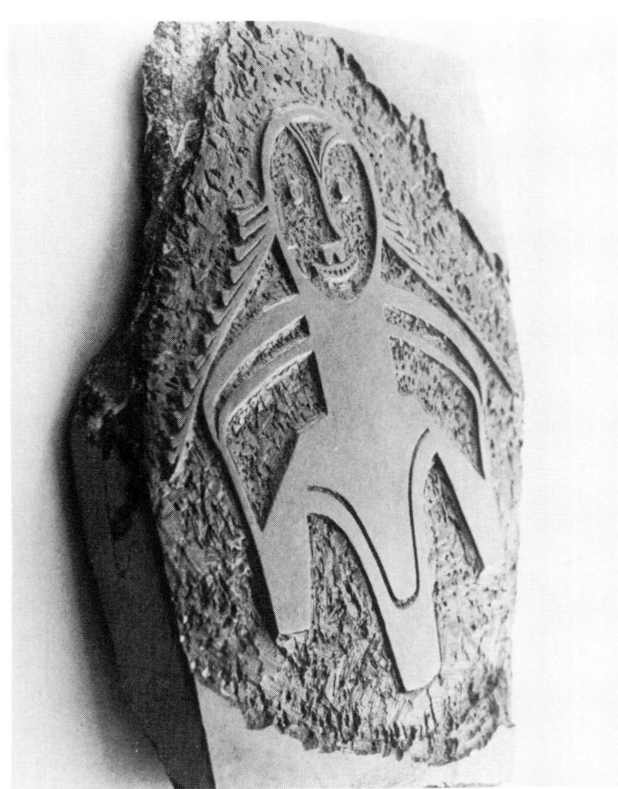

The design for the stonecut print 'Day Spirit'. Slabs of stone imported from southern Quebec are used at Baker Lake.

A separate stencil is cut for each colour in the drawing. To make the print, one stencil is placed over a sheet of printing paper on a flat surface and held in place with masking tape. The printing ink to be used is a lithograph ink especially processed for use in hand-done printing techniques. The colour is mixed on a glass palette and usually thinned slightly with turpentine. The colour is applied to the printing paper through the cut areas or lines of the stencil. The colour can be applied with a stiff short-bristled stencil brush as in *Animals* by Anguhadluq, Mannik. Very heavy application of ink can result in areas of flat strong colour, *Woman* by Oonark, Mannik, or thinner application can produce light airy tones or areas which graduate from dark to light, *Kudloopudlooalook* by Oonark, Ruby Angrna'naaq. Another method of handling is to spatter the colour onto the print surface by flicking the loaded bristles of the

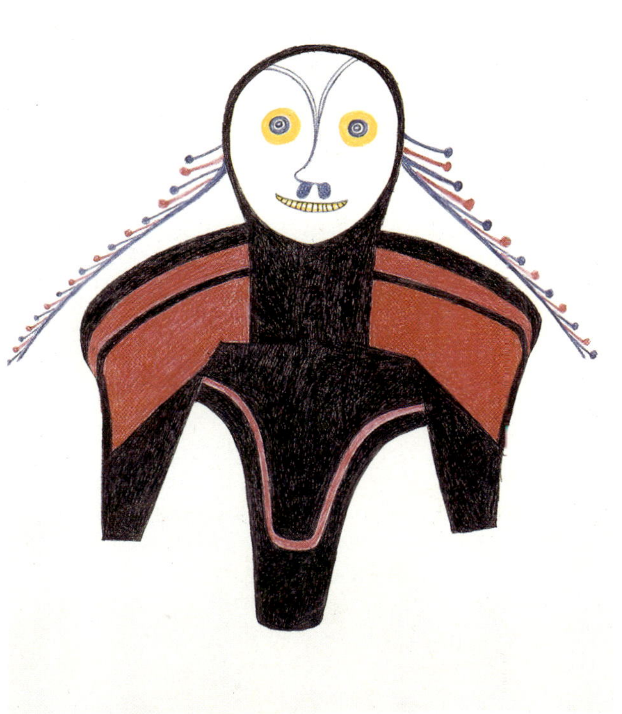

The original drawing of 'Day Spirit' by Oonark.

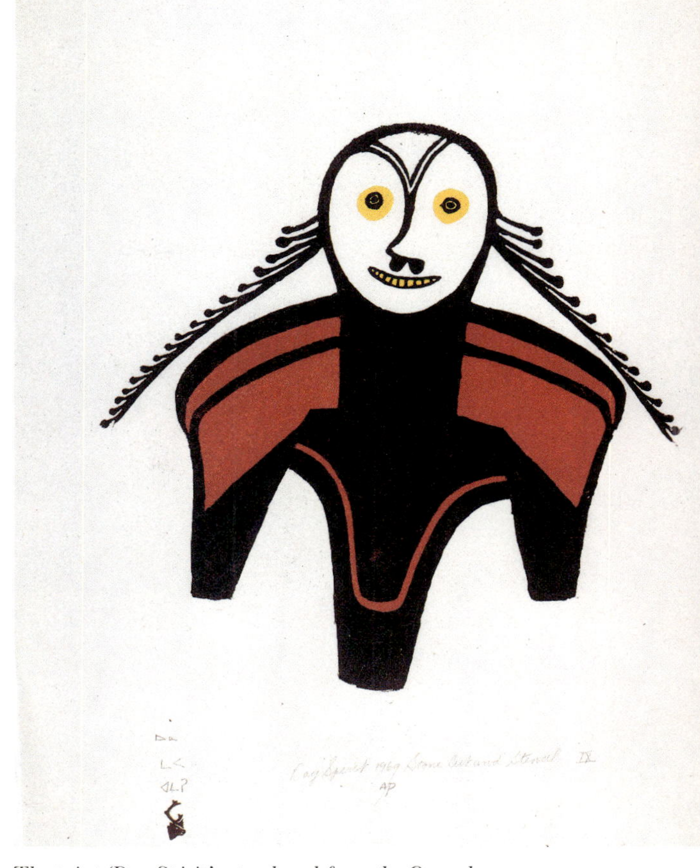

The print 'Day Spirit' reproduced from the Oonark drawing by printers Makpaaq and Amarook.

brush with the finger, *Dream* by Kukiiyaut, Aningrniq. Often special colour effects are obtained by printing one colour with the brush and then spattering another colour over it as in *Dream.* And of course, as in any print media, the desired effect must be repeated exactly for each print in the edition. This process has the distinct advantage that very little in the way of equipment is really needed, an important factor in the North where shipping is expensive and erratic.

The stonecut process is slightly more involved, technically, but is still one of the most direct and simple of the various hand-printing processes. Large flat slabs of stone are, of course, indispensable. Since printmaking had been briefly attempted in Baker Lake prior to our arrival in 1969, several slabs of stone for printmaking were already in place in the craft shop. No local stone deposits suitable for quarrying in the form of the necessary large slabs existed in the Baker Lake area. The stone we worked on had been quarried in southern Quebec and shipped to Baker by sea. These stone slabs vary in size but are approximately 24" x 36" and about 5" thick. The face is filed and sanded down to a level surface. It is soft enough to be cut with a penknife or paring knife. As with the stencil process, tracing the drawing is the first step in making the stone cut. Generally the surface is first painted white to make the tracing more visible and to make the emerging image clearer as the cutting proceeds. All areas which do not appear in the drawing are cut away, the lines and shapes to be printed remaining level with the face of the slab. Some areas may be treated with a scratched surface line to create a textural effect, such as the fur texture in *Wolf Man,* 1971, by William Noah, Oosuaq and Martha Noah. The ink is the same as is used in the stencil prints; it is mixed on a glass palette and rolled onto the cut surface of the stone with a rubber brayer. A sheet of paper is placed on the inked surface of the block and the back of the paper is rubbed until the inked design transfers to the paper. The Baker Lake printers have made their own tools from caribou antler to use in applying the rubbed pressure necessary to transfer the inked image to the paper. Some examples of stonecut line are *Celebration* by H. Kigusiuq, Iksiraq, and *The Pleasures of Eating Fish* by Tookoome. Additional colours may be added by cutting separate stones for each colour and printing successively one colour over the next. When the edition is completed, the surface of the stone slab is filed and sanded by hand to clear the surface for use in making another print. So each block is used to make many prints until it becomes too thin to be sanded down.

One of the immediate needs was for more drawings. The old sketchbooks stored in the loft of the shop served to get the project started but we needed new sources if the production of the prints was to grow. We handed out drawing paper and pencils to anyone, any age, who wanted to try and we promised to buy all drawings that came back as a result of our talent hunt. The results were absolutely incredible. And for most of these people these were the first drawings they had ever made in their lives. Some of the artists discovered in those first few weeks were Anguhadluq, Annaqtuusi, Iisa, Ittuluka'naaq, Janet Kigusiuq, William Noah, Mamnguqsualuk, and Qarliksaq. This is not to say that everyone in Baker lake who took pencil in hand immediately made beautiful images. We did make aesthetic quality judgements and the people did accept our decisions without rancour since drawing was a 'white' idea anyway. Our decisions were made by virtue of the pay scale. We paid more money for those drawings which showed promise and very little for poorer efforts. Everyone in the shop enjoyed seeing the drawings come in and we had gala occasions inspecting and discussing the new efforts. The story content in particular was of great interest to everyone in the shop and I am sure that some of the young 'hip' teenagers heard the traditional legends for the first time while looking at drawings in the craft shop.

In short order printmaking became a spectator sport, second only in popularity to the Friday night movies. The transition from spectator to participant was also swift and painless. We offered $2.00 per hour for trainees to work while learning for one week. Afterwards they would be paid by the job. Some of the first trainees were Thomas Mannik, Martha Noah, William Kannak, Francis Kaluraq, Michael Amarook, Vital Makpaaq, Alexis Pameok, Barnabas Oosuaq. The Baker Lake printshop has had a fluid organization from the first. Of the first printers some have since left for other jobs, some have worked as printers for as long as they could stand the lack of freedom involved in wage employment, and then have returned when the responsibilities and the indoor environment could again be tolerated. Others have worked continuously with the project from the beginning.

Ruby Angrna'naaq c. 1970.

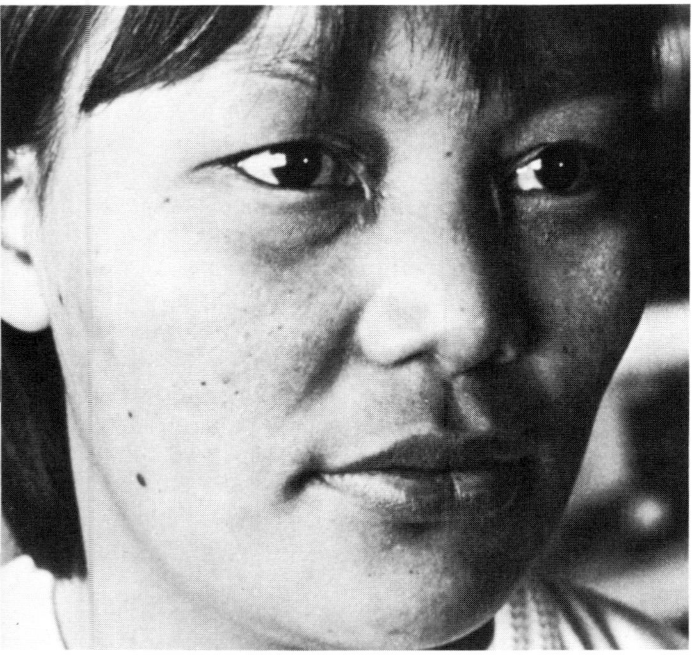

Michael Amarook and William Kannak were the only printers to have had previous experience with printmaking. Michael's introduction to the 1971 Baker Lake print catalogue states: 'In 1964 the people picked Akkanarshoonark and me to go to Winnipeg for the first exhibition of Baker Lake carvings. A year later I started on printmaking. We ran out of paper and there was no one to help us so we never printed again until 1969.' The drawings we were using for our first prints had been made in connection with earlier government projects designed to add prints to the sculpture output of Baker Lake. There were few to work with and they were mostly on rather poor quality paper in large sketchbooks. We found drawings by Jessie Oonark, Luke Iksiktaaryuk, Victoria Mamnguqsualuk and Hannah Kigusiuq.

The rationale for the making of multiples was a difficult concept to put across. It had a kind of magic of its own but was exceedingly tedious to the visually sensitive printers who, although they did not think of themselves as artists, were all capable of and willing to make variations and elaborations of the image they were printing. No one had ever considered attempting to reproduce a carving exactly, and why pictures should be different was difficult to explain to a group of people totally innocent of knowledge regarding the history of printmaking in the western world. They more or less accepted on faith the idea that once a successful image had been created, then it must be repeated. Right from the beginning, however, we did not present printing as an operation limited to an exact reproduction of a drawing. The printing was a creative process in its own right, and we worked together, making many proofs, changing colours or strength of line, leaving out parts of drawings in some cases, adding spattered stencil effects, until the strongest image could be agreed upon. For this reason the final prints are signed by both artist and printer. In many cases the drawing itself was the merest suggestion of a contour line. One that comes to mind in particular from the first collection of Baker prints is *Keeveeok's Journey* by Mamnguqsualuk and Ruby Angrna'naaq. In my notebook which I kept at that time I find a little notation at the bottom of the page for 12 September 1969: 'Pick one for Ruby where she can use her watermark idea.'

Ruby had spilled coffee on a piece of print paper which was thrown in the garbage. Later she mentioned to me how beautifully the edge of the coffee stain had dried, making a shape with a slightly darker sinuously curved edge. I suggested right away that this effect could be used to advantage in a print and *Keeveeok's Journey* was the result of our joint experimentations, beginning with a drawing which was only a delicate pencil outline. In many cases colour was added to black and white drawings. At the beginning this was done either in exclusively stencil prints as in *Scraping Caribou Skin* by Arngnatqik, Taviniq, or in stonecut prints where colours were added by additional over-printing with stencils, as in *Day Spirit* by Oonark, Makpaaq, Amarook. The problems of registration involved in overprinting two or more stonecuts was more difficult and was not used until 1971 in *On the Land* by Anguhadluq, Mannik.

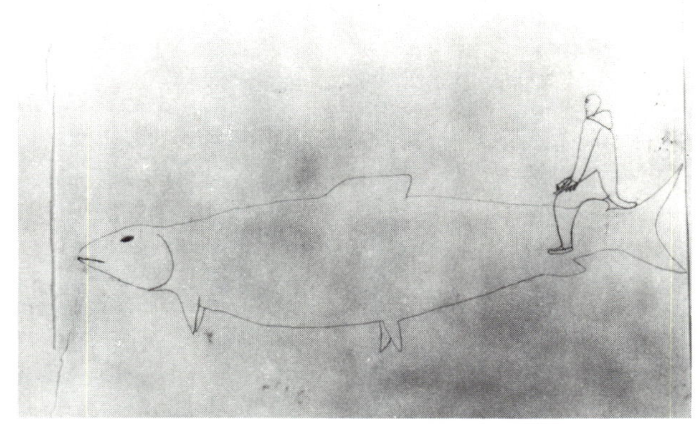

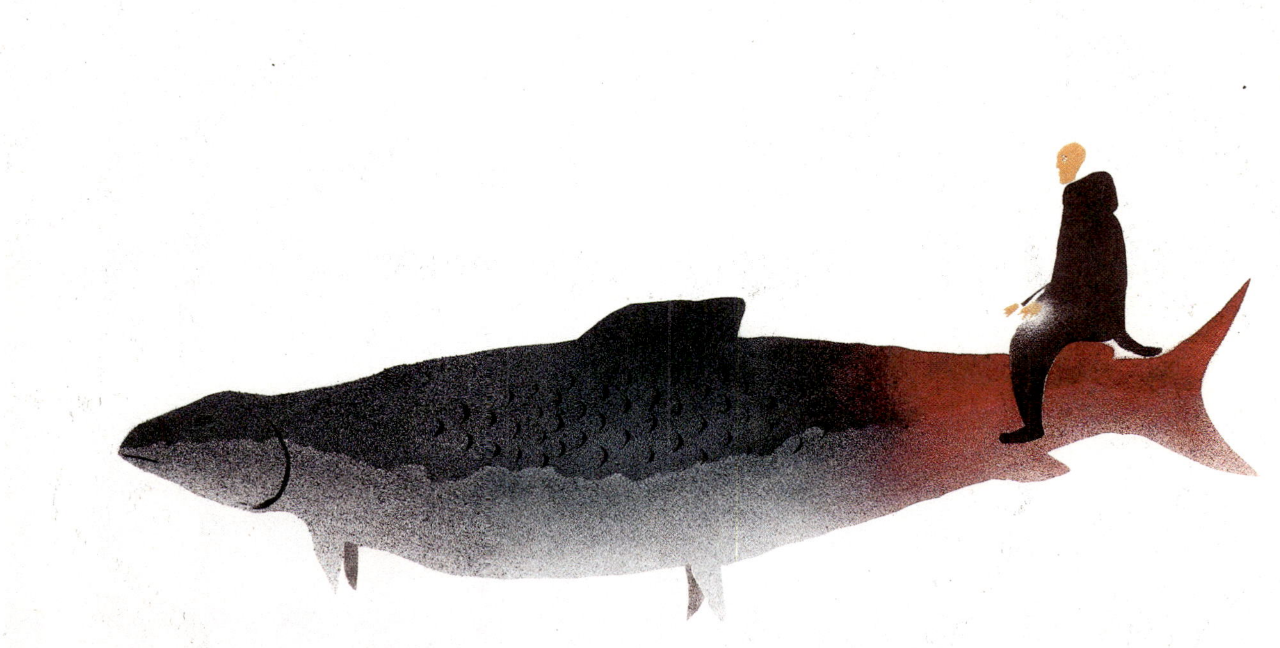

'Keeveeok's Journey' – a print inspired by a coffee stain – by Mamnguqsualuk and Ruby Angrna'naaq. At the top of the page is the original drawing of the design.

We had been asked to submit a report on our progress to the industrial department in Churchill, less than three weeks after our arrival and we dutifully reported to the area administrator on 18 July 1969.

The printmaking project is off to a good beginning. There are five people working on stonecuts. The first editions of good prints are in progress. Sheila has introduced stencil prints and six people are working on them. There are eight different stencils in progress and several look saleable to me. C.A.P.'s [Canadian Arctic Producers] procedures for prints and Cape Dorset's analysis of labour costs and local sales policies would be a great help to me in planning the break-down of labour costs to produce prints here. I would appreciate any effort to rush our order for stencil paper as the stencil print project will soon come to a stand-still without it. ...As yet our trunk and the coffee maker for the shop have not arrived.

By the end of the second week in August our trunk still had not arrived, but after the results of our talent search for drawings, we had definitely decided that our dreams of moving to Vancouver were a thing of the past. We had had little communication from the Churchill office, but we had been offered a contract to stay for seven more months. We agreed, although with some trepidation since we had as yet received no money, neither travelling allowance nor salary and we were literally almost down to our last nickel. Another dilemma was that we had several loose ends in the south. Our car was on temporary loan to a friend in Pittsburgh, we had shipped a few things to a friend in Vancouver and had some other things stored in a friend's basement awaiting shipment to Vancouver. Most of the things, including the car, could not be re-routed to the Arctic. We felt that we had to return to Winnipeg for a week to clear up all these loose ends before we could organize ourselves for a seven-month stay in Baker.

Two other problems, new to us then, were to continue as the major worries for months to come. We were almost out of crucial supplies at the shop: stencil paper, printing paper and ink. There had only been odds and ends to start with anyway. Repeated telexes on this subject to Churchill had gone unanswered. The other area of concern was that we did not have a reliable budget for the project—weekly, month, or yearly. We had been told to get the printmaking underway and to spend what was needed. We enquired in the settlement about usual rates of pay, hired people to begin work, paid them until funds were gone and then waited for money, sometimes tiding the project over with cash from our own pockets. We had no way of determining how many people we could hire, how much we could realistically expect to spend on materials or how to divide the expenses between carving and printmaking.

The lack of a continuing reliable source of funds and the lack of response to our requisitions for supplies were two sources of frustration and concern during our three years at Baker Lake. They were followed closely by a third: the difficulty of lack of communication with the South. Mail was often slow due to bad flying weather. Reception over radiophone was very poor and often radio communication would be completely out for days at a time. With government telex we were only permitted to communicate with the next link in the chain of command and whether our messages were acted upon or passed on or even read was something we had no way of knowing. We could do very little to communicate with sources of supply, the marketing agency for the art our shop was producing, or with the gallery dealers who were engaged in selling the prints and sculpture. But, in August, 1969, only the tip of the iceberg was revealed with regard to these problems and we thought that a week in Winnipeg would enable us to straighten out our affairs in the South and at the same time discuss some of these issues person-to-person with the people in Churchill. We sent a telex on 16 August 1969 to the Regional Administrator at Churchill.

> My cheque for July has not arrived—remember—please make reservations Transair to Winnipeg and Churchill Hotel for two adults, one child, out August 22, 23, return August 31, Sept. 1—short of cash for trip—can Transair bill me, pay later—also want to buy supplies for Craft Shop maximum $500.—please advise. K.J. Butler.

By August 22 we had received no money, no trunk and no answer to our telexes. We did not have enough to pay our fare to Churchill but we decided to go out to the airstrip, get on the plane and try to talk about it in Churchill. The buying and checking of airline tickets was a little more casual in Baker Lake than it is in the South so we were indeed able to fly to Churchill with no ticket and to explain to a very disgruntled Transair clerk that we just had to run over to the government office for a minute before we could pay for our flight. I would not like to try repeating this little scenario in Toronto or Vancouver, but fortunately for us it worked in Churchill. At the government office our next-in-line superior was out of town and the man behind the desk gave us the 'I just work here' routine. Rising to his full, menacing, 115-pound bulk, Jack suggested that someone better damn well find us a pay cheque somewhere or all three of us would move into the office since we had no money for a hotel. A little menace seemed to go a long way and a few secretarial scurryings produced a cheque for our long-overdue travel allowance and a month's pay.

Returning to the airport we paid for our flight and inquired about our trunk. It was suggested that we could look around for it in the hangar if we wanted to. We soon found the much desired trunk stashed in a corner where it had obviously been for a good while and arranged to have it put on the next plane to Baker. We proceeded the next day to Winnipeg where we duly burned our bridges behind us and returned to the Arctic at the end of the week. On September 3 we submitted another monthly report:

> The printmaking project is continuing to grow. There is a core group of printers and cutters for stone and stencil prints who are rapidly developing technical skill. Over three dozen experimental prints have been tried and ten signed, complete editions are ready for presentation to the C.E.A.C. ... The 'talent hunt' described in July's report has produced many potentially good draftsmen and eight very talented artists whose drawings we are now using for prints. When adequate and permanent drawing materials have arrived, these people may produce drawings that are saleable.

Shortly after our return from Winnipeg a very happy event occurred which gave real impetus to the burgeoning printmaking project. The Industrial Department in Churchill suggested that it would be possible to raise funds to send one of the Eskimo printmakers from Cape Dorset to Baker Lake for a visit if we were interested. We were very enthusiastic and so, early in September, Iyola arrived in Baker Lake. The Baker Lake printers were impressed with his self-assurance and although there was some problem in communication due to the two different Inuit dialects, it seemed to work out well enough.

We wrote to the Regional Industrial Superintendent at Churchill on 17 September 1969 to express

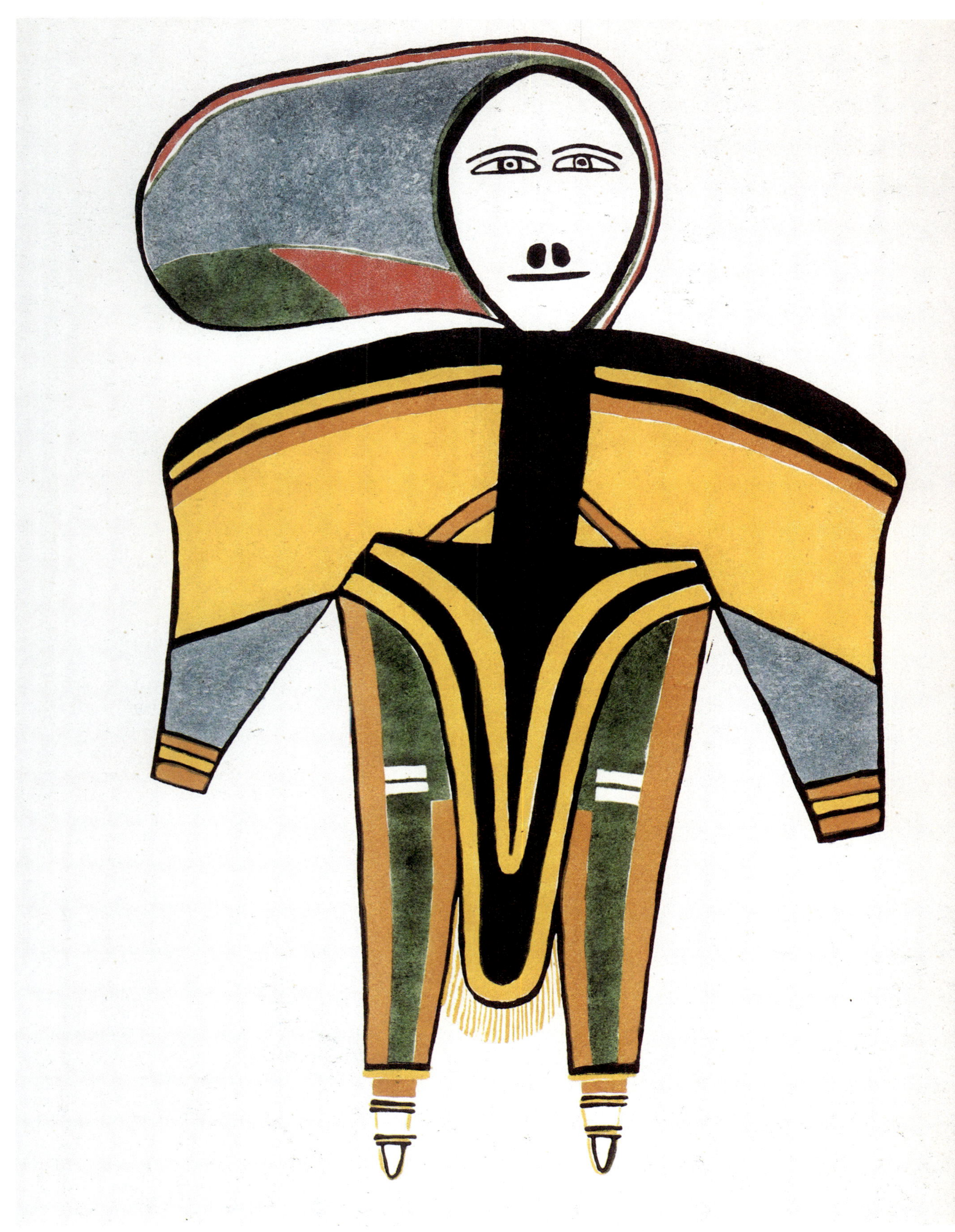

'Woman' by artist Oonark and printer Mannik. A very heavy application of ink was used to achieve the areas of flat strong colour.

our appreciation to the Canadian Eskimo Arts Council and the West Baffin Co-operative for sending Iyola to Baker Lake.

His stay here served as a catalyst for our new printmaking program. ... He was very helpful technically, knowing how to turn the available files and knives into first-class printmaking tools. But more important, he was a rich source of information about the whole West Baffin print experience.

Later that same month we reported that a selection of completed stencil prints and stonecuts was sent to the Council to be reviewed.

On November 3 and 4, the Canadian Eskimo Arts Council met in Yellowknife. One of the items on their agenda was the viewing of the first small group of Baker Lake prints. It had not been customary in the past for craft officers to attend meetings of the Council. The Regional Industrial Supervisor attended and relayed Council's comments, but since he was not an artist, and knew nothing about printmaking, this arrangement seemed less than satisfactory. Jack requested permission to attend the meeting to discuss the prints in person and his request was granted. A vote of confidence by the Council would indicate that the prints were of sufficient quality to begin marketing. The minutes of the Council's November meeting record:

The Council examined 31 Baker Lake prints, presented by Mr Jack Butler. These prints had been produced in the past 3 1/2 months under Mr. Butler's guidance. The Council was very impressed with the results which he had achieved, and felt that the quality was sufficient to warrant a special exhibition of Baker Lake prints in the Spring, 1970. After some discussion as to the appropriate centre for such an exhibition, it was agreed that Mrs Alma Houston should explore the possibilities of an exhibition at the Edmonton Art Gallery, in April, 1970.

Mr Poliquin suggested that Mr Butler might give consideration to better placing of the designs within the framework of the sheet. Other than this, the Council found the technical aspects of the prints most encouraging.

The vote of confidence by the Council was important and put us in a better position to discuss continuing employment in Baker Lake. As early as September 30 we had written to Churchill:

Our two principal responsibilities at Baker Lake are to insure the growth of a producing Art and Crafts Centre and to develop Eskimo leadership capable of assuming the management burden of the centre as soon as possible. These two functions are inseparable if art and crafts production is to become financially and socially successful here.

The Crafts Shop may not have been ready for Eskimo direction in the past, but in our opinion Eskimo leadership must take first priority now. We recommend the establishment of a new position, 'Director of Art and Crafts', to be held only by an Eskimo resident of Baker Lake. His responsibility should be the complete operation of the Craft Centre and all its functions. He should be given assistance in quality control by government appointed special projects officers, technical assistants, etc. This puts the responsibility on Eskimo shoulders where it belongs and opens the way for an art and crafts producing organization independent of government support.

We recommend John Naryagek for this position. He is at present under contract to assist in the operation of the centre. His duties are to keep records, to pack shipments of finished work, to arrange for display of work and inventory, and to supervise and maintain the shop when called upon to do so. He has performed all of the above in varying degrees for the last seven years. He has often been called upon to direct the whole operation including the appraisal of sculpture and artifacts and has done considerable interpreting and translation as well.

In the same line of thought we have invented an unofficial position, 'Director of Printmaking'. The print program is technically complex and requires continuous supervision. Michael Amarook is holding this position. He was one of the first people to try printmaking here in 1965 and is an experienced stone cutter and printer. He has demonstrated considerable initiative and to the full extent of his present knowledge and experience has made contributions at the organizational level. He has also redesigned the printing and cutting rooms to better serve our needs. At present his salary is paid from the purchase budget, but a separate contract and salary would be preferable.

For both men, official recognition would give them a secure position from which to gain the additional knowledge and education necessary for the independent management of the Baker Lake Crafts program.

Even in the short time we had been in Baker, we could see that the people with whom we were working were sincerely grateful for an alternative to the welfare office. But since the crafts program was for most adults the only alternative to welfare, we wondered to what extent people were trying to be artists simply because there was no alternative. At any rate, we believed that they had to have a real stake in the project before they could reasonably decide whether or not art was the right alternative. They had to take on some of the real worries and responsibilities of management. For the first three printmaking years, John Naryagek and Michael Amarook were the managerial backbone of the organization and fundamental movers in the eventual establishment of the Sanavik Co-operative Association which now manages the printmaking and sculpture production in Baker Lake. So as 1970 began, we optimistically felt that the worst hurdles had been cleared. The idea of eventual Inuit management had been initiated with formal contracts for Michael and John, we had contracts to continue in Baker, the Council had been happy with the prints, and an official opening was definitely set for April. It only remained to complete the printing of the editions in time to ship the prints out of Baker by the beginning of March at the latest.

Money had been a nagging problem all along with sometime more, sometimes less money to work with and always the promise that soon a permanent

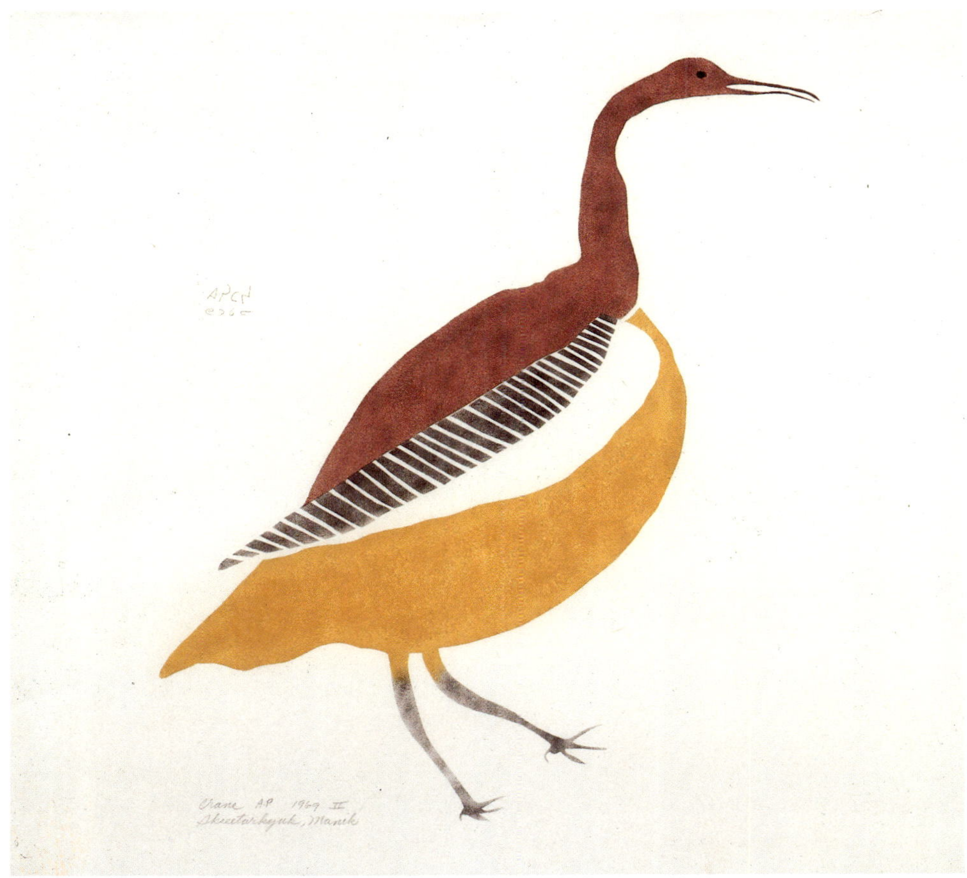

'Crane', the first Baker Lake stencil print by Iksiktaaryuk/Mannik.

revolving account would be set up for the project with a fixed monthly amount for expenditure that could be counted on. Then in January (near the close of the fiscal year when federal funds were low) we were told by telex that we should cease to write cheques. This, at the eleventh hour, was hard to take, especially since we had lost printing time in November and December while waiting for the rice paper to come. It was a hard blow to the morale of printers and artists who had been responding to our appeals to take their project into their own hands. The artistic worth of the prints and their value in the southern market had not yet been demonstrated to the printers and artists. Withdrawal of funds to them seemed to indicate the unworthiness of the work they were producing. After the initial moments of disbelief we immediately set to work sending imploring letters, telegrams, telexes to Churchill, to the marketing agency, to the Canadian Eskimo Arts Council, to our mothers and to anyone we could think of who might be sympathetic. We met that week's payday out of our own pockets while we waited for some kind of response from someone. After a few more weeks of sweating it out in the arctic silence, the response came in the form of an even smaller, but at least renewed budget. The first collection of prints was finished in time and the opening was a great success. Jack attended with two of the printers, Barnabas Oosuaq and William Kannak. The Edmonton Art Gallery bought the entire first collection and virtually sold out a second collection. The printmakers returned with a very favourable impression—badly needed to help them believe in the usefulness of their work. With the successful presentation of a year's work in the form of the 1970 collection of Baker Lake prints, the experience had come full circle. An excerpt from a letter we wrote to an old friend at that time is a good indication of how we felt.

At first there was so much unfamiliar in the whole experience of living here. We were forced to remain open to anything that came along and there were half a dozen new things a minute. Bringing our organizational powers to bear on the machinery of the Craft Shop and trying to sensitively administrate a large-scale production without violating what we know of Eskimo psyche, also teaching (always the subtlest of games—permitting learning to happen in those who want it to happen) and just plain living in such a severe and isolated scene were totally occupying. Now the major structure of the Craft Shop is organized and functioning—it takes continual attention to implement new discoveries and it takes great care not to over-organize and thus impose, or more accurately, close out an Eskimo-generated organization and style—now the shoe is on the other foot and the Eskimos can serve as the best teachers. ♦

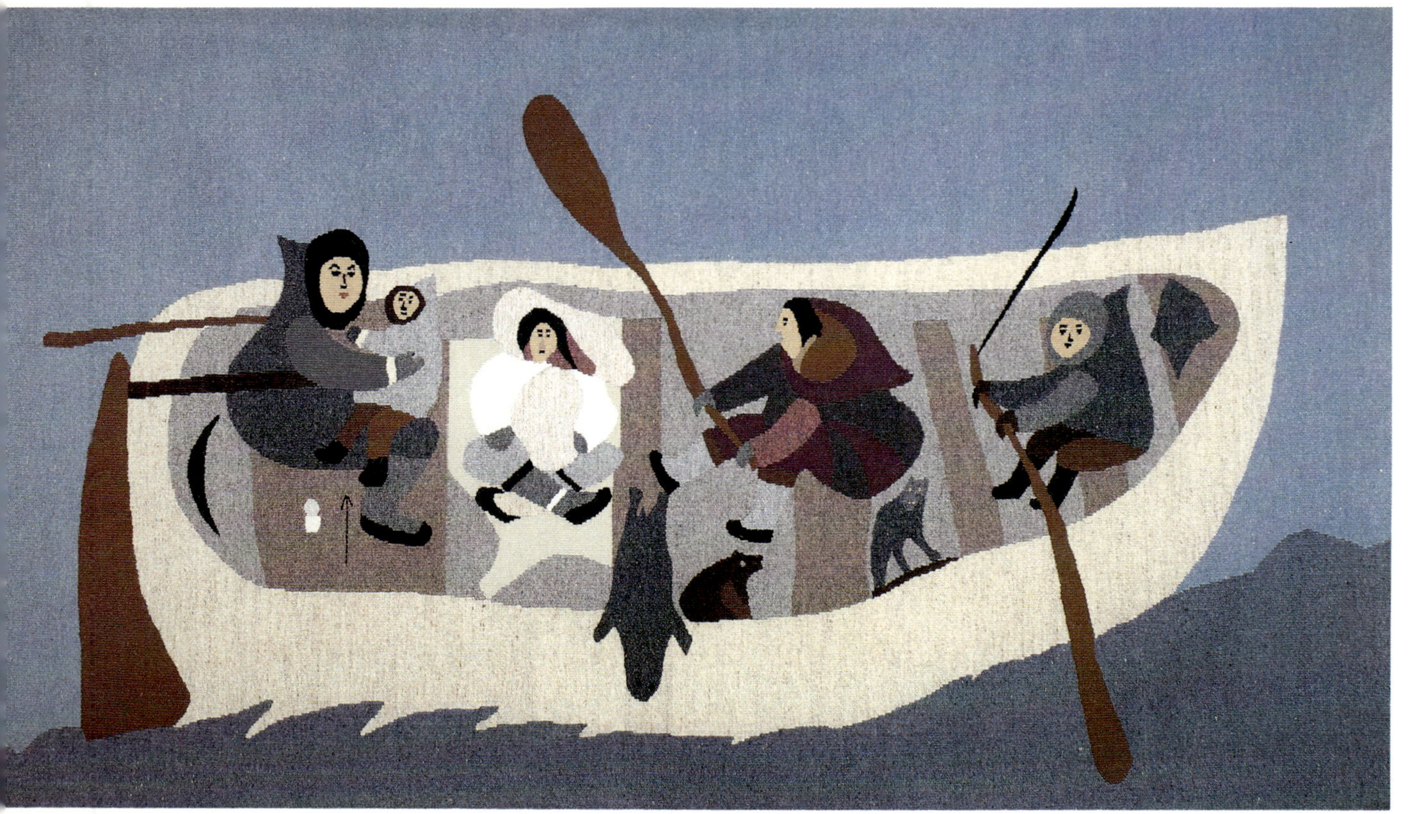

'Umiaktuktu-Boating': designer Annie Kilabuk; weaver Agah Etooangat. 75" wide x 42" deep.

The Pangnirtung Tapestries

By Charlotte and Edward Lindgren

Photographs by Campbell & Chipman, Winnipeg. The tapestries shown with this article are from an exhibition held in May 1981, at the Upstairs Gallery, Winnipeg. Most of the tapestries shown here are reproduced in editions of ten.

From *The Beaver,* Autumn 1981.

VISITORS TO BAFFIN ISLAND who take either the ancient DC-3 or the new Twin Otter from Frobisher over the mountains and Cumberland Sound to Pangnirtung, never forget the experience. Many stories are told by travellers about that adventure; the one thing they have in common is the description of the breath-taking beauty of the fiord with the mountains plunging into the sea.

In recent times visitors have been discovering the weaving shop at Pangnirtung and spreading the word about the beautiful, but hitherto little-known tapestries. Tourists from Canada, the United States, Sweden, New Zealand, Japan and Germany have taken these works of art home with them; enquiries have been made about showing them and having dealer representation in Europe.

Now in its twelfth year of operation, the weaving program was sponsored initially by the federal government and taken over by the Northwest Territories government in 1970. With Karen Bulow of Montreal as consultant and Don Stuart as manager, the weaving was launched as an economic venture to create employment in the community. First, there were sashes or belts, employing the traditional skills of finger-weaving; scarves, ties, rugs, blankets and parka braid followed. Finally tapestries were started and the first show, held at the Canadian Guild of Crafts Gallery in Montreal in 1972, was an economic and artistic triumph.

Pangnirtung Weaving Shop

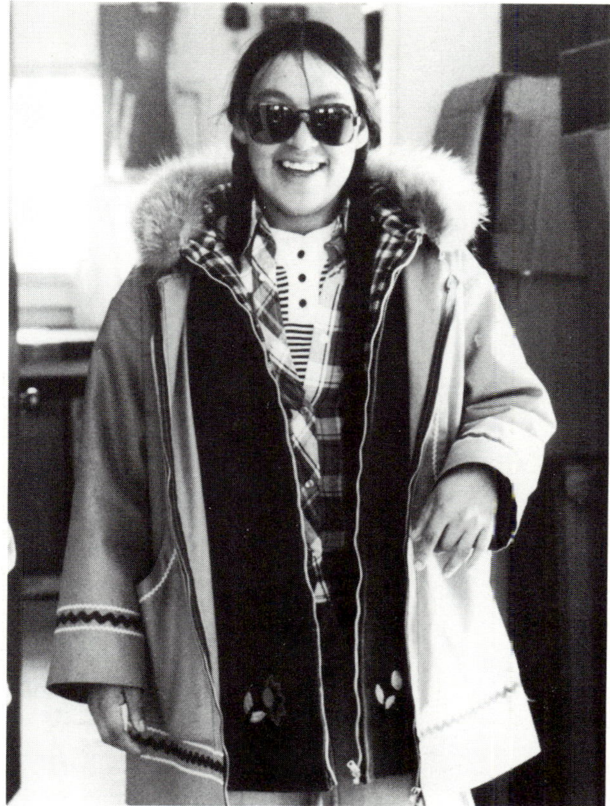

Kawtysee Kakee, who brought her gift for colour to the weaving of the first edition of 'Umiaktuktu-Boating'.

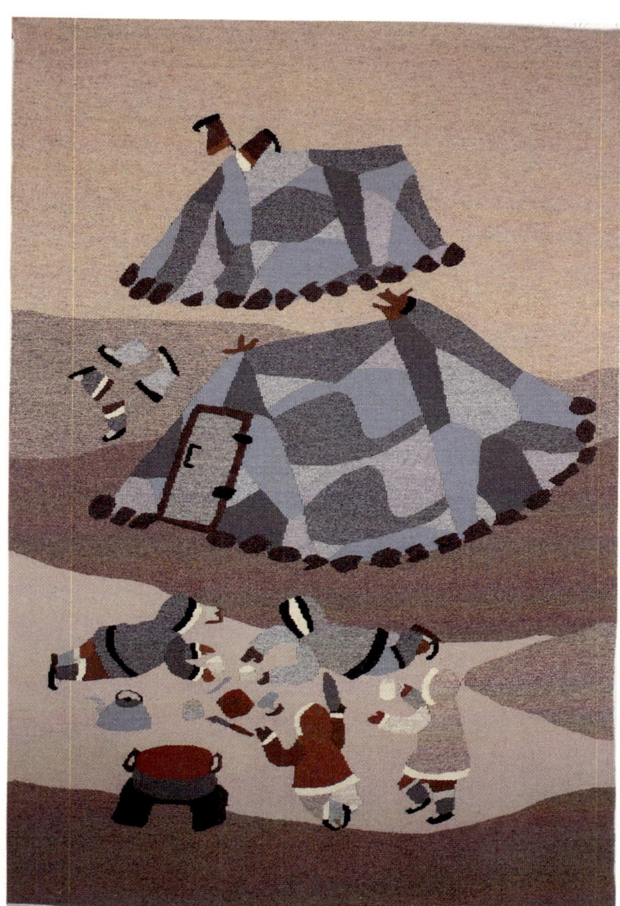

'Children at the Summer Camp': designer Malaya Akulukjuk; weaver Kawtysee Kakee. 40" wide x 55" deep.

The next significant exhibition of Pangnirtung tapestries was in 1978 at the Snow Goose Gallery in Ottawa. Then followed a series of shows in major cities across Canada and the United States. When Virginia Watt, managing director of Crafts Gallery in Montreal, presented her second exhibition of the Pangnirtung tapestries this year she stated that 'these tapestries are light years away from the first ones'. A recent exhibition was mounted by Faye Settler of the Upstairs Gallery in Winnipeg in May 1981. There, Robert Enright reviewed the show for the *Free Press*, commenting that the finest tapestry was *Frightened Owl*: 'its nocturnal aspect seems burned into the bright-yellow background'.

It is remarkable that these dynamic world-class tapestries come from a community of only 900 inhabitants—400 of whom are children. The people of Pangnirtung had not seen the achievements of their weaving studio until an exhibition sale was held in the local school in November 1980. As a result of the show, the community realized that the weavers had indeed achieved a level of importance and performance equal to the Pangnirtung printers. It was an affirmation that the weaving shop was producing work not only for the South but for the North as well. Of equal importance was the development of a closer relationship with the Pangnirtung print-making shop. Recently the printmakers have started coming to see the work of the weavers, displaying a growing respect, and testifying to the strength of their achievement.

The Pangnirtung show marked an important change in the marketing of the tapestries in the North. Previous policy had opposed this, and with good reason. It was important for the shop to make a significant impact on the southern market by sending its best work out and to maintain proper ethical standards with the established Inuit art dealers. If the tapestries could be bought locally, then the best work would be acquired by local people, tourists, or roving dealers.

Now the tapestry shop is able, through a system of editions, to satisfy its growth objectives, pace its production, and have exhibitions and sales in the community. Instead of making every tapestry different, the shop will reproduce a number of the best designs in limited editions of up to twenty tapestries. This gives dealers across Canada and the United States a chance to have the best work. Editions are a guarantee of quality and availability.

The decision on which tapestries are to be reproduced is made collectively by the tapestry weavers and the manager. New designs are carefully chosen; each one has an appropriate size, medium, and technique. Not all of the weavers are artists. All, however, are competent to recognize good design. Thus in the collective decision-making they have

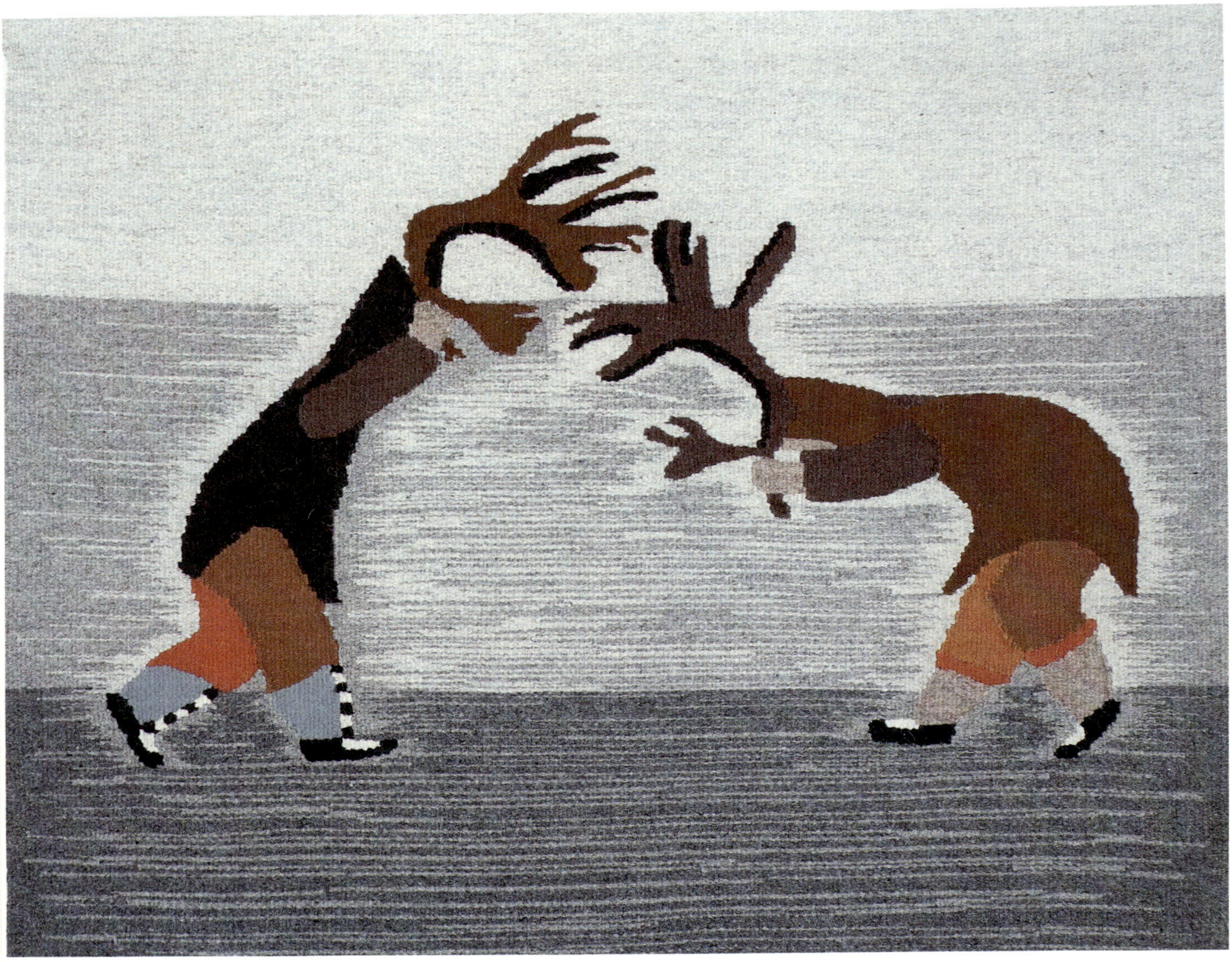

'Antler Fighting': designer Gyta Isheemylee; weaver Towkee Etooangat. 33" wide x 27" deep.

tremendous creative input. Inevitably, they will make deletions from a design or simplifications based on the technical limitations and possibilities of the weaving process. Lines that involve fussy weaving or embroidery may be reduced or removed.

They will also decide whether the tapestry be woven lengthwise or widthwise. The overall proportions and treatment of background are arrived at by discussion too. The dimensions are set and a drawing the actual size of the tapestry is made.

This highly creative, studied approach gives to the first number of an edition an importance and excitement that is felt by everyone in the shop. Nevertheless, subsequent repeats are considered for possible refinements or improvements. As a result, no two numbers of an edition are perfectly identical. Sometimes the differences may be due simply to the need of the weaver to avoid the monotony of repetition; or, when the series is done over a long period of time, various editions are usually woven by different people.

In the translation of a design to a woven tapestry the art of the weaver is evident. A black line drawing on white paper becomes a composition of colour and

Towkee Etooangat

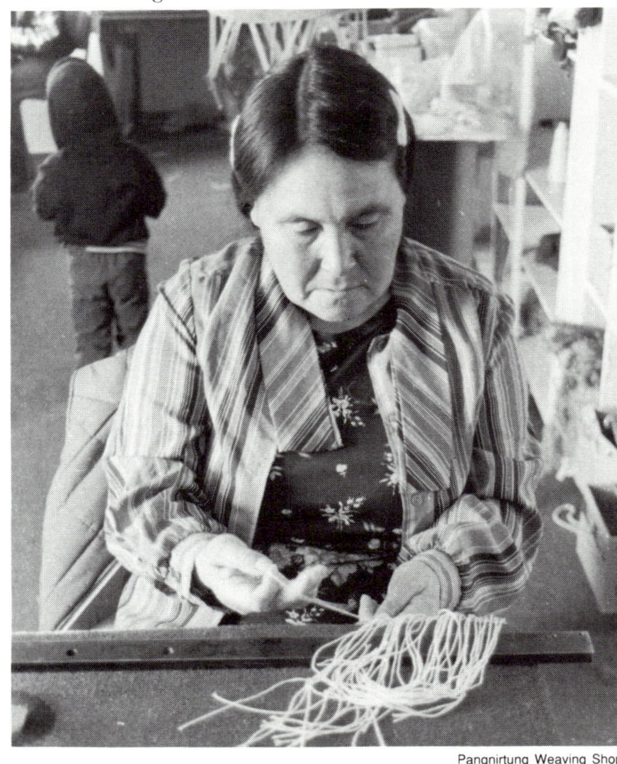

Pangnirtung Weaving Shop

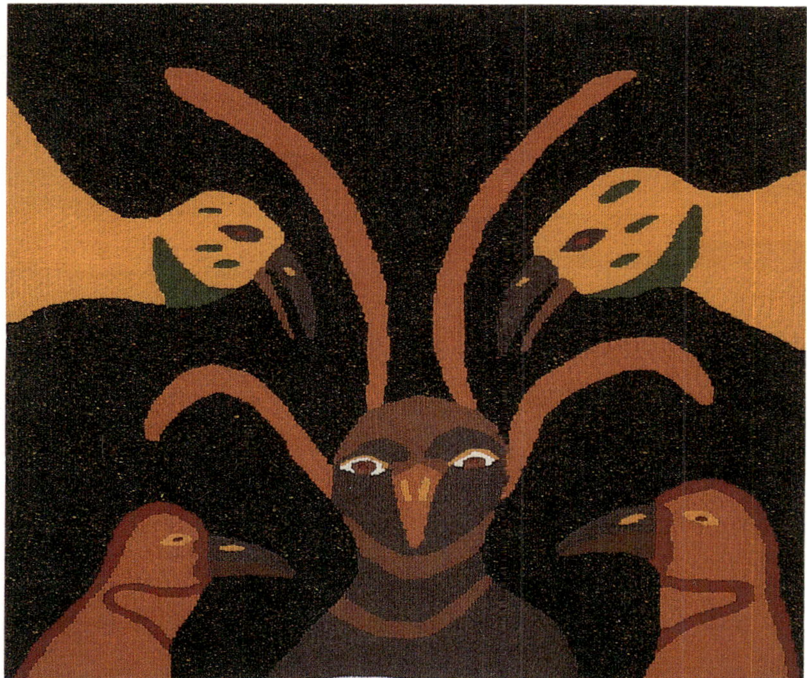

'Monster With Four Birds': designer Malaya Akulukjuk; weaver Towkee Etooangat. 33" wide x 28" deep.

depth; a figure in a landscape of white becomes a figure in a composition of shades of white. It is interesting to see how the weaver differentiates arms or legs crossing each other by changing the colour of one; and it is exciting to see how a face that had been defined with lines and dots in the sketch is translated into planes of colour that model the features and suggest three dimensions.

Adjacent colour areas may be woven with different colour wefts interlocking in such a way as to produce a blurred line. Or an outlining technique might be used by twining weft of a third colour to join two colour areas with a continuous line. The third technique, one most often used at Pangnirtung, is the practice of the slit technique. Slits between colours are left open to give a stronger definition and depth to the design; they are sewn closed only when necessary.

To express light qualities such as snow, fog and ice glare, transitional colour changes are made using the technique of hatching, as in *Antler Fighting* and *A Dog Is Harnessed.* It is likely that some of the most interesting developments will come as the weavers explore the possibilities and problems in depicting snow in all its variations that the Inuit know so well.

What is evident in the Pangnirtung tapestries is that superb design is married to superb weaving. The standard of weaving is uncompromisingly high, and the finishing is so perfect that it is difficult to tell the front from the back when the tapestry comes off the loom. The master weavers who are judged skilful enough to weave tapestries are indeed the first who should be credited with the success of the Pangnirtung shop. Among these, two people deserve to be singled out.

Olassie Akulukjuk, who has been weaving tapestries longer than anyone in Pangnirtung, deserves recognition for her exceptional work. She wove the first edition of *Frightened Owl, Antler Fighting, Exploring a Cave,* and *Creeping Up.*

Kawtysee Kakee has a special gift for colour. When a large tapestry is to be woven she often does the first one, for she has the capability of working out the complex relationships that a large tapestry presents. She wove the first edition of *Umiaktuktu-Boating* and *Raven Scares Creatures.* The first edition of the best tapestry in the Montreal show of March 1981—Kawtysee's *Going Fishing* was purchased by the federal department of Indian and Northern Affairs. The next copy of this design will be displayed in the Frobisher Bay show in November 1981 at Baffin Kamutauyait.

Attention to detail is typical of the Pangnirtung weavers. The changes in the kind of sleeve that is made is a case in point. In the early tapestries the top and bottom were folded over. This was simple and provided sleeves where support rods could be inserted. But the Aubusson technique produces a very flat work and these bulky hems were not consonant with the elegant flatness of the tapestry itself. As well, the edges were vulnerable to wear.

Now the warp ends are neatly terminated by a thin line of Swedish braid at top and bottom; then a linen cloth sleeve covers and firmly anchors the ends. This type of braid and linen sleeve are in the best tradition of the ancient art of tapestry-making. As well, the

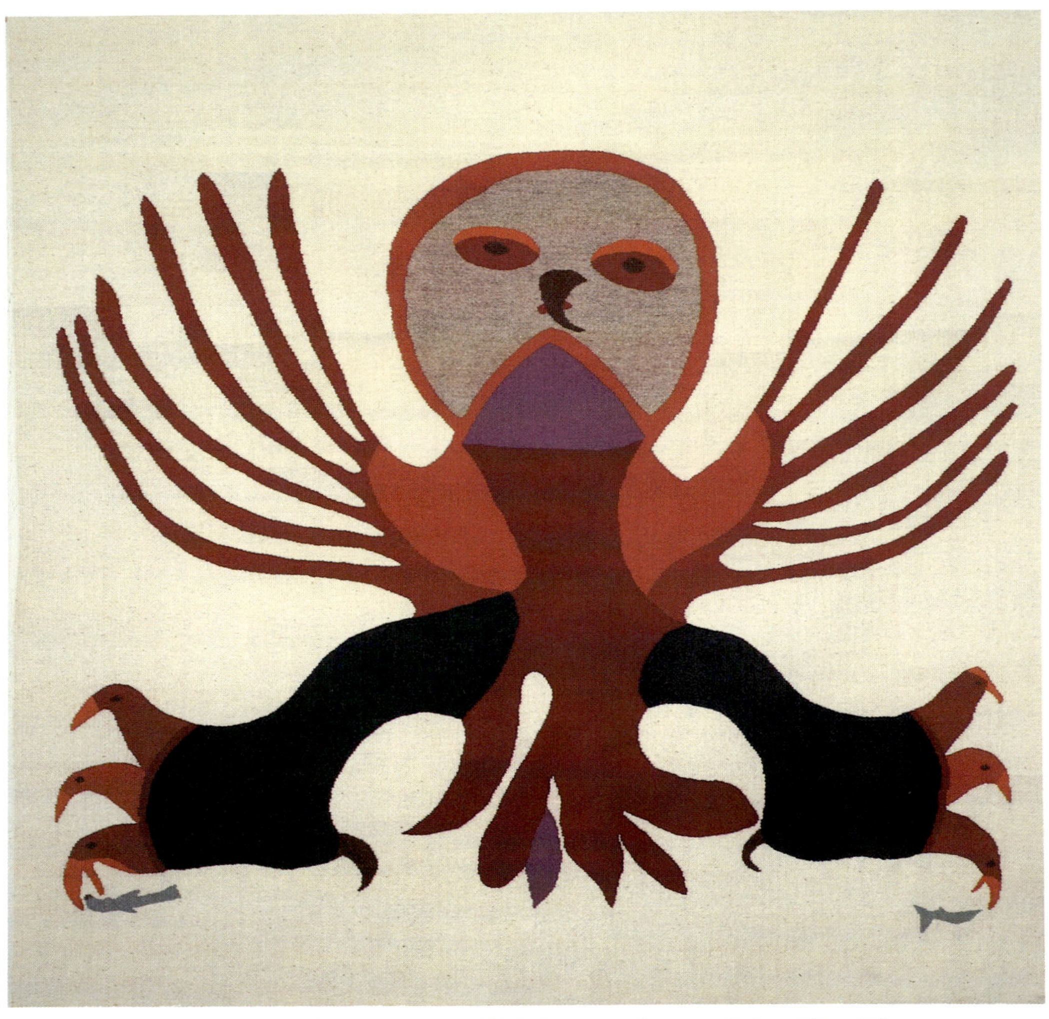

'Frightened Owl': designer Annie Kilabuk; weaver Kawtysee Kakee. 60" x 60".

linen sleeve provides a surface for information about the tapestry, which is written with indelible ink, in English and syllabics.

The designers, too, should be given credit for their contribution. The tapestries now being made are more varied than in the past. There are fewer single-figure designs now, and fewer that could be classed as merely decorative; most often they tell a story. For several years the shop used the drawings of just one artist, Malaya Akulukjuk. Now drawings by a number of people are used so there is a greater variety of style and subject matter.

Some designers live on the land in outlying camps; others live in town. Some remember the old ways, some depict the legendary myths, and some, the magnificent landscape of Pangnirtung fiord.

In such works as *Creeping Up* and *Where They Go Caribou Hunting* the aerial view illustrates the unusual ability of the Inuit to visualize freely without European pictorial conventions. For example they are able to make absolutely accurate maps utilizing this ability to 'see' the land as if viewed from above. The community recognizes something of itself in these works, sees its world in its own way.

The contribution of the managers (or co-ordinators) has been another factor in the shop's growth. The previous manager, Megan Williams, was trained in the art of weaving. With her expertise she increased the weavers' technique and aesthetic vocabulary. The present manager, Deborah Hickman, is an art college graduate and weaver. Her organizational skills are bringing together the various aspects of production and marketing.

In her association with the weavers, Hickman too has become interested in the way the new weaving terminology has been adapted to the Inuit language. 'In most cases,' she writes, 'words have been borrowed from skills familiar before the introduction of weaving. The word for the verb "weave", for example, is "nuvisa" which is the same as the verb "knit". The word "loom" is "nuvisavu" which also means "knitting needles" or literally "an instrument for putting yarns together". ... Weft threads are wound around bobbins before use and take the name "nuvilauti" which

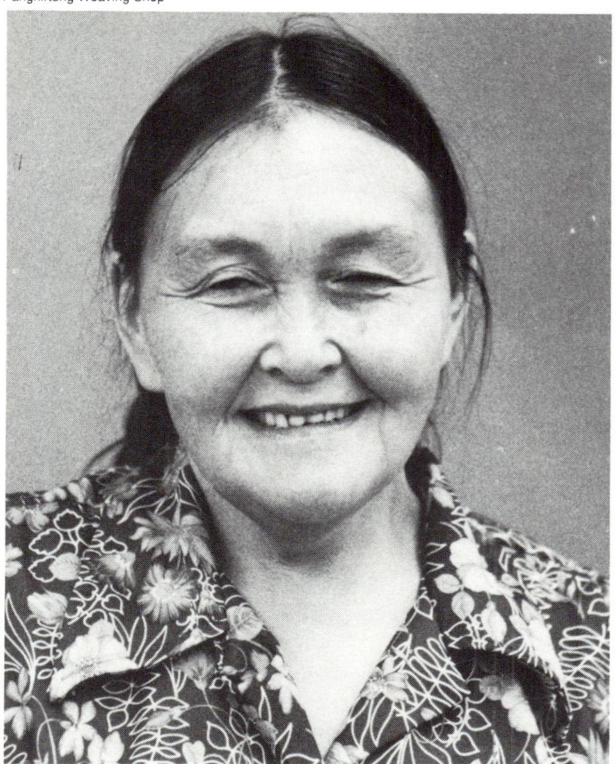

Annie Kilabuk.

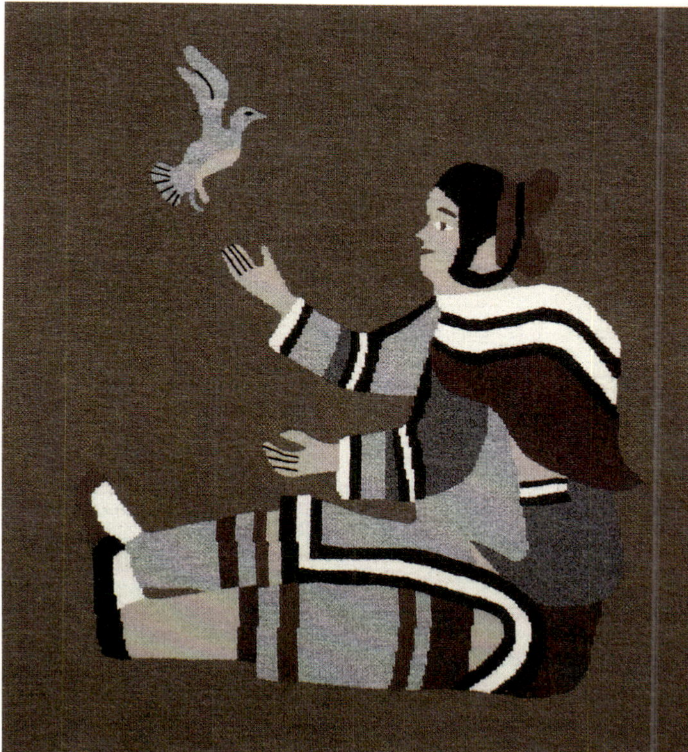

'Lady with Bird': designer Malaya Akulukjuk; weaver Geela Akulukjuk. 34" x 34".

means "to wind around". Warp threads, however, encounter a more humorous adaptation. As these threads are chained together into a coil before transfer to the loom, the word for "warp" is "inaluguat" meaning "looks like intestines".'

It is likely that a firmer sense of being in charge will come to the Inuit when one of their own people holds the title of manager. It is also certain that a southern connection will still be needed to handle the transactions of ordering supplies, delegating weavers and designers and doing business with the South in general.

This year two entirely new products were introduced: after-ski boots, and a jacket that is based on the traditional women's garment named 'akujulik' (a-koo-joo-lik) meaning 'parka with a little tail'. The nearby sewing shop was enthusiastic about the design and spontaneously made a matching nylon shell.

Another new venture is rug making. These are made only on order and distributed mainly through the network of tapestry dealers already established. Two rugs were exhibited with the tapestries at the Innuit Gallery in Toronto in September 1981, and the first woven Pangnirtung rug was commissioned by that gallery for a client's office in New York.

Tapestries have a special quality: presence—a combination of material and size. In the earlier years the maximum size was 45" but now larger tapestries are being made and are much in demand. This may be a natural response to the impact of the art form. Anyone who has seen a large tapestry on a large wall is aware of how the tapestry can dominate an area. A tapestry on a wall seems to warm a room, to give it a special aura with its sound-and-light-absorbing properties.

When it comes down to the final analysis it is not the technique or the subject matter that is vital; it is the fact that the tapestries are memorable works of art. Some critics suggest that the Inuit tapestries are 'borrowed' art forms because there is no tradition of weaving in the Inuit culture. In my opinion, it is irrelevant that weaving is not indigenous to the Inuit. The fact is that the Inuit have survived over the centuries because they can adapt. What is their tradition is the taking of whatever means there are at hand to make a better life.

In their struggle for survival they were forged into a people who had marvelous manual dexterity, patience, and a sense of humour. They were not able to lose touch with the elemental in life, and this is what is genuine in their art; it is not the medium but the force of the imagery that brings renown to Inuit art, in all its forms. ♦

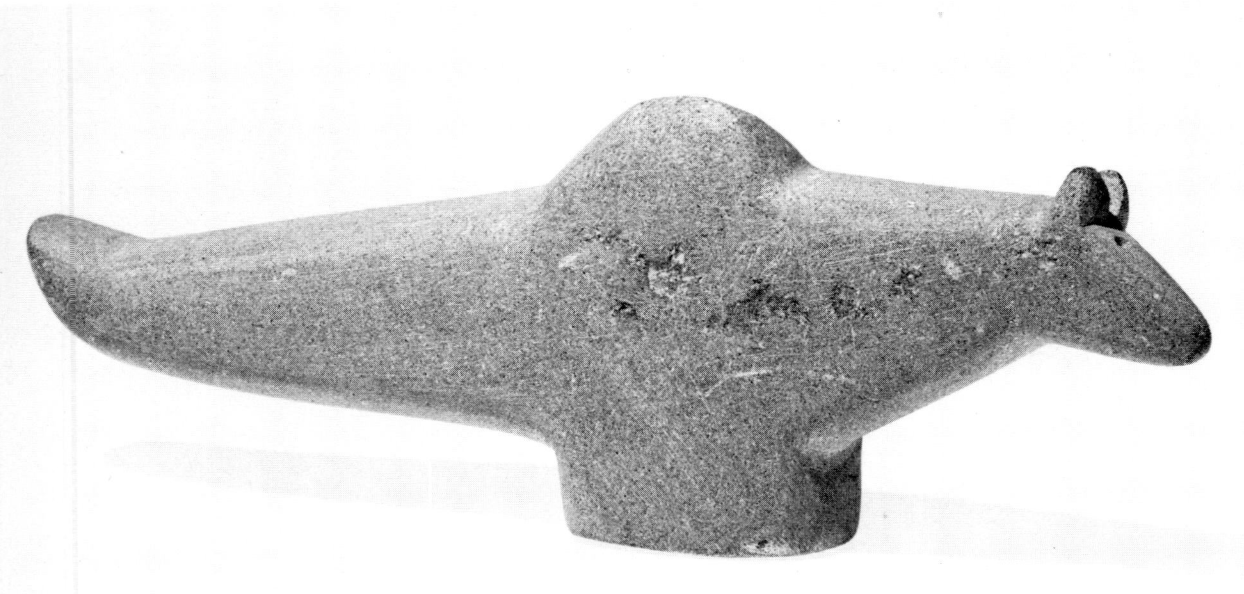

Ernest Mayer

'Animal', undated, by Miki of Eskimo Point. The artist is one 'whose works are either thoroughly enjoyed or simply don't appeal—there is no middle ground.' Jerry Twomey Collection, Winnipeg Art Gallery.

Reflections on Inuit Art

By Betty Bell

THE GALLERY SHOP of the Vancouver Art Gallery first came into being in 1964 under the auspices of the women's auxiliary to the Vancouver Art Gallery and with the blessing of Richard Simmins, the director at that time. At first, there was no thought of attempting to become involved in the sale of original works of art. The first tentative steps taken by the committee on the way to eventually becoming recognized dealers in Inuit art was the placing, around 1965, of a trial order through the Hudson's Bay Company for about a dozen inexpensive carvings—a conspicuously hesitant beginning, but one which led to far greater involvement.

Shortly after that experiment, which had resulted in an immediate sell-out, George Swinton happened to drop into the shop and when asked about a regular source for carvings from the Arctic he immediately advised us of Canadian Arctic Producers, the wholesale outlet for the work from the arctic co-operatives in the Northwest Territories. That began a period of a year or so when Mary Craig or one of her assistants in Ottawa selected occasional shipments of up to thirty or so small to medium-sized carvings for us, and I was lucky enough to be the one who looked after them. We almost went into shock the first time it was necessary to price a piece of sculpture at $100. We were still cautiously feeling our way.

From *The Beaver*, Spring 1981.

Ernest Mayer

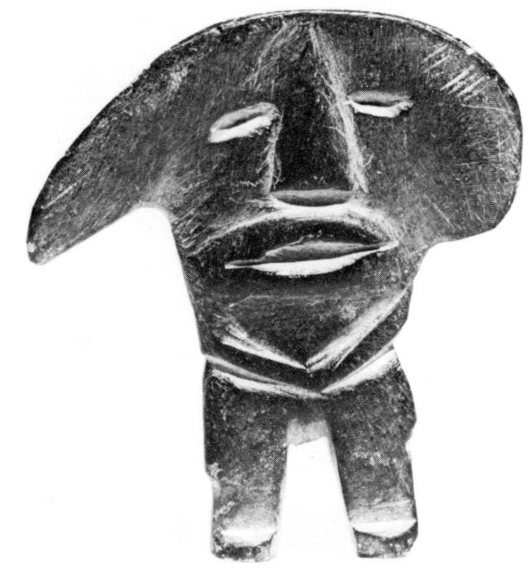

'Parka Image', 1964, by John Kavik of Rankin Inlet. George Swinton Collection in the Winnipeg Art Gallery.

Ernest Mayer

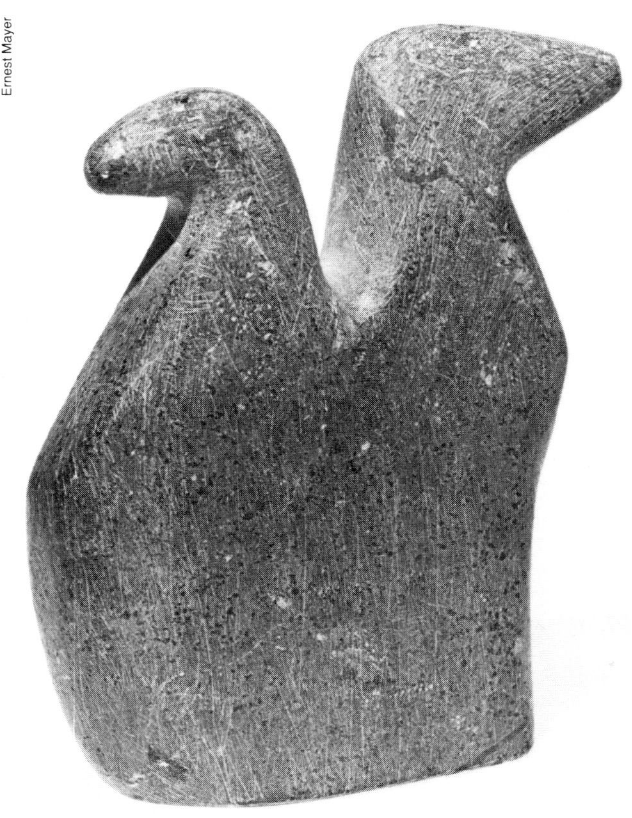

'Two Bird Figures', 1970, by Miki. George Swinton Collection, Winnipeg Art Gallery.

As business increased, it was decided that two of us would follow up one of our buying trips to the Toronto Gift Show by visiting Ottawa ourselves to pick out a supply of carvings sufficient to last for several months or even a year. That, at least, was our expectation. It turned out to be rather a bewildering day. Facing shelf after shelf packed with heavy stone figures, stumbling over large sculptures on the floor, and having the responsibility for the first time of personally choosing suitable pieces was an overwhelming experience. That first day there were many hesitations and qualms before the final selections were made. From then on, we found it necessary to renew our stock with increasing frequency and to choose a larger portion of important pieces as the shop grew into a respected dealership. Finally we achieved the near impossible by becoming, one year, the customer with the largest volume at Canadian Arctic Producers.

Once the move of the wholesale depot from Catherine Street to the building near the Ottawa airport was made (CAP has since moved to Winnipeg), the selection of suitable works became infinitely more simple; one could see and even walk around most of the carvings, and it was then that I established my own way of buying.

There were two main criteria: the Vancouver Art Gallery's standards must always be kept in mind, and nothing should be bought that I myself did not really like (although there were naturally degrees of approval, ranging from considering a work pleasant and well made to being personally immensely excited by it). There was also the necessity of making sure that sufficient choice in size and price within these guidelines could be offered to suit a varied public. After all, not everyone who enters an art gallery shop wants or is able to leave with a major purchase, although I know some visitors surprised themselves and us by succumbing to an important work on impulse. But apart from aiming to attract casual buyers, it was also necessary to keep in mind our growing list of collectors and returning customers, many of whom were, not too much later than ourselves, developing their feeling and appreciation for outstanding carvings.

What caught my eye increasingly, the longer I was a buyer, was a carving with individuality and originality and also, and I suppose most particularly, with some of the marks of the tool. This is a preference not confined to Inuit works, but to sculpture in general. There are, of course, many exceptions—in Inuit carving, for instance, the intimate ivory pieces obviously appreciate in beauty with their finish—but I do feel a considerable portion of the recent stone sculpture is overly tidy and too highly polished for my taste. The simple and meaningful earlier pieces (usually fetishes or toys handled and re-handled until smooth and seductive to hold) are another exception to the preference for tool-marks. The availability of power tools must make it very tempting to overdo the glossiness of a carving, and obviously this shiny finish has great appeal for many people and is most saleable. But ruggedness (frequently, it is recognized, caused by harder stone) is something I myself find much more exciting as a rule. Again, there are always exceptions and some of the impressive works by the best-known artists are very desirable in spite of showing no tool marks and being painstakingly finished.

So, while I never blinded myself to the smoother work and certainly bought good pieces of various sorts, I was most attracted by and looking for the rougher and more powerful works, and those were what were picked out so quickly at Canadian Arctic Producers. It usually turned out, after our first couple of years as dealers, that the shop displays included many pieces from Baker Lake, Rankin Inlet, Eskimo Point, Spence Bay and Pangnirtung and a few from Lake Harbor or Belcher Islands, though it was recognized that most of the works so passed by were as well carved and as saleable as those that I myself happened to prefer.

Another preference was for works standing on their own feet. The effect of a pedestal being carved as part of a sculpture seems to inevitably detract from the piece, even though it obviously makes it more secure. Many of the ivories, of course, have to be set into stone or bone and this practically never affects the beauty of the work. How else, for instance, could a group of minute sea-birds be displayed? But for larger stone or whale-bone works those splayed-out stands, unfortunately becoming more numerous as time goes by, seem almost, without exception, interferences with the carvings themselves.

Whale-bone carvings always caught my eye and held attraction for the material, apart from the carving, because of the variations of colour and texture, so far fewer whale-bone than stone carvings were without any particular interest. I felt, perhaps without foundation, that the artists themselves often got more inspiration from working in the bone and this resulted in a higher percentage of really creative works in that material. There would certainly be a great challenge in using the contrasts between the denser and the more perforated areas in an imaginative way, and I feel sure that these variations, as well as the shape of the bones, frequently suggested the eventual forms. This also must have been a reason for so many intense 'spirit' pieces being carved from whale bone. One particularly compelling work of this nature, obviously influenced by the bone's shape, was created at Arctic Bay in 1964 by Kongaseretook (also known as Elijah Kuppaq). It makes an unforgettable impression on one and refuses to be ignored. Luckily this unique piece, which actually has three sets of eyes, was not one that was taken away to some other country, but remains a treasured object in a private Vancouver collection. When on a buying trip, whale bone was always high on my list because of its many attractions.

Robert Keziere

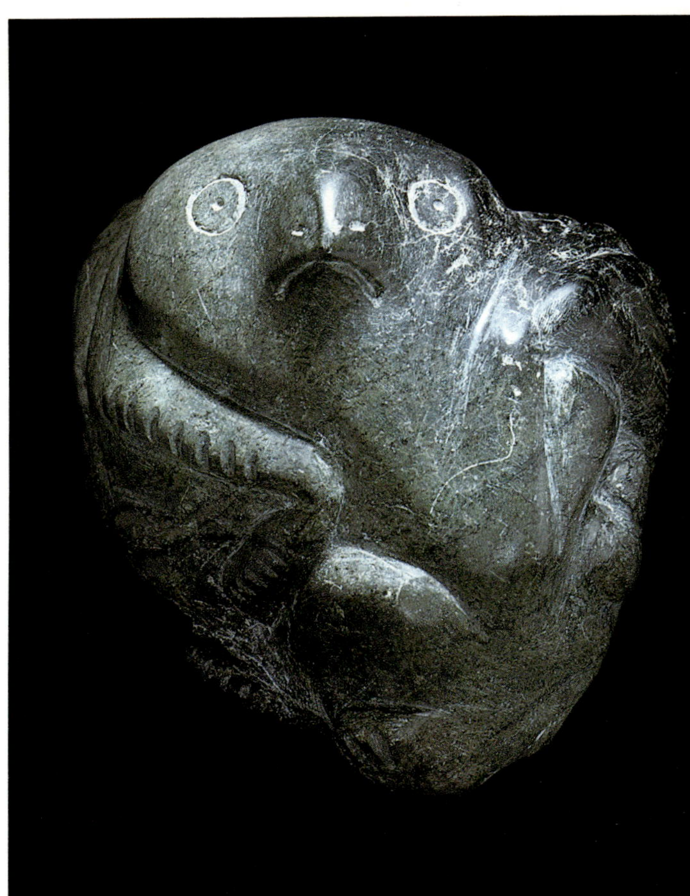

'Owl', c. 1960, by Pudlo of Cape Dorset. From the collection of the Vancouver Art Gallery.

These were my guidelines, or perhaps some would consider them prejudices, when choosing carvings, but there was never complete rigidity because, it is stressed again, there are always exceptions and one would be extremely foolish to exclude a fine and attractive work because it did not comply with all one's personal criteria. But having such a definite sense of what I wanted did lead to much speedier selection.

Having decided on my objectives, I found out, somewhat to my surprise, that buying very fast and depending on first impressions gave me the best results. This sometimes shocked other people who thought it a careless or flippant approach; but I seldom regretted having worked in that way—moving quite quickly through the displays and picking out carvings to right and left as anything attracted my eye. Then I went back more slowly on my tracks to find any good pieces which had eluded me on the first round. I sometimes found it hard to believe that I would spend $6,000 in two or three hours. Once in a while I discovered later that, because of this method of selecting, some small carving refused to stand up, had lost a spear or possibly its antlers, or even had some minor defect on closer observation.

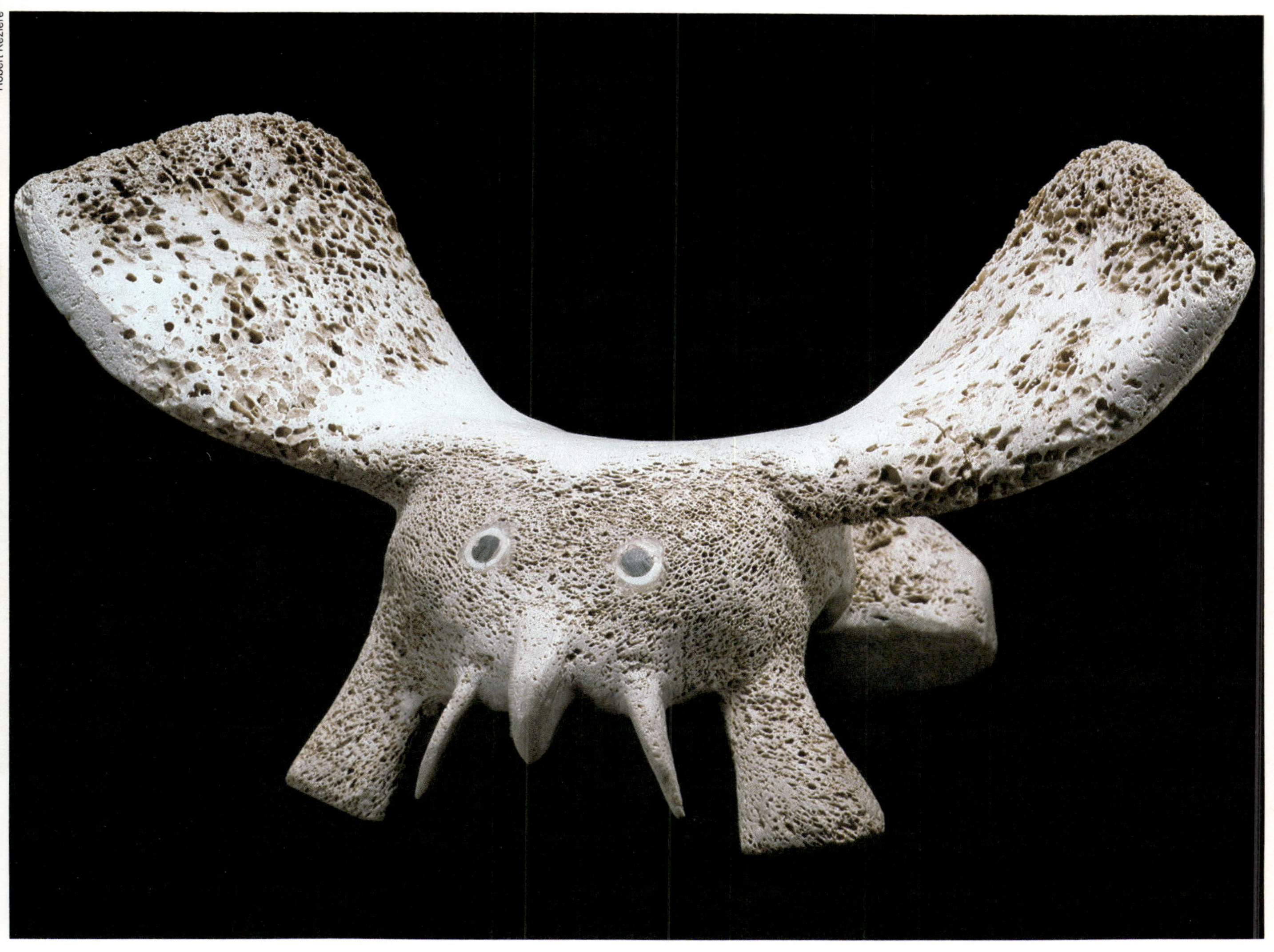

Robert Keziere

'Spirit', 1964, whale bone and stone, by Kongaseretook (also known as Elijah Kuppaq) of Arctic Bay. From a private collection in North Vancouver.

But in almost all cases I continued to agree with my own first impressions.

There was much more satisfaction to be gained from feeling that other people were being offered things I myself believed in, rather than in just selling for the sake of making money—though we were most anxious to support the Gallery and did, over the years, contribute between a quarter million and a half million dollars to the Gallery's budget.

It was always rewarding to find an appreciative home for a particularly fine piece and I tried, as I am sure all dealers do in the case of really exceptional works, to see if they could be placed in a worthy private collection or better still, a public one. Sales to galleries or museums are, of course, the most satisfying, as one then knows that a great many people will be able to enjoy the works through the years and that they will be properly cared for and preserved. But those sales do not turn up every day.

Customers naturally varied considerably and one was always curious to see what would appeal to each of them. Some just wanted a souvenir or small gift, or even two similar carvings to use as book ends. But others, though uninitiated, proved much more interesting to serve, perhaps picking up an attractive small bird or animal to begin with, then spotting something considerably more subtle and ending up by buying one of the best (not necessarily major in size) carvings in the shop. As is well recognized, being enthusiastic about what one is selling can be contagious, and I still sometimes worry in case my personal excitement about certain works caused anyone to make a purchase which was later regretted.

In the course of time, we accumulated a group of steady customers who became familiar to us. A handful only wanted to be shown works by the 'big name' artists and so lost the opportunity of discovering and collecting fine carvings by people who were then less well known. It was difficult not to show at least a touch of impatience when someone peered briefly into the well-stocked display area saying 'Have you a Pauta bear?' Or 'Are there any pieces by Latcholassie?' Or some such thing. What a dull and insensitive way to buy something to live with and enjoy!

It never ceased to be surprising when customers expected that works they had seen and admired elsewhere in a shop in Ontario or in a friend's house in Vancouver, for instance, could be duplicated like commercial reproductions or tins of vegetables. Again and again through the years, I was asked if I could find a 'carbon copy' of a particular carving which someone described or illustrated for me. Of course, that was almost impossible and many hours at the wholesale outlet were wasted trying to locate the unattainable. To my amazement, once there was total success. An Australian visitor on his way back home drew a picture of a bird he had seen and admired in Eastern Canada and which, when he returned to buy it, had been sold. As usual, he was told it was most unlikely anything could be done for him, but, lo and behold, on the next buying trip, there waiting on a display stand was an exact likeness of the one he had drawn, and what was more, it was a very good carving. Naturally, I jumped at it and later had it photographed for the customer. Finally it arrived at his home in Australia after we had personally delivered it to the dockside and started it on the long ocean voyage. He was immensely pleased with the carving and the service, but probably never realized how lucky he was to have received exactly what he wanted.

One summer day a young tourist from Germany allowed himself to fall for a stone figure weighing about twenty pounds. He was carrying an overnight bag and just leaving for the airport, so we agreed to mail all the bag's contents to Europe, in order that he could board his plane with the carving, trying valiantly to look as though his carry-on luggage only contained the usual overnight accessories.

Many of us became very fond of the strange imaginative beasts carved by Miki at Whale Cove and Eskimo Point and once we had a fascinating one-man show of his works. As a result, some of his finest and most unusual carvings are now in Vancouver collections. Miki seems to be an artist whose works are either thoroughly enjoyed or simply don't appeal—there is no middle ground. I suppose it depends on the viewer's own imagination and perception.

Pudlo—that free spirit—was a personal favourite of mine, in spite of the occasional uneven quality of his work. Throughout the ten or so years that I was privileged to buy and sell Inuit art several really stunning works by Pudlo were handled by the shop, one of which (an owl, though it looks more like the spirit of all owls) was, with a bit of persuasion, bought by a patron and donated to the Vancouver Art Gallery's collection, and gained the distinction of being included in the Masterworks Exhibition. Another, a creamy white soapstone bear, is the

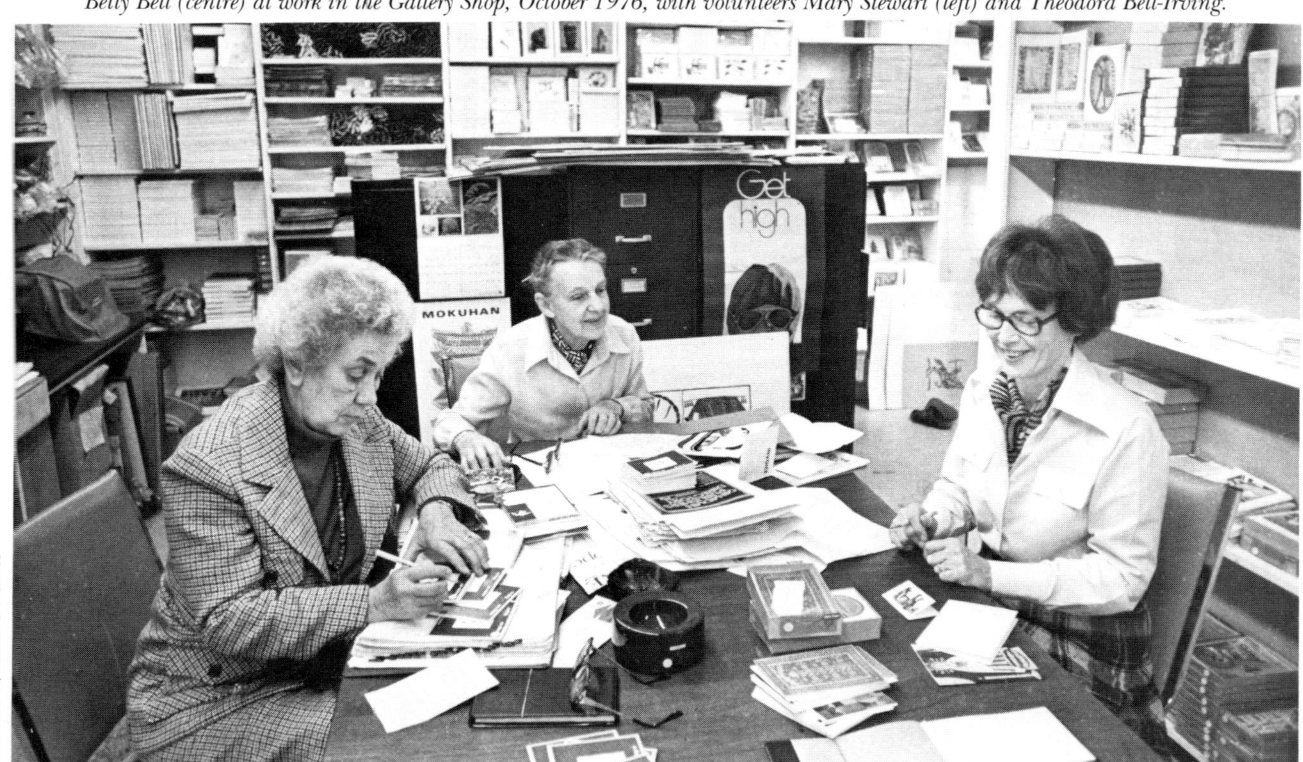

Betty Bell (centre) at work in the Gallery Shop, October 1976, with volunteers Mary Stewart (left) and Theodora Bell-Irving.

John Deniston, Vancouver Province

centrepiece of a private Vancouver collection and has also been publicly exhibited at least once. So I am able to feel completely satisfied when I think of those two outstanding works.

One lone carving by the famous Tiktak—a timeless figure obtained directly from Rankin Inlet—passed through our hands and is now in the Inuit art collection at Simon Fraser University; and two other fine sculptures from the shop—one an exceptionally large abstract piece by George Arluk, and the other, a big rugged, even jagged, figure in dark stone by Kavik, both emanating from Rankin Inlet—joined the Pudlo owl in the Vancouver Art Gallery's collection. Several important and compelling whale-bone carvings from Pangnirtung—two or three being by Manaipik, a carver who always impressed me, were sold a year or so before the end of our operation of the shop; the majority of them, like countless other fine works, went to the United States before the shipment of whale bone across the border was prohibited. Some visiting physicists from Ann Arbor, Michigan, taking part in a gathering at the University of British Columbia, are now the owners of several of the strongest of Manaipik's sculptures, including the largest piece of his that I have seen—a haunting figure of a man. Mathematicians and physicists so often seemed to be among our most perceptive customers for Inuit art. Much as one liked to see the best works remain in Canada, I think it was often equally important to me to know that these special carvings were going where they would obviously be intensely appreciated. Whatever their final destination, I missed some of them for a long time after they found new homes.

Apart from the important large sculptures already mentioned, I particularly remember some smaller but exceptional carvings, such as a classic bear in serpentine from Cape Dorset, possibly by Kaka, dating from the mid-sixties. Luckily that piece caught the eye of discriminating friends of mine, so from time to time I can still see and admire it. A small but most unusual bird's nest from Baker Lake, complete with simplified baby birds with beaks agape—which sounds like a most unlikely motif—also continues to stay in my mind, and one really tiny but beautiful piece by Anaija of Spence Bay proved irresistible and has just been returned to my mantelpiece after its inclusion in an exhibition arranged by the Department of Indian and Northern Affairs. The subject is Sedna, holding a stone lamp in front of her as she swims. But hundreds of pieces of all sizes and descriptions, which I have loved, are scattered far and wide.

My work as a member of the Gallery Shop Committee wasn't all involved with shopkeeping. For instance, a day might sometimes be taken up with arrangements for shipping Inuit carvings abroad. These were only occasional events, but to someone who loves ships and has travelled on a freighter, it was always exciting to track down through the various shipping agencies a vessel about to leave for some particular distant port. Then when a ship had been found and the forwarding of our crate arranged, we visited the agent for the vessel and filled out the countless forms for the shipping company, insurance firms and customs. By the time we took our crate down we almost felt we were embarking on a voyage ourselves.

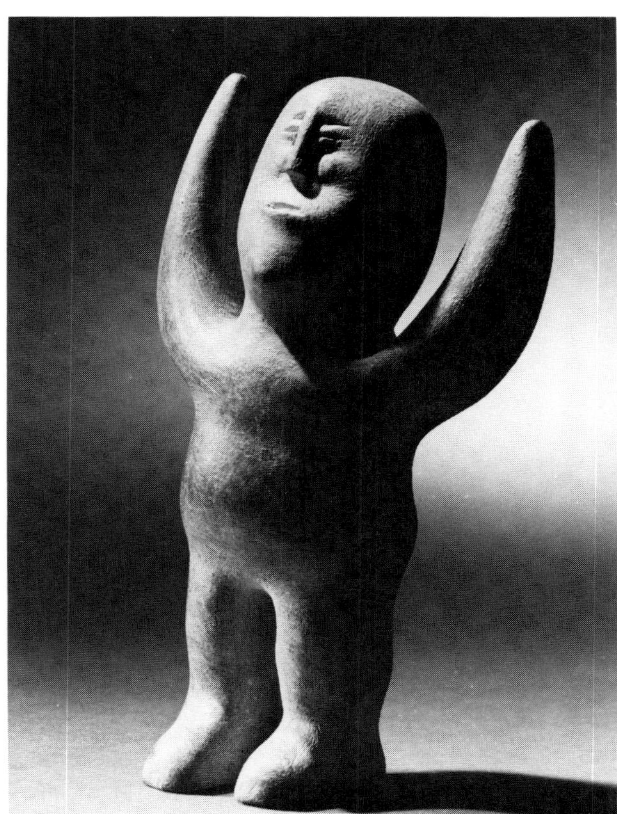

'Man', 1960s, by Tiktak of Rankin Inlet. From a private collection, Winnipeg.

I once spent another and totally different, out-of-the-way morning down in the bowels of the Vancouver Police Station. We had been notified that a quantity of stolen property was being held there and that the suspect had offered the information that some of the Inuit carvings included in his loot came from the Gallery Shop. Trying to identify a dozen or so small carvings which had been shop-lifted over a period of months or years was pretty difficult. One particular piece (a very tender black stone bird from Baker Lake) caught my eye at once. I had been particularly attracted by it and had no idea it had been stolen. But some of the very small birds and animals, which were certainly ones I might have selected, were far less simple to be certain of, although I was quite positive I had never chosen a number of them. I tried to be honest, but on the other hand it seemed to me (perhaps erroneously) that the police appeared anxious for me to identify more than I honestly could. I am sure they wanted to clear the matter up and I gathered that people from other shops which had also suffered losses to this particular shop-lifter were equally uncertain of

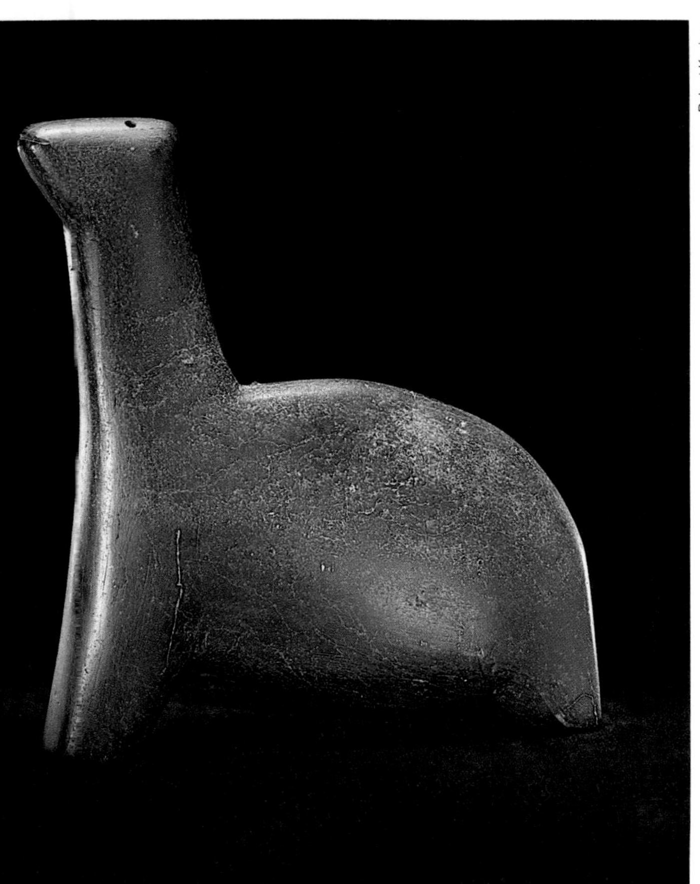

Robert Keziere

'Imaginary Animal', 1960s, by Miki. From a private collection, Vancouver.

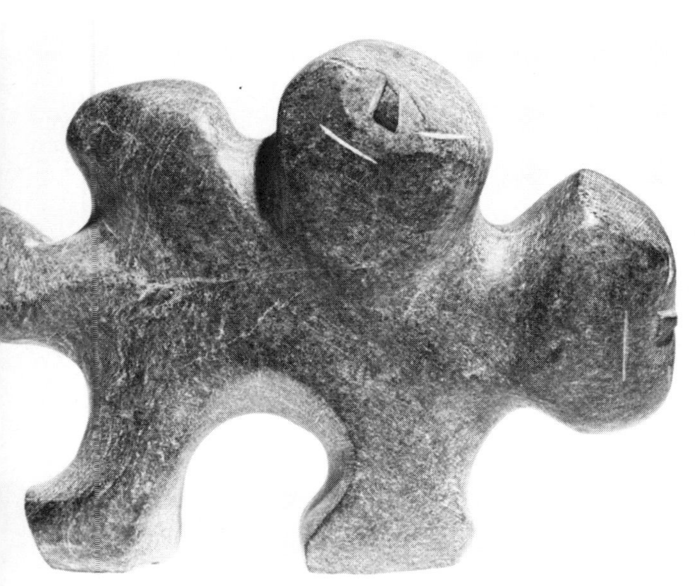

Ernest Mayer

'Figure with Two Heads', 1972, by George Arluk, Rankin Inlet. From the George Swinton Collection in the Winnipeg Art Gallery.

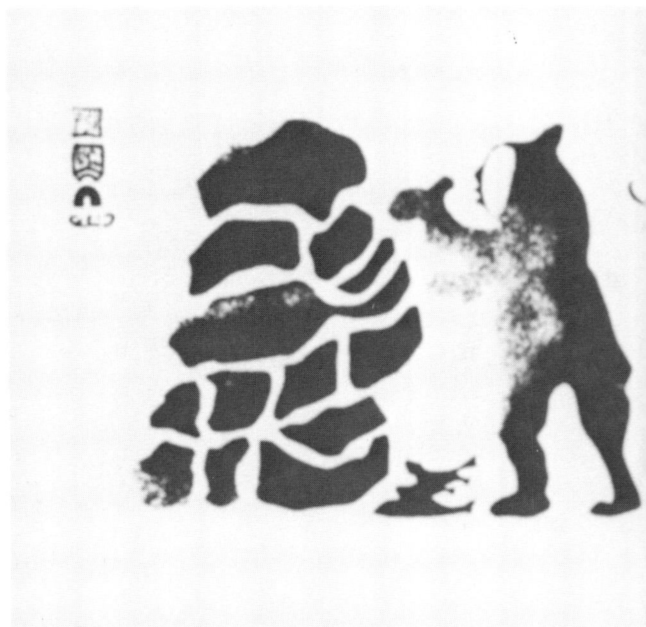

which piece was or was not from their stock. I still remember that day and how claustrophobic it was down there as door after door was unlocked and then clanged to behind me.

Print openings were, as they are for all the dealers, a wild scramble. I am sure I am right in saying that we initiated, for Vancouver outlets, the system of giving numbered tickets to customers in order of their arrival, so as to prevent scenes when two people claimed the same print. In spite of the precaution there often seemed to be some contretemps. Print collectors are an intense and competitive group. We even once had several prospective customers lying at the head of the Art Gallery steps on camp-cots all night, awaiting the hour of the sale. Kenojuak's prints, as was the case everywhere for years, were the most sought after, though seldom my favourites. Her lovely *Enchanted Owl* certainly was responsible for a lot of greed after it brought astronomical prices on the resale market; it gave a tremendous boost to the popularity and appreciation of the prints in general. By far the most exciting to me of all the prints that we ever stocked were those compelling and direct Cape Dorset intaglios and stone-cuts from the early sixties which were lying unsold in drawers at Canadian Arctic Producers and many of which we had the good fortune to handle later. I am thinking of the 1961 and 1963 prints by Parr, Kiakshuk, Ottochie and Kananginak, among others, and of my excitement when I was first shown these in Ottawa and permitted to select some for the shop. It seemed the most amazing treasure trove.

In retrospect it seems that perhaps the occasion I enjoyed the most during those years was arranging a special display for the sake of the delegates to the Habitat Conference in 1975. Our idea was to show

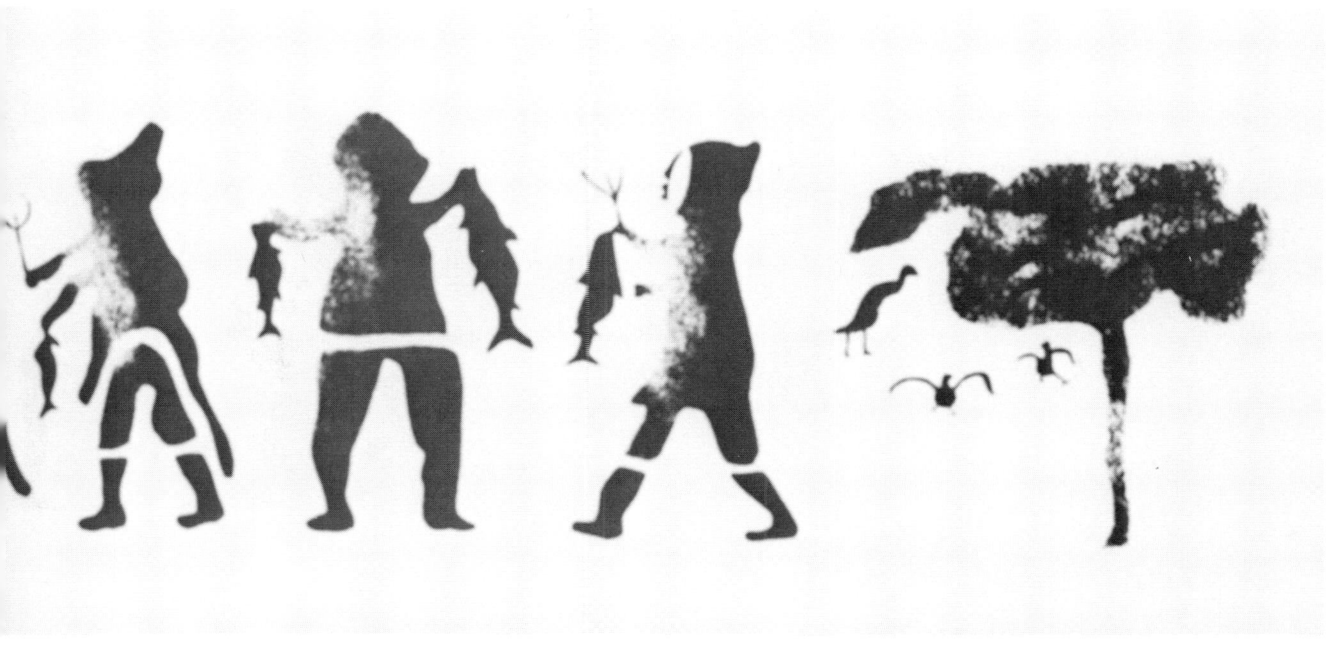

'Eskimo Family Catching Fish', sealskin print, 1961, by Kiakshuk of Cape Dorset.

these thoughtful people from all the corners of the earth an outstanding collection of works by Canadian native artists, as well as the best of British Columbia's crafts. With the help of our suppliers we did gather together in the Inuit department a stunning display, including (apart from selected carvings and our stock of prints) some of those lovely embroidered garments, dolls and birds made at Spence Bay under Judy McGrath's direction; a group of the rare and expertly made baskets from Nouveau Quebec, as well as some of their sumptuously dressed dolls; and great bold and exciting Baker Lake wall hangings with their embroidered and appliqued designs. With everyone making a special effort in each of our departments, the shop looked more elegant than it had ever done before and the visitors were impressed and most complimentary; but few had much money to spend (as we had more or less anticipated).

So while the objective of letting the visitors see the best work we could accumulate was accomplished, the big sale of these beautiful things came a little later as the summer tourists arrived. I think that all my special and expensive stock was sold before autumn, except for some of the Baker Lake hangings. This was very satisfying and also a bit of a relief. There was always the possibility of going overboard in one's enthusiasm.

In 1977, by mutual agreement, the volunteer operation of the Gallery Shop came to an end after thirteen strenuous but rewarding years, and it is now being run professionally. But for all the time when it was in our care, it was a fulfilling and exciting experience to be spending my days amongst memorable works by Inuit artists, and to have had countless unforgettable contacts with people from round the globe. ♦

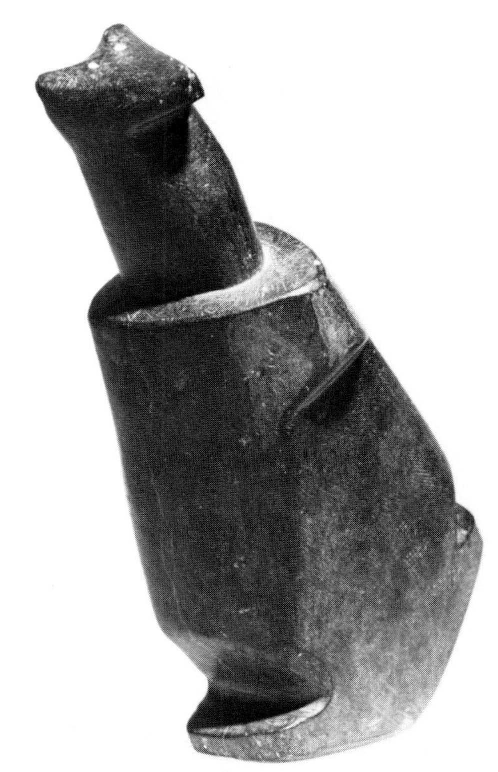

'Animal Stone', undated, by Miki. From the collection of Stanley and Jean Zazelenchuk, in the Winnipeg Art Gallery.

Index

PEOPLE

PLACES

ILLUSTRATIONS